Technician Units 8 and 9

MANAGING PERFORMANCE AND CONTROLLING RESOURCES

For assessments in December 2003 and June 2004

Interactive Text

In this May 2003 new edition

- For assessments under the **new standards**
- Layout designed to be easier on the eye – and easy to use
- Clear language and presentation
- Activities checklist to tie in each activity to specific knowledge and understanding, performance criteria and/or range statement
- Thorough reliable updating of material to 1 April 2003

FOR 2003 AND 2004 EXAM BASED ASSESSMENTS

First edition May 2003

ISBN 0 7517 1131 4

British Library Cataloguing-in-Publication Data
A catalogue record for this book
is available from the British Library

Published by

BPP Professional Education
Aldine House, Aldine Place
London W12 8AW

www.bpp.com

Printed in Great Britain by Ashford Colour Press Ltd
Unit 600
Fareham Reach
Fareham Road
Gosport
Hampshire
PO13 0FW

We are grateful to the Lead Body for Accounting for permission to reproduce extracts from the Standards of Competence for Accounting, and to the AAT for permission to reproduce extracts from the mapping and Guidance Notes.

Contents

Introduction

How to use this Interactive Text – Technician qualification structure – Unit 8 Standards of competence – Unit 9 Standards of competence – Assessment strategy

		Page	Answers to activities

PART A A foundation for your studies

		Page	Answers to activities
1	An introduction to management accounting	3	415
2	The behaviour, recording and reporting of costs	25	416
3	Collecting data	43	420
4	Analysing data	69	424
5	Forecasting	95	432

PART B Core theme 1: standard costing

		Page	Answers to activities
6	Calculating variances	139	440
7	Analysing variances	193	455

PART C Core theme 2: budgeting

		Page	Answers to activities
8	Budgeting	221	464
9	Budget preparation	237	468
10	Budgetary control	273	479
11	Further aspects of budgeting	301	487

Page Answers to activities

PART D Core theme 3: measurement of performance

12 Performance measurement 323 491
13 Further aspects of performance measurement 345 495

PART E Core issues

14 Cost management I 373 499
15 Cost management II 387 500

Answers to activities 413

Index 503

Order form

Review form & free prize draw

Introduction

How to use this Interactive Text

Aims of this Interactive Text

To provide the knowledge and practice to help you succeed in the assessments for Technician Unit 8 *Contributing to the Management of Performance and the Enhancement of Value* and Unit 9 *Contributing to the Planning and Control of Resources.*

To pass the assessment successfully you need a thorough understanding in all areas covered by the standards of competence.

To tie in with the other components of the BPP Effective Study Package to ensure you have the best possible chance of success.

Interactive Text

This covers all you need to know for the exam based assessments for Unit 8 *Contributing to the Management of Performance and the Enhancement of Value* and Unit 9 *Contributing to the Planning and Control of Resources.* Numerous activities throughout the text help you practise what you have just learnt.

Assessment Kit

When you have understood and practised the material in the Interactive Text, you will have the knowledge and experience to tackle the Assessment Kit for Unit 8 *Contributing to the Management of Performance and the Enhancement of Value* and Unit 9 *Contributing to the Planning and Control of Resources*. This aims to get you through the AAT's exam-based assessments for these units.

Passcards

These short memorable notes focused on key topics for Units 8 and 9 are designed to remind you of what the Interactive Text has taught you.

Recommended approach to this Interactive Text

(a) To achieve competence in Units 8 and 9 (and all the other units), you need to be able to do **everything** specified by the standards. Study the Interactive Text carefully and do not skip any of it.

(b) Learning is an **active** process. Do **all** the activities as you work through the Interactive Text so you can be sure you really understand what you have read. There is a checklist at the end of each chapter to show which areas of knowledge and understanding, performance criteria and/or range statements are covered by each activity.

(c) After you have covered the material in the Interactive Text, work through the **Assessment Kit**.

(d) Before you take the assessments, check that you still remember the material using the following quick revision plan for each chapter.

  (i) Read and learn the **key learning points**, which are a summary of the chapter. This includes key terms and shows the sort of things likely to come up in assessments.

  (ii) Do the **quick quiz** again. If you know what you're doing, it shouldn't take long.

  (iii) Go through the **Passcards** as often as you can in the weeks leading up to your assessments.

This approach is only a suggestion. Your college may well adapt it to suit your needs.

Quick quizzes

These include multiple choice questions, true/false and other formats not used by the AAT. However, these types of questions are usually very familiar to students and are used to help students adjust to otherwise unfamiliar material.

Remember this is a **practical** course.

(a) Try to relate the material to your experience in the workplace or any other work experience you may have had.

(b) Try to make as many links as you can to your study of the other Units at Technician level.

(c) Keep this text, (hopefully) you will find it invaluable in your everyday work too!

Technician qualification structure

The competence-based Education and Training Scheme of the Association of Accounting Technicians is based on an analysis of the work of accounting staff in a wide range of industries and types of organisation. The Standards of Competence for Accounting which students are expected to meet are based on this analysis.

The AAT issued new standards of competence in 2002, which take effect from 1 July 2003. This Text reflects the **new standards.**

The Standards identify the key purpose of the accounting occupation, which is to operate, maintain and improve systems to record, plan, monitor and report on the financial activities of an organisation, and a number of key roles of the occupation. Each key role is subdivided into units of competence, which are further divided into elements of competences. By successfully completing assessments in specified units of competence, students can gain qualifications at NVQ/SVQ levels 2, 3 and 4, which correspond to the AAT Foundation, Intermediate and Technician stages of competence respectively.

Whether you are competent in a Unit is demonstrated by means of:

- *Either* an Exam Based Assessment (set and marked by AAT assessors)
- *Or* a Skills Based Assessment (where competence is judged by an Approved Assessment Centre to whom responsibility for this is devolved)
- Or *both* Exam *and* Skills Based Assessment

Below we set out the overall structure of the Technician (NVQ/SVQ Level 4) stage, indicating how competence in each Unit is assessed. In the next two sections there is more detail about the Standards of Competence and the Assessments for Units 8 and 9.

All units at Technician level are assessed by Exam Based Assessment, except for Units 10, 15, 17 and 22, which are assessed by Skills Based Assessment.

NVQ/SVQ Level 4

Group 1 Core Units – All units are mandatory.

Unit 8 Contributing to the Management of Performance and the Enhancement of Value	Element 8.1	Collect, analyse and disseminate information about costs
	Element 8.2	Monitor performance and make recommendations to enhance value
Unit 9 Contributing to the Planning and Control of Resources	Element 9.1	Prepare forecasts of income and expenditure
	Element 9.2	Produce draft budget proposals
	Element 9.3	Monitor the performance of responsibility centres against budgets
Unit 10 Managing Systems and People in the Accounting Environment	Element 10.1	Manage people within the accounting environment
	Element 10.2	Identify opportunities for improving the effectiveness of an accounting system
Unit 22 Contribute to the Maintenance of a Healthy, Safe and Productive Working Environment	Element 22.1	Contribute to the maintenance of a healthy, safe and productive working environment
	Element 22.2	Monitor and maintain an effective and efficient working environment

NVQ/SVQ Level 4, continued

Group 2 Optional Units – Choose **one** of the following **four** units.

Unit 11 Drafting Financial Statements (Accounting Practice, Industry and Commerce)	Element 11.1 Draft limited company financial statements
	Element 11.2 Interpret limited company financial statements
Unit 12 Drafting Financial Statements (Central Government)	Element 12.1 Draft Central Government financial statements
	Element 12.2 Interpret Central Government financial statements
Unit 13 Drafting Financial Statements (Local Government)	Element 13.1 Draft Local Authority financial statements
	Element 13.2 Interpret Local Authority financial statements
Unit 14 Drafting Financial Statements (National Health Service)	Element 14.1 Draft NHS accounting statements and returns
	Element 14.2 Interpret NHS accounting statements and returns

NVQ/SVQ Level 4, continued

Group 3 Optional Units – Choose **two** of the following **four** units.

Unit 15 Operating a Cash Management and Credit Control System	Element 15.1	Monitor and control cash receipts and payments
	Element 15.2	Manage cash balances
	Element 15.3	Grant credit
	Element 15.4	Monitor and control the collection of debts
Unit 17 Implementing Auditing Procedures	Element 17.1	Contribute to the planning of an audit assignment
	Element 17.2	Contribute to the conduct of an audit assignment
	Element 17.3	Prepare related draft reports
Unit 18 Preparing Business Taxation Computations	Element 18.1	Prepare capital allowances computations
	Element 18.2	Compute assessable business income
	Element 18.3	Prepare capital gains computations
	Element 18.4	Prepare Corporation Tax computations
Unit 19 Preparing Personal Taxation Computations	Element 19.1	Calculate income from employment
	Element 19.2	Calculate property and investment income
	Element 19.3	Prepare Income Tax computations
	Element 19.4	Prepare Capital Gains Tax computations

Units 8 and 9 Standards of competence

The structure of the Standards for Unit 8 and Unit 9

The Units commence with statements of the **knowledge and understanding** which underpin competence in the Units' elements.

The Units of Competence are then divided into **elements of competence** describing activities which the individual should be able to perform.

Each element includes:

(a) A set of **performance criteria.** This defines what constitutes competent performance.

(b) A **range statement.** This defines the situations, contexts, methods etc in which competence should be displayed.

The elements of competence for Unit 8 *Contributing to the Management of Performance and the Enhancement of Value* and Unit 9 *Contributing to the Planning and Control of Resources* are set out below. Knowledge and understanding required for each unit are listed first, followed by the performance criteria and range statements for each element. Performance criteria are cross-referenced below to chapters in this Units 8 and 9 *Managing Performance and Controlling Resources* Interactive Text.

Unit 8: Contributing to the Management of Performance and the Enhancement of Value

Unit commentary

This unit is about collecting, analysing and interpreting information of help to managers in controlling costs and improving the performance of operations. There are two elements.

The first element focuses on the identification and analysis of costs that may be of help to managers. You will have to monitor and analyse costs against trends, standards and organisational needs, and explain any difference between actual and planned or expected costs. In addition, you will have to demonstrate your understanding of forecasting techniques as an aid to cost analysis and control.

The second element is concerned with monitoring the performance of an organisation or parts of an organisation and making recommendations that will enhance the organisation's value. In this element you have to identify and calculate performance indicators, monitor the performance of part or all of the organisation and make proposals that will enhance the value of the organisation.

You will have to obtain information from a variety of internal and external sources and monitor costs, performance indicators and movements in prices over an appropriate timescale. You will also be required to use the information to prepare and present management reports. As well as being familiar with manually developing information, you will also need to know how computer spreadsheets can assist you in preparing cost and performance information.

Knowledge and understanding

The business environment

1 External sources of information on costs and prices: government statistics, trade associations, financial press, quotations, price lists (Elements 8.1 and 8.2)

2 General economic environment (Elements 8.1 and 8.2)

Accounting techniques

3 Basic statistical methods: index numbers; sampling techniques; time series analysis (moving averages, linear regression and seasonal trends) (Element 8.1)

4 Use of relevant computer packages (Elements 8.1 and 8.2)

5 Methods of presenting information in graphical, diagrammatic and tabular form (Element 8.1)

6 Performance indicators: efficiency, effectiveness, productivity; balanced scorecard, benchmarking; unit costs; control ratios (efficiency, capacity and activity), scenario planning ('what-if' analysis) (Element 8.2)

7 Standard costing (Element 8.1)

Accounting principles and theory

8 Marginal and absorption costing: cost recording, cost reporting, cost behaviour (Elements 8.1 and 8.2)

9 Cost management: life cycle costing; target costing (including value engineering); activity based costing; principles of Total Quality Management (including cost of quality) (Element 8.2)

10 The use and limitation of published statistics (Element 8.1)

11 Effect of accounting controls on behaviour of managers and other employees (Elements 8.1 and 8.2)

The organisation

12 How the accounting systems of an organisation are affected by its organisational structure, its administrative systems and procedures and the nature of its business transactions (Elements 8.1 and 8.2)

13 The organisation's external environment and specific external costs (Element 8.1)

14 The contribution of functional specialists in an organisation (e.g. marketing, design, engineering, quality control, etc.) to cost reduction and value enhancement (Element 8.2)

Element 8.1 Collect, analyse and disseminate information about costs

Performance criteria		**Chapters in this Text**
A	Identify valid, relevant **information** from internal and external sources	3
B	Monitor and analyse on a regular basis current and forecast trends in prices and market conditions	5
C	Compare trends with previous experience and identify potential implications	5
D	Compare standard costs with actual costs and analyse any **variances**	6, 7
E	Analyse the effect of organisational accounting policies on reported costs	2, 15
F	Consult relevant staff in the organisation about the analysis of trends and variances	5
G	Present reports to management that **summarise data**, present information using appropriate **methods** and highlight significant trends	4

Range statement

Information: 3

- Movements in prices charged by suppliers, competitors, and providers of services
- General price changes

Methods of summarising data: 3, 4, 5

- Time series (moving averages, linear regression, seasonal variations)
- Index numbers and sampling

Methods of presenting information in reports: 4

- Written analysis and explanation
- Tables
- Diagrams

Variance analysis: 6, 7

- Material price and usage variances
- Labour rate and efficiency variances
- Fixed overhead expenditure, volume, capacity and efficiency variances
- Subdivision of variances

The build up of costs: 2, 15

- Absorption costing
- Marginal costing
- Activity-based costing

Element 8.2	**Monitor performance and make recommendations to enhance value**	
Performance criteria		**Chapters in this Text**
A	Analyse routine cost reports, compare them with other sources of information and identify any implications	12
B	Prepare and monitor relevant **performance indicators**, interpret the results, identify potential improvements and estimate the value of potential improvements	12, 13
C	Consult relevant specialists and assist in identifying ways to reduce costs and enhance value	14, 15
D	Prepare exception reports to identify matters which require further investigation	12
E	Make specific **recommendations** to management in a clear and appropriate form	15
Range statement		
Performance indicators to measure: • Financial, customer, internal business, and learning and growth perspectives • Efficiency, effectiveness and productivity • Unit costs; resource utilisation • Profitability • Quality of service • Cost of quality		12, 13, 15
Recommendations: • Efficiencies • Modifications to work processes • Benchmarking		13, 14, 15

Unit 9 Contributing to the Planning and Control of Resources

Unit commentary

This unit focuses on the planning and control of resources in an organisation. There are three elements.

In the first element, you have to develop forecasts of demand, turnover, resources to be consumed and their cost.

The second element requires you to use forecasts to prepare draft budgets for income and expenditure. This may involve you changing your initial budget to take account of revised information about factors that limit the operations of the organisation.

The final element relates to part of the control function in organisations. You will be required to compare the actual performance of all or part of an organisation against what was planned to happen and advise managers of possible reasons for any difference.

You will need to ensure all relevant data has been included in your budgets and that all relevant staff have been consulted. In addition, you will need to ensure that transactions have been accurately recorded and appropriate accounting methods have been used for both the planning and monitoring of budgets. As well as being familiar with manually developing forecasts and budgets, you will also need to know how computer spreadsheets can help you in their development.

Knowledge and understanding

The business environment

1. External sources of information on costs, prices, demand and availability of resources (Elements 9.1, 9.2 and 9.3)
2. General economic environment (Elements 9.1, 9.2 and 9.3)

Accounting techniques

3. Basic statistical methods: time series (moving averages, linear regression and seasonal variations), sampling techniques; index numbers (Element 9.1)
4. Use of relevant computer packages (Elements 9.1, 9.2 and 9.3)
5. Development of production, resource and revenue budgets from forecast sales data
6. Co-ordination of the budget system (Elements 9.2 and 9.3)
7. The effect of capacity constraints, other production constraints and sales constraints on budgets; limiting (key or budget) factor (Elements 9.2 and 9.3)
8. Budgets for control: flexible budgets, marginal costing
9. The effect of budgetary systems on the behaviour and motivation of managers and other employees (Element 9.2)
10. Analysing the significance of budget variances and possible responses required by managers (Element 9.3)
11. Presentation of budget data in a form that satisfies the differing needs of budget holders

Accounting principles and theory

12. Marginal and absorption costing: cost recording, cost reporting, cost behaviour (Elements 9.2 and 9.3)
13. Uses of budgetary control: planning, co-ordinating, authorising, cost control (Elements 9.1, 9.2 and 9.3)
14. Relationship between budgets, forecasts and planning and product-life cycles (Elements 9.1, 9.2 and 9.3)
15. Different types of budgets: budgets for income and expenditure; resource budgets (production, material, labour and other resource budgets); capital budgets (Elements 9.2 and 9.3)

The organisation

16. How the accounting systems of an organisation are affected by its organisational structure, its administrative systems and procedures and the nature of its business transactions (Elements 9.1, 9.2 and 9.3)
17. The structure of the organisation and its responsibility centres and an understanding of the inter-relationships between departments and functions is required (Elements 9.1, 9.2 and 9.3)
18. Responsibility centres: expense centres; profit centres; investment centres (Element 9.3)

Element 9.1 Prepare forecasts of income and expenditure

	Performance criteria	Chapters in this Text
A	Identify relevant **data** for projecting **forecasts** from internal and external sources	3, 8
B	Communicate with relevant individuals and give them the opportunity to raise queries and to clarify forecasts	5
C	Prepare forecasts in a clear format with explanations of assumptions, **projections** and adjustments	5
D	Review and revise the validity of forecasts in the light of any significant anticipated changes	5

Range statement

	Chapters in this Text
Data: • Accounting information • Wage and salary information • Information about suppliers and availability of inputs • Information about customers and markets • General economic information	3, 8
Forecasts: • Income • Expenditure	5, 8
Projections: • Trends • Seasonal variations • Market research	5, 8

Element 9.2 Prepare draft budget proposals

Performance criteria		**Chapters in this Text**
A	Present to management draft **budget** proposals in a clear and appropriate format and on schedule	9
B	Verify that draft budget proposals are consistent with organisational objectives and include all relevant **data** and assumptions	9
C	Break down budgets into periods appropriate to the organisation	9
D	Communicate with budget holders in a manner which maintains goodwill and ensure budget proposals are agreed with budget holders	9, 11
Range statement		
Types of budgets: • Budgets for income and expenditure • Resource budgets (production budget, material budget, labour budget, fixed overhead budget) • Capital budgets		9
Data: • Accounting information • Wage and salary information • Market information • General economic information • Strategic plans		8, 9

Element 9.3 Monitor the performance of responsibility centres against budgets

Performance criteria		**Chapters in this Text**
A	Check and reconcile **budget** figures on an ongoing basis	10
B	Correctly code and allocate actual cost and revenue data to **responsibility centres**	10
C	Clearly and correctly identify **variances** and prepare relevant reports for management	10
D	Discuss with budget holders and other managers any significant variances and help managers take remedial action	10
Range statement		
Types of budgets: Budget for income and expenditure Resource budget Fixed and flexible budgets		10
Responsibility centres: Expense centres Profit centres		10
Variances: Actual Potential		10

Assessment strategy

Unit 8 and Unit 9 are assessed by **exam based testing** only.

An exam-based assessment is a means of collecting evidence that you have the **essential knowledge and understanding** which underpins competence. It is also a means of collecting evidence across the **range of contexts** for the standards, and of your ability to transfer skills, knowledge and understanding to different situations. Thus, although exam-based assessments contain practical tests linked to the performance criteria, they also focus on the underpinning knowledge and understanding. You should in addition expect each exam-based assessment to contain tasks taken from across a broad range of the standards.

Because exam-based assessments aim to cover the breadth of Units 8 and 9, an area of competence may be **assessed in one way in one assessment** and a **different way in later one**. This has two main implications.

- There is little point in memorising the answers to previous assessment tasks.
- You need to be able to apply your knowledge and understanding in a variety of different situations.

Tasks will assess your ability to **apply basic management accounting techniques** in simple organisational situations and to **make recommendations** to management in a clear and appropriate form.

Unit 8 Contributing to the Management of Performance and the Enhancement of Value

Unit 8 will be assessed using an unseen examination that is set and marked by the AAT. The examination will be divided into two sections. It will last for three hours (plus 15 minutes' reading time) and will test a broad range of the performance criteria from the Standards.

Normally, there will be two tasks in each section and candidates have to reach a minimum standard in each section to be assessed as competent in the whole unit. Sometimes, however, there may be more than two tasks per section. This does not mean more work. Extra tasks will only be asked where they make the tasks clearer or where it reduces the amount of data to be considered before answering.

Each task will normally be a mini case study. The candidate will be given a realistic workplace-type problem and asked to solve it. Sometimes the techniques to apply will be obvious – as when candidates are asked to calculate standard costing variances. At other times, candidates may have to identify the technique or knowledge and understanding for themselves.

The two sections will **not** be the same as the two elements because some performance criteria can either be:

- logically assessed in either section; or
- assessed together because they are closely connected.

Generally, the first section will be concerned with the management of costs, the second with the wider aspects of management of performance and enhancement of value. An indicative guide to how the knowledge and understanding of Unit 8 relates to the two sections is shown below. Candidates must, however, remember that this is indicative only. It is neither exhaustive nor exclusive.

Section 1

- Standard costing

Section 2

- Performance indicators: efficiency, effectiveness, productivity; balanced scorecard, benchmarking; unit costs; control ratios (efficiency, capacity and activity), scenario planning ('what-if' analysis)

Either section

- External sources of information on costs and prices: government statistics, trade associations, financial press, quotations, price lists.
- General economic environment.
- Basic statistical methods: index numbers; sampling techniques; time series analysis (moving averages, linear regression and seasonal trends).
- Use of relevant computer packages.
- Methods of presenting information in graphical, diagrammatic and tabular form.
- Marginal and absorption costing: cost recording, cost reporting, cost behaviour.
- Cost management: life cycle costing; target costing (including value engineering); activity based costing; principles of Total Quality Management (including cost of quality).
- The use and limitation of published statistics.
- Effect of accounting controls on behaviour of managers and other employees.
- How the accounting systems of an organisation are affected by its organisational structure, its administrative systems and procedures and the nature of its business transactions.
- The organisation's external environment and specific external costs.
- The contribution of functional specialists in an organisation (e.g. marketing, design, engineering, quality control, etc.) to cost reduction and value enhancement.

Unit 9 Contributing to the Planning and Control of Resources

Unit 9 will be assessed using an unseen examination that is set and marked by the AAT. The examination will be divided into two sections. It will last for three hours (plus 15 minutes' reading time) and will test a broad range of the performance criteria from the Standards.

Normally, there will be two tasks in each section and candidates have to reach a minimum standard in each section to be assessed as competent in the whole unit. Sometimes, however, there may be more than two tasks per section. This does not mean more work. Extra tasks will only be asked where they make the tasks clearer or where it reduces the amount of data to be considered before answering a task.

Each task will normally be a mini case study. The candidate will be given a realistic workplace-type problem and asked to solve it. Sometimes the techniques to apply will be obvious – as when candidates are asked to prepare a flexible budgeting statement. At other times, the candidate may have to identify the technique or knowledge and understanding themselves.

The two sections will **not** directly relate to the three elements because some performance criteria can either be:

- logically assessed in either section; or
- assessed together because they are closely connected.

Generally, the first section will be concerned with planning budgets, the second with the control of resources. A guide to how the knowledge and understanding of Unit 9 relates to the two sections is shown below. Candidates must, however, remember that this is indicative only. It is neither exhaustive nor exclusive.

Section 1

- Relationships between budgets, forecasts and planning and product-life cycles.
- Basic statistical methods: time series (moving averages, linear regression and seasonal variations, sampling techniques; index numbers).
- Development of production, resource and revenue budgets from forecast sales data.
- Co-ordination of the budget system.
- The effect of capacity constraints, other production constraints and sales constraints on budgets; limiting (key or budget) factor.
- Different types of budgets: budgets for income and expenditure ; resource budgets (production, material, labour and other resource budgets); capital budgets.

Section 2

- Budgets for control: flexible budgets, marginal costing.
- Analysing the significance of budget variances and possible responses required by managers.
- The effect of budgetary systems on the behaviour and motivation of managers and other employees.
- Responsibility centres: expense centres; profit centres; investment centres.

Either section

- External sources of information on costs, prices, demand and availability of resources.
- General economic environment.
- Use of relevant computer packages.
- Presentation of budget data in a form that satisfies the differing needs of budget holders.
- Marginal and absorption costing: cost recording, cost reporting, cost behaviour.
- Uses of budgetary control: planning, co-ordinating, authorising, cost control.
- How the accounting systems of an organisation are affected by its organisational structure, its administrative systems and procedures and the nature of its business transactions.
- The structure of the organisation and its responsibility centres and an understanding of the inter-relationships between departments and functions.

PART A

A foundation for your studies

chapter 1

An introduction to management accounting

Contents

1 Introduction
2 Why management accounting is different
3 Management accounting and Units 8 & 9
4 A systems approach to management accounting
5 Management accounting as a human system
6 Objectives
7 Effectiveness, productivity and efficiency

Performance criteria, range statement and knowledge and understanding

This chapter serves as an introduction to Technician-level management accounting in general and to the key themes of Units 8 and 9 in particular. As such it touches both on performance criteria from across the units and on a wide range of areas of knowledge and understanding. In particular, however, the Unit 8 and Unit 9 knowledge and understanding point 'How the accounting systems of an organisation are affected by its organisational structure, its administrative systems and procedures and the nature of its business transactions' is covered here. The performance criteria and other areas of knowledge and understanding are covered in far greater depth in subsequent chapters, however, and are referenced specifically to those chapters.

Signpost

You should read this introductory chapter whether you are studying **Unit 8** or **Unit 9**.

1 Introduction

As its title suggests, this chapter provides you with an introduction to **management accounting**, the subject of Units 8 and 9. But do you know what management accounting is? You've met financial accounting in your earlier studies, but this is something **new**, something **different** and something very **exciting**!

Sections 2 and 3 provide you with an idea of what management accounting is, and of the aspects of particular relevance to Units 8 and 9.

Sections 4 and 5 are probably the **most important** in the chapter as they provide a perspective for many of the techniques associated with the three core themes of Units 8 and 9 (standard costing, budgeting and performance indicators). If you fully understand this section you will find it a lot easier to grasp the concepts and ideas we study in later chapters.

In **Section 6** we introduce some of the **wider, behavioural issues** associated with management accounting, while in **Section 7** we provide you with a framework for your studies of one of the key themes, **performance indicators**.

All of the topics in this chapter will be examined in greater depth in the remaining chapters of this text. Here they provide you with a platform from which you can safely plunge into the wonderful world of management accounting.

2 Why management accounting is different

Before studying the subject, students often have the idea that management accounting is just some part of financial accounting. Nothing could be further from the truth!

2.1 A history lesson

Long before there was any need or requirement for financial statements, **management accounting was *the* accounting**. It was developed to help managers (be they landowners, the Church or small businesses) to manage their assets and resources.

As businesses grew, more people became involved and the owners could no longer keep track of all their activities and transactions. And so there developed a need from within the organisation for some form of financial reporting, if only to verify the honesty of managers (stewards) who were running the business on a daily basis.

Stewards had to give regular accounts of their activities to the owners of businesses. This involved providing a reconciliation between the resources under their control at the beginning of the period (say £5,000) and those at the end (say £4,000). Only by valuing the expenditure at **historical cost** could an owner be sure that a misappropriation had not taken place.

The **first management accountants** were therefore the medieval clerks **recording** the **transactions** of what today we would call **managers**.

2.1.1 Other uses of 'management accounting'

The early management accounts could also have provided managers with answers to the following questions.

- 'Will we do better or worse next year?' (assistance with planning)
- 'Did we do as well as expected?' (assistance with control)

We return to the issue of planning and control in the next section.

2.1.2 Organisational and accounting developments

The way in which organisations then developed had an impact on accounting.

In organisations	In accounting
The increased **complexity** of manufacturing required expensive **fixed assets** which could be used for many years.	The **matching concept** enabled the cost of a fixed asset to be charged over a number of years.
Production volumes were **not** necessarily the **same** as **sales volumes**.	**Stock valuation methods** developed.
Companies had sometimes many **shareholders** to make possible the purchase of expensive fixed assets. **Managers** rather than owners therefore **controlled** organisations on a **day to day** basis.	**Financial statements** were prepared by the managers for the owners, initially voluntarily but later in line with legislation and professional rules.

Financial accounting therefore **developed out of management accounting**. Modern day published **financial statements** include the profit and loss account, the balance sheet and the cash flow statement. These provide users (shareholders, creditors, tax authorities and so on) with an overview of the organisation as a whole but they are **not particularly useful** as a basis **for managing the future activities** of the organisation. Management accounting, which was not superseded by financial accounting but continued to flourish in its own right, is.

2.2 Financial accounting versus management accounting

Financial accounts	Management accounts
Prepared on an **historical cost** basis, which may **not** be **suitable** for **planning** and managing the future.	Incorporate **modified recorded historical cost data** and/or **data** from **outside** the rigid framework of the **double entry system** for recording transactions. (Budgets, for example, which you will encounter later in this text, are short-term plans, the data for which cannot be recorded in the double entry system as the transactions are not certain to take place.)
Provide **aggregate data** about the **whole organisation** to **external stakeholders** and **cannot answer** questions such as: • What did it cost to operate department A last year? • How much profit did product C produce? • If we subcontract canteen operations, what will be the effect on profit?	Focus on the **individual businesses** and **segments** which make up the organisation and provide **information** to **help managers manage.**

Financial accounts	Management accounts
Prepared according to **law, SSAPs and FRSs.**	**Format entirely at management's discretion.** No strict rules govern the way they are prepared or presented. Management accounts are **driven by utility**, by their own usefulness to management, and each organisation can devise its own management accounting system and format of reports. There is no right or wrong approach – it all depends on circumstances and the management needs in question.

The **information provided by the management accountant** must therefore be **useful**, nothing more and nothing less. There are **no rules and regulations** to follow as there are in financial accounting. To study management accounting effectively you therefore need to understand the various options open to the management accountant and apply what you believe to be the most appropriate in the circumstances. This text will provide guidance on how to do that!

3 Management accounting and Units 8 & 9

Basically, **management accounting is all about helping managers to do their jobs.**

Obviously the work done by management is extremely wide ranging and so consequently management accounting has a variety of aspects.

- Scorekeeping
- Planning
- Co-ordinating
- Control
- Decision making

It is with planning and control that we are particularly concerned, however,

3.1 Planning and control

We all have to think ahead, even if it is only planning what bus to catch to get us to work on time, what to buy at the supermarket so that we have enough food for the week, how much money to save for an annual holiday.

But what happens if we regularly miss the bus, often have no food in the fridge or have not saved enough money for our annual holiday? In such circumstances we have to rethink our plans, perhaps leaving home earlier in the morning, making a shopping list for when we visit the supermarket or saving a little extra every month. In short, we have to **revise the plan.**

Suppose, by revising plans, we are only late for work if the bus is late, only run out of food at the very end of the week and only have a small shortfall between our savings and the cost of the holiday. Revising our plans would have resulted in what actually happened being very close to, or the same as, what we planned to happen.

The process of **looking at what we planned to do and comparing it with what we actually did** is called **feedback.** And the **action taken to try to make what we did the same as what we planned** to do is **control.**

In much the same way, **managers have to plan for their organisations**. There is one fundamental difference, however. Most organisations are sufficiently large and hence of such a complexity that plans cannot be made by just one manager or kept in one manager's head. Organisational planning involves a number of people and so has to be a **formalised** process. Likewise an organisation's **control process** must be **formalised** to ensure that plans are changed before any serious damage to the organisation's future occurs.

3.1.1 Management accounting and planning and control

It is the **ways in which management accountants can help management to plan and control** that provide the **core themes** of Unit 8 and 9. These themes are all **based on** what are known as **planning and control systems**, an introduction to which is provided in the next section.

4 A systems approach to management accounting

Managers of small organisations can often keep the information needed to run the organisation in their heads. Managers of **larger organisations** are unable to do this, however. **Formal systems** (including management accounting) are therefore needed to **provide management** with the **information** they need to run the organisation – be it a major supermarket chain such as Tesco in the UK, a charity such as the Red Cross, a government body such as the Inland Revenue or an educational establishment such as Liverpool University. The management accounts system provides much of this information.

4.1 Systems

4.1.1 Definition of a system

The word 'system' is impossible to define satisfactorily (think of all the examples – the tax 'system', the respiratory 'system', the class 'system'), but basically it means **something that connects things up**.

4.1.2 The component parts of a system

A system has three component parts.

Part of system	Detail
Inputs	Provide the system with what it needs to be able to operate. May vary from matter (in a manufacturing operation this might be adhesives or rivets), energy, humans (typing an instruction booklet or starting a piece of machinery) to information.
Process	Transforms an input into an output. May involve tasks performed by humans, plant, computers, chemicals and/or a wide range of other action.
Outputs	The results of the process

We can show this diagrammatically.

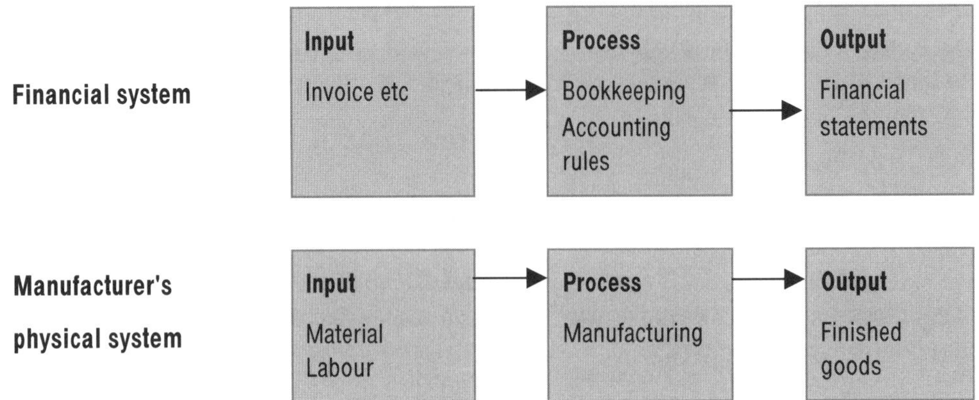

These two systems should be **run in parallel** and the **financial system** should directly **shadow** the **manufacturer's physical system.** This does not often occur in practice, however: physical stock very rarely equals book stock; cash in the bank is usually different to the cash balance in the accounts.

4.2 Control systems

Control is required because **unpredictable disturbances** can arise and enter a system, so that **actual results** (outputs of a system) **deviate from expected results or goals**. Here are some examples of **disturbances in a business system**.

- The entry of a powerful new competitor into the market
- An unexpected rise in costs
- The failure of a supplier to deliver materials
- The tendency of employees to stop working to gossip

To have a control system, there has to be a **plan, standard, budget, rule book or other sort of target or guideline** towards which the system as a whole should be aiming.

Budgets, **standards** and **performance targets**, the core areas of management accounting which we will cover in this text, are all **types of plan or target**.

4.2.1 Components of a control system

Component	Description	Examples in management accounting
Standard	The targets at which the organisation is aiming	Budgeted/expected material costs or performance targets such as the number of claims under warranty
Sensor	Device or person by which information or data is collected and measured	Computer turn-around documents
Feedback	Measurement of differences between planned results and actual results	Management reports

Component	Description	Examples in management accounting
Comparator	Means by which actual results of the system are measured against the predetermined plans	Managers. They are expected to make some judgement on the results of the calculation of the comparison, to decide whether any differences (variances) need to be investigated and then (after investigation) whether control action is required.
Effector or activator	The device or means by which control action is initiated	A manager's instruction and a subordinate's action

The diagram below illustrates a control system. Notice how **corrective action impacts** on both **inputs and planned performance**.

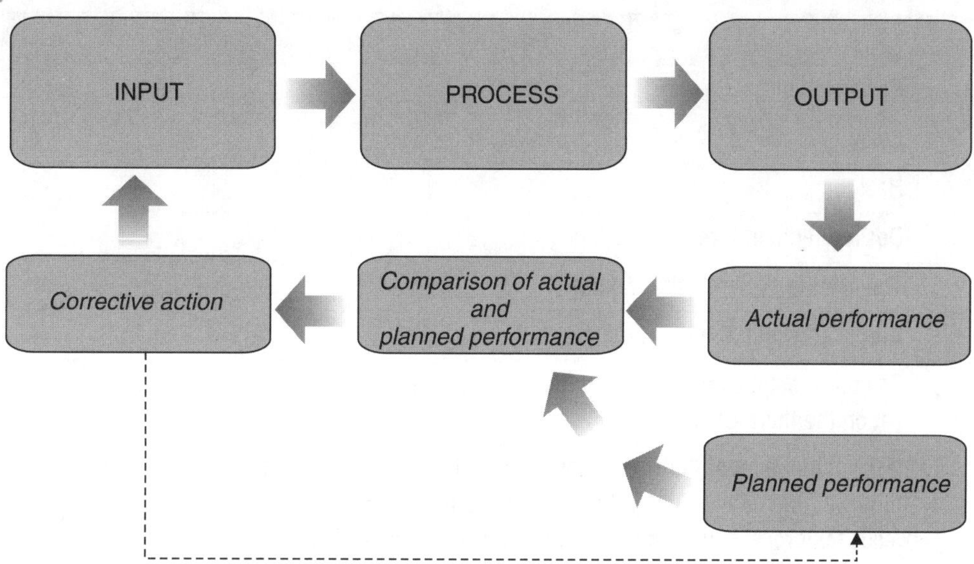

4.2.2 Management accounting example of a control system

This example might help to make the idea of a control system easier to understand.

Component	Example
Standard	A sales budget or plan is prepared for the year.
Sensor	The costing system records actual results.
Feedback	At the end of each month, actual results (units sold, revenue and so on) are reported back to management.
Comparator	Managers compare actual results against the plan.
Effector	Where necessary, managers take corrective action to adjust the workings of the system, probably by amending the inputs to the system. For example, sales people might be asked to work longer hours or new price discounts might be decided. Where appropriate, the sales plan might be revised to take account of the results of control action.

IMPORTANT POINT

The control process does not stop with the calculation of the differences between planned and actual results (which are called variances). Management action is then required in the form of investigation and if necessary, corrective action. Given that exam tasks reflect the workplace, you can therefore expect to have to **calculate variances** (differences) and **provide an interpretation** of their meaning and significance and/or **suggestions for control action**. Don't worry. This text will show you how to do this.

4.2.3 A practical example

If you still find these ideas and concepts too vague, think in terms of a central heating system.

Component	Central heating system example
Input	Power (oil or gas)
Process	Boiler
Output	Heat
Standard	Desired temperature
Sensor	The heating system's thermostat
Feedback	Produced within the thermostat
Comparator	The thermostat compares the actual heat being produced by the boiler with the desired temperature set on the thermostat.
Effector	If the actual temperature is too low, the feedback message to the thermostat is to increase the input of power and convert it into heat. If it is too high, the feedback message is to stop input. The feedback process will continue until the desired temperature is achieved.

4.3 Feedback

4.3.1 Negative feedback

Negative feedback indicates that the system is deviating from the planned course and that control action is needed to bring it back on course.

This feedback is **negative** because the aim of the **control action** would be to **reverse the direction of the system** back towards its planned course.

For example, suppose planned sales for a department for June and July were £100,000 in each month. If the report of actual sales in June showed that only £90,000 of goods had been sold, this negative feedback would indicate that control action was needed to raise sales in July to £110,000 in order to get back on the planned course.

4.3.2 Positive feedback

Positive feedback results in **control action** that **causes actual results to maintain or increase their path of deviation from planned results**.

For example, if actual sales demand is greater than expected sales demand, control action could result in production being increased to meet the increased demand and in additional advertising expenditure to maintain the high level of sales.

4.4 Open and closed systems

Think back to the central heating system that we used to illustrate the idea of a control system.

Suppose flat A is directly under flat B. The owners of both flats have gone on holiday in search of the sun to escape the bitterly cold weather at home. A water pipe in flat B freezes and bursts. Cold water starts to drip into flat A, causing the temperature to fall. The central heating thermostat therefore receives a feedback message to input more power to increase the temperature. The heat output rises, with the result that even more water leaks into flat A. This continues until the owners return from their holiday.

The **central heating system** is therefore a **closed system** because **it cannot interact with its environment**. If it could, it would have realised there was a burst pipe, closed down the system and called for a plumber.

An **open system**, on the other hand, can **interact with the environment**. A **business** is an open system, where management decisions are influenced by or have an influence on suppliers, customers, competitors, society as a whole, the government and so on.

4.5 Management accounting as a system

Throughout this section we have referred to management accounting examples. You do not need to have a detailed understanding of our three core themes of standard costing, budgetary control or performance indicators at this point. You simply need to realise that the **management accounting systems** we will be looking at involve the **comparison of some form of plan with actual results** and that **differences between planned and actual results (which are often called variances) need to be investigated** and **control action taken if necessary**.

Despite the usefulness of the central heating example, it is important to realise that management accounting systems are not as mechanical and are still very much **dependant on human beings** – despite advances in information technology. This has important implications, as we will now discover.

5 Management accounting as a human system

Mechanical systems, such as central heating systems, are relatively **simple**.

- They have **one objective** (maintain the actual temperature at the desired temperature).
- **Feedback** messages are **clear** and **unambiguous** (the actual temperature is twenty five degrees, a degree warmer than desired).
- Any necessary **control action** (add no more power to the boiler) is **automatic** and **exact**.

Management accounting systems are part of human organisational systems and are therefore **much more complex**.

5.1 Multiple objectives

In **organisations** there is likely to be **conflict between more than one objective**.

In **profit-making** organisations there might be conflict between a **long-term** objective such as to ensure that all staff are able to use computers and a **short-term** objective to cut costs (and hence training costs).

A **charity** might have an objective to help as many sufferers of a disease as possible. This might conflict with the objective to increase funds put into research of the causes of the disease, however.

Managers' objectives might **conflict** with **those of the organisation**. For example, a manager might choose to purchase components more cheaply from outside the organisation in the interests of his own department's profit, even if purchasing them from another department of the organisation would be more profitable for the organisation overall.

We revisit the subject of objectives at the end of the chapter.

5.2 The importance of motivation

There is **no automatic response** to feedback information in a management accounting system. **Managers need to be motivated to investigate any difference between planned and actual results (variance)** and to take the appropriate control action. This topic is covered in detail later in the text.

5.3 Problems in understanding feedback information

Managers might be appropriately motivated but they may not know the correct action to take in response to a particular variance.

For example, suppose the difference between the planned cost of materials for the production of product A (£4,000) and the actual cost of materials (£4,500) is £500. This difference or variance is **adverse** (A) because **the actual cost was greater than the planned cost**. If **the actual cost had been less than the planned cost** the variance would have been described as **favourable (F)**. The existence of this adverse variance does not necessarily mean that the system has gone wrong and someone needs to take the blame for the overspend, however.

5.3.1 Measurement errors

In exam tasks there is generally no question of the information about actual results that you are given being wrong. In practice, however, it may be extremely difficult to establish that 1,000 units of product A used 400 kgs of raw material X8.

- Scales may be misread.
- Pilferage or wastage of materials may go unrecorded.
- Items may be wrongly classified (as material X3, say, when material X8 was used in reality).
- Employees may make 'cosmetic' adjustments to their records to make their own performance look better than it was.

An investigation may show that **control action** is required to **improve** the **accuracy of the recording system** so that measurement errors do not occur.

5.3.2 Incorrect plan/standard/budget

The plan may have been wrong.

- The plan might have assumed that wastage levels of material X8 would fall as employees' experience increased but in reality the employees might not have learnt at the rate expected.
- Planned prices are likely to become out of date quickly in periods of high inflation. If there had been a world-wide price increase of material X8 of 15% the planned cost should have been £4,600, so that the variance would have been £100 (F).

Such variances are likely to **occur in closed systems**. Open systems would have recognised the change in price or the alternative rate of learning and amended the plan.

Investigation of such variances is likely to highlight a general change in market prices or the need to review and update plans frequently, rather than operating efficiencies or inefficiencies.

The appropriate control action when prices are becoming out of date because of high inflation would be to encourage purchasing despite the adverse variance (because the actual cost is less than the expected cost taking world-wide increases into account).

5.3.3 Caused by one department, reported in another

The feedback information might be reported to the manager of one department but the variance might be caused by the manager of another.

For example, suppose the purchasing manager forgot to order enough material X8 so that he had to buy some at short notice from an alternative supplier. This material turned out to be of a much lower quality than that normally supplied with the result that wastage levels were far higher than usual. The **purchasing manager** would therefore have **caused** the **cost of the extra material** but the **cost (of the high wastage)** would be **reported** as the **responsibility** of the **production manager**.

Investigation should therefore be centred on the **department causing the variance** rather than on the one reporting the variance.

5.3.4 Random or chance fluctuations

The **planned figure** is only management's best guess of what should happen, an **average** if you like. **Actual results** are therefore quite likely to **deviate unpredictably within a small range.** A small variance could therefore be the result of random or chance fluctuation. Alternatively it might be an indication of greater problems to come. Management are therefore faced with the difficult decision of whether or not to investigate. The decision will be based on a number of factors such as the cost of investigation. We return to this point in Chapter 7.

5.4 Deliberate distortion

Another problem with human systems such as management accounting systems is that **managers** might **deliberately try to distort the variance**.

5.4.1 Distortion of the planned (standard/budget/target) figure

Managers might deliberately **overstate planned costs** so that **favourable variances** are reported. Alternatively they might deliberately **understate planned costs** in order to **impress senior management** but are then unable to carry out all necessary operations without cutting corners or incurring large adverse variances.

5.4.2 Manipulation of actual results

- Keep back invoices to keep the apparent level of spending low.
- Delay discretionary expenditure such as training, advertising and research and development.
- Reduce levels of quality (and hence save costs) in ways that are not immediately apparent to customers.
- Achieve favourable variances at the expense of adverse variances occurring elsewhere in the organisation. For example, a manager might decide to use cheaper and hence lower quality materials in a component transferred to and used in the production process of a second department. While the first department reports favourable material variances, the second might report adverse labour variances as the production workers have difficulty using the component.

ATTENTION!

The paragraphs above make it clear that there is no one reason why planned performance differs from actual performance. And because they attempt to simulate the workplace, this is as true in exams as it is in real life. What's more, a manager would not look down a list of possible causes if asked to explain why a variance had occurred. Likewise, there is **little point in you rote learning lists** for the exam.

TOPIC LINK

Forecasting and Total Quality Management

Even better than a perfectly operating control system would be a situation in which **no variances** occurred at all. By looking into the future (**forecasting** – covered in Chapter 5) and designing out errors before they occur (**Total Quality Management** – covered in Chapter 15) differences between planned and actual performance can be minimised, if not eliminated.

5.5 Summary of Sections 4 and 5

This brief overview of systems will have given you a framework within which to study management accounting. It has provided a view of organisations, has touched on the key topics that we will be looking at in the remainder of this text,

has illustrated how they fit together, and has shown how difficult it is in the real world to interpret variances. You will find the introduction of these concepts of great use as we begin our look at management accounting.

6 Objectives

In simple terms, an **objective** of an organisation is an **aim that can be expressed in quantitative terms (ie numerically)**.

For example, if the aim of an organisation is to provide a quality product, an associated objective might be to ensure a defect rate of less than 0.5%. Likewise, if a university has an aim 'to seek truth', an objective might be for research hours to increase by 20% in the coming academic year.

It is often **difficult** to **incorporate objectives into control systems** such as budgets. When this happens, the **target** established by the control system is often **not consistent with the objective**. An added problem occurs if **staff** put their **own interpretation on objectives**, often acting against the underlying spirit of the objective.

Here's an **example** courtesy of the assessor.

A centrally-imposed objective of an NHS ambulance trust was that an ambulance and qualified attendant should quickly reach any patient dialling 999. The target associated with this objective was that an ambulance should get to the emergency within 12 minutes of receiving the call.

Ambulance drivers often found that they could not get to the patient within 12 minutes, however, because of traffic congestion, but senior management still demanded that ambulances took the target time. The drivers then realised that the 12 minutes started when they acknowledged that they had taken the call and ended when they arrived at the scene. They therefore took to radioing in that they had accepted the call only when they were already on their way to the scene and that they had arrived at the scene shortly before they actually had.

Management also found it difficult to meet the target. Financial and other pressures meant that it was not always possible to use medically-trained paramedics. To appear to be meeting the target management therefore used unqualified ambulance drivers – those who normally transported senior citizens and similar patients to and from hospital and medical appointments – to go to emergencies.

IMPORTANT POINT

This example illustrates two **key issues.**

- The difficulties in setting reasonable and operational targets within control systems to ensure that objectives are met
- The way in which staff and management may act against the spirit of the underlying objective to ensure that the control system target is met

We return to these issues when we look at the behavioural issues of budgeting (Chapter 11) and performance measurement (Chapters 12 and 13).

7 Effectiveness, productivity and efficiency

Performance measurement is a topic we will return to in Part D, but if we look at the basic ideas here, in this introductory section, you will be able to understand more fully standard costing and budgeting (the subjects of Parts B and C of the text).

Productivity, efficiency and effectiveness are the overall areas of performance that control systems aim to measure.

7.1 Effectiveness

Effectiveness is **about meeting targets and objectives**.

Suppose a factory in the former Soviet Union with a workforce of 100 manufactured 50,000 socks a month. The factory was asked to increase output to 60,000 socks a month. It employed another 100 workers and was able to meet the target.

The factory has therefore been effective because it has met the target.

7.2 Productivity

But what is your overall impression of the factory's performance? What do think of the fact that the workforce doubled but output only increased by 20%? It can't be good, can it?

There is no doubt that output has increased. But what about the output per employee? Before the change the **output per employee** was 500 socks per month. After the change it was just 300 socks per month. There had therefore been a considerable drop in the productivity of the workforce.

Productivity is **a measure of output relative to some form of input**.

- The output might be socks, cars, meals served in a restaurant or telephone calls answered in a customer service department.
- The input might be the workforce, raw materials or machinery.

Productivity measures compare the **output achieved from a certain amount of input**. Here are some examples.

- Number of customers served per employee per day
- Number of components produced per machine per month
- Number of litres of orange juice made per tonne of oranges used in production
- Number of hotel rooms occupied as a percentage of rooms available
- Passenger miles travelled as a percentage of train miles available

Productivity measures might also compare the output achieved per £ of labour, per £ of fixed assets and so on. Output can **also be expressed in financial terms** so revenue per £ of labour is a useful measure of productivity.

Activity 1.1

A service business has collected some figures relating to its year just ended.

	Budget	*Actual*
Customer enquiries		
New customers	6,000	9,000
Existing customers	4,000	3,000
Business won		
New customers	2,000	4,000
Existing customers	1,500	1,500
Types of services performed		
Service M	875	780
Service N	1,575	1,850
Service P	1,050	2,870
Employees		
Service M	5	4
Service N	10	10
Service P	5	8

Task

Calculate figures that illustrate productivity.

IMPORTANT POINT

An increase in production does not necessarily mean there has been an increase in productivity, as the example about the socks above illustrates.

7.3 Efficiency

Suppose another sock-making factory in the former Soviet Union also produced 50,000 socks per month using a workforce of 100, but managed to increase production to 60,000 socks per month by employing just two extra workers. Despite this **increase in productivity**, the factory's **profitability** actually **fell** because there was **no demand** for the extra socks.

Increasing production and increasing productivity was therefore not the most efficient use of the factory's resources because the resulting output could not be sold and so **profitability actually fell** (because there was no new revenue to cover the extra costs).

Efficiency also looks at **output relative to input**, but it is not the same as productivity because the **output is considered in terms of financial gain or value to the organisation**.

In the example above, if the financial value of the output (the revenue from selling the socks) had been greater than the financial value of the inputs (raw material and labour to make the socks) the factory would have been operating efficiently.

In most organisations, the **value generated** is **normally** some kind of **profit**. Other measures of efficiency might look at profitability relative to labour costs or profitability relative to capital invested.

Activity 1.2

Hersham Products Ltd's workforce of 24 usually produces 12,000 components each period. These sell for £600,000 and cost £360,000 to produce. Senior management have set a target of 12,400 units for period 6 and have employed an additional worker to help meet this target. The workforce has been informed that they will receive a bonus if they can increase their productivity by 3%. The actual output in period 6 of 12,460 units sold for £49 each and cost £373,800 to produce.

Tasks

(a) Decide whether the workforce was effective during period 6.

(b) State whether or not the productivity bonus should be paid.

(c) Explain whether or not Hersham Products Ltd was more or less efficient in period 6 than in previous periods (using an efficiency measure based on profit and costs).

IMPORTANT POINT

Something **might be effective** but that **does not mean that it is efficient**. For example, if you wanted to purchase some apples grown in New Zealand and so travelled to New Zealand for this sole purpose you would have achieved your objective and so the action would have been effective. If those apples could have been purchased at your local supermarket the action would not have been particularly efficient, however, because of the additional costs you would have incurred.

Activity 1.3

Randall Stationery Products Ltd carries out much of its selling effort by means of telemarketing (the marketing of products or services by means of a telephone sales force) and many firm sales orders are secured by telephone. The company also has a field sales force to back up the telemarketing staff. The field sales staff visit customers who have been telephoned by telemarketing staff and who have indicated a possible interest in making an order.

Task

Given that the following information is available, provide one measure of productivity, one measure of efficiency and one measure of effectiveness.

Information available

Telemarketing staff (man days)
Field sales force (man days)
Number of working days in the year
Number of telephone calls made
Target number of sales orders: telemarketing
Target number of sales orders: field sales force
Actual number of sales orders: telemarketing
Actual number of sales orders: field sales force
Salary costs: telemarketing
Salary costs: field sales force
Total costs: telemarketing
Total costs: field sales force
Costs: telephone charges
Sales commission: field sale force
Value of sales: telemarketing
Value of sales: field sales force

7.4 Unit cost

Another way of **comparing outputs with inputs** is to calculate the cost per unit of output. This can be applied to both products and services provided output can be measured in some way.

Unit cost = cost of input ÷ units of output

The cost may be total cost or may be a particular element of cost such as material (so that material cost per unit is calculated).

Key learning points

- ☑ **Management accounting** exists in its own right. It is not some part of financial accounting.
- ☑ Financial accounting information is used by parties external to the organisation. **Management accounting information** is **used** by an organisation's **management** to help them run the business. We are particularly interested in how management accounting helps with **planning** and **control**.
- ☑ The core themes covered in this text are based on **planning and control systems**. In general, such systems compare actual results with planned results (feedback) and initiate control action if necessary.
- ☑ **Feedback** is the measurement of differences between planned results and actual results.
- ☑ **Negative feedback** indicates the system is deviating from the planned course and that control action is needed to bring it back on course.
- ☑ **Positive feedback** results in control action that causes actual results to maintain or increase their path of deviation from planned results.
- ☑ **Closed systems,** such as central heating systems, cannot interact with their environment. **Open systems** can.
- ☑ **Management accounting systems** are **part** of **human organisational systems** and hence are far **more complex** than mechanical systems. Four particular **problems** were noted.
  - Multiple objectives
  - The importance of motivation
  - Understanding feedback information
  - Deliberate distortion of variances
- ☑ There are a number of **reasons why variances may occur.**
  - Measurement errors
  - Incorrect plan/standard/budget
  - Caused by one department, reported in another
  - Random or chance fluctuations
- ☑ In simple terms, an **objective** of an organisation is an aim that can be expressed in quantitative terms (ie numerically). We considered two important points about objectives.
  - The difficulties in setting reasonable and operational targets within control systems to ensure objectives are met
  - The way in which staff and management may act against the spirit of the underlying objective to ensure that a control system target is met
- ☑ **Effectiveness, productivity and efficiency** are the overall areas of performance that control systems aim to measure.
  - Effectiveness is about meeting targets and objectives.
  - Productivity is a measure of output relative to some form of input.
  - Efficiency looks at output (in terms of financial gain or value) relative to input.

  It is vital that you can distinguish between productivity and efficiency.

Quick quiz

1 When preparing management accounting information, there are rules and regulations to follow in the same way as there are in financial accounting. *True or false?*

2 What are the three component parts of a system?

A Control, output, action
B Inputs, control, feedback
C Inputs, process, outputs
D Process, feedback, output

3 *Insert the labels listed below onto the diagram.*

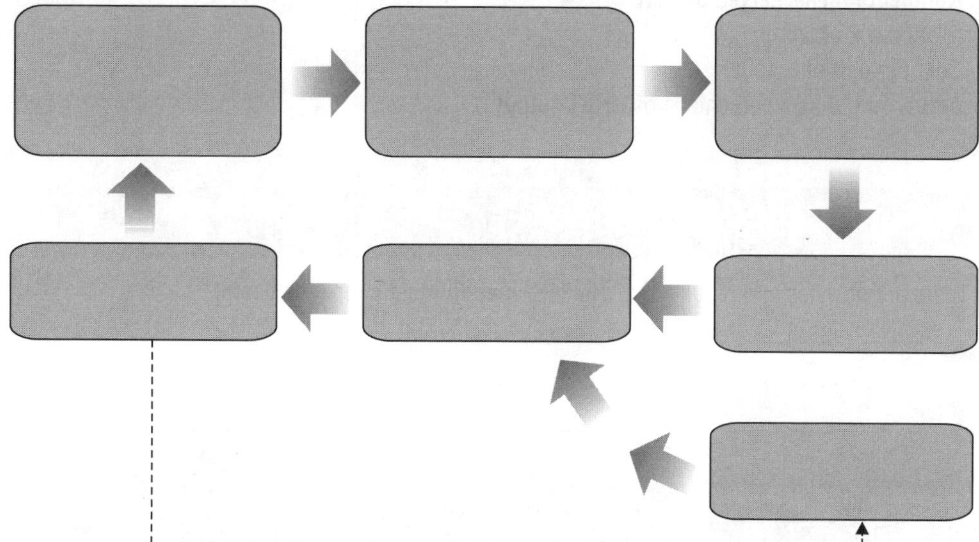

Labels for diagram
Actual performance
Corrective action
Input
Output
Comparison of actual and planned performance
Planned performance
Process

4 *Match the appropriate control action to the relevant cause of variances.*

Causes	*Control action*
Measurement errors	Frequently review and update plans
Incorrect plan/standard/budget	Probably nothing
Random/chance fluctuations	Improve accuracy of recording systems

5 List four ways in which management can manipulate actual results.

- ....
- ....
- ....
- ....

6 *Choose the correct word from those highlighted.*

An objective is an aim that can be expressed in **qualitative/quantitative** terms

7 Which of the following is a measure of efficiency?

A Number of meals served per day
B Profit per £ of labour
C Cost per unit of output
D Actual output as a percentage of target output

Answers to quick quiz

1 False. There are no rules and regulations. The information must simply be useful.

2 C

3

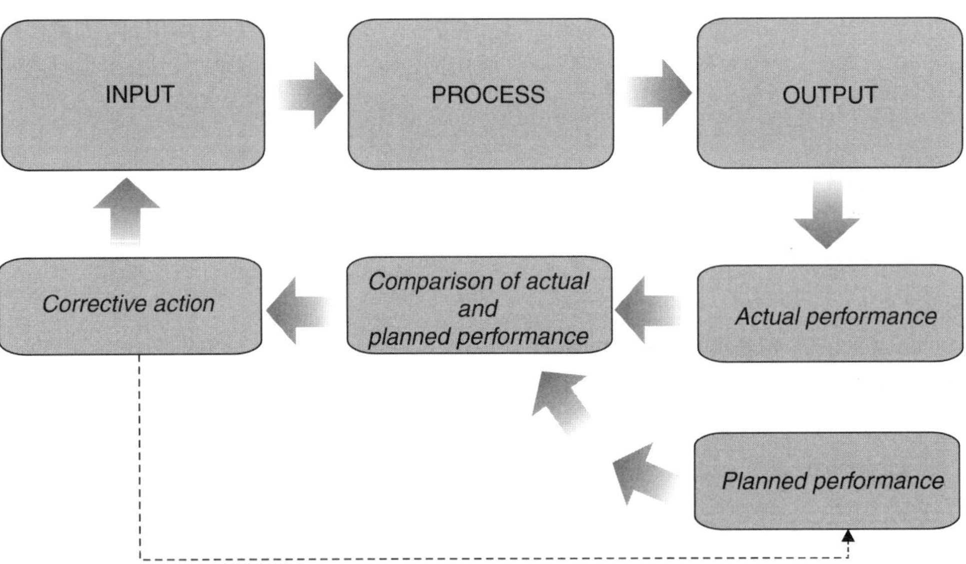

4 Measurement errors – improve accuracy of recording system
Incorrect plan/standard/budget – frequently review and update plans
Random/chance fluctuations – probably nothing

5
- Keep back invoices to keep the apparent level of spending low.
- Delay discretionary expenditure on, for example, training, advertising, research and development.
- Reduce levels of quality (and hence save costs) in ways that are not immediately apparent to customers.
- Achieve favourable variances at the expense of adverse variances occurring elsewhere in the organisation.

6 An objective is an aim that can be expressed in quantitative terms.

7 B

ASSESSMENT KIT ACTIVITIES

The following activity in the BPP Assessment Kit for Units 8 & 9 includes topics covered in this chapter.

Activity 1

Activity checklist

This checklist shows which performance criteria, range statement or knowledge and understanding point is covered by each activity in this chapter. Tick off each activity as you complete it.

Activity		
1.1	☐	This activity deals with Performance Criteria 8.2B regarding the preparation of performance indicators, Range Statement 8.2: performance indicators and Unit 8 Knowledge & Understanding point (6): performance indicators.
1.2	☐	This activity deals with Performance Criteria 8.2B regarding the preparation of performance indicators, Range Statement 8.2: performance indicators and Unit 8 Knowledge & Understanding point (6): performance indicators.
1.3	☐	This activity deals with Performance Criteria 8.2B regarding the preparation of performance indicators, Range Statement 8.2: performance indicators and Unit 8 Knowledge & Understanding point (6): performance indicators.

chapter 2

The behaviour, recording and reporting of costs

Contents

1 Introduction
2 Cost behaviour
3 Recording and reporting of costs – absorption costing
4 Recording and reporting of costs – marginal costing
5 Marginal costing versus absorption costing
6 Manipulating performance

Performance criteria

8.1E Analyse the effect of organisational accounting policies on reported costs

Range statement

8.1 The build up of costs: absorption costing; marginal costing

Knowledge and understanding

Unit 8 Accounting principles and theory

8 Marginal and absorption costing: cost recording, cost reporting, cost behaviour

Unit 9 Accounting principles and theory

12 Marginal and absorption costing: cost recording, cost reporting, cost behaviour

Note that the contents of this chapter represent an important aspect of knowledge and understanding in both Unit 8 and Unit 9. Relevance to particular performance criteria will be apparent in subsequent chapters.

Signpost

You should read this introductory chapter whether you are studying **Unit 8** or **Unit 9**.

1 Introduction

This chapter offers you a chance to clarify your understanding of a number of topics covered in your earlier cost accounting studies (namely **cost behaviour** and **absorption costing).** You need to be competent in these topics to be able to deal with techniques introduced in later chapters.

The chapter also considers in Section 4 an alternative to absorption costing called **marginal costing** (which you may or may not have covered already, depending on when you sat previous exams). In particular you will need to be aware of the **implications on profit** of using absorption costing and marginal costing. This will be of particular relevance in Chapter 10, when we look at flexible budgeting.

2 Cost behaviour

Cost behaviour underpins a number of ideas and techniques we will be looking at as we work through this text. Although you covered cost behaviour in your earlier studies, you need to check that you remember the main points set out in the REMEMBER box below.

REMEMBER...

Cost behaviour

Variable (or marginal) costs

- Tend to vary directly with the level of output (so that there is a linear relationship between variable cost per unit and output)
- Variable cost **per unit** is the same amount for each unit produced but **total** variable cost increases as volume of output increases
- Example: materials

Fixed costs

- Tend to be unaffected by increases or decreases in the level of output
- Relate to a span of time and so are a **period charge** (as the time span increases so too will the cost)
- Only constant at all levels of output within the **relevant range** of output (the range of output at which the organisation has had experience of operating in the past and for which cost information is available)
- Examples: local government taxes for commercial properties (rates) and UK road fund licence

Semi-variable (or semi-fixed or mixed) costs

- Made up of a fixed cost element and a variable cost element and so partly affected by changes in the level of activity

REMEMBER... (cont'd)

Stepped costs

- Behave like fixed costs within certain ranges of activity
- Example: rent (of an organisation's one factory) may be a fixed cost if production remains below 1,000 units a month, but if production exceeds 1,000 units a second factory may be required and the cost of rent (on two factories) would go up a step
- Do not behave like variable costs and so, continuing the example above, if monthly output is 1,500 units, two factories are required – not 1.5 factories

These descriptions of cost behaviour are **factual statements.**

TOPIC LINK

Cost behaviour and budgeting

A good knowledge of cost behaviour is vital when you come on to studying flexible budgeting in Chapter 10 in particular and budget preparation in general.

3 Recording and reporting of costs – absorption costing

There are two basic approaches for recording and reporting costs, marginal costing and absorption costing. (A third, activity based costing, is a variation of absorption costing, and is covered in Chapter 15.)

Absorption costing is a **method of determining the cost of products**. It aims to **include in the total cost of a product an appropriate share of an organisation's total overhead**.

You should be familiar with absorption costing from your earlier studies of both cost accounting and financial accounting. Read through the following 'REMEMBER' box for a summary of the main points. We then look at under/over absorption and timing differences in a little more detail.

REMEMBER...

Absorption costing

- Divide costs into direct costs and indirect costs.
  - A **direct cost** is a cost that can be traced in full to the product, service or department that is being costed.
  - An **indirect cost** or **overhead** is incurred in the course of making a product, providing a service or running a department but it cannot be traced directly and in full to the product, service or department.

Direct costs can therefore be allocated to the cost of a product immediately. **Overheads** need to be **divided between (or absorbed into) products** using the following approach.

- Either allocate an overhead to a particular cost centre (if the overhead relates solely to that cost centre) or apportion it to a number of cost centres using a fair apportionment basis (if the overhead relates to a number of cost centres). For example, heating and lighting costs might be apportioned on the basis of volume of space/floor area occupied by each cost centre.

REMEMBER... (cont'd)

- Apportion the overheads which have been accumulated in service cost centres (canteen, maintenance and so on) to production cost centres that benefit from the service provided. For example, the cost of a canteen might be apportioned on the basis of the number of employees in the production departments.
- **Absorb overheads** which have been **accumulated in production cost centres** into units of output using a **predetermined absorption rate** based on expected activity level (labour hours, machine hours and so on). If the absorption basis is labour hours, the greater the number of labour hours the product requires, the greater the amount of budgeted overhead absorbed by the product.
- A product cost determined using absorption costing is therefore a **'full' cost** in that it includes both direct and indirect costs.

Activity 2.1

A direct labour employee's wage in week 5 is made up as follows.

		£
(a)	Basic pay for normal hours worked, 36 hours at £4 per hour =	144
(b)	Pay at the basic rate for overtime, 6 hours at £4 per hour =	24
(c)	Overtime shift premium, with overtime paid at time-and-a-quarter ¼ × 6 hours × £4 per hour =	6
(d)	A plus payment under a group bonus (or 'incentive') scheme – bonus for the month =	30
Total gross wages in week 5 for 42 hours of work		204

Task

Decide which costs are direct and which are indirect.

Activity 2.2

List as many possible bases of absorption (or 'overhead recovery rates') which you can think of.

Activity 2.3

Redhill Ltd has just begun the manufacture of a product, the NK7.

(a) The following is taken from the company's budget for year 1.

	Department	
	A (machinery)	*B (finishing)*
Production overhead cost	£24,000	£21,000
Direct material cost	£50,000	£30,000
Direct labour hours	2,500	30,000
Direct labour rate per hour	£10	£5
Machine hours	10,000	500

Department A is heavily automated, with machines doing most of the work. Individual workers in each department earn different rates of pay, and occasionally work overtime.

Task

Calculate an appropriate production overhead absorption rate for each department.

(b) During year 1, Reagale Ltd order an NK7. Production data is as follows.

Direct materials		£100
Direct labour	(department A)	2 hours
	(department B)	12 hours
Machine time	(department A)	20 hours
	(department B)	10 hours

Task

Calculate the cost of the order.

(c) Employee B works in Department B. He is paid £5 per hour (basic) and £7.50 per hour for any overtime. In week 47, he was paid for 42 hours, although he only worked 20 as the machine he uses broke down. Before the break down, he had worked two hours overtime, which are included in the 42 hours paid for.

Task

Calculate employee B's wage for week 47, and the amount that would be classified as direct labour cost.

Activity 2.4

An organisation has budgeted production volume of 5,000 units, actual production volume of 5,300 units and budgeted fixed overheads of £100,000. What are the fixed overheads absorbed into production?

3.1 Over and under absorption

Estimated overheads are **included** in the **actual cost of production** using an **absorption rate based on expected activity level** (units, labour hours, machine hours and so on).

Unless actual activity level and **actual overheads** are the **same** as those **expected**, the **overhead absorbed** into the cost of production **will not be the same** as the **overhead incurred**. This means that at the end of the period, **profit** either needs to be **reduced (over-absorbed overhead) or increased (under-absorbed overhead)** by an amount which, along with the overhead absorbed in the cost of production, totals actual overhead expenditure.

Remember that under-absorbed and over-absorbed overhead are simply **bookkeeping adjustments** to **ensure** that the **overhead absorbed equals the overhead incurred**.

Try the following activity to ensure that you can remember how to deal with under and over absorption.

Activity 2.5

MH Ltd has a budgeted production overhead of £180,000 and a budgeted activity of 45,000 machine hours.

Task

Calculate the under-/over-absorbed overhead, and note the reasons for the under/over absorption in the following circumstances.

(a) Actual overheads cost £170,000 and 45,000 machine hours were worked.
(b) Actual overheads cost £180,000 and 40,000 machine hours were worked.
(c) Actual overheads cost £170,000 and 40,000 machine hours were worked.

Activity 2.6

County Consumables Ltd uses absorption costing. The predetermined overhead absorption rate for year 7 was set at £10 per direct labour hour. The company's year 7 profit calculation showed a figure for overheads of £23,840 and a figure for under-absorbed overhead of £1,790.

Task

Calculate County Consumables Ltd's budgeted and actual activity levels for year 7.

3.2 Timing differences

Not all the overhead absorbed into the cost of production is charged against the period's profit. The cost of production is made up of the cost of sales and the cost of closing stock. The **overhead included in the cost of sales is charged**

against the period's profit, but the **overhead included in closing stock** is **carried forward** and set against the profit of subsequent periods.

Suppose that an organisation's actual overhead costs were the same as budgeted overhead costs but the actual volume of output was less than the budgeted volume of output. The following diagram sets out **how the overhead is charged against profit**.

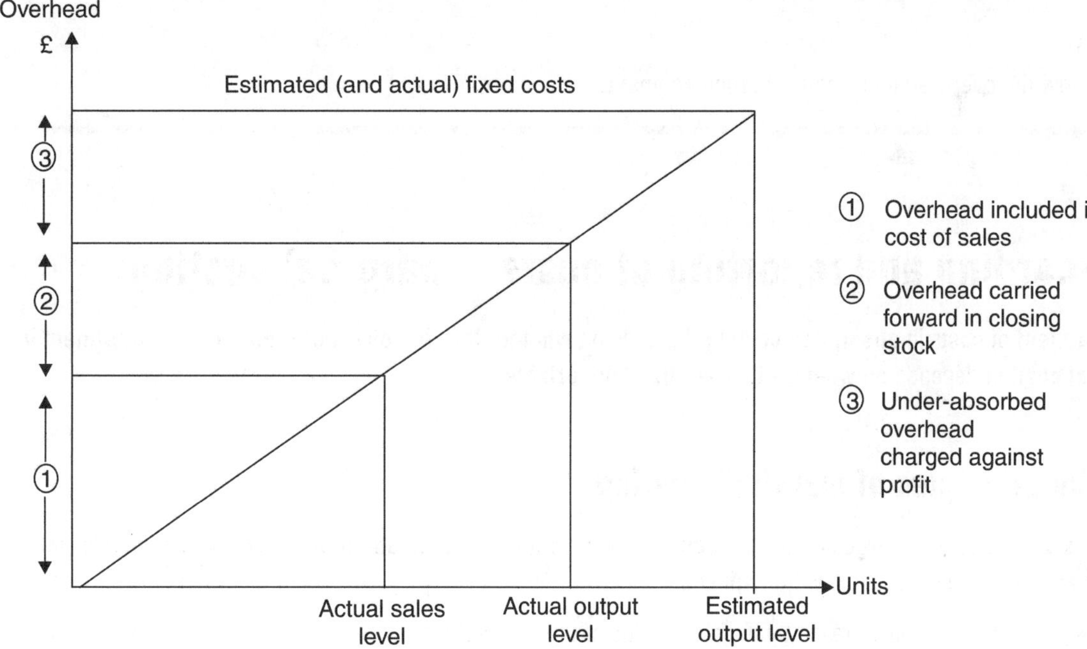

As you can see, the overhead incurred is charged against profit in three ways.

1. In the period in question, in cost of sales (the overhead absorbed by the units sold)
2. In a subsequent period, when units of closing stock are sold (the overhead absorbed by those units produced but not sold)
3. In the period in question, via a bookkeeping adjustment which ensures that 1 + 2 + 3 = overhead incurred

The **charging of some overhead in the current period** and **some in a later period** is just a **timing difference**. **Over time all overhead incurred** will be **charged** against profit.

IMPORTANT POINT

Make sure that you really understand the diagram above as you will find it an invaluable help in your understanding of fixed overhead variances (Chapter 6) and flexible budgeting (Chapter 10).

Activity 2.7

Suppose the expected level of activity for Hamilton Ltd is 5,000 units per year and the estimated annual overheads are £25,000. Actual overheads were £25,000, the number of units actually produced was 6,000, while 5,500 units were sold. There were no opening and closing stocks of materials or finished goods. Hamilton Ltd uses absorption costing.

Task

Set out how the overhead incurred is charged against profit.

4 Recording and reporting of costs – marginal costing

The **treatment** of costs in **absorption costing** depends on **whether** they are **direct** or **indirect**. Their **treatment** in **marginal costing** depends on **whether** they are **fixed** or **variable**.

4.1 The principles of marginal costing

Fixed costs are a period charge and are the **same for any volume of sales and production** (within the relevant range). So if an extra unit is sold the following happens.

- Revenue will increase by the sales value of the item sold.
- Costs will increase by the variable cost per unit.
- Profit will increase by the **difference between sales value per unit and variable cost per unit (contribution).**

Therefore **only variable costs** are **charged** to the **cost of sales**.

Fixed costs are **deducted** from **total contribution** (the difference between sales revenue and the cost of sales) **to derive profit** for the period.

When a unit of product is made, the extra costs incurred in its manufacture are the variable production costs. Fixed costs are unaffected – no extra fixed costs are incurred when output is increased. The **valuation of units of output** and hence **closing stocks** is therefore at **variable production cost** because these are the only costs properly attributable to the product.

Activity 2.8

A particular electrical good is sold for £1,009.99. The direct material cost per unit is £320, the direct labour cost per unit is £192 and the variable production overhead cost per unit is £132. Fixed overheads per annum are £100,000 and the budgeted production level is 1,000 units.

Task

Calculate the contribution per unit of the electrical good.

Example: marginal costing

Gamma Ltd makes a product, the delta, which has a variable production cost of £6 per unit and a sales price of £10 per unit. At the beginning of April Year 3, there were no opening stocks and production during the month was 20,000 units. Fixed costs for the month were £45,000. There were no variable marketing costs.

Task

Calculate the contribution and profit in April Year 3 using marginal costing principles if 10,000 deltas were sold.

Solution

The **first** stage in the profit calculation must be to **identify the variable cost of sales**, and **then** the **contribution. Fixed costs** are **deducted** from the total contribution to derive the profit. All **closing stocks** are **valued** at **marginal production cost** (£6 per unit).

	£	£
Sales (at £10)		100,000
Opening stock	0	
Variable production cost	120,000	
	120,000	
Less value of closing stock (at marginal cost)	60,000	
Variable cost of sales		60,000
Contribution		40,000
Less fixed costs		45,000
Profit/(loss)		(5,000)
Profit/(loss) per unit		£(0.50)
Contribution per unit		£4

Activity 2.9

Look at the example above. Calculate the contribution and profit in April Year 3 using marginal costing principles if (a) 15,000 deltas and (b) 20,000 deltas had been sold.

5 Marginal costing versus absorption costing

One of the reasons an organisation uses a costing system is to put a value on closing stock that can be incorporated into profit statements. As we have seen, absorption costing and marginal costing give different unit costs. This means that stock valuations will be different and so, consequently, will profits.

REMEMBER....

If you are having trouble understanding why the valuation of closing stock affects profit, think back to the following formula you should have encountered in your financial accounting studies.

Cost of sales = opening stock + cost of production – closing stock

The cost of sales is set against sales revenue to arrive at profit and the value of cost of sales depends in part on the value of closing stock. Hence stock valuation will have a significant impact on the profit reported.

Let's have a look at the effect the two approaches have on reported profit.

5.1 When production equals sales

Suppose the expected level of activity for K Ltd is 5,000 units per year and the estimated annual fixed overhead costs are £25,000. Sales revenue was £64,000, material and labour cost £7.50 per unit, actual fixed overhead costs were £28,000 and the number of units actually produced was 4,000. There were no opening and closing stocks of materials or finished goods.

Activity 2.10

Draw up the profit statement for K Ltd above using absorption costing.

What is highlighted by the absorption costing profit statement?

- Because there are **no opening and closing stocks**, the **cost of production** is the **same** as the **cost of sales**.

- The **fixed overhead charged** to the cost of production (£20,000) is **less** than the **fixed overhead incurred** (£28,000) for two reasons.

  The **actual production level** was **less** than the **planned production level**, with the result that (1,000 × £5) £5,000 of overhead was not absorbed into the cost of production.

  Actual fixed overheads were £3,000 **more** than **budgeted fixed overheads**.

The difference of £8,000 must be charged to the profit and loss account (via under-absorbed overheads) so that overhead charged equals overhead incurred.

Now let's use the same information about K Ltd and draw up a marginal costing profit statement.

Marginal costing profit statement

	£	£
Revenue		64,000
Variable cost of production		
Material and labour	30,000	
Cost of sales		30,000
Contribution		34,000
Fixed overheads		28,000
Profit		6,000

What is highlighted by the marginal costing profit statement?

- Because there are **no opening and closing stocks**, the **cost of production** is the **same** as **the cost of sales**.
- The **fixed overhead costs** are **charged in full** against contribution and hence profit.

5.1.1 Summary

As you can see, the marginal costing profit is the same as the absorption costing profit because £28,000 fixed overhead has been charged against profit in both cases.

5.2 Production is not equal to sales

Now suppose K Ltd had actually produced 5,000 units but had only sold 4,000 of them, with all other data remaining the same.

Activity 2.11

Draw up a profit statement using absorption costing using this new information about K Ltd.

What is highlighted by the absorption costing profit statement?

- The variable cost of production has increased because the level of production has increased.
- The amount of fixed overhead absorbed is based on the production level of 5,000 units
- The closing stock is valued at the absorbed cost per unit.
- Cost of sales is not the same as cost of production because 1,000 units have not been sold but remain in closing stock.
- The fixed overhead charged to the cost of production is £3,000 less than the fixed overhead incurred. This under absorption is due simply to the difference between budgeted overhead of £25,000 and actual overhead of £28,000. There is no under or over absorption due to production volume because actual production volume was the same as budgeted production volume.
- The £28,000 of overhead has been accounted for as follows.
  - In cost of sales (4,000 × £5) £20,000
  - In closing stock (1,000 × £5) £5,000
  - In under-absorbed overhead £3,000

  This means that only £23,000 has been charged against profit, the rest being carried forward in closing stock to be charged against the next period's profit.

Activity 2.12

Draw up the marginal costing profit statement for the same example.

What is highlighted by the marginal costing profit statement?

- The **variable cost of production** has **increased** because the volume of **production** has **increased**.
- The **closing stock** is **valued** at **variable cost** only.
- The **fixed overhead costs** incurred are **charged in full** against contribution and hence profit.

This time, however, the marginal costing profit is not the same as the absorption costing profit, the absorption costing profit being higher by £5,000. Why is this?

- The revenue is the same in each statement.
- The variable costs are the same in the two statements (£37,500 in cost of production and £7,500 in closing stock).
- £23,000 of fixed overhead has been charged against absorption costing profit but £28,000 has been charged against marginal costing profit.

The **absorption costing profit** is therefore **higher** than the **marginal costing** profit **by the amount of fixed overhead carried forward in closing stock** (1,000 × £5).

IMPORTANT POINT

When **opening and closing stock levels differ**, marginal costing and absorption costing will report different profits.

- If **stock levels increase**, as in the example above, **absorption costing** will report a **higher profit** than marginal costing because more of the fixed overheads are carried forward in closing stock to be set against profit in a future period.
- If **stock levels fall, absorption costing** will report a **lower profit** than marginal costing because, as well as fixed overheads incurred in the current period, some fixed overheads incurred in a previous period are set against profit.
- If **stock levels** are **constant** there is **no difference** in the profits reported using the two methods.

Again, the differences in reported profits are just **timing differences**. Over time the total profits reported are the same because over time the overheads reported are the same.

TOPIC LINK

Absorption/marginal costing and flexible budgeting

Your understanding of the differences between absorption and marginal costing and the implications on reported profit will be tested when we look at flexible budgeting in Chapter 10.

6 Manipulating performance

As we have seen, **absorption costing profits** can **vary with the volume** of **production**, even when the volume of sales is constant. Management can therefore **manipulate** budgeted and/or actual performance (in terms of **profit**) simply **by changing output and stock levels.**

Let's look at another example just to make sure you have grasped this idea. Suppose James Hardy Ltd uses absorption costing and budgeted to make and sell 10,000 units of its product in 20X1. The selling price is budgeted at £10 per unit and the variable cost at £4 per unit. Fixed production overheads are budgeted at £50,000 per year.

During 20X1 it became apparent that sales demand would be only 8,000 units. The management, concerned about the apparent effect of the low volume of sales on profits, decided to increase production for the year to 15,000 units. Actual fixed overheads were still expected to be £50,000 in spite of the significant increase in production volume. Actual selling price and variable cost were as budgeted.

Here are some profit calculations.

Original budgeted profit

	£
Sales (10,000 × £10)	100,000
Cost of production (10,000 × £(4 + 5))	(90,000)
	10,000

Profit if production had not been increased

	£	£
Sales (8,000 × £10)		80,000
Cost of production (10,000 × £9)	(90,000)	
Closing stock (2,000 × £9)	18,000	
Cost of sales		(72,000)
Profit		8,000

Actual profit

	£	£
Sales (8,000 × £10)		80,000
Cost of production (15,000 × 9)	135,000	
Less: closing stock (7,000 × £9)	(63,000)	
Cost of sales	72,000	
Over-absorbed overhead (5,000 × £5)	(25,000)	
Total costs		(47,000)
Profit		33,000

By **increasing production in excess of sales**, management have been able to **increase** the actual **profit** from the £8,000 that would have been recorded to £33,000. Despite sales being lower than budgeted, the actual profit is £23,000 greater than the £10,000 budgeted.

This example highlights the fact that favourable variances can occur for reasons other than improved efficiency.

Key learning points

- ☑ Descriptions of **cost behaviour** are factual statements.
- ☑ Costs tend to behave in **variable**, **fixed**, **semi-variable/semi-fixed/mixed** or **stepped** fashion.
- ☑ The treatment of costs in **absorption costing** depends on whether they are **direct** or **indirect/overheads**. Their treatment in **marginal costing** depends on whether they are **fixed** or **variable**.
- ☑ When **absorption costing** is used, overhead incurred in a period is charged against profit in three ways.
  - In the period in question, in cost of sales
  - In a subsequent period, when closing stock is eventually sold
  - In the period in question, via under-/over-absorbed overhead
- ☑ **Marginal costing** charges the fixed costs (which include fixed overheads) incurred in a period against the profit for the period.
- ☑ The different approaches to charging fixed overheads cause **timing differences** in profit reported if opening and closing stock levels differ.
  - If stock levels increase, absorption costing reports the higher profit because fixed overheads are carried forward in closing stock to be set against future profit.
  - If stock levels fall, absorption costing reports the lower profit because, as well as fixed overheads incurred in the period, some fixed overheads incurred in a previous period are set against profit.
  - If stock levels are constant, there is no difference in the profits reported using marginal costing and absorption costing.

  Over time all fixed overhead incurred will be charged against profit and so over time total profits reported are the same.
- ☑ Management can **manipulate profit** when using absorption costing by increasing production in excess of sales.

Quick quiz

1 The behaviour of fixed costs depends on whether marginal costing or absorption costing is being used. *True or false?*

2 *Match the number on the graph to the descriptions of how overhead is charged if absorption costing is used.*

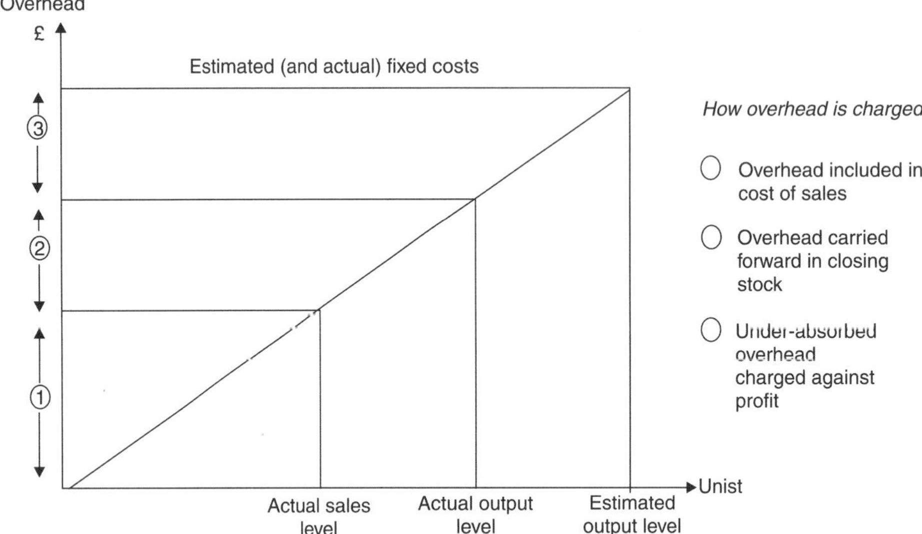

3 *Fill in the blanks.*

In marginal costing, ... are deducted from total contribution (sales revenue minus ....) to derive .... Units of closing stock are valued at .... cost.

4 *Choose the correct words from those highlighted.*

If stock levels **fall/rise,** absorption costing will report a higher profit than marginal costing.

Answers to quick quiz

1 False. The behaviour of fixed costs remains the same regardless of the costing system being used. It is the recording and reporting of costs that varies.

2

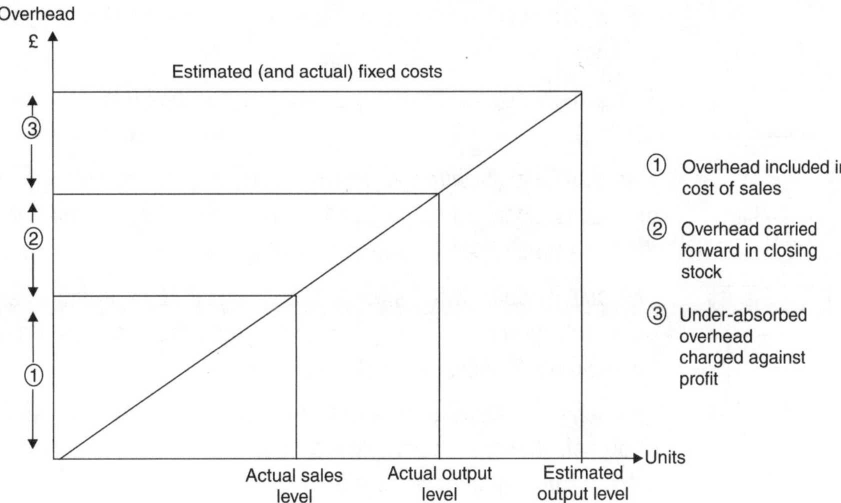

3 In marginal costing, fixed costs are deducted from total contribution (sales revenue minus variable costs) to derive profit. Units of closing stock are valued at variable or marginal cost.

4 If stock levels **rise**, absorption costing will report a higher profit than marginal costing.

ASSESSMENT KIT ACTIVITIES

The following activities in the BPP Assessment Kit for Units 8 & 9 include topics covered in this chapter.

Activities 2 and 3 and lecturers' practice activity 1

Activity checklist

This checklist shows which performance criteria, range statement or knowledge and understanding point is covered by each activity in this chapter. Tick off each activity as you complete it.

Activity		
2.1	☐	This activity deals with Range Statement 8.1: the build up of costs (absorption costing).
2.2	☐	This activity deals with Range Statement 8.1: the build up of costs (absorption costing).
2.3	☐	This activity deals with Performance Criteria 8.1E regarding analysis of the effect of organisational accounting policies on reported costs and Range Statement 8.1: the build up of costs (absorption costing)
2.4	☐	This activity deals with Performance Criteria 8.1E regarding analysis of the effect of organisational accounting policies on reported costs and Range Statement 8.1: the build up of costs (absorption costing).
2.5	☐	This activity deals with Performance Criteria 8.1E regarding analysis of the effect of organisational accounting policies on reported costs and with Range Statement 8.1: the build up of costs (absorption costing).
2.6	☐	This activity deals with Range Statement 8.1: the build up of costs (absorption costing).
2.7	☐	This activity deals with Performance Criteria 8.1E regarding analysis of the effect of organisational accounting policies on reported costs and Range Statement 8.1: the build up of costs (absorption costing).
2.8	☐	This activity deals with Range Statement 8.1: the build up of costs (marginal costing).
2.9	☐	This activity deals with Performance Criteria 8.1E regarding analysis of the effect of organisational accounting policies on reported costs and Range Statement 8.1: the build up of costs (marginal costing).
2.10	☐	This activity deals with Performance Criteria 8.1E regarding analysis of the effect of organisational accounting policies on reported costs and Range Statement 8.1: the build up of costs (absorption costing).
2.11	☐	This activity deals with Performance Criteria 8.1E regarding analysis of the effect of organisational accounting policies on reported costs, Range Statement 8.1: the build up of costs, Unit 8 Knowledge & Understanding point (8): marginal and absorption costing and Unit 9 Knowledge & Understanding point (12): marginal and absorption costing.
2.12	☐	This activity deals with Performance Criteria 8.1E regarding analysis of the effect of organisational accounting policies on reported costs, Range Statement 8.1: the build up of costs, Unit 8 Knowledge & Understanding point (8): marginal and absorption costing and Unit 9 Knowledge & Understanding point (12): marginal and absorption costing.

chapter 3

Collecting data

Contents

1 Introduction
2 Data
3 Sampling
4 Random sampling
5 Quasi-random sampling
6 Non-random sampling
7 Sources of data
8 Primary external sources of data – surveys
9 Secondary external sources of data

Performance criteria

8.1A Identify valid, relevant information from internal and external sources

9.1A Identify relevant data for projecting forecasts from internal and external sources

Range statement

8.1 Information: movements in prices charged by suppliers, competitors and providers of services; general price changes

8.1 Methods of summarising data: sampling

9.1 Data: accounting information; wage and salary information; information about suppliers and availability of inputs; information about customers and markets; general economic information

Knowledge and understanding

Unit 8 The business environment

1 External sources of information on costs and prices: government statistics, trade associations, financial press, quotations, price lists

2 General economic environment

Knowledge and understanding (cont'd)

Unit 8 Accounting techniques

3 Basic statistical methods: sampling techniques

Unit 8 Accounting principles and theory

10 The use and limitation of published statistics

Unit 8 The organisation

13 The organisation's external environment and specific external costs

Unit 9 The business environment

1 External sources of information on costs, prices, demand and availability of resources

Unit 9 Accounting techniques

3 Basic statistical methods: sampling techniques

Signpost

The topics covered in this chapter are relevant to **Unit 8** and **Unit 9**.

1 Introduction

In this chapter we will be considering methods for collecting data. The **data**, once **collected**, can then be **analysed** (see Chapter 4) to become **useful information**.

Here we look at the basic principles involved. Application of the methods in terms of the contents of Units 8 and 9 we will look as we work through the text.

This chapter's contents **do not constitute core issues** of the management accounting units but instead **underpin** the key themes of standard costing, budgeting and performance indicators.

Tasks in previous exams have incorporated various aspects of data collection on occasions but this is **not an area that was regularly examined** under the previous version of the standards.

2 Data

2.1 What is data?

Data is a 'scientific' term for **facts, figures, information and measurements**.

Data includes the following.

- The number of goals scored by each football team in the second division
- The profit after tax for the past ten years of the four biggest supermarket chains

2.2 Types of data

2.2.1 Quantitative and qualitative data

Quantitative data is data that can be **measured**. Here are some examples.

- The **temperature** on each day of August (which can be measured in degrees Fahrenheit or Celsius)
- The **time** it takes you to travel to work each day this week (which can be measured in hours and minutes)

Qualitative data is data that **cannot be measured** but reflects some **quality** of what is being observed.

Whether somebody is **male or female** is an example of **qualitative data**: there is no measure of *how* male or *how* female somebody is. 'This bed is **very comfortable'** is another example.

2.2.2 Primary and secondary data

Primary data is data **collected specifically** for the purpose you have in mind.

Secondary data is data which has **already been collected elsewhere**, for some other purpose, but which can be used or adapted for your purpose.

What are the **advantages** of using **primary data**?

- The source of the data, the circumstances under which it is collected and any limitations or inadequacies in the data are known to you.
- The data is tailor-made to your requirements and likely to be more up-to-date than anything from a published source.
- You might not be aware of any limitations in secondary data because you did not collect it.
- Secondary data may not be entirely suitable for your purpose.

Secondary data can sometimes be **used** despite its inadequacies because it is **available cheaply** (the extra cost of collecting primary data outweighing its extra value) and because you, as a private individual or representative of your firm, are **unlikely to have direct access to the primary data** sources. It is essential that you **believe** that the data is **reliable and accurate** if you are to use it, however.

Examples of secondary data include the following.

- **Published statistics**. We examine these in Section 9.
- **Historical records**. The type of historical record used depends on why it is required. An accountant producing an estimate of future company sales might use historical records of past sales.

2.3 Why collect data?

Organisations collect data because they **need information in order to function.** Managers need information to enable them to make plans, set targets, make decisions and control operations.

Information is **data** that has been **processed** in such a way as to be **meaningful** to the person who receives it.

Information is sometimes referred to as **processed data**. The terms 'information' and 'data' are often used interchangeably.

2.3.1 Turning data into information

Consider the following situation in which data is collected and then processed in order to produce meaningful information.

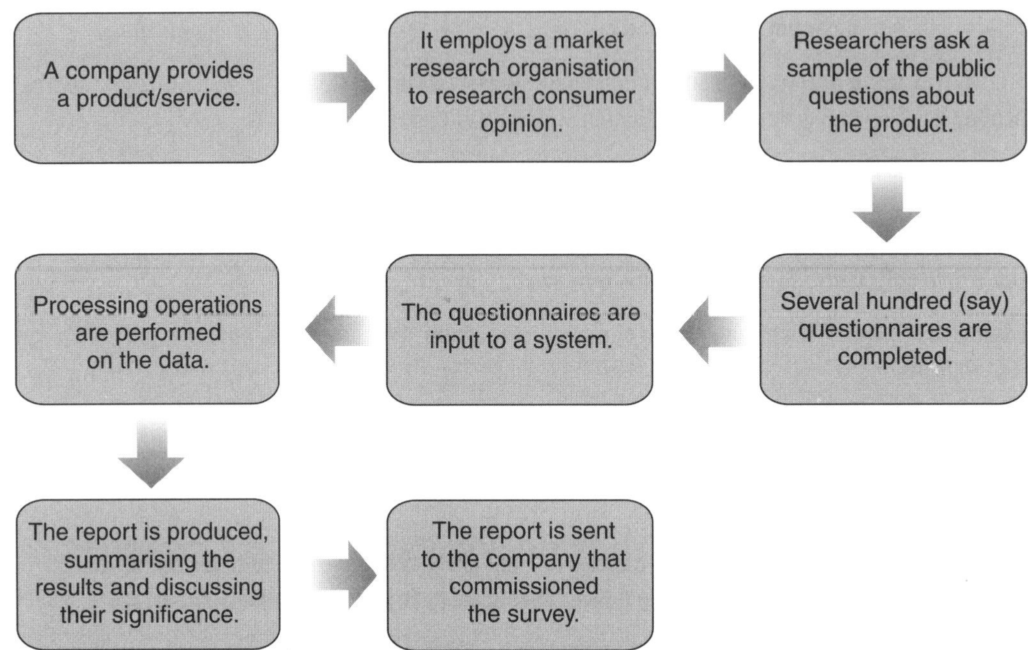

Individually, a completed questionnaire would not tell the company very much, only the views of one consumer. In this case, the **individual questionnaires are data**. Once they have been **processed**, and **analysed**, the resulting report is **information**. The company will use it to inform its decisions regarding the product. If the report revealed that consumers disliked the product, the company would scrap or alter it.

The **quality of source data affects the value of information**. Information is worthless if the source data is flawed. If the researchers filled in questionnaires themselves, inventing the answers, then the conclusions drawn from the processed data would be wrong, and poor decisions would be made.

3 Sampling

3.1 Populations

When collecting primary data, we need to define the population we are interested in. This is not as obvious as it sounds. **We have to be extremely specific** in our definition, especially if part-time market research interviewers are to do some of the data collection.

- If you tell your interviewers to question 'accountants', does this mean qualified accountants or students in training?
- Does the term include certified, management and chartered accountants and accounting technicians?

If you intended the term to be interpreted in one particular way and your interviewers interpret it differently your results may be invalid and even misleading and biased.

Example: Defining a population

Years ago in the United States, somebody was asked to conduct a survey on whether the next president was likely to be a Democrat or a Republican. The survey was carried out, but in an inappropriate way. The survey officer *telephoned* people, and in those days far more Republican than Democrat voters had telephones. The survey was useless, because it had not been planned properly.

The reason why the opinion poll turned out so badly was that the population for the survey had not been defined properly. The opinion poll should have used the population 'all Americans of voting age' whereas it actually used the population 'all Americans with a telephone'.

3.2 Censuses and samples

It is unlikely that we will be able to collect information from *every* member of our defined population. If **all members of a population are examined** we are conducting a **census**. The advantage of a census is that it should give a completely accurate view of the population but it is usually impractical and too costly.

Here are some **disadvantages of a census**.

- In practice, a 100% survey (census) never achieves the completeness required.
- The higher cost of a census may exceed the value of results.
- Even if you carry out a census, it could well be out of date by the time you complete it.

It therefore makes sense to study only a portion or sample of the population and hope that the results we get from our sample will not be too far from those which would apply to the population as a whole. In fact, if we select our sample in the right way we can be quite precise about how reliable the results we get will be.

It is possible to **ask more questions** with a sample and it can be shown mathematically that once a certain sample size has been reached, **very little extra accuracy is gained by examining more items**.

3.2.1 Bias

One of the most important requirements of **data** is that it **should be complete**. That is, the data should cover all areas of the population to be examined. If this requirement is **not met**, then the sample will be **biased** and any conclusions drawn from analysing the results of the sample will be invalid and misleading.

Example: Biased samples

Suppose you wanted to survey the productivity of workers in a factory, and you went along every Monday and Tuesday for a few months to measure their output. But that data would not be complete. You might have gathered very thorough data on what happens on Mondays and Tuesdays, but you would have missed out the rest of the week. It could be that the workers, keen and fresh after the weekend, work better at the start of the week than at the end. Your data would then give a misleadingly high productivity figure. Careful attention must therefore be given to the sampling method employed to produce a sample.

Activity 3.1

Suppose an organisation's sales department contacted customers about their expected future demand for the organisation's products.

Task

Briefly describe possible ways in which bias might be introduced into the data collected.

3.2.2 Sampling error

Sampling error arises when a **population sample is not representative of the population from which it is drawn**.

For example, if a sample of the population of a city was composed entirely of babies less than three months old, the sample would obviously not be representative of the population of the city. Again, conclusions drawn from analysing the results of the sample will be invalid and misleading.

Activity 3.2

What are the implications for the relevance of the information provided from a small sample? Provide an example linked to the scenario in Activity 3.1 to illustrate your answer.

3.3 Sampling methods

Sampling methods fall into three main groups: random sampling; quasi-random sampling; non-random sampling.

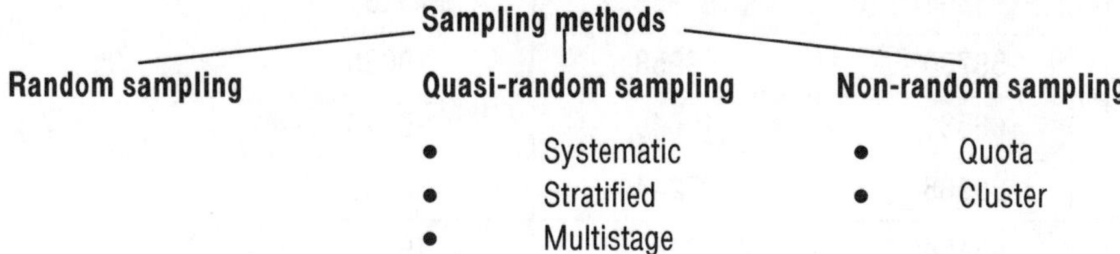

4 Random sampling

To ensure that the sample selected is **free from bias**, random sampling must be used. Inferences about the population being sampled can then be made validly.

A simple **random sample** is a sample selected in such a way that **every item in the population has an equal chance of being included**.

For example, if you wanted to take a random sample of library books, it would not be good enough to pick them off the shelves, even if you picked them at random. This is because the books which were out on loan would stand no chance of being chosen. You would either have to make sure that all the books were on the shelves before taking your sample, or find some other way of sampling (for example, using the library index cards).

A random sample is not necessarily a perfect sample. For example, you might pick what you believe to be a completely random selection of library books, and find that every one of them is a detective thriller. It is a remote possibility, but it could happen. The only way to eliminate the possibility altogether is to take a 100% survey (a census) of the books, which, unless it is a tiny library, is impractical.

4.1 Sampling frames

If random sampling is used then it is necessary to construct a sampling frame. A **sampling frame** is simply a **numbered list of all the items in the population**. Once such a list has been made, it is easy to select a random sample, simply by generating a list of random numbers. One way of achieving such a list is by numbering every member of the population, putting their numbers on pieces of paper, mixing up the pieces of paper in a hat and drawing out the numbers of those to be used in the sample. Alternatively, **random number tables** can be used.

4.1.1 Random number tables

Set out below is part of a typical random number table.

93716	16894	98953	73231
32886	59780	09958	18065
92052	06831	19640	99413
39510	35905	85244	35159
27699	06494	03152	19121
92962	61773	22109	78508
10274	12202	94205	50380
75867	20717	82037	10268
85783	47619	87481	37220

The sample is found by selecting groups of random numbers with the number of digits depending on the total population size, as follows.

Total population size	Number of random digits
1 – 10	1
1 – 100	2
1 – 1,000	3

The items selected for the sample are those corresponding to the random numbers selected.

The starting point on the table should be selected at random. After that, however, numbers must be selected in a consistent manner. In other words, you should use the table row by row or column by column. By jumping around the table from place to place, personal bias may be introduced.

In many practical situations it is more convenient to use a computer to generate a list of random numbers, especially when a large sample is required.

Example: random number tables

An investigator wishes to select a random sample from a population of 800 people, who have been numbered 000, 001, ...799. As there are three digits in 799 the random numbers will be selected in groups of three. Working along the first line of the table given earlier, the first few groups are 937 161 689 498 953 732. Numbers over 799 are discarded. The first four people in the sample will therefore be those numbered 161, 689, 498 and 732.

ATTENTION!

Although you will not be required to **use** random number tables in the exam, the assessor has stated that you must be aware of **how** they are used to determine a sample.

Sometimes it is not possible to draw up a sampling frame. For example, if you wanted to take a random sample of Americans, it would take too long to list all Americans. Two readily available sampling frames for the human population of Great Britain are the **council tax register** (list of dwellings) and the **electoral register** (list of individuals).

4.2 Drawbacks of random sampling

- The selected items are subject to all the variation inherent in the population.
- An unrepresentative sample may result.
- The sample may be scattered over a wide area, adding to costs and difficulties.
- An adequate sampling frame might not exist.
- The numbering of the population might be laborious.

In many situations it might be too expensive to obtain a random sample, in which case quasi-random sampling is necessary, or else it may not be possible to draw up a sampling frame. In such cases, non-random sampling has to be used.

5 Quasi-random sampling

Quasi-random sampling, which provides a **good approximation to random sampling**, necessitates the existence of a sampling frame. The main methods of quasi-random sampling are systematic sampling, stratified sampling and multistage sampling.

5.1 Systematic sampling

Systematic sampling may provide a good approximation to random sampling. It works by **selecting every nth item after a random start**. For example, if it was decided to select a sample of 20 from a population of 800, then every 40th (800 ÷ 20) item after a random start in the first 40 should be selected. The starting point could be found using the lottery method or random number tables. If (say) 23 was chosen, then the sample would include the 23rd, 63rd, 103rd, 143rd ... 783rd items. The gap of 40 is known as the **sampling interval**.

The **advantages** of systematic sampling are that it is easy to select the sample items given a sampling frame and it is reasonably random, providing there is no pattern to the distribution of items.

Systematic sampling has a number of **limitations**, however.

- It requires a sampling frame.
- It requires access to the whole population.
- If there is a regular pattern to the distribution of items, the sample may be biased.
- It may be expensive to select the required sample (every nth item).

5.2 Stratified sampling

In many situations stratified sampling is the best method of choosing a sample. The **population must be divided into strata or categories**. If we took a random sample of all AAT students in the country, it is conceivable that the entire

sample might consist of AAT students working in public companies. Stratified sampling removes this possibility as random samples could be taken from each type of employment, the number in each sample being proportional to the total number of AAT students in each type (for example those in partnerships, those in public companies and those in private companies).

Example: stratified sampling

The number of AAT students in each type of work in a particular country are as follows.

Partnerships	500
Public companies	500
Private companies	700
Public sector	800
	2,500

If a sample of 20 was required the sample would be made up as follows.

		Sample
Partnerships	(500/2,500) × 20	4
Public companies	(500/2,500) × 20	4
Private companies	(700/2,500) × 20	6
Public sector	(800/2,500) × 20	6
		20

The **strata frequently involve multiple classifications**. In social surveys, for example, there is usually stratification by age, sex and social class. This implies that the sampling frame must contain information on these three variables before the threefold stratification of the population can be made.

Here are some **advantages** of stratification.

- It ensures a representative sample since it guarantees that every important category will have elements in the final sample.
- The structure of the sample will reflect that of the population if the same proportion of individuals is chosen from each stratum.
- Each stratum is represented by a randomly chosen sample and therefore inferences can be made about each stratum.

Stratification requires prior knowledge of each item in the population but sampling frames do not always contain this information. Stratification from the electoral register as to age structure would not be possible because it does not contain age information.

5.3 Multistage sampling

Multistage sampling is normally **used to cut down the number of investigators and the costs** of obtaining a sample. An example will show how the method works.

Example: multistage sampling

A survey of spending habits is being planned to cover the whole of Britain. It is obviously impractical to draw up a sampling frame, so random sampling is not possible. Multi-stage sampling is to be used instead.

The country is divided into a number of areas and a small sample of these is selected at random. Each of the areas selected is subdivided into smaller units and again, a smaller number of these is selected at random. This process is repeated as many times as necessary and finally, a random sample of the relevant people living in each of the smallest units is taken. A fair approximation to a random sample can be obtained.

Thus, we might choose a random sample of eight areas, and from each of these areas, select a random sample of five towns. From each town, a random sample of 200 people might be selected so that the total sample size is $8 \times 5 \times 200 =$ 8,000 people.

There are two main **advantages** of this method.

- It does not require a sampling frame of the whole population.
- It is relatively cheap, because samples may be collected quickly.

The main **disadvantages** are that it is **not truly random**, as once the final sampling areas have been selected, the rest of the population cannot be in the sample and the sample **may be biased** if only a small number of regions are selected.

The sampling methods looked at so far have required a sampling frame but it is often impossible to identify a satisfactory one and so other sampling methods have to be employed.

6 Non-random sampling

There are two main methods of non-random sampling. Quota sampling and cluster sampling are **used when a sampling frame cannot be established**.

6.1 Quota sampling

Quota sampling is a sampling method commonly used by market researchers, and involves **stratifying the population and restricting the sample to a fixed number in each strata**.

Investigators are told to interview all of the people that they meet up to a certain quota. The quota may be further divided to ensure that the sample mirrors the structure or stratification of the population. The actual choice of the individuals to be interviewed is left to the investigator. The selection is therefore not done on a random basis, which is how quota sampling differs from stratified sampling.

Here are some **advantages** of quota sampling.

- It is cheap and administratively easy.
- A much larger sample can be studied, and hence more information can be gained at a faster speed for a given outlay.

- A fairly detailed knowledge of the population is required, but no sampling frame is necessary as the interviewer questions every person he meets up to the quota.
- It may be the only possible approach (eg television audience research).
- Given suitable, trained and properly briefed field workers, quota sampling yields enough accurate information for many forms of commercial market research.

There is a **disadvantage** to quota sampling. The method can result in certain biases. For example, if interviewers are asked to choose respondents in a shopping centre, those people who seldom or never go shopping will be excluded from the sample. (These biases can often be allowed for and/or may be unimportant for the purpose of the research, however.)

Quota sampling is unsatisfactory if it is important that theoretically valid results are obtained, but if other large sources of error exist, such as non response, it is pointless to worry too much about sampling error.

Example: quota sampling

Consider the figures in the example on stratified sampling, but with the following additional information relating to the sex of AAT students.

	Male	*Female*
Partnerships	300	200
Public companies	400	100
Private companies	300	400
Public sector	300	500

An investigator's quotas might be as follows.

	Male	*Female*	*Total*
Partnerships	30	20	50
Public companies	40	10	50
Private companies	30	40	70
Public sector	30	50	80
			250

Using quota sampling, the investigator would interview the first 30 male AAT students in partnerships that he met, the first 20 female AAT students in partnerships that he met and so on.

6.2 Cluster sampling

Cluster sampling involves **selecting one definable subsection of the population as the sample**, that subsection taken to be representative of the population in question. The pupils of one school might be taken as a cluster sample of all children at school in one county.

Cluster sampling benefits from **low costs** in the same way as multistage sampling. It is a **good alternative to multistage sampling** if a satisfactory sampling frame does not exist and it is **inexpensive** to operate because little organisation or structure is involved. There is **potential for considerable bias**, however.

Activity 3.3

Describe four methods a manufacturer could employ to test the market for a new coffee. Discuss the relative advantages and disadvantages of each method chosen.

ATTENTION!

In an exam you won't have to calculate sample sizes but you must be aware of the way in which the various types of sample are determined and, as the assessor has stated, you must have a good qualitative grasp of the benefits and limitations of sampling.

7 Sources of data

Data may be obtained from either an internal (in-house) source or from an external source.

7.1 Internal (in-house) sources of data

7.1.1 The financial accounting records

You should by now be very familiar with the idea of a system of sales ledgers and purchase ledgers, general ledgers, cash books and so on. These records provide a history of an organisation's monetary transactions. Some of these data are of great value outside the accounts department, for example sales data for the marketing function. Other data, like cheque numbers, are of purely administrative value within the accounts department.

You should also know that to maintain the integrity of its financial accounting records, an organisation of any size will have systems for and **controls over transactions**. These also **give rise to valuable data**. A stock control system, for example, will include purchase orders, goods received notes, goods returned notes and so on, and these can be analysed to provide management information about speed of delivery, say, or the quality of supplies.

7.1.2 Other internal sources

Here are some examples.

- Data about personnel can be sourced from the **payroll system** if, say, a project is being costed and it is necessary to ascertain the availability and rate of pay of different levels of staff.
- A lot of data will be produced by a **production department** about machine capacity, fuel consumption, movement of people, materials, and work in progress, set up times, maintenance requirements and so on.
- A **marketing department** would be able to provide market surveys, information about salesmen's performance and trends in discounts.

- A **personnel department** would be able to provide information about overtime, sickness, absence and lateness rates.
- Many **service businesses** – notably accountants and solicitors – need to keep **detailed records of the time spent** on various activities, both to justify fees to clients and to assess the efficiency of operations.

In fact, all departments in an organisation are important sources of data.

TOPIC LINK

Collecting data and control systems

The **sensor** (think back to Chapter 1 and control systems) within standard costing, budgeting and performance measurement control systems will need to record a wide range of internal data such as the cost of labour and the number of labour hours worked.

7.2 External sources of data

An organisation's files are full of invoices, letters, advertisements, quotations, price lists and so on received *from* customers and suppliers. But there are many occasions when an active search outside the organisation is needed. In this connection we need to define two terms.

- A **primary source** of data is, as the term implies, as close as you can get to the origin of an item of data: the eyewitness to an event, the document under scrutiny.
- A **secondary source**, again logically enough, provides 'second-hand' data: books, articles, verbal or written reports by someone else.

8 Primary external sources of data – surveys

Although surveys (which are often used for market research purposes) offer a quick, efficient and cost-effective way of obtaining the required data, they are not straightforward. Without skill, tact and expertise the results may easily become contaminated with bias and error and the conclusions subsequently drawn will be useless.

There are two main types of survey, interviews and postal questionnaires.

8.1 Interviews

There are basically two types of interview that can be used to collect data.

- Personal (face to face) interview
- Telephone interview

8.1.1 Personal (face to face) interviews

In a personal interview, an **interviewer asks a number of questions from a questionnaire**.

These interviews have a number of advantages.

- Interviewers are able to reduce anxiety and embarrassment of respondents.
- There is an increased response rate.
- There is increased accuracy of responses.
- Interviewers can ask for clarification of answer given.
- Questions can be asked in a fixed order.
- Answers can be recorded in a standard manner.
- Standardisation of questions means less skilled (cheaper) interviewers may be used.
- Pictures, signs and objects can be used.
- Routing of questions is easier.

But they also have disadvantages.

- They are time consuming.
- Cost per completed interview can be higher than with other survey methods.
- Questionnaires can be difficult to design.

Store/shopping mall intercept surveys are face-to-face interviews that are carried out in busy town centres, especially shopping centres/malls. The interviewer tends to stand in one position and approaches potential respondents as soon as the previous interview is completed, thereby eliminating time between interviews. The interview needs to be brief, however, as respondents are unlikely to want to stop for more than ten minutes.

Focus groups (otherwise known as **group discussions**) are useful in providing qualitative data. They usually consist of seven to ten respondents and an interviewer. The interviewer introduces topics for discussion and intervenes as necessary to encourage respondents or to direct discussions if they threaten to wander too far off the point.

Focus groups have a number of **advantages**.

- Inexpensive
- Quick
- Provide useful, timely data
- Less intimidating than one-to-one interviews

But, of course, they have **disadvantages**.

- Dependant on the skill of the interviewer
- Can inhibit some people from making a full contribution
- May require audio/video taping for later analysis/interpretation

8.1.2 Telephone interviews

Telephone interviews are most **useful** when only a **small amount of information is required**. **CATI (computer-assisted telephone interviewing)** has been used successfully by a wide range of organisations, including insurance services and banks. The telephone interviewer calls up a questionnaire on screen and reads questions to the respondent. Answers are then recorded instantly on computer. Complex questions with questionnaire routing may be handled in this way.

Telephone interviews have a number of **advantages**.

- The response is rapid.
- It is relatively cheap.
- A wide area can be covered by an interviewer in a central location.
- It may be easier to ask sensitive or embarrassing questions.
- The interview does not take up much of the respondent's time.

They also have **disadvantages**, however.

- A biased sample may result (it won't include people with no telephones).
- It is not possible to use 'showcards' or pictures.
- The refusal rate is much higher than with face-to-face interviews.
- It is not possible to see the interviewee's expression and it is difficult to develop a rapport.
- The interview must be short.
- Respondents may be unwilling to participate for fear of being sold something.

8.2 Postal questionnaires

Postal questionnaires have a number of **advantages over personal interviews**.

- The cost per person is likely to be less, so more people can be sampled.
- It is usually possible to ask more questions because the people completing the forms (the respondents) can do so in their own time.
- All respondents are presented with questions in the same way. The interviewer cannot influence responses or misrecord them.
- It may be easier to ask personal or embarrassing questions in a postal questionnaire.
- Respondents may need to look up information for the questionnaire. This will be easier if the questionnaire is sent to their home or place of work.

On the other hand, the use of **personal interviews** does have certain **advantages** over the use of postal questionnaires.

- Large numbers of postal questionnaires may not be returned or may be returned only partly completed. This may lead to biased results if those replying are not representative of all people in the survey.
- Misunderstanding is less likely with personal interviews because the interviewer can explain questions which the interviewee does not understand.
- They are more suitable for deep or detailed questions since the interviewer can take the time required to explain the implications of the question, probe for further information and encourage the respondent to think deeper.

ATTENTION!

In the December 1997 exam candidates had to explain why telephone sampling might be preferable to using postal questionnaires for an organisation trying to collect data for forecasting purposes.

8.3 The advantage of primary external sources of information

The advantage of using a primary source of data is that the **user of the information knows where it came from, the circumstances under which it was collected, and any limitations or inadequacies in it**.

Activity 3.4

One of the problems associated with both interviews and postal questionnaires is that of non-response. In what ways could the level of non-response be reduced?

TOPIC LINK

Primary external data and control systems

Primary external data is often used to draw up the 'standard' within a control system. For example, data from surveys of customers may provide the basis for sales targets for an organisation's sales force.

9 Secondary external sources of data

In contrast to primary external data sources, secondary external sources of data have four **limitations**.

- The user will be unaware of any limitations in the data.
- The data may not be suitable for the purpose it is being used for.
- The data may be out of date.
- The geographical area covered may not be appropriate.

Example: Limitations of secondary external sources of data

The British government proposed an 'industrial services' category for official economic statistics. Economists, statisticians and opposition figures alike protested, however, accusing the government of trying to introduce a measure that would merely disguise the degree of the recession in manufacturing.

Manufacturing output had declined year-on-year by 5.4%, faster than at any time since the previous recession. If activities which manufacturing organisations outsourced to organisations in the service sector were included under 'manufacturing', however, the proportion of manufacturing in the economy would immediately have risen by a third without UK workers producing a single extra product.

Secondary data sources may be satisfactory in certain situations, or they may be the only convenient means of obtaining an item of data. It is essential that there is good reason to believe that the secondary external source used is accurate and reliable, however.

Let us take a brief look at the types of data which are supplied by the **main secondary external data sources**.

9.1 Governments

One of the most important external sources of data in many countries is official statistics which are supplied by many Governments. In Great Britain, official statistics are supplied by the **Office for National Statistics (ONS)**.

Population data is published by many Governments around the world, and includes data on that country's population, such as population numbers, births, deaths, marriages and so on. In Britain the Government carries out a full census of the whole population every ten years, the results of which are published.

9.2 Banks

The Bank of England issues a quarterly magazine which includes data on banks in the UK, the money supply and Government borrowing and financial transactions.

9.3 Financial newspapers

There are a number of financial newspapers which contain detailed business data and information. Financial newspapers include the *Financial Times,* the *Wall Street Journal,* the *Singapore Business Times* and the *Nikkei Weekly.* Such newspapers provide data on foreign exchange rates, interest rates, gilts and other stock prices. They are a valuable source of data which are relevant to the business world.

9.4 Trade journals

Most industries are served by one or more trade journals which can provide invaluable information to those working within the industry.

Journals contain information on new developments in the industry, articles about competitors' products, details of industry costs and prices and so on.

One edition of *Commercial Motor* contained information about the rise in truck sales. This might lead truck manufacturers to rethink their forecasts and budgets.

An edition of *Marketing Week* included an article on salaries in the marketing industry. Such information could be highly relevant to a marketing organisation: they would be able to assess whether they were paying more or less than the average salary, information which might be vital in future salary negotiations and in setting budgets if it is anticipated that a salary increase may be necessary.

Activity 3.5

Find out what trade journals your organisation subscribes to. Look through a number of them and note the type of information they contain and assess how that information may be used by both you and other members of your organisation.

9.5 Other sources

- **Advice or information bureaux** provide enquirers with information in their own particular field, in the form of advice, or information leaflets and fact sheets. Examples include Consumer Standards Offices and Tourist Information bureaux.
- There are also **consultancies** of all sorts.
    - There are general market research organisations like MORI and Gallup, as well as a great many specialist market research companies providing market intelligence for specific industries.
    - Accounting firms have management consultancy divisions.
    - Many organisations have their own information 'desk' which can be contacted for details of a non-confidential nature about themselves or their field.
- **Specific reference works** are used in a particular line of work. For example, in a tax department of a firm of accountants you would use published lists of dividends and fixed interest payments for publicly quoted securities.
- **Libraries and information services** may be part of the free public library system, or associated with a learned or professional institution like the AAT.
- **Electronic sources of information** are invaluable. Besides local and national radio and TV, and teletext services there are also more specialised forms. Topic, for example, offers information on the stock market.
- Increasingly businesses can use each other's systems as sources of information, via **electronic data interchange (EDI)** which, in simple terms, involves the exchange of routine business documents between the computers of suppliers and their customers.

9.5.1 The Internet

The **Internet** is a global network connecting millions of computers. The Internet allows any computer with a telecommunications link to **send and receive information** to and from any other suitably equipped computer.

A **website** is a collection of images and text that **provide information** which may be viewed on the World Wide Web. Most organisations now have a website. Some sites are able to **process transactions** (known as electronic commerce or **e-commerce**).

Connection to the Internet is made via an **Internet Service Provider** (ISP). ISPs, such as AOL and Virgin, provide their **own information services** in addition to Internet access and e-mail capability.

Users access the Internet through interface programs called **browsers.** The most popular and best known is **Microsoft Internet Explorer**.

Browser software packages provide a facility to **store Internet addresses** so that users can access frequently-visited sites without having to go through a long search process. So in business use, if you **regularly need up-to-date information**, say, on stock market movements, new government legislation, or the activities of a competitor, you can simply click on the appropriate entry in a personal 'favourites' directory and be taken straight to the relevant site.

Searching the Net is done using a **search engine** such as Yahoo!, Google or AltaVista. These guide users to destinations throughout the web: the user simply types in a word or phrase to find related sites and documents.

All search engines work in a similar way. The illustrations that follow show the opening ('home') page of Google.co.uk. To perform a search, you simply click in an empty box (if the cursor isn't flashing there already), type in a word or words and click on Search or, for Google, on Google Search.

In the following example, the user is using the Google.co.uk search engine to find web pages from the UK containing information regarding share prices.

The results of the search are shown below.

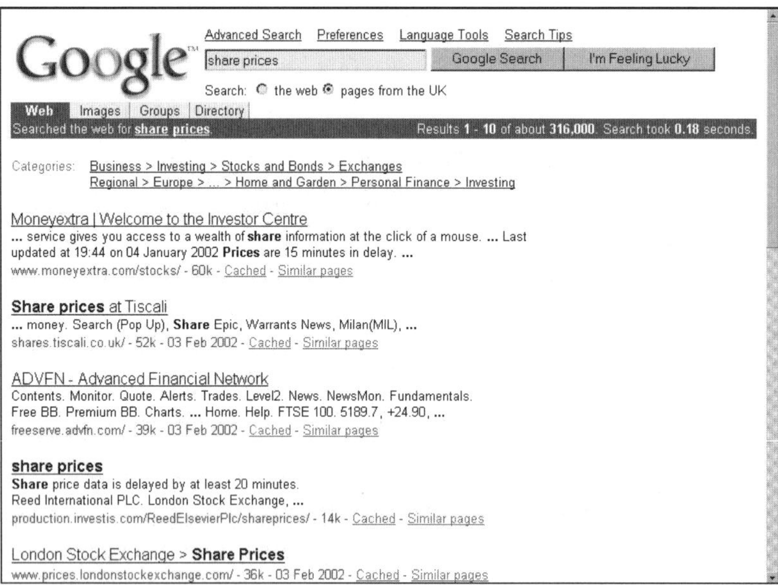

Google found hundreds of websites or documents relating to share information. To view a document, you simply click on the highlighted document title.

Remember, when you are looking at information on the Internet it is **not necessarily good information**, just because it is 'published'. **Anybody** can put information on the Internet. The **reliability** and **reputation** of the **provider is important**. For example, The Financial Times site, FT.com, is a respected source of financial information. On the other hand, a site such as 'Fred's Financial Advice' may contain unreliable information.

TOPIC LINK

Secondary external data and control systems

As you can imagine, the role of secondary external data in providing standards or targets within a control system is crucial. For example, secondary external data provides information on suppliers' prices.

Activity 3.6

Identify which of the following are secondary external sources of data.

(a) *Economic Trends* (published by the Office for National Statistics in the United Kingdom).

(b) The *Singapore Business Times.*

(c) Data collected for a survey which was commissioned in order to determine whether Donald Ltd should launch a new product.

(d) Historical records of expenditure on canteen costs in a hospital in order to prepare current forecasts.

Activity 3.7

Describe how an organisation could structure and implement formal methods and procedures for gathering information to monitor its external environment.

Activity 3.8

Distinguish between primary and secondary data, discussing the advantages and disadvantages of each and giving examples in each case of the use of such data to business organisations.

ATTENTION!

In the exam, you could face a scenario based on a industry or sector in which you have not worked. But just because you do not work in a particular area, it does not mean you have no experience of it. You might work for a manufacturing organisation and the scenario could be based on the non-profit-making or service sectors. But you have been to school and/or college, used doctors and/or hospitals, you might have donated money to a charity, booked a holiday through a travel agent, shopped in a supermarket and so on. So do not panic because you think you know nothing about the wider environment of the scenario. You probably know a lot more than you think.

Key learning points

- ☑ **Quantitative data** is data that can be measured.
- ☑ **Qualitative data** is data that cannot be measured but reflects some quality of what is being observed.
- ☑ **Primary data** is data collected specifically for the purpose you have in mind.
- ☑ **Secondary data** is data which has already been collected elsewhere, for some other purpose, but which can be used or adapted for your purpose.
- ☑ When collecting primary data, the **population** in question must be very carefully **defined**.
- ☑ **Samples** from populations will be **biased** if the population is not complete.
- ☑ **Sampling error** arises when a population sample is not representative of the population from which it is drawn.
- ☑ A simple **random sample** is a sample selected in such a way that every item in the population has an equal chance of being included.
- ☑ A **sampling frame** is simply a numbered list of all the items in a population.
- ☑ A random sample can be picked using the **lottery method** or **random number tables**.
- ☑ There are three methods of **quasi-random sampling** (**systematic sampling**, **stratified sampling** and **multistage sampling**).
- ☑ **Systematic sampling** works by selecting every nth item after a random start.
- ☑ **Stratified sampling** involves taking random samples from all strata or categories into which the population has been divided.
- ☑ **Multistage sampling** works by selecting random samples from smaller and smaller samples which have themselves been selected randomly.
- ☑ When a sampling frame cannot be established, a **non-random sampling** method (**quota sampling** or **cluster sampling**) should be used.
- ☑ **Quota sampling** involves stratifying the population and restricting the sample to a fixed number in each strata.
- ☑ **Cluster sampling** involves selecting one definable subsection of the population as the sample, that subsection taken to be representative of the population in question.
- ☑ You need to be aware of the validity of a particular form of sampling to a particular scenario.
- ☑ Data may be obtained from either an **internal source** or from an **external source**.
- ☑ There are two main types of **survey**, **interviews** and **postal questionnaires**. Interviews include **personal (face to face)** interviews and **telephone** interviews.
- ☑ The main **secondary external data sources** are governments, banks, newspapers, trade journals and the Internet.

Quick quiz

1 The weights of the pupils in a school are an example of qualitative data. *True or false?*

2 Which of the following is an advantage of systematic sampling?

A It is reasonably random.
B It does not require a sampling frame of the whole population.
C It is cheap.
D There is no chance of bias.

3 *Match the type of sampling to the correct description. Note that one type of sampling does not have a corresponding description.*

Types of sampling	Descriptions
Systematic Stratified Multistage Quota Cluster	(a) Divide the population into groups and take a random sample from each group. (b) Divide the population into groups and restrict the sample to a fixed number in each group. (c) Select every nth item after a random start. (d) Select one definable subsection of the population as the sample.

4 The eyewitness to an event will be a primary source of data. *True or false?*

5 *Choose the correct words from those highlighted.*

Personal interviews/shopping mall intercept surveys/focus groups/telephone interviews usually consist of seven to ten respondents and an interviewer.

6 Which of the following is an advantage of personal interviews over the use of postal questionnaires?

A Misunderstanding is more likely.
B They are more suitable for deep or detailed questions.
C The cost per person is likely to be less.
D It may be easier to ask personal or embarrassing questions.

7 *Choose the correct words from those highlighted.*

An example of a primary source of data is **trade journals/EDI/the Internet/the government/postal questionnaires.**

Answers to quick quiz

1 False

2 A

3 Systematic – (c)
Stratified – (a)
Quota – (b)
Cluster – (d)

4 True

5 Focus groups

6 B

7 Postal questionnaires

ASSESSMENT KIT ACTIVITIES

The following activities in the BPP Assessment Kit for Units 8 & 9 include topics covered in this chapter.

Activities 4, 5, 10 and 28
Lecturers' practice activity 2

Activity checklist

This checklist shows which performance criteria, range statement or knowledge and understanding point is covered by each activity in this chapter. Tick off each activity as you complete it.

Activity		
3.1	☐	This activity deals with Performance Criteria 8.1A regarding the identification of valid relevant information from internal and external sources and Performance Criteria 9.1A regarding the identification of relevant data from internal and external sources.
3.2	☐	This activity deals with Performance Criteria 8.1A regarding the identification of valid relevant information from internal and external sources and Performance Criteria 9.1A regarding the identification of relevant data from internal and external sources.
3.3	☐	This activity deals with Range Statement 8.1: methods of summarising data (sampling), Unit 8 Knowledge & Understanding point (3): basic statistical methods (sampling techniques) and Unit 9 Knowledge & Understanding point (3): basic statistical methods (sampling techniques).
3.4	☐	This activity deals with Performance Criteria 8.1A regarding the identification of valid relevant information from internal and external sources and Performance Criteria 9.1A regarding the identification of relevant data from internal and external sources.
3.5	☐	This activity deals with Range Statement 8.1: information, Range Statement 9.1: data, Unit 8 Knowledge & Understanding point (1): external sources of information on costs and prices and Unit 9 Knowledge & Understanding point (1): external sources of information on costs, prices, demand and availability of resources.
3.6	☐	This activity also deals with the Knowledge & Understanding points covered in Activity 3.5.
3.7	☐	This activity deals with Unit 8 Knowledge & Understanding point (13): the organisation's external environment and specific external costs.
3.8	☐	This activity deals with Unit 8 Knowledge & Understanding point (10): the use and limitation of published statistics.

chapter 4

Analysing data

Contents

1 Introduction
2 Patterns in numbers
3 Presentation of data
4 Introducing index numbers
5 Using indices
6 Index numbers and practical issues
7 Good information

Performance criteria

8.1G Present reports to management that summarise data, present information using appropriate methods and highlight significant trends

Range statement

8.1 Methods of summarising data: index numbers

8.1 Methods of presenting information in reports: written analysis and explanation; tables; diagrams

Knowledge and understanding

Unit 8 Accounting techniques

3 Basic statistical methods: index numbers

5 Methods of presenting information in graphical, diagrammatic and tabular form

Unit 9 Accounting techniques

3 Basic statistical methods: index numbers

Signpost

The topics covered in this chapter are relevant to **Unit 8** and **Unit 9**.

1 Introduction

This chapter looks at ways in which data collected using the approaches set out in Chapter 3 can be **analysed** so as to provide **useful information**.

Section 2 is very **important**. If you are either not adept at dealing with numbers or are not used to dealing with numbers, the information will be of significant help. You need to be able to **work with numbers effectively** during the exam and this section provides you with some pointers.

We then see how data that has been collected can be presented so that its key features are highlighted. You have covered **data presentation** formats in your previous studies and the assessor has yet to require any format other than a table. Glance though the section, however, just to remind yourself of the key points. Attempt the activities if you feel that you need to practise using the different formats.

Later sections of the chapter cover **index numbers**. Index numbers are used throughout the text **in conjunction with standard costing, budgeting and performance indicators**, the key themes of Units 8 and 9. You must be able to deal with them in any of the wide variety of situations in which they could appear and so a thorough understanding of them from the outset is vital.

The final section of the chapter describes the qualities that **good information** should possess. You need to bear them in mind when you are providing information in exams!

2 Patterns in numbers

In a wide variety of tasks you will need to be able to see 'patterns in numbers'. You have to be able to manipulate numbers and deal with them efficiently. But don't worry – this is not anywhere near as complicated as it sounds!

LOOK OUT FOR...

Rearranging equations

You need to be aware of the following terminology.

- An **equation** says that one thing (say turnover) is equal to another (say price multiplied by volume).
- A **variable** in this context is a letter representing an unknown numerical value in an equation.

Suppose you are given figures for price and sales volume and you are asked to calculate turnover. You know instinctively that turnover = price x sales volume. You can therefore solve the equation and find turnover. But do you know how to solve the equation to find selling price (p) if you are given figures for turnover and sales volume?

For example, suppose that turnover is £150,000 and sales volume is 15,000 units.

£150,000 = p × 15,000

We need to find a value for the variable p such that when it is multiplied by 15,000 we get £150,000. With trial and error we get p = £10.

There is an easier way to solve equations, however.

To **solve an equation** you need to get it into the following form:

Unknown variable = something with just numbers in it, that you can work out

You therefore need to get the unknown variable on one side of the = sign, and everything else on the other side.

The rule is that you **can do what you like to one side of an equation, so long as you do the same thing to the other side straightaway.** The two sides are equal, and they will stay equal so long as you treat them in the same way.

For example, you could do any of the following.

- Add 37 to both sides
- Subtract 6p from both sides (if p is the letter representing the unknown value)
- Multiply both sides by –5.67
- Divide both sides by 4.5p

So if £150,000 = p × 15,000, we can divide both sides by 15,000
£150,000/15,000 = p × 15,000/15,000
£10,000 = p

Here are some more general examples.

(a) £172 = £350 – c
£172 + c = £350 (add c to each side)
c = £350 – £172 (subtract £172 from each side)
c = £178 (work out the right hand side)

(b) 450 = 3x + 72 (initial equation: x unknown)
450 – 72 = 3x (deduct 72 from each side)
$\frac{450-72}{3} = x$ (divide each side by 3)
126 = x (work out the left hand side)

(c) 3y + 2 = 5y – 7 (initial equation: y unknown)
3y + 9 = 5y (add 7 to each side)
9 = 2y (subtract 3y from each side)
4.5 = y (divide each side by 2)

You may need to rearrange equations in a wide range of situations. Here are a couple of examples of the sort of calculations you might need to carry out.

(a) An organisation had output of 100 units in 20X2 and used 587 litres of material. How many litres of material were used per unit of output?

Output x litres of material per unit = usage of material
100 × litres of material per unit = 587
100 × litres of material per unit/100 = 587/100 divide both sides by 100
Litres of material per unit = 5.87 litres

(b) The cost of labour during control period 13 was £13,500, during which time 900 labour hours were worked and paid for. What was the labour cost per hour?

Number of hours × rate per hour = cost of labour
900 × rate per hour = £13,500
900 × rate per hour/900 = £13,500/900 divide both sides by 900
Rate per hour = £15

Efficient calculations

This leads on from the advice above.

In a number of exam tasks about performance indicators, candidates have been asked to calculate cost per unit. Task data has never provided a figure for total costs, however, but has given turnover, a list of costs, and profit.

An inefficient and time-consuming way to derive cost per unit is to add up all the costs and divide by the number of units. A more efficient approach is to deduct profit from turnover and then divide by the number of units.

This example shows how, using knowledge you already have (turnover – costs = profit), you can obtain new information efficiently and quickly.

Always look at the workings we provide and make sure that you understand how we have dealt with the numbers.

Activity 4.1

(a) Find the value of j if $\frac{72j + 16}{16} = 10$

(b) During control period 7, M Ltd spent £29,700 on compound A. Each kg of compound A costs £16.50. How many kgs of compound A were purchased?

3 Presentation of data

This is a topic you will have covered in your earlier studies and so we have provided a brief reminder of both the main presentation formats and the rules for drawing graphs.

ATTENTION!

The standards do not explain the meaning of the word 'diagram'. The choice of type of diagram you use (if you are required to use diagrammatic presentation of data) is therefore left to you. Clearly the term includes charts, illustrations and graphs.

The assessor has therefore confirmed that you will **not** be asked to explain what any particular diagram is, nor will you be asked to use a particular type of diagram. It will be up to you to choose the format most appropriate in the circumstances.

REMEMBER ...

Tabulation

You could be asked to present performance indicators in a table, as candidates had to do in the June 1997 exam. You'll need to apply the following guidelines for tabulation, a topic covered in your earlier studies.

- Tables are two dimensional and so can only show **two variables** (such as performance indicators and years). One dimension (rows or columns) represents one variable (say the performance indicators), the other dimension represents the other variable (such as years).

Performance indicators for A Ltd

	20X0	*20X1*	*20X2*	*20X3*
Sales per employee	X	X	X	X
Profit margin	X	X	X	X
Asset turnover	X	X	X	X
Creditors' period	X	X	X	X
Debtors' days	X	X	X	X

- The table should be given a clear **title**.
- All columns should be clearly **labelled**.
- Where appropriate, there should be clear **sub-totals**.
- Where appropriate, a **total column** should be used; this would normally be the right-hand column.
- **Do not include too much information** otherwise reading the table will be difficult.

Activity 4.2

The total sales revenue of a certain trading company in Year 8 was £10,000,000. Sales were made to three different regions, A, B and C. £6,000,000 of sales were to region A and £3,000,000 were to region B. The organisation makes four products, the alpha, the beta, the gamma and the delta. Sales of the alpha totalled £1,100,000, sales of the beta also totalled £1,100,000, while sales of the gamma totalled £2,900,000.

Sales to region A were £3,500,000 of the delta, £1,500,000 of the gamma and £500,000 of the alpha, whilst in region B, sales of the delta totalled £1,000,000, sales of the gamma totalled £1,100,000 and sales of the alpha £500,000.

Task

Draw up a table to show all the details of sales in the organisation. Interpret the data by providing suitable secondary statistics to describe the distribution of sales across the regions.

Activity 4.3

Draw up a table using the information in Activity 4.2 but this time interpret the information by adopting an alternative approach.

Activity 4.4

(a) Convert the information given below into tabular form.

The number of televisions sold in a country in 1960 was 5,246,000. Ten years later in 1970 the number was 6,830,000, and by 1980 the total sold in that year was 12,654,000. Another ten years later the number for 1990 was 10,194,000. In 1960 Best View Ltd sold 2,114,000 of its televisions, more than any other kind; Accurate Vision Ltd was second with 1,810,000; Clear Cut Ltd third with 448,000; and the 'all others' group accounted for 874,000. In 1970 Accurate Vision Ltd was in first position with 3,248,000; Clear Cut Ltd was second with 1,618,000; Best View Ltd third with 1,288,000; and the 'all others' group sold fewer televisions than ten years earlier: 676,000. In 1980 Accurate Vision Ltd's sales alone, 5,742,000, exceeded total sales of just 20 years earlier. Best View Ltd was in second position with 3,038,000; Clear Cut Ltd third with 2,228,000; and the 'all others' group sold just 1,646,000. 1990 data indicated that relative positions remained the same since 1980 with Accurate Vision Ltd at 4,932,000, Best View Ltd at 3,138,000, Clear Cut Ltd at 1,506,000 and 'all others' at 618,000.

(b) Interpret the data in (a) by calculating and further tabulating appropriate percentages to show comparisons of televisions sold by the producers in the four years given.

(c) Comment on the percentage trends in (b).

REMEMBER ...

Diagrams

- Diagrams convey information in a way that will demonstrate its meaning or significance more clearly than a table would. They are not always more appropriate than tables, and the **most suitable way of presenting information will depend on the following**.
  - **What the information is intended to show**. Visual displays usually make one or two points quite forcefully, whereas tables usually give more detailed information.
  - **Who is going to use the information**. Some individuals might understand visual displays more readily than tables.

  This is an important point to bear in mind when deciding what information presentation format to use and/or when recommending a suitable format.

REMEMBER... (cont'd)

- **Pictograms**
  - A pictogram is a diagram in which quantities are represented by pictures or symbols.
  - The symbols should be clear and simple.
  - The quantity that each symbol represents should be clearly shown in a key.
  - Bigger quantities ought to be shown by more symbols, not by bigger symbols.
  - **Disadvantage.** Pictograms lack precision. Each symbol must represent quite a large number of items, otherwise a pictogram would contain too many symbols. Using portions of a symbol to represent smaller quantities gives some extra precision but not much.

If
represents 1,000 men then
represents less than 1,000 men, but how many? 400? 500? 600?

- **Pie charts**
  - A pie chart is a method of showing the relative sizes of the components of a total.
  - **Disadvantage.** Pie charts have sectors of varying sizes, and you need to be able to draw sectors fairly accurately. To do this, you need a protractor (and so it is unlikely you will need to draw one in an exam). Working out sector sizes involves converting parts of the total into equivalent degrees of a circle.
  - Pie charts show only the relative sizes of elements.
- **Bar charts**
  - A bar chart is a method of presenting information in which quantities are shown in the form of bars on a chart, the length of the bars being proportional to the quantities.
  - A **simple** bar chart is a chart consisting of one or more bars, in which the length of each bar indicates the magnitude of the corresponding information. They show the actual magnitude of each item and they allow magnitudes to be compared.
  - Alternatively a bar chart can give a **breakdown of each total into its components.** Each total bar is split into sections representing the components of the total and so the chart shows how the totals change and how the components change. The total length of each bar (and the length of each component in it) indicates magnitude. A bigger amount is shown by a longer bar.
  - In a bar chart **based on percentages**, total magnitudes are not shown. If two or more bars are drawn on the chart, the total length of each bar is the same. The only varying lengths are the lengths of the sections of a bar, which vary according to the relative sizes of the components.
  - A bar chart can be drawn in which **two or more separate bars** are used to **present sub-divisions of information**. Several bars are used for each total. The bars are usually drawn vertically but they can be horizontal. They do not show the grand total, but they do illustrate the comparative magnitudes of the components.
- **Line charts**
  - A line chart is similar to a bar chart but with lines instead of bars. The length of the line is proportional to the value represented.

Activity 4.5

Material costs of Carlton Ltd's two products during March Year 2 were as follows.

	Standard product		*Deluxe product*	
	£'000	%	£'000	%
Wood	700	35	500	20
Metal	300	15	1,250	50
Plastic	900	45	500	20
Glass	100	5	250	10
	2,000	100	2,500	100

Task

Show the relative material costs of the two products in diagrammatic form.

Activity 4.6

Revenue for DO Ltd in Year 1, Year 2 and Year 3 is made up as follows.

	Year 1	*Year 2*	*Year 3*
	£'000	£'000	£'000
Sales of the Albertine (A)	3,579	2,961	2,192
Sales of the Kensington (K)	857	893	917
Sales of the Edward (E)	62	59	70

Task

Present the above data using the form of bar chart you consider most appropriate in each of the following circumstances.

(a) To show how total revenue has changed over the three years

(b) To show how both total revenue and revenue from each product have changed over the three years

(c) To show how the relative proportions of the products' sales have changed over the three years

(d) To show changes in the revenue of the individual products rather than changes in total revenue over the three years

Activity 4.7

Zoom Ltd, a motorbike manufacturer, has undertaken an attitude survey of recent buyers of motorbikes in Great Britain. As a part of this study, 100 recent buyers of British motorbikes and 100 recent buyers of non-British motorbikes were asked to agree or to disagree with a number of statements. One of the summary tables from the survey is shown below.

	Buyers of British motorbikes		Buyers of non-British motorbikes	
Statements	**Agree**	**Disagree**	**Agree**	**Disagree**
British motorbikes are:				
easy to get serviced	65	35	46	54
economical	81	19	55	45
reliable	76	24	48	52
comfortable	69	31	61	39
Non-British motorbikes are:				
easy to get serviced	32	68	60	40
economical	61	39	83	17
reliable	74	26	85	15
comfortable	35	65	58	42

Task

Draft an appraisal of the most significant features of these data, illustrating your analysis with tables and diagrams.

REMEMBER ...

Drawing graphs

- A graph shows, by means of either a straight line or a curve, the **relationship** between two variables.
- The value of a **dependent variable** is determined by the value of an **independent variable**. If y = mx +c, y is the dependent variable because its value depends on that of x. If x = 3y – 5, x is the dependent variable.
- The **horizontal axis** on a graph is for the **independent** variable, the **vertical axis** is for the **dependent** variable. If **time** is one variable, it is always treated as the **independent** variable.
- Select a **scale** so that as much of the paper is used as possible. Do not cramp a graph into one corner.

REMEMBER... (cont'd)

- In some cases it is best not to start a scale at zero so you can avoid having a large area of wasted paper. To avoid confusion you can **break the axes**.

Sales

Time

- The scales on the **axes** should be **marked**. For example, if the vertical axis relates to amounts of money, the axis should be marked at every £1 or £1,000 interval or at whatever interval is appropriate. The axes must be marked with values to give an idea of the size of the values on the graph.
- A graph should **not be overcrowded** with too many lines. Graphs should always give a **clear, neat** impression.
- A graph must always have a **title** and, where appropriate, a reference should be made to the source of data.
- If the data to be plotted is derived from calculations, make sure that there is a neat **table** in your working papers.

Activity 4.8

The figure below purports to show the profits of four divisions within a firm during the period from Year 1 to Year 6.

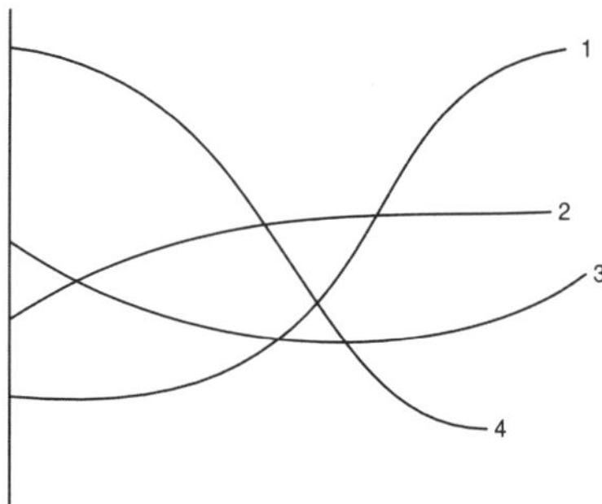

Tasks

(a) Criticise the graph by outlining a series of rules for correct graphical presentation.
(b) Suggest briefly some alternative methods of presenting these data.

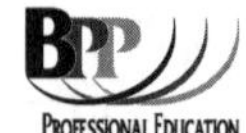

REMEMBER ...

Reports

- At the top of every report you should include the **title** of the report (its subject), **who** has **prepared it**, for **whom** it is **intended** and the **date** of completion.

REPORT

To:	Chief accountant
From:	Assistant accountant
Date:	17 January 20X1
Subject:	Overview of results of period 13

- If you are reporting to senior management you will need to adopt a fairly formal style, but you can adopt a more informal tone in a report for your line manager.
- You should always offer an introduction and recommendations / summary / conclusion.
- Try to divide the report into a number of clearly marked sections (for example, background, findings and conclusion for informal reports, with additional sections such as procedure / method in more formal reports).
- You may be able to use the various requirements of the task as the sections of your report.
- If you want to, you can include calculations and workings in appendices, with clear referencing to such appendices in the main body of the report.
- An ordinary memo can be used for flexible, informal reports. Despite their informality, memos should have headings and some sort of structure too.
- If you need to cover a number of issues in a memo, letter or report, perhaps because the task has a number of parts, you need to make it clear which issues you are covering, perhaps by identifying the task number in the margin and/or by providing a subheading to each task.

Activity 4.9

When writing a report, what can you do to ensure that the particular needs and abilities of the users of your report will be met?

Activity 4.10

What basic questions should you ask yourself before writing a report?

Activity 4.11

Rewrite the following sentence so that it is more suitable for inclusion into a report.

'I've had a good hard look but try as I might I've not been able to find out who's been nicking money from the petty cash box. I'd prefer it if you'd take over now.'

4 Introducing index numbers

If we want to look at trends in costs and prices, we need to take account of the fact that organisations operate within an economic environment in which general shifts in costs (ie prices) take place.

- If a business achieves an increase in sales of 10% in monetary (cash) terms over a year, this result becomes less impressive if we are told that there was general price inflation (increase) of 15% over the year.
- If the business has raised its prices in line with this inflation rate of 15%, then a 10% increase in sales in cash terms indicates a fall in the physical volume of sales. The business is now selling less at the new higher prices.

4.1 What is an index number?

Index numbers are a **way of comparing figures** over time. Those figures might be costs, prices, volume of output, quantities used and so on.

An example is the **'cost of living' index**. This is made up of a large variety of items including bread, butter, meat, rent, insurance and so on. The raw data giving the prices of each item for successive years would be confusing and useless to most people, but a **simple index** stating that the cost of living index is 300 for 2000 compared with 150 for 1990 is easily understood. It is evident that prices have doubled.

Perhaps the most well-known index in the UK is the **Retail Prices Index (RPI).** This measures changes in the costs of items of expenditure of the average household (it used to be called the 'cost of living' index) and hence gives an indication of inflation. Another example which you may have heard reported in the news is the FT-SE (or 'footsie') 100 share index, which measures how the top 100 share prices in general have performed from one day to the next.

4.2 Index points

Index points are a **measure of the difference in the index value in one year with the index value in another year**.

For example, suppose that the index of food prices in Year 1 was 180 and in year 6 was 336.

The index has risen 156 points between Year 1 and Year 6. This is an increase of (156/180) × 100% = 86.7%. Food prices have therefore increased by 86.7% in the six-year period.

Activity 4.12

Suppose the RPI stood at 370 at the beginning of 20X0 and 395 at the beginning of 20X1.

(a) What is the increase in index points?
(b) What is the percentage increase in the RPI?
(c) What is price inflation?

4.3 The base period

To construct an index, all other values are compared against the value in the base period. The value in the base period is usually taken as 100. For example, the base period of the RPI is January 1987, when the index value was 100.

The choice of a base period is not significant, except that it should be 'representative'. In an index which looks at changes in prices, the base year must not be one in which there were abnormally high or low prices. For example, a year in which there was a potato famine would be inadvisable as a base period for a vegetable price index.

4.4 Constructing an index

An index is constructed as:

(value in time period in question/value in base period) × 100

For example, suppose sales for a company over the last five years were as follows.

Year	*Sales*
	£'000
5	35
6	42
7	40
8	45
9	50

The managing director has decided that he wants to set up a sales index (ie an index which measures how sales have changed from year to year), using Year 5 as the base year. The £35,000 of sales in Year 5 is given the index 100. What are the indices for the other years?

The Year 5 sales of £35,000 = 100.

- Index in Year 6, when sales are £42,000 = (42,000/35,000) × 100 = 120
- Index in Year 7, when sales are £40,000 = (40,000/35,000) × 100 = 114
- Index in Year 8, when sales are £45,000 = (45,000/35,000) × 100 = 129
- Index in Year 9, when sales are £50,000 = (50,000/35,000) × 100 = 143

Sales revenue has therefore increased by 43 index points or ((143 – 100)/100) × 100% = 43% in the five-year period.

Example: index 1

If the price of a cup of coffee in the Café Lucille was 40p in Year 0, 50p in Year 1 and 76p in Year 2, using Year 0 as a base point the price index numbers for Year 1 and Year 2 would be:

Year 1 price index = $(50/40) \times 100 = 125$
Year 2 price index = $(76/40) \times 100 = 190$

Example: index 2

Similarly, if the Café Lucille sold 500,000 cups of coffee in Year 0, 700,000 cups in Year 1, and 600,000 in Year 2, then quantity index numbers for Year 1 and Year 2, using Year 0 as a base year, would be:

Year 1 quantity index = $(700{,}000/500{,}000) \times 100 = 140$
Year 2 quantity index = $(600{,}000/500{,}000) \times 100 = 120$

4.5 Composite index numbers

Most practical indices **cover more than one item** and are hence termed composite index numbers. The RPI, for example, considers components such as food, alcoholic drink, tobacco and housing. An index of motor car costs might consider components such as finance payments, service costs, repairs, insurance and so on.

Suppose that the cost of living index is calculated from only three commodities: bread, tea and caviar, and that the prices for Year 1 and Year 2 were as follows.

	Year 1	Year 2
Bread	20p a loaf	40p a loaf
Tea	25p a packet	30p a packet
Caviar	450p a jar	405p a jar

The index would need to take account of both **the amounts** of bread, tea and caviar consumed (and hence the importance of each item), **and the units** to which the prices refer. If, for example, the price of a cup of tea is used rather than the price of a packet of tea, the index would be different.

To overcome both the problem of quantities in different units and the need to attach importance to each item, we can use weighting which reflects the importance of each item.

To decide the weightings of different items in an index, it is necessary to **obtain information**, perhaps by market research, about the relative importance of each item. In our example of a simple cost of living index, it would be necessary to find out how much the average person or household spends each week on each item to determine weightings.

5 Using indices

You will need to use indices in a large variety of tasks and so you will encounter **topic link** boxes for indices and **variances**, indices and **budgeting** and indices and **performance measurement** as we work through this text.

Usually you will be using indices because you need to **bring a figure 'more up to date'** because of changes in costs, prices or quantities.

The basic technique is to **multiply the figure in question by (recent index number/older index number)**. We will see how to apply this to particular situations in the chapters which follows.

5.1 Exchange rates

Exchange rates should be one of the most familiar of all indices to you. If you have taken a holiday abroad you will be aware of how important they are. And even small organisations often either purchase or sell abroad. So the problem of exchange rate movements is one faced by management accountants in many organisations.

Exchange rates are merely a special form of price index – the cost of one currency in terms of another (rather than the price of a product in term of its price at a particular point in time).

Suppose that the exchange rate between currency 1(£) and currency 2($) is $X.

- To convert an amount from currency 2 to currency 1, divide by the exchange rate.
- To convert an amount from currency 1 to currency 2, multiply by the exchange rate.

If the exchange rate is 0.5 dollars to the pound, $10 = £(10/0.5) = £20, whereas £15 = $(15 × 0.5) = $7.5.

Activity 4.13

Suppose ABC Ltd decides to buy product X from an American company for $100, when the exchange rate between the UK pound and the American dollar is $2. The company actually pays when the exchange rate is $2.20. What is the difference in £ between the planned cost of product X and the actual cost?

6 Index numbers and practical issues

6.1 Retail Prices Index (RPI)

The Retail Prices Index (RPI) **measures the monthly change in the cost of living in the UK**.

The RPI is published monthly. The index shows the percentage changes, month by month, in the average level of prices of **'a representative basket of goods'** purchased by the great majority of households in the United Kingdom. Since it measures the monthly change in the cost of living its **principal use is as a measure of inflation.**

From information gathered by a continuing survey conducted by the Department of Employment into the general characteristics of households, their income and their expenditures, the representative basket of goods is divided into main groups. Each group is weighted according to information from the survey to account for its relative importance in the basket. The weights in 2001 were as follows.

Food	116
Catering	53
Alcoholic drink	68
Tobacco	29
Housing	205
Fuel and light	29
Household goods	71
Household services	57
Clothing and footwear	53
Personal goods and services	43
Motoring expenditure	140
Fares and other travel	23
Leisure goods	49
Leisure services	64
	1,000

The weights are always calculated to add to 1,000.

Certain items of expenditure are not included in the RPI. These include the following.

- Income tax and National Insurance payments
- Insurance and pension payments
- Mortgage payments for house purchase (interest payments are included)
- Gambling, gifts, charity

The items and their weights in the basket of goods are continually revised to ensure that they remain as representative as possible.

6.2 What items to include

The purpose to which the index is to be put must be carefully considered. Once this has been done, the **items selected** must be as **representative as possible**, taking into account this purpose. Care must be taken to ensure that the items are **unambiguously defined** and that their **values are readily ascertainable**.

For some indices, the choice of items might be relatively straightforward. For example, the FT Actuaries All-Share Index, compiled jointly by the Financial Times, the Institute of Actuaries and the Faculty of Actuaries, is made up of the share prices of approximately 800 companies quoted on The Stock Exchange.

For other indices, the choice of items will be more difficult. The Retail Prices Index is an excellent example of the problem. It would be impossible to include all items of domestic spending and a selective, representative basket of goods and services must be found.

6.3 Collecting the data

TOPIC LINK

Indices and data collection

We looked at data collection in Chapter 3. You need to think about the issues covered there when considering data collection for indices. For the RPI, for example, prices are collected all over the United Kingdom from different types of retail outlet by Department of Employment staff each month. What would be the best method of collecting this data? Face-to-face interviews? Telephone interviews?

Data is required to determine the values for each item and the weight that will be attached to each item. Consider as an example a cost of living index. The prices of a particular commodity will vary from place to place, from shop to shop and from type to type. Also the price will vary during the period under consideration. The actual prices used must obviously be some sort of average. The way in which the average is to be obtained should be clearly defined at the outset.

When constructing a price index, it is common practice to use the quantities consumed as weights; similarly, when constructing a quantity index, the prices may be used as weights. Care must be taken in selecting the basis for the weighting. For example, in a cost of living index, it may be decided to use the consumption of a typical family as the weights, but some difficulty may be encountered in defining a typical family.

6.4 Limitations of index numbers

Index numbers are easy to understand and fairly easy to calculate, so it is not surprising that they are frequently used. However, they are not perfect and it is as well to bear in mind the following points.

- **Index numbers are usually only approximations** of changes in price (or quantity) over time, and must be interpreted with care and reservation.
- **Weighting factors become out of date as time passes**. They will gradually cease to reflect the current 'reality'.
- **New products or items may appear, and old ones cease to be significant.** For example, spending has changed in recent years, to include new items such as mobile phones and PCs, whereas the demand for large black and white televisions has declined. These changes would make the original weightings of a retail price index for consumer goods out of date.
- **Sometimes, the data used to calculate index numbers might be incomplete, out of date, or inaccurate.** For example, the quantity indices of imports and exports are based on records supplied by traders which may be prone to error or even falsification.
- The base year of an index should be a 'normal' year, but there is probably no such thing as a perfectly normal year. **Some error in the index will be caused by untypical values in the base period.**
- **The 'basket of items' in an index is often selective.** For example, the Retail Prices Index (RPI) is constructed from a sample of households and, more importantly, from a basket of only about 600 items.

- **A national index cannot necessarily be applied to an individual town or region.** For example, if the national index of wages and salaries rises from 100 to 115, we cannot state that the following are necessarily true.
  - The wages and salaries in, say, Birmingham, have gone up from 100 to 115.
  - The wages and salaries of each working individual have gone up from 100 to 115.
- **An index may exclude important items**, for example, the RPI excludes payments of income tax out of gross wages.

If you are asked to explain why the use of a particular index in certain circumstances may be inappropriate, you must apply the general limitations above to the specific scenario details.

6.5 Limitations of specific indices

6.5.1 Index of producer prices (PPI)

The PPI **measures manufacturers' prices**. The various index numbers produced are calculated from the price movements of about 10,000 closely defined materials and products representative of goods purchased and manufactured by United Kingdom industry. They are quoted for main industrial groupings, such as motor vehicles and parts, food manufacturing industries, the textile industry and so on.

It may not always be appropriate to use a general index of production costs to make an organisation's costs more 'up to date' if the resources used to compile the index do not reflect those used by the organisation.

6.5.2 Average earnings index

There are two main limitations of using an average earnings index to assess the reasonableness of wages.

- The mix of skills and experience in the organisation may be different to the national average.
- The rate of pay in the local area might have risen at a different rate to the national rate.

6.5.3 Index of retail sales

Published monthly, this index **covers the retail trades (excluding the motor trades) in Great Britain**. Indices are given for both volume and value of sales as a result of major enquires into retailing. Each month a sample of approximately 5,000 retailers fill out statistical returns covering volume and value of sales. Mail order firms are included in the panel.

Here are some problems for organisations using such an index.

- The organisation's product range might not be typical.
- The index might not reflect the seasonality of an organisation's sales.

6.5.4 Index of labour rates

An organisation might use some sort of index of labour rates. The index will be a weighted average of many different labour rates for many different levels of skill, but the weighted average may not be appropriate for the organisation.

ATTENTION!

Index numbers are a useful way of summarising a large amount of data in a single series of numbers. Remember, however, that any summary hides some detail and so you should interpret any index numbers presented in a exam with caution.

As you work through the remainder of this text remember that you will need to use index numbers in conjunction with other techniques. So make sure that you are happy with the topic before you move on to the next chapter.

7 Good information

We end this chapter on the analysis of data with a look at the general features of the information needed for management accounting.

Management accounting information should possess the attributes and principles of what is known as **good information.**

- It should be **relevant** for its purpose.
- It should be **complete** for its purpose.
- It should be sufficiently **accurate** for its purpose.
- It should be **clear** to the manager using it.
- The manager using it should have **confidence** in it.
- It should be **communicated** to the appropriate manager.
- It should not be excessive, its **volume** should be **manageable**.
- It should be **timely** (in other words communicated at the most appropriate time).
- It should be communicated by an appropriate **channel of communication.**
- It should be provided at a **cost which is less than the value of the benefits** it provides.

Let's have a look at the qualities in a bit more detail

7.1 Relevance

Information must be relevant to the purpose for which a manager wants to use it.

In practice, far too many reports **fail to 'keep to the point'** and contain **purposeless, irritating paragraphs** which only serve to annoy the managers reading them.

The consequences of irrelevant information are that managers might be confused by the information and might waste time.

7.2 Completeness

A manager should have all the information he needs to do his job properly. **If he does not have a complete picture of the situation, he might well make bad decisions**.

Suppose that the debt collection section of a company is informed that a customer owes £10,000 and the debt is now four months overdue. A strongly-worded letter is sent to the customer demanding immediate payment. If an important piece of information had been kept from the debt collection section, for example that the customer had negotiated special credit terms of six months, sending a demand for payment is not a correct course of action.

7.3 Accuracy

Using incorrect information could have serious and damaging consequences. However, information should only be **accurate enough for its purpose** and there is no need to go into unnecessary detail for pointless accuracy.

Some tasks of supervisors and clerical staff might need information that is accurate to the nearest penny, second or kilogram.

- A cashier will do a bank reconciliation to the exact penny and purchase ledger staff will pay creditors exactly what they are owed.
- Much financial accounting information for day-to-day transactions must indicate amounts to the exact penny.

Middle managers might be satisfied with revenues and costs rounded to the nearest £100 or £1,000, since greater detail would serve no purpose. For example, in budgeting, revenue and cost figures are often rounded to the nearest £1,000. Trying to be more exact would not improve the usefulness of the information.

Senior managers in a medium-sized to large organisation might be satisfied with figures to the nearest ten thousand pounds, or even hundred thousand or million pounds. Estimates to the nearest pound at this level of decision making would be inappropriate and unnecessary.

7.4 Clarity

If the manager does not understand information properly he cannot use it properly. Lack of clarity is one of the causes of a breakdown in communication. It is therefore important to choose the most appropriate presentation medium or channel of communication.

7.5 Confidence

Information must be **trusted by the managers who are expected to use it**.

Not all information is certain, however. An important issue is therefore how to take account of uncertainty and incorporate it into the information, in order to make the information realistic. Some information, such as long-term planning information, is uncertain because of the time span involved. If the assumptions underlying the information are clearly stated, however, this should improve the level of confidence the user will have in the information.

7.6 Communication

Within any organisation, **individuals are given the authority to do certain tasks, and they must be given the information they need to do them.** An office manager might be made responsible for controlling expenditures in his office, and given an expenditure limit for the year. As the year progresses, he might try to keep expenditure in check but

unless he is told throughout the year what is his current total expenditure to date, he will find it difficult to judge whether he is keeping within budget or not.

Information that is needed **might be communicated to the wrong person**. It might be communicated to a person who does not have the authority to act on it, or who is not responsible for the matter and so does not need it.

7.7 Volume

There are physical and mental limitations to what a person can read, absorb and understand properly before taking action. An enormous mountain of information, even if it is all relevant, cannot be handled. Reports to management must therefore be **clear and concise**.

In many systems, control action works on the **'exception' principle** (attention is focused on those items where performance differs significantly from standard or budget). This is especially true of information for management control.

7.8 Timing

Information which is **not available until after a decision is made** will be useful only for comparisons and longer-term control, and **may serve no purpose** even then.

Information prepared **too frequently** wastes resources. If, for example, a decision is taken at a monthly meeting about a certain aspect of a company's operations, information to make the decision is only required once a month, and weekly reports would be a time-consuming waste of effort.

The **frequency** with which information is provided should **depend on the needs of the managers for whom it is provided.**

7.9 Channel of communication

There are **occasions when using one particular method of communication will be better than others.**

- Job vacancies should be announced in a medium where they will be brought to the attention of the people most likely to be interested. The channel of communication might be the company's in-house journal, a national or local newspaper, a professional magazine, a job centre or school careers office.
- Some internal memoranda may be better sent by 'electronic mail'.
- Some information is best communicated informally by telephone or word-of-mouth, whereas other information ought to be formally communicated in writing or figures.

7.10 Cost

The **benefits obtainable from the information must exceed the costs of acquiring it.** Whenever management is trying to decide whether or not to produce information for a particular purpose (for example whether to computerise an operation), a cost/benefit study ought to be made. For information to have value, it must lead to a decision to take action which results in reducing costs, eliminating losses, increasing sales, better utilisation of resources and so on.

Key learning points

- ☑ You must be able to **manipulate numbers**. When **rearranging equations**, the rule is that you can do what you like to one side of an equation, so long as you do the same thing to the other side straight away.
- ☑ **Tables** are a simple way of presenting information about two variables.
- ☑ Make sure that you are able to construct **pictograms, pie charts, bar charts** and **line charts.**
- ☑ Always follow the **rules for drawing graphs.**
- ☑ You will not be told to use a particular diagrammatic format. You should use the one most suitable to the scenario in the task.
- ☑ Certain general principles should be followed in planning and giving structure to a **report.**
- ☑ **Index numbers** are a way of comparing figures over time.
- ☑ **Index points** are a measure of the difference in the index value in one year with the value in another year.
- ☑ The **base period / year** has the value against which all other values are compared in order to construct an index.
- ☑ An index is constructed as (**value in time period in question/value in base period**) × 100.
- ☑ When constructing composite index numbers, **weighting** can be used to overcome the problems of quantities in different units and the need to attach importance to each item.
- ☑ To bring a figure 'up to date' you multiply it by (recent index number/older index number).
- ☑ **Exchange rates** are a special form of price index.
- ☑ The **Retail Prices Index (RPI)** measures the change in the cost of living.
- ☑ Index numbers have a range of **limitations.**
- ☑ Management accounting information should have the qualities of **good information**.

Quick quiz

1 Rearrange the following equation to find the value of x.

1,930 – 4.7x = 1,900.39

2 Choose the correct word from those highlighted.

In the equation m = 3p – 2, m is the **independent/dependent** variable.

3 A memo format should be used for a formal report. *True or false*?

4 Fill in the blank.

The exchange rate between currency 1 and currency 2 is X. To covert an amount from currency 2 to currency 1 you .... by the exchange rate.

5 Why might it be inappropriate to use an average earnings index to assess the reasonableness of wage payments?

A Because the mix of skills and experience in the organisation may be different to the national average
B Because the rate of pay in the local area might have risen at the same rate as the national rate
C Because the RPI should be used
D Because there is no such index as an average earnings index

6 Fill in the blanks in the statements below to describe the principles and attributes of good information.

(a) It should be .... for its purpose.
(b) It should be .... for its purpose.
(c) It should be sufficiently .... for its purpose.
(d) It should be .... to the manager using it.
(e) The manager using it should have .... in it.
(f) It should be .... to the appropriate manager.
(g) It should not be excessive, its .... should be manageable.
(h) It should be............. (in other words communicated at the most appropriate time).
(i) It should be communicated by an appropriate..
(j) It should be provided at a ....it provides.

Answers to quick quiz

1 1,930 – 4.7x = 1,900.39

$$\begin{aligned} 1{,}930 - 4.7x - 1{,}930 &= 1{,}900.39 - 1{,}930 \\ -4.7x &= -29.61 \\ x &= -29.61/-4.7 = 6.3 \end{aligned}$$

2 m is the **dependent** variable as its value depends on the value of p.

3 False. Memos are used for informal reports.

4 Divide by the exchange rate

5 A

6

(a)	relevant	(f)	communicated
(b)	complete	(g)	volume
(c)	accurate	(h)	timely
(d)	clear	(i)	channel of communication
(e)	confidence	(j)	cost which is less than the value of the benefits

ASSESSMENT KIT ACTIVITIES

The following activities in the BPP Assessment Kit for Units 8 & 9 include topics covered in this chapter.

Activities 6, 13, 16, 17, 18, 19, 26, 42 and 43
Lecturers' practice activity 3

Activity checklist

This checklist shows which performance criteria, range statement or knowledge and understanding point is covered by each activity in this chapter. Tick off each activity as you complete it.

Activity		
4.1	☐	This activity deals with Unit 8 Knowledge & Understanding point (3): basic statistical methods and Unit 9 Knowledge & Understanding point (3): basic statistical methods.
4.2	☐	This activity deals with Performance Criteria 8.1.G regarding the presentation of reports to management that summarise data, the presentation of information using appropriate methods and the highlighting of significant trends, Range Statement 8.1: methods of presenting information in reports (written analysis and explanation; tables), and Unit 8 Knowledge & Understanding point (5): methods of presenting information (tabular form).
4.3	☐	This activity deals with Performance Criteria 8.1.G regarding the presentation of reports to management that summarise data, the presentation of information using appropriate methods and the highlighting of significant trends, Range Statement 8.1: methods of presenting information in reports (written analysis and explanation; tables), and Unit 8 Knowledge & Understanding point (5): methods of presenting information (tabular form).
4.4	☐	This activity deals with Performance Criteria 8.1G regarding the presentation of reports to management that summarise data, the presentation of information using appropriate methods and the highlighting of significant trends, Range Statement 8.1: methods of presenting information in reports (written analysis and explanation; tables), and Unit 8 Knowledge & Understanding point (5): methods of presenting information (tabular form).
4.5	☐	This activity deals with Performance Criteria 8.1G regarding the presentation of reports to management that summarise data, the presentation of information using appropriate methods and the highlighting of significant trends, Range Statement 8.1: methods of presenting information in reports (diagrams) and Unit 8 Knowledge & Understanding point (5): methods of presenting information (diagrammatic form).
4.6	☐	This activity deals with Performance Criteria 8.1G regarding the presentation of reports to management that summarise data, the presentation of information using appropriate methods and the highlighting of significant trends, Range Statement 8.1: methods of presenting information in reports (diagrams) and Unit 8 Knowledge & Understanding point (5): methods of presenting information (diagrammatic form).

Activity checklist (cont'd)

4.7	☐	This activity deals with Performance Criteria 8.1G regarding the presentation of reports to management that summarise data, the presentation of information using appropriate methods and the highlighting of significant trends, Range Statement 8.1: methods of presenting information in reports (written analysis and explanation; tables; diagrams) and Unit 8 Knowledge & Understanding point (5): methods of presenting information (diagrammatic and tabular form).
4.8	☐	This activity deals with Unit 8 Knowledge & Understanding point (5): methods of presenting information (graphical form).
4.9	☐	This activity deals with Range Statement 8.1: methods of presenting information in reports (written analysis and explanation).
4.10	☐	This activity deals with Range Statement 8.1: methods of presenting information in reports (written analysis and explanation).
4.11	☐	This activity deals with Range Statement 8.1: methods of presenting information in reports (written analysis and explanation).
4.12	☐	This activity deals with Range Statement 8.1: methods of summarising data (index numbers), Unit 8 Knowledge & Understanding point (3): basic statistical methods (index numbers) and Unit 9 Knowledge & Understanding point (3): basic statistical methods (index numbers).
4.13	☐	This activity deals with Range Statement 8.1: methods of summarising data (index numbers), Unit 8 Knowledge & Understanding point (3): basic statistical methods (index numbers) and Unit 9 Knowledge & Understanding point (3): basic statistical methods (index numbers).

chapter 5

Forecasting

Contents

1 Introduction
2 Time series analysis: the components of time series
3 Time series analysis: finding the trend
4 Time series analysis: finding the seasonal variations
5 Time series analysis: deseasonalisation
6 Time series analysis: forecasting
7 Linear regression analysis
8 Cost forecasting
9 Forecasting problems

Performance criteria

8.1B Monitor and analyse on a regular basis current and forecast trends in prices and market conditions

8.1C Compare trends with previous experience and identify potential implications

8.1F Consult relevant staff in the organisation about the analysis of trends and variances

9.1B Communicate with relevant individuals and give them the opportunity to raise queries and to clarify forecasts

9.1C Prepare forecasts in a clear format with explanations of assumptions, projections and adjustments

9.1D Review and revise the validity of forecasts in the light of any significant anticipated changes

Range statement

8.1 Methods of summarising data: time series (moving averages, linear regression, seasonal variations)

9.1 Forecasts: income; expenditure

9.1 Projections: trends; seasonal variations; market research

Knowledge and understanding

Unit 8 Accounting techniques

3 Basic statistical methods: time series analysis (moving averages, linear regression and seasonal trends)

Unit 9 Accounting techniques

3 Basic statistical methods: time series (moving averages, linear regression and seasonal variations)

Signpost

The topics covered in this chapter are relevant to **Unit 8** and **Unit 9**.

1 Introduction

Another way in which **collected data can be analysed** to provide useful management information is by applying **forecasting** techniques. Forecasting involves **analysing past data** in order to **predict and quantify what will happen** in the future. The resulting **forecasts** can be used to **establish plans and targets** representing what should happen against which actual results are compared in control systems.

You need a full understanding of the way in which forecasts are derived so in this chapter we look at the **general approach** to various forecasting techniques. In particular we look at time series analysis and linear regression analysis. Forecasting often forms part of a wider task in the exam, however, and so in later chapters we will see how forecasting can be applied in connection with the core themes of Units 8 and 9.

2 Time series analysis: the components of time series

A **time series** is a **series of figures or values recorded over time**.

The following are examples of time series.

- Output at a factory each day for the last month
- Monthly sales over the last two years
- The Retail Prices Index each month for the last ten years

A **graph of a time series** is called a **historigram**.

Note the 'ri'; this is *not* the same as a histogram. For example, consider the following time series.

Year	0	1	2	3	4	5	6
Sales (£'000)	20	21	24	23	27	30	28

The historigram is as follows.

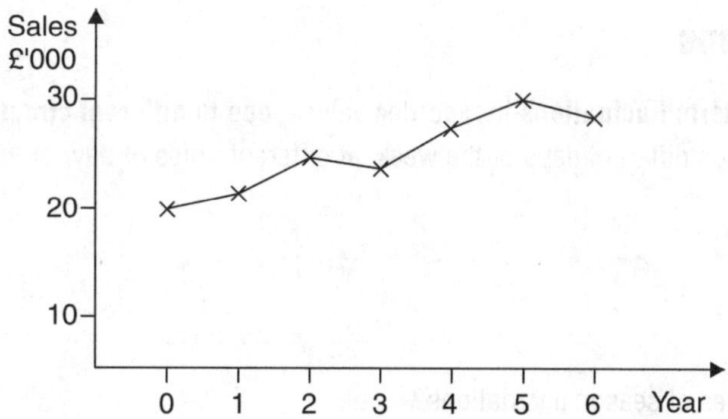

The horizontal axis is always chosen to represent time, and the vertical axis represents the values of the data recorded.

There are several **components of a time series** which it may be necessary to identify.

- A **trend**
- **Seasonal variations** or fluctuations
- Cycles, or **cyclical variations**
- Non-recurring, **random variations**. These may be caused by unforeseen circumstances such as a change in government, a war, technological change or a fire.

2.1 The trend

The trend is the **underlying long-term movement over time in values of data recorded**.

In the following examples of time series, there are three types of trend.

Year	*Output per labour hour*	*Cost per unit*	*Number of employees*
	Units	£	
4	30	1.00	100
5	24	1.08	103
6	26	1.20	96
7	22	1.15	102
8	21	1.18	103
9	17	1.25	98
	(A)	(B)	(C)

- In time series **(A)** there is a **downward trend** in the output per labour hour. Output per labour hour did not fall every year, because it went up between Year 5 and Year 6, but the long-term movement is clearly a downward one.
- In time series **(B)** there is an **upward trend** in the cost per unit. Although unit costs went down in Year 7 from a higher level in Year 6, the basic movement over time is one of rising costs.
- In time series **(C)** there is **no clear movement up or down**, and the number of employees remained fairly constant. The trend is therefore a static, or level one.

2.2 Seasonal variations

Seasonal variations are **short-term fluctuations** in recorded values, **due to different circumstances which affect results at different times** of the year, on different days of the week, at different times of day, or whatever.

Activity 5.1

Can you think of some examples of seasonal variations?

'Seasonal' is a term which may appear to refer to the seasons of the year, but its meaning in time series analysis is somewhat broader, as the examples given in the activity above show.

Example: a trend and seasonal variations

The number of customers served by a company of travel agents over the past four years is shown in the following historigram.

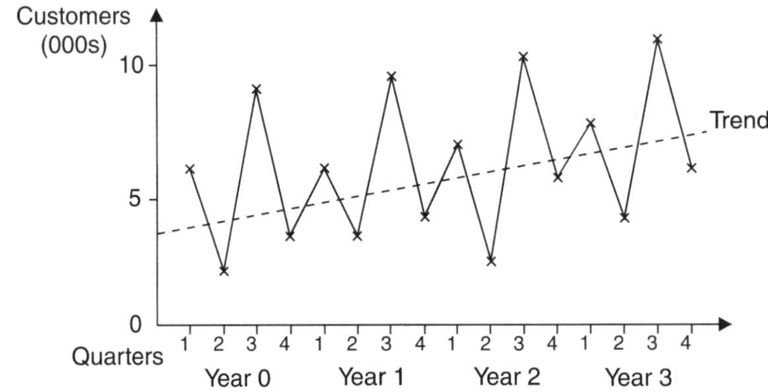

In this example, there would appear to be large seasonal fluctuations in demand, but there is also a basic upward trend.

2.3 Cyclical variations

Cyclical variations are **fluctuations which take place over a longer time period than seasonal variations**.

It may take several years to complete a cycle, as in the case of the 'trade cycle'. Economists observed in the late 19th century that the level of economic activity or output often fluctuated over a cycle of approximately nine years in length (although the length of the cycle has not been changed).

2.4 Summarising the components

In practice a time series could incorporate all four of the features we have been looking at and, to make reasonably accurate forecasts, the four features often have to be isolated. We can begin the process of isolating each feature by summarising the components of a time series by the following equation.

$$Y = T + S + C + I$$

where **Y = the actual time series**
T = the trend series
S = the seasonal component
C = the cyclical component
I = the random, non-recurring component

Though you should be aware of the cyclical component, you will not be expected to carry out any calculation connected with isolating it. The mathematical model which we will use, the **additive model** of a time series, therefore excludes any reference to C and is **Y = T + S + I.**

Note. A **mathematical model** is simply a **mathematical relationship or formula which aims to represent a 'real-world' situation**. Here the additive model attempts to represent how the components of a time series are related.

Activity 5.2

Consider the following time series.

(a) The state of the world's economy since 1950 as measured by economic output

(b) Monthly sales of new cars over the last ten years

(c) Weekly sales of a chocolate mousse during the year in which, in the space of two days, 57 people found slivers of glass in tubs of the mousse

(d) Quarterly sales of Christmas crackers over the last four years

(e) Monthly sales of mobile phones over the last three years

(f) The number employed in heavy manufacturing industries in Great Britain over the last forty years

Task

Which of the following will be the most obvious feature of each of the time series (a) to (f) above?

An increasing trend
A decreasing trend
Seasonal variations
Cyclical variations
Random variations

We will begin by looking at how to find the trend in a time series.

3 Time series analysis: finding the trend

Look at these monthly sales figures.

Year 6	August	September	October	November	December
Sales (£'000)	0.02	0.04	0.04	3.20	14.60

It looks as though the business is expanding rapidly – and so it is, in a way. But when you know that the business is a Christmas card manufacturer, then you see immediately that the January sales will no doubt slump right back down again.

It is obvious that the business will do better in the Christmas season than at any other time – that is the seasonal variation. Using the monthly figures, how can you tell whether or not the business is doing well overall – whether there is a rising sales trend over time other than the short-term rise over Christmas?

One possibility is to compare figures with the equivalent figures of a year ago. However, many things can happen over a year to make such a comparison misleading – new products might now be manufactured and prices will probably have changed.

In fact, there are a number of ways of overcoming this problem of distinguishing trend from seasonal variations. One such method is called **moving averages**. This method **attempts to remove seasonal (or cyclical) variations from a time series by a process of averaging so as to leave a set of figures representing the trend.**

3.1 Finding the trend by moving averages

A **moving average** is an **average of the results of a fixed number of periods**.

Since it is an average of several time periods, a moving average is **related to the mid-point of the overall period.**

Example: moving averages

Year	*Sales*
	Units
0	390
1	380
2	460
3	450
4	470
5	440
6	500

Task

Take a moving average of the annual sales over a period of three years.

Note. By taking the moving average over three years, we are saying that there are three distinct 'seasons' within that three-year period. If you take a moving average over 5 periods, you are saying there are five 'seasons' within the five year period.

Solution

(a) Average sales in the three year period Year 0 – Year 2 were (390 + 380 + 460)/3 = 1,230/3 = 410. This average relates to the middle year of the period, Year 1.

(b) Similarly, average sales in the three year period Year 1 – Year 3 were (380 + 460 + 450)/3 = 1,290/3 = 430. This average relates to the middle year of the period, Year 2.

(c) The average sales can also be found for the periods Year 2 – Year 4, Year 3 – Year 5 and Year 4 – Year 6, to give the following.

Year	*Sales*	*Moving total of 3 years' sales*	*Moving average of 3 year's sales (÷ 3)*
0	390		
1	380	1,230	410
2	460	1,290	430
3	450	1,380	460
4	470	1,360	453
5	440	1,410	470
6	500		

Note the following points.

- The moving average series has five figures relating to the years 1 to 5. The original series had seven figures for the years 0 to 6.
- There is an upward trend in sales, which is more noticeable from the series of moving averages than from the original series of actual sales each year.

Activity 5.3

Check the moving average figures shown in the table in solution part (c) above, using the method set out in solution parts (a) and (b).

The above example averaged over a three-year period. Over what period should a moving average be taken? The answer to this question is that the **moving average which is most appropriate will depend on the circumstances and the nature of the time series.**

- A moving average which takes an **average of the results in many time periods will represent results over a longer term** than a moving average of two or three periods.

- On the other hand, with a moving average of results in many time periods, the **last figure in the series will be out of date by several periods**. In our example, the most recent average related to Year 5. With a moving average of five years' results, the final figure in the series would relate to Year 4.
- When there is a **known cycle** over which seasonal variations occur, such as all the days in the week or all the seasons in the year, the **most suitable moving average would be one which covers one full cycle**.

3.1.1 Moving averages of an even number of results

In the previous example, **moving averages were taken of the results in an *odd* number of time periods**, and the **average then related to the mid-point of the overall period.**

If a **moving average** were taken of results in an **even number of time periods**, the basic technique would be the same, but the mid-point of the overall period would not relate to a single period. For example, suppose an average were taken of the following four results.

Spring	120	
Summer	90	
Autumn	180	average 115
Winter	70	

The average would relate to the mid-point of the period, between summer and autumn.

The trend line average figures need to relate to a particular time period; otherwise, seasonal variations cannot be calculated. To overcome this difficulty, we **take a moving average of the moving average**. An example will illustrate this technique.

Example: moving averages over an even number of periods

Calculate a moving average trend line of the following results of Andy Ltd.

Year	*Quarter*	*Volume of sales* '000 units
Year 5	1	600
	2	840
	3	420
	4	720
Year 6	1	640
	2	860
	3	420
	4	740
Year 7	1	670
	2	900
	3	430
	4	760

Solution

A moving average of four will be used, since the volume of sales appears to depend on the quarter of the year, and each year has four quarterly results. The moving average of four does not relate to any specific time period and so a second moving average of two will be calculated on the first moving average trend line.

Year	*Quarter*	*Actual volume of sales* '000 units (A)	*Moving total of 4 quarters' sales* '000 units (B)	*Moving average of 4 quarters' sales* '000 units (B ÷ 4)	*Mid-point of 2 moving averages Trend line* '000 units (C)
Year 5	1	600			
	2	840			
	3	420	2,580	645.0	650.00
	4	720	2,620	655.0	657.50
Year 6	1	640	2,640	660.0	660.00
	2	860	2,640	660.0	662.50
	3	420	2,660	665.0	668.75
	4	740	2,690	672.5	677.50
Year 7	1	670	2,730	682.5	683.75
	2	900	2,740	685.0	687.50
	3	430	2,760	690.0	
	4	760			

By taking a mid point (a moving average of two) of the original moving averages, we can relate the results to specific quarters (from the third quarter of Year 5 to the second quarter of Year 7).

Activity 5.4

What can you say about the trend in sales of Andy Ltd above?

3.2 Moving averages on graphs

One way of displaying the trend clearly is to show it by plotting the moving average on a graph.

Example: moving averages on graphs

Actual ice cream sales for Year 5 and Year 6 were as follows.

	Sales	
	Year 5	*Year 6*
	£	£
January	100	110
February	120	130
March	200	220
April	200	210
May	240	230
June	250	240
July	210	250
August	210	300
Soptombor	200	160
October	110	110
November	90	80
December	50	40
	1,980	2,070

Task

Calculate the trend in the ice cream sales and display it on a graph.

Solution

		Sales	Annual moving total	Moving average	Mid-point of 2 moving averages
		£	£	£	
Year 5	January	100			
	February	120			
	March	200			
	April	200			
	May	240			
	June	250			
			1,980	165.00	
	July	210			165.415
			1,990	165.83	
	August	210			166.250
			2,000	166.67	
	September	200			167.500
			2,020	168.33	
	October	110			168.750
			2,030	169.17	
	November	90			168.750
			2,020	168.33	
	December	50			167.915
			2,010	167.50	
Year 6	January	110			169.165
			2,050	170.83	
	February	130			174.580
			2,140	178.33	
	March	220			176.250
			2,090	174.17	
	April	210			174.170
			2,090	174.17	
	May	230			173.750
			2,080	173.33	
	June	240			172.915
			2,070	172.50	
	July	250			
	August	300			
	September	150			
	October	110			
	November	80			
	December	40			

The moving data on ice cream sales could be drawn on a graph as follows.

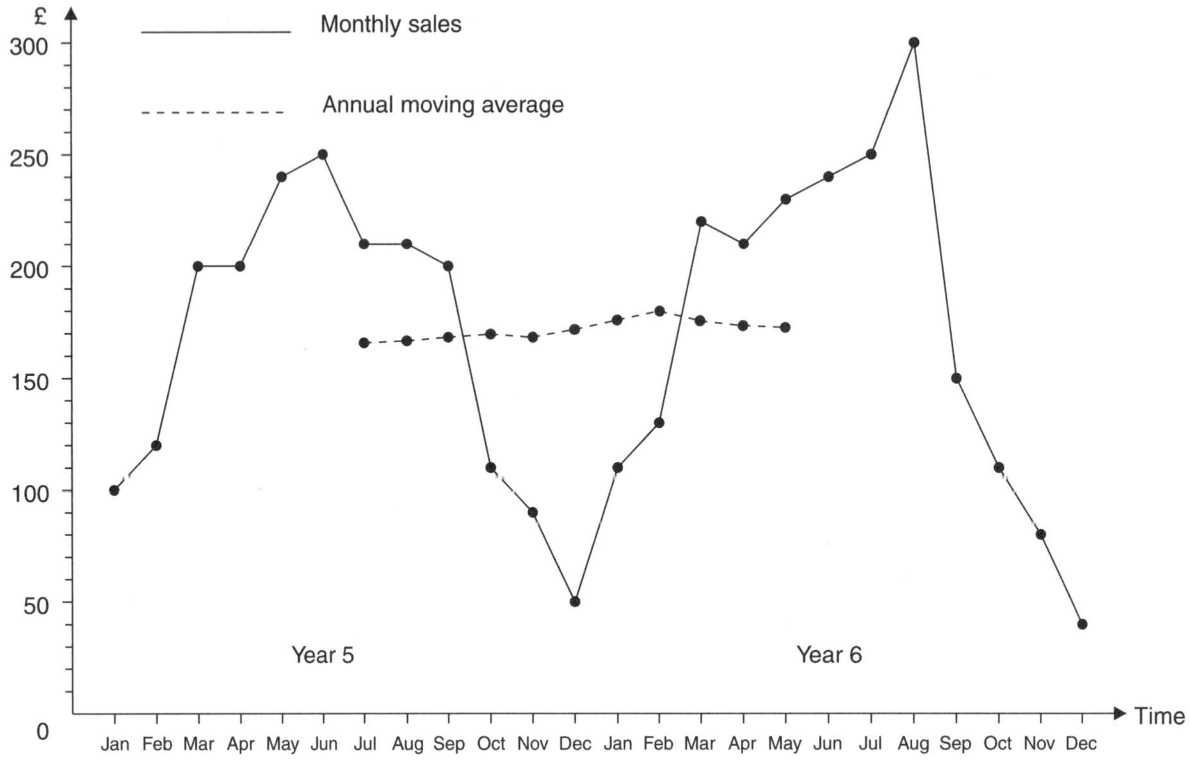

Points to note about this graph

- The annual moving average can only be plotted from July Year 5 to May Year 6 as we have no data prior to January Year 5 or after December Year 6.
- The moving average has the effect of smoothing out the seasonal fluctuations in the ordinary sales graph (which is the reason why moving averages are used).

4 Time series analysis: finding the seasonal variations

4.1 Seasonal variations and the additive model

Once a trend has been established, we can find the seasonal variations.

- As we saw earlier, the additive model for time series analysis is Y = T + S + I.
- We can therefore write Y – T = S + I. In other words, if we deduct the trend series from the actual series, we will be left with the seasonal and random components of the time series.
- If we assume that the random movements component is relatively small, and hence negligible, the **seasonal component can be found as S = Y – T**, the **de-trended series**.

The actual and trend sales for Andy Ltd (as calculated in Section 3.1.1) are set out below. The difference between the actual results for any one quarter (Y) and the trend figure for that quarter (T) will be the seasonal variation for that quarter.

Year	*Quarter*	*Actual (Y)*	*Trend (T)*	*Seasonal variation (Y – T)*
Year 5	1	600		
	2	840		
	3	420	650.00	–230.00
	4	720	657.50	62.50
Year 6	1	640	660.00	–20.00
	2	860	662.50	197.50
	3	420	668.75	–248.75
	4	740	677.50	62.50
Year 7	1	670	683.75	–13.75
	2	900	687.50	212.50
	3	430		
	4	760		

The variation between the actual result for a particular quarter and the trend line average is not the same each year, but an **average of these variations can be taken.**

	Q_1	Q_2	Q_3	Q_4
Year 5			–230.00	62.50
Year 6	–20.00	197.50	–248.75	62.50
Year 7	–13.75	212.50		
Total	–33.75	410.00	–478.75	125.00
Average (÷ 2)	–16.875	205.00	–239.375	62.50

Variations around the basic trend line should cancel each other out, and add up to zero. At the moment, they do not. We **therefore spread the total of the variations (11.25) across the four quarters (11.25 ÷ 4) so that the final total of the variations sums to zero.**

	Q_1	Q_2	Q_3	Q_4	*Total*
Estimated quarterly variations	– 16.8750	205.0000	–239.3750	62.5000	11.250
Adjustment to reduce variations to 0	–2.8125	–2.8125	–2.8125	–2.8125	–11.250
Final estimates of quarterly variations	–19.6875	202.1875	–242.1875	59.6875	0

These might be rounded as follows.

QI: –20,	QI: 202,	QI:-242,	QI: 60,	Total: 0

4.1.1 A weakness in moving average analysis and the additive model

The moving average calculations described so far are based on an **additive model** which means that we add the values for a number of periods and take the average of those values.

The model assumes that the components of the series are independent of each other so that, for example, an increasing trend does not affect the seasonal variations and make them increase as well.

An additive model therefore has an important drawback: **when there is a steeply rising or a steeply declining trend, the moving average trend will either get ahead of or fall behind the real trend.**

For example, consider a three-period moving average of the following sales figures.

	Actual sales	*Three-year moving total*	*Moving average*
	£'000	£'000	£'000
Year 1	1,000		
Year 2	1,200	3,700	1,233
Year 3	1,500	4,800	1,600
Year 4	2,100	6,600	2,200
Year 5	3,000	9,300	3,100
Year 6	4,200	12,900	4,300
Year 7	5,700	18,000	6,000
Year 8	8,100		

In this example sales are on a steeply rising trend, which means that the moving average value for each year consistently overstates sales because it is partly influenced by the value of sales in the next year. The moving average value for Year 7, for example, is £6,000, which is £300 above actual sales for Year 7. This is because the moving average is partly based on the higher sales value in Year 8. This means that the trend sales is not a good representation of actual sales and that the trend will probably be unsuitable for forecasting.

4.2 Seasonal variations using the proportional model

The alternative to using the additive model is to use the **proportional (or multiplicative) model** in which each actual figure is expressed as a percentage of the trend.

The proportional (multiplicative) model summaries a time series as $\mathbf{Y = T \times S \times I}$.

Note that the **trend** will be the **same whichever model is used** but the values of the **seasonal and random components** will **vary according to the model** being applied.

The above example about Andy Ltd can be reworked on this alternative basis. The trend is calculated in exactly the same way as before but we need a different approach to calculating the seasonal variations. The proportional model is $Y = T \times S \times I$ and, just as we calculated $S = Y - T$ for the additive model, we can calculate $\mathbf{S = Y/T}$ for the proportional model.

Year	*Quarter*	*Actual* (Y)	*Trend* (T)	*Seasonal percentage* (Y/T)
Year 5	1	600		
	2	840		
	3	420	650.00	0.646
	4	720	657.50	1.095
Year 6	1	640	660.00	0.970
	2	860	662.50	1.298
	3	420	668.75	0.628
	4	740	677.50	1.092
Year 7	1	670	683.75	0.980
	2	900	687.50	1.309
	3	430		
	4	760		

The summary of the seasonal variations expressed in proportional terms is as follows.

	Q1	*Q2*	*Q3*	*Q4*
Year 5			0.646	1.095
Year 6	0.97	1.298	0.628	1.092
Year 7	0.98	1.309	–	–
Total	1.95	2.607	1.274	2.187
Average	0.975	1.3035	0.637	1.0935

Instead of summing to zero, as with the additive approach, the averages should sum (in this case) to 4.0, 1.0 for each of the four quarters. They actually sum to 4.009 so 0.00225 has to be deducted from each one.

	Q1	*Q2*	*Q3*	*Q4*
Average	0.97500	1.30350	0.63700	1.09350
Adjustment	–0.00225	–0.00225	–0.00225	–0.00225
Final estimate	0.97275	1.30125	0.63475	1.09125
Rounded	0.97	1.3	0.63	1.09

Note that the **proportional model is better than the additive model for forecasting when the trend is increasing or decreasing over time.** In such circumstances, seasonal variations are likely to be increasing or decreasing too. The additive model simply adds absolute and unchanging seasonal variations to the trend figures whereas the proportional model, by multiplying increasing or decreasing trend values by a constant seasonal variation factor, takes account of increasing or decreasing seasonal variations.

ATTENTION!

Both the additive and multiplicative models are examinable so make sure that you can use both of them.

Activity 5.5

The trend in a company's quarterly sales figures has been analysed using moving averages.

Year	*Quarter*	*Actual*	*Trend*
		£'000	£'000
Year 1	1	350	366
	2	380	370
	3	400	380
	4	360	394
Year 2	1	410	406
	2	430	414
	3	450	418
	4	370	423

Task

Find the average seasonal variation for each quarter, using the proportional model.

Activity 5.6

A home improvement store opens seven days per week and the daily takings are given in the table below.

	Sunday	*Monday*	*Tuesday*	*Wednesday*	*Thursday*	*Friday*	*Saturday*
	£'000	£'000	£'000	£'000	£'000	£'000	£'000
Week 1	13	5	7	9	11	14	23
Week 2	14	5	9	10	11	16	25
Week 3	15	6	8	12	13	17	27

Task

By means of a moving average find the trend and the daily variation factors.

5 Time series analysis: deseasonalisation

Economic statistics, such as unemployment figures, are often **'seasonally adjusted'** or **'deseasonalised'** so as to ensure that the overall trend (rising, falling or stationary) is clear.

Seasonally-adjusted or deseasonalised data have had **seasonal variations (derived from previous data) taken out**, to **leave a figure** which could be viewed as the **trend**.

Example: deseasonalisation

Actual sales figures for the four quarters of Year 1, together with appropriate seasonal adjustment factors derived from previous data, are as follows.

		Seasonal adjustments	
Quarter	*Actual sales*	*Additive model*	*Multiplicative model*
	£'000	£'000	
1	148	+3	1.02
2	154	+4	1.03
3	153	–2	0.99
4	155	–5	0.97

Task

Deseasonalise these data.

Solution

Additive model: $Y = T + S$

We want to find T.

$\mathbf{T = Y - S}$

Multiplicative model: $Y = T \times S$

We want to find T.

$\mathbf{T = Y/S}$

		Deseasonalised sales	
Quarter	*Actual sales*	*Additive model*	*Multiplicative model*
	Y	*Y – S*	*Y/S*
	£'000	£'000	£'000
1	148	145	145
2	154	150	150
3	153	*155	155
4	155	160	160

* $T = 153 - (-2) = 153 + 2$

The seasonally-adjusted figures show an increase of £5,000 per quarter. The trend will therefore show an increase of £5,000 per quarter.

6 Time series analysis: forecasting

6.1 Using time series analysis in practice

The analysis of a time series allows historical aspects of data to be monitored. In other words, it is possible to observe how a variable has performed over the period of time being monitored. So, for example, the cost of raw materials, the price of a particular bought-in component or the rate per hour paid to labour can be monitored and analysed.

Equally, if not more important, however, is the potential to use the historical data once analysed to forecast future performance, which is a necessary part of business planning.

6.2 Forecasting

6.2.1 Using the additive model

We know that Y = T + S.

∴ **Forecast Y = forecast T + S.**

So if we can **forecast the trend** value and **adjust by the seasonal variation** we will have our forecast.

6.2.2 Using the multiplicative model

We know that Y = T × S.

∴ **Forecast Y = forecast T × S.**

So, again, if we forecast the trend value and adjust by the seasonal variation we will have our forecast.

6.2.3 In general

Forecasts can therefore be made using time series analysis data as follows.

- **Find a trend** by using moving averages (as covered in Section 3) or by seasonally-adjusting a time series (as covered in Section 5).
- Use the trend line to **forecast future trend values.** This involves projecting the trend outside the range of known data. This is known as **extrapolation**.
- **Adjust the forecast trend values by the seasonal variation** applicable to the future period, to determine the forecast.

There are three principal methods of extrapolating a trend.

- **'By eye'** on a graph
- Using a common sense approach
- Using linear regression analysis (see Section 7)

Let's use the following example to illustrate the first two methods.

Example: forecasting using moving averages

The quarterly sales (in £'000) by BW Ltd are as follows.

Quarter	*Year 4*	*Year 5*	*Year 6*	*Year 7*
	£'000	£'000	£'000	£'000
First		8	20	40
Second		30	50	62
Third		60	80	92
Fourth	24	20	40	

Tasks

(a) Find the centred moving average trend.

(b) Find the average seasonal variation for each quarter using the additive model.

(c) Predict sales for the last quarter of Year 7 and the first quarter of Year 8, stating any assumptions, using the following methods.

   (i) Extrapolation of the trend 'by eye'
   (ii) Common sense approach

Solution

(a)

	Quarter	*Actual*	*4 quarter moving total*	*Centred moving total*	*Moving average(÷4)*	*Seasonal variation*
Year 4	4	24				
Year 5	1	8				
			122			
	2	30		120	30	-
			118			
	3	60		124	31	29
			130			
	4	20		140	35	–15
			150			
Year 6	1	20		160	40	–20
			170			
	2	50		180	45	5
			190			
	3	80		200	50	30
			210			
	4	40		216	54	–14
			222			
Year 7	1	40		228	57	–17
			234			
	2	62				
	3	92				

(b) **Seasonal variations**

		Quarter			
	1	*2*	*3*	*4*	*Total*
Year 5		0.00	+29.00	–15.00	
6	–20.00	+5.00	+30.00	–14.00	
7	–17.00	–	–		
Total	–37.00	+5.00	+59.00	–29.00	
Average	–18.50	+2.50	+29.50	–14.50	–1
Adjust total variation to nil	+0.25	+0.25	+0.25	+0.25	+1
Average seasonal variation	–18.25	+2.75	+29.75	–14.25	

(c) **Extrapolation of the trend 'by eye'**

We plot the trend values on a graph and extrapolate the **trend line** 'by eye' so that it **appears to lie evenly between the plotted trend points.**

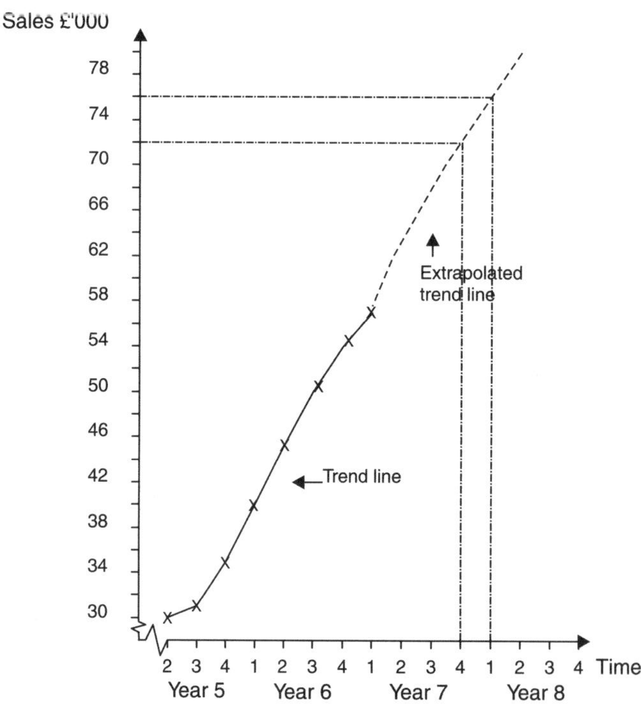

From the extrapolated trend line we can **take readings and adjust them by the seasonal variations.**

We are using the **additive model** and so **Y = T + S**

∴ **'Forecast' Y = 'forecast' T + S**

	Extrapolated trend line reading Forecast T	*Seasonal variation S*	*Forecast Y*
	£'000	£'000	£'000
Year 7 Q4	72	–14.25	57.75
Year 8 Q1	76	–18.25	57.75

Rounding to the nearest thousand pounds, the forecast sales are £58,000 for each of the two quarters.

Common sense 'rule-of-thumb' approach

This method is simply to **guess what future movements** in the trend line might be, **based on movements in the past**. It is not a mathematical technique, merely a common sense approach.

In past exam tasks it has been immediately obvious that the trend is increasing by, say, £2,000 per quarter or, say, 500 units per week. In this example, however, we might guess that the trend line is rising steadily, by (57 – 40)/4 = 4.25 per quarter in the period 1st quarter Year 6 to 1st quarter Year 7 (57 being the prediction in 1st quarter Year 7 and 40 the prediction in 1st quarter Year 6). Since the trend may be levelling off a little, a quarterly increase of +4 in the trend will be assumed.

		Forecast trend	*Seasonal variation*	*Forecast*
1st quarter	Year 7	57		
4th quarter	Year 7 (+ (3 × 4))	69	–14.25	54.75
1st quarter	Year 8 (+ (4 × 4))	73	–18.25	54.75

Rounding to the nearest thousand pounds, the forecast sales are £55,000 for each of the two quarters.

Example: forecasting using seasonally-adjusted data

Look back at the deseasonalisation example in Section 5. Assuming a similar pattern of sales in the future, forecast the likely sales figures for the first two quarters of Year 1.

Solution

We noted in the solution to the example that the trend shows an increase of £5,000 per quarter. We will use both the additive model (Y(forecast) = T + S) and the proportional model (Y(forecast) = T × S).

Period	*Trend*	*Additive seasonal variations*	*Proportional seasonal variations*	*Additive forecast*	*Proportional forecast*
Q1	£165,000*	+ £3,000	1.02	£168,000	£168,300
Q2	£170,000**	+ £4,000	1.03	£174,000	£175,100

*£(160,000+5,000)

**£(165,000+5,000)

WATCH OUT FOR ...

Different forms of multiplicative model seasonal components

You may be given a multiplicative model seasonal component as a percentage, such as 15% or –15%.

This simply means that the actual figure is either 15% above the trend or 15% below the trend.

Think about it: Y = T × S and so if the trend (T) is £10,000 and the seasonal variation (S) is –7%, the forecast (Y) will be 7% below the trend of £10,000, ie £10,000 × (100 – 7)% = £10,000 × 93% = £9,300.

WATCH OUT FOR ... (cont'd)

If the seasonal variation is +7%, however, the forecast will be 7% above the trend of £10,000, ie £10,000 × 107% = £10,700.

Alternatively you might need to find the trend. Suppose that S is 12% of T.

Forecast Y = 112% of T = 112/100 × T
∴ 100/112 × Y = T

Likewise, suppose S is –12% of T.

Forecast Y = (100 – 12)% of T = 88% of T = 88/100 × T
∴ 100/88 × Y = T

Activity 5.7

If the trend figure for week 13 is £47,500 and the appropriate seasonal variation is –13.3%, what is the forecast value for week 13?

Let's look at an example which incorporates the percentage form of seasonal components described in the 'Watch out for ...' box above.

Example: forecasting and percentage seasonal components

The following trend in sales of product X over a six-month period was determined using moving averages. Seasonal variations are also shown.

Month	*Sales* Units	*Seasonal variation*
1	500	–10%
2	600	–5%
3	720	0
4	864	5%
5	1,037	10%
6	1,244	0

These figures show that the trend is increasing by 20% per month. Check this for yourself (eg ((720 – 600)/600) × 100% = 20%).

The forecast trend for month 7 is therefore 1,244 × 120% = 1,493 units

Assuming that sales vary on a six-monthly basis, the forecast for month 7 is

1,493 × (100 – 10)% = 1,344 units

Activity 5.8

What is the forecast sales level of product X (see example above) in month 9 and month 11?

In the next activity, remember that the seasonal adjustment shows whether the forecast should be lower than the trend (a negative seasonal adjustment) or above the trend (a positive seasonal adjustment).

Activity 5.9

Your organisation's sales manager had made some progress in preparing the sales forecasts for year 5 when she unexpectedly needed to take leave for personal reasons.

She has left you the following memo.

MEMORANDUM

To: Assistant Management Accountant   Date: 12 December Year 4
From: Sales Manager
Subject: Sales forecasts for year 5

In preparing the sales volume forecasts for year 5, I have got as far as establishing the following trend figures and average seasonal variations.

	Quarter 1	*Quarter 2*	*Quarter 3*	*Quarter 4*
	Units	Units	Units	Units
Year 3 – trend figures	3,270	3,313	3,358	3,407
Year 4 – trend figures	3,452	3,496	3,541	3,587
Average seasonal variation	–50	+22	+60	–32

As a basis for extrapolating the trend line, I forecast that the trend will continue to increase in year 5 at the same average amount per quarter as during year 4.

Sorry to leave you with this unfinished job, but it should be possible to prepare an outline forecast for year 5 with this data.

Tasks

(a) Briefly explain what is meant by the following.

(i) Seasonal variations
(ii) Extrapolating a trend line

Use the data from the memorandum to illustrate your explanations.

(b) Prepare a forecast of sales volumes for each of the four quarters of year 5, based on the data contained in the analyst's memo.

6.3 Residuals

A residual is the difference between the results which would have been predicted (for a past period for which we already have data) by the trend line adjusted for the average seasonal variation and the actual results for the past period.

- The residual is therefore the difference which is not explained by the trend line and the average seasonal variation.
- It gives some indication of how much actual results were affected by other factors.
- Large residuals suggest that any forecast is likely to be unreliable.
- It is a good idea to calculate the residual series (Y – T – S) in order to assess the adequacy of predictions.

Look back at the first example of this section (BW Ltd).

- The 'prediction' for the first quarter of Year 7 would have been 57 – 18.25 = 38.75. As the actual value was 40, the residual was 40 – 38.75 = 1.25.
- The residual for the fourth quarter of Year 6 was 40 – (54 – 14.25) = 0.25.
- An analysis of all the residuals associated with a particular time series will indicate whether the predictions based on the time series are reliable. Our predictions appear fairly reliable.

Activity 5.10

You work as the assistant to the management accountant for Henry Limited, a medium-sized manufacturing company. One of their products, product P, has been very successful in recent years, showing a steadily increasing trend in sales volumes.

Sales volumes for the four quarters of last year were as follows.

	Quarter 1	*Quarter 2*	*Quarter 3*	*Quarter 4*
Actual sales volume (units)	420,000	450,000	475,000	475,000

A new assistant has recently joined the marketing department and she has asked you for help in understanding the terminology which is used in preparing sales forecasts and analysing sales trends.

She has said: 'My main problem is that I do not see why my boss is so enthusiastic about the growth in product P's sales volume. It looks to me as though the rate of growth is really slowing down and has actually stopped in Quarter 4. I am told that I should be looking at the deseasonalised or seasonally adjusted sales data but I do not understand what is meant by this.'

You have found that product P's sales are subject to the following seasonal variations.

	Quarter 1	*Quarter 2*	*Quarter 3*	*Quarter 4*
Seasonal variation (units)	+ 25,000	+ 15,000	0	– 40,000

Tasks

(a) Adjust for the seasonal variations to calculate deseasonalised or seasonally adjusted sales volumes (ie the trend figures) for each quarter of last year.

(b) Assuming that the trend and seasonal variations will continue, forecast the sales volumes for each of the four quarters of next year.

(c) Prepare a memorandum to the marketing assistant which explains

(i) what is meant by seasonal variations and deseasonalised or seasonally adjusted data; and

(ii) how they can be useful in analysing a time series and preparing forecasts.

Use the figures for product P's sales to illustrate your explanations.

7 Linear regression analysis

Linear regression analysis is a statistical **technique for finding the equation of the trend line**. The technique is based on the assumption that the trend line is a straight line and therefore has the form **y = a + bx (a *linear* equation)** where:

y is the sales level at a particular point in time
x is that point in time (where x = 1 is the first period of time in the past data provided)
a and b are constants

You will not be required to determine the values of a and b. You will be given them in the exam. All you are then likely to have to do is to substitute appropriate values of x for future time periods in the equation incorporating a and b and adjust the resulting trend forecast by the seasonal variations provided.

Example: linear regression analysis and forecasting

The trend in sales of product B can be described by the linear regression equation y = 18.23 + 0.56x, where x is the quarter of the year (with the third quarter of year 1 as x = 1) and y is the volume of sales in the quarter, in thousands of units. Seasonal variations in quarterly sales volume (in thousands of units) are as follows.

Q1	*Q2*	*Q3*	*Q4*
–0.1	+12.4	+1.3	–13.4

Tasks

(a) Forecast sales volumes of product B for each quarter of year 4.

(b) Identify the forecast quarterly percentage increases or decreases in sales volume during year 4.

Solution

(a) The forecasts for year 4 *before* seasonal adjustments (that is, the trend line forecasts only) are as follows.

Year 4 quarters	*x value*	*y value where y = 18.23 + 0.56x*
1	11*	24.39
2	12	24.95
3	13	25.51
4	14	26.07

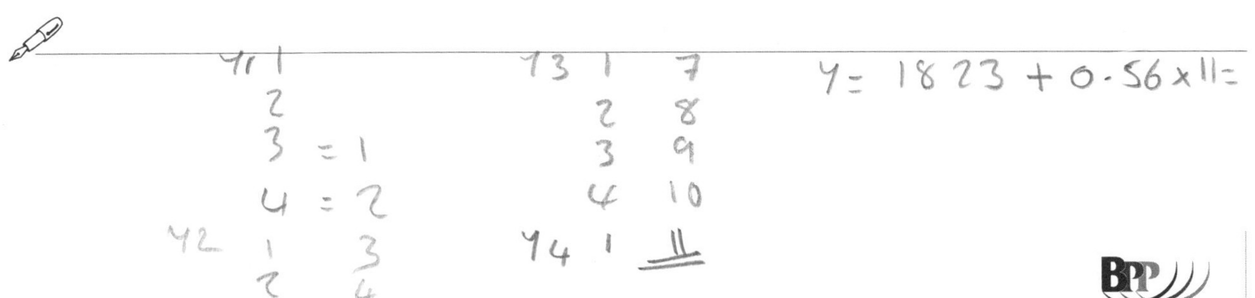

* Yr 1 Q3, x = 1; Yr 1 Q4, x = 2; Yr 2 Q1, x = 3 and so on and therefore for Yr 4 Q1, x = 11.

Seasonal variations should now be incorporated to obtain the final forecast.

Year 4 quarters	*Trend line forecasts*	*Seasonal variation*	*Final forecast*
	'000 units	'000 units	'000 units
1	24.39	–0.1	24.29
2	24.95	+12.4	37.35
3	25.51	+1.3	26.81
4	26.07	–13.4	12.67

(b)

	Q1	*Q2*	*Q5*	*Q7*
Forecast ('000 units)	24.29	37.35	26.81	12.67
Increase/(decrease)		*53.77%	**(28.22)%	***(52.74)%

* (37.35 – 24.29)/24.29 × 100%

** (26.81 – 37.35)/37.35 × 100%

*** (12.67 – 26.81)/26.81 × 100%

Activity 5.11

Suppose that a trend line, found using linear regression analysis, is y = 300 – 4.7x where x is time (in quarters) and y = sales level in thousands of units. Given that x = 0 represents Year 0 quarter 1 and that the seasonal variations are as set out below, forecast the sales level of Year 5 quarter 4.

	Q_1	Q_2	Q_3	Q_4
Seasonal variations ('000 units)	–20	–8	+4	+15

Activity 5.12

The linear regression equation y = 100 + 5x (where y denotes sales volume and x denotes the quarterly time period) has been found to describe the trend in sales of product A1, one of the products manufactured by B plc. An analysis of historical data has resulted in the following average seasonal variations for product A1.

	Quarter			
	First	*Second*	*Third*	*Fourth*
Seasonal effect	0	–20%	+40%	–20%

Tasks

(a) Using the regression equation and the seasonal variations, produce forecasts for sales volumes of product A1 for the four quarters of Year 1, where the x value of the first quarter of Year 1 is 20.

(b) Produce forecasts for actual sales revenue for the four quarters of Year 1 given that the unit price of product A1 is £1,000 during the first quarter of Year 1. This price is revised every quarter to allow for inflation, which is running at 2% per quarter.

(c) If the exchange rate between the UK pound and the Danish Kroner is forecast to be 9.77 Danish Kroner to the pound in the third quarter of Year 1, determine the forecast revenue for the third quarter in Danish Kroner.

(d) Briefly explain the assumptions upon which your forecasts in (b) are based.

(e) Explain briefly how product A1 has been performing to date.

Note that linear regression equations do not simply describe the relationship between sales and time. In general terms the linear regression equation y = a + bx represents the relationship between a **dependent variable y**, the value of which depends on the value of an **independent variable x**.

Let's consider some examples.

If the equation represents the relationship between sales value and time, the **value of sales will depend on the particular time period we are considering.** (In other words, sales value changes as time changes.)

- **Sales is therefore the dependent variable, y, in the equation.**
- **Time is the independent variable, x.**

Suppose a linear regression equation represents the relationship between the cost of producing product X and the volume of output of product X. The cost will depend on the volume of output, rather than the volume of output depending on the cost. (In other words, costs change as volume of output changes.)

- **Cost** is therefore the **dependent** variable.
- **Volume of output** is the **independent** variable.

The dependent variable in a linear regression equation representing the relationship between advertising expenditure and sales volume would be sales volume. (The level of sales depends on the level of advertising expenditure.)

Activity 5.13

What would be the dependent and independent variables in a linear regression equation describing the relationship between hours of study and examination results?

---

8 Cost forecasting

Cost forecasting involves the measurement of historical costs to predict future costs. The techniques used range from simple arithmetic and visual methods to advanced computer-based statistical systems. The sophisticated techniques are likely to be more reliable but, in practice, the **simple techniques are more commonly found** and should **give estimates that are accurate enough for their purpose.**

All three techniques that we will be looking at involve splitting costs into their fixed and variable components and using those components to forecast total cost.

8.1 Scattergraph method

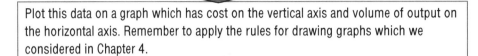

Collect data of past volumes of output and the associated cost of production.

Plot this data on a graph which has cost on the vertical axis and volume of output on the horizontal axis. Remember to apply the rules for drawing graphs which we considered in Chapter 4.

Draw a line of best fit through the middle of the plotted points so that the distance of points above the line is the same as the distance of points below the line. This line represents the total cost at different volumes of output.

The intersection of the line of best fit on the vertical axis is the fixed cost (since the fixed cost is the cost of production when the volume of output is zero).

The variable cost per unit can be calculated as (total cost – fixed cost)/number of units, using a point very close to the line of best fit.

Line of best fit

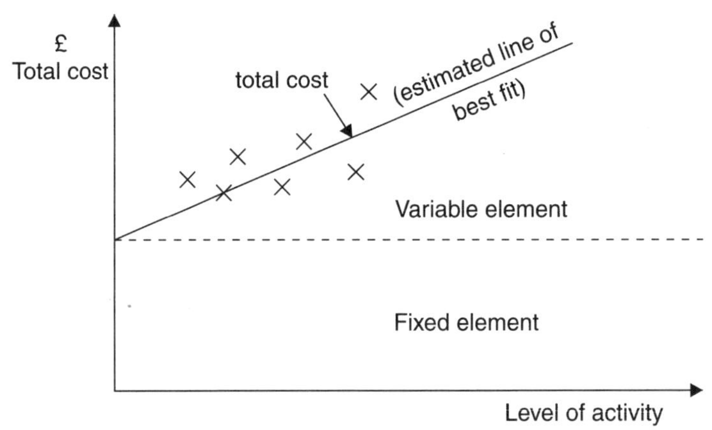

Suppose the fixed cost is £500 and that one of the plotted points (which is very close to the line or actually on it) represents output of 100 units and total cost of £550. The variable cost of 100 units is therefore calculated as £(550 – 500) = £50 and so the variable cost per unit is £0.50.

Activity 5.14

The intersection of the line of best fit on the vertical axis of a scattergraph is £3,750. A point on the line of best fit represents output of 4,500 units at a total cost of £5,100. What is the variable cost per unit?

8.1.1 Forecasting with the scattergraph method

Continuing with the example in Section 8.1 above, if the forecast volume of output is 200 units then the fixed cost is forecast to be £500 and total variable costs are forecast to be 200 × £0.50 = £100, giving a total forecast cost of £600. Alternatively, the total forecast cost can be read directly from the total cost line, provided that the expected volume of output is contained within the range covered by the scattergraph.

Activity 5.15

Prepare a scattergraph of the following cost and volume data and forecast the total cost of production if the budgeted production volume in month 5 is 6,900 units.

Month	*Production cost*	*Production volume*
	£	Units
1	110,000	7,000
2	115,000	8,000
3	111,000	7,700
4	97,000	6,000

This method **uses all of the data available**. Its principal disadvantage is that the line of best fit is only a **subjective** approximation of the total cost line.

8.2 High-low method

8.2.1 Algebraic approach

Review records of costs in previous periods and select the costs of the periods with the highest and lowest levels of activity.

(**Note**. These periods may not be the periods of highest/lowest cost.)

Determine the variable cost of the difference in activity levels (= **the difference between the total cost at the high level of activity and the total cost at the low level of activity**, since the same fixed cost is included in each total cost).

Calculate the variable cost per unit from this (difference in total costs ÷ difference in activity levels), and then determine the fixed cost (total cost at either output level – variable cost for output level chosen).

Example: the high-low method

Crispy Ltd has recorded the following total costs during the last five years.

Year	*Output volume*	*Total cost*
	Units	£
Year 4	65,000	145,000
Year 5	80,000	160,000
Year 6	90,000	170,000
Year 7	60,000	140,000
Year 8	75,000	155,000

Task

Calculate the total cost that should be expected in Year 9 if output is 85,000 units.

Solution

(a) Begin by noting high and low activity levels and costs.

	Output		*Total cost*
			£
High activity level	90,000 units		170,000
Low activity level	60,000 units		140,000
Variable cost of	30,000 units	=	30,000

∴ Variable cost per unit = £1

(b) By deducting the variable cost of 90,000 units from the total cost we can determine the fixed cost.

	£
Total cost of 90,000 units	170,000
Variable cost of 90,000 units (× £1)	90,000
Fixed costs	80,000

(c) Now we can calculate costs in Year 9 for 85,000 units.

	£
Variable costs	85,000
Fixed costs	80,000
Total costs	165,000

Activity 5.16

Using the high-low method and the following information, determine the cost of power in July if 2,750 units of power are consumed.

Month	*Cost*	*Electricity consumed*
	£	Units
January	204	2,600
February	212	2,800
March	200	2,500
April	220	3,000
May	184	2,100
June	188	2,200

8.2.2 Graphical approach

This involves plotting on a graph the points representing the highest and lowest activity levels and joining them with a straight line to represent total cost.

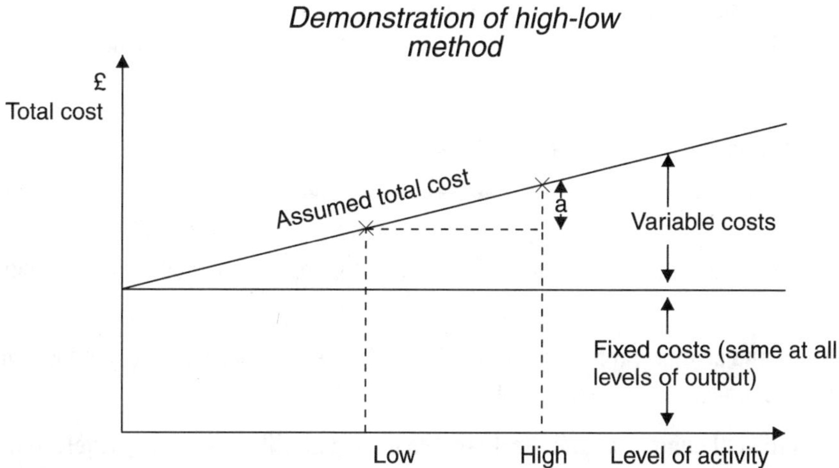

As with the scattergraph method, the fixed cost is the intercept of the total cost line with the vertical axis and the variable cost per unit can be determined using one of the two plotted points.

Forecasting using the graphical high-low method is the same as when using the scattergraph method.

- Forecasts of total cost can be read directly from the graph if the activity level is within the range covered by the graph.
- Alternatively the fixed cost and variable unit cost can be determined from the graph and then the variable cost for the forecast activity level calculated and added to the fixed cost to arrive at a forecast total cost.

Activity 5.17

What are the major drawbacks of the scattergraph and high-low methods of forecasting?

The **advantage** of the high-low method is its relative simplicity. Its **disadvantage** is that **only two historical cost records are used**. Unless these two records are a reliable indicator of costs throughout the relevant range of output (which is unlikely), you will only obtain a loose approximation of the fixed and variable cost elements of a semi-fixed cost.

8.3 Linear regression analysis

We saw how a linear regression equation can be used in sales forecasting in Section 7, but it can also be used in cost forecasting.

Activity 5.18

Using linear regression analysis, the relationship between production costs and production volume of product C has been estimated as $y = 28 + 2.6x$ where y = total cost (in thousands of pounds) and x = output (in thousands of units).

Task

Determine budgeted costs if 17,000 units of product C are produced.

Linear regression analysis is an alternative technique to the high-low and scattergraph methods, and it should be used in the following circumstances.

- **When the high-low and scattergraph methods** are thought to be **too unreliable** so that they might produce serious inaccuracies in the estimate of costs
- When there is a **sufficient number of historical records of cost at different activity levels** to make it capable of providing a more reliable estimate of costs

As with all forecasting techniques, the results from regression analysis will not be wholly reliable. Reliability of forecasts will be affected by a number of factors.

8.3.1 The reliability of linear regression analysis forecasts (1)

Linear regression analysis **assumes a linear relationship** between the two variables (since it produces an equation in the linear format) whereas a non-linear relationship might exist.

8.3.2 The reliability of linear regression analysis forecasts (2)

The technique **assumes that the value of one variable, y, can be predicted or estimated from the value of one other variable, x.** In reality the value of y might depend on several other variables, not just x.

When used for sales forecasting for example, it assumes that sales can be predicted or estimated from the period of time, which may not be true. Is demand for mobile phones simply related to time or do other variables have an impact?

8.3.3 The reliability of linear regression analysis forecasts (3)

When it is used for forecasting, it **assumes that what has happened in the past will provide a reliable guide to the future**. For example, if a line is calculated for total costs of production, based on historical data, the estimate could be used to budget for future costs. However, future costs of production might bear no relation to costs in the past if there has been:

- Inflation
- A productivity agreement
- A move to new premises
- The dismissal of large numbers of staff
- The introduction of new equipment

8.3.4 The reliability of linear regression analysis forecasts (4)

When calculating a line of best fit, a range of values for x are used. For example, a linear regression equation y = 28 + 2.6x might have been drawn up with output values ranging from x = 16 to x = 24.

- We might safely use the estimated line of best fit to predict values for y in the future, provided that the value of x remains within the range 16 to 24.
- We would be on less safe ground if we used the formula to predict a value for y when x = 10, or 30, or any other value outside the range 16 to 24, because we would have to assume that the trend line applies outside the range of x values used to establish the line in the first place.

  When linear regression analysis is **used for sales forecasting** (when the x values represent time) **we have to assume that the trend line can be extrapolated into the future, however**. (**Extrapolation** means **using a line of best fit to predict a value outside the two extreme points of the observed range of data**.) This might not necessarily be a good assumption to make.

(**Note**. **Interpolation** means **using a line of best fit to predict a value within the two extreme points of the observed range of data.**)

Vodafone, the world's largest mobile phone operator, has enjoyed 50% annual growth over the last few years and has now reached the 100 million customer landmark. Would it be wise for Vodafone to base future forecasts on such high levels of growth? Probably not. Estimates set growth at just 5% for the current quarter.

8.3.5 The reliability of linear regression analysis forecasts (5)

As with any forecasting process, the **amount of data available is very important.** Although any forecast should be regarded as being somewhat unreliable, if the sample of past data being used is small, the forecast is likely to be even less reliable.

ATTENTION!

Exam tasks for both Unit 8 and Unit 9 can require you to question the validity/strength/weakness of techniques. In the December 2000 exam, candidates were required to identify limitations of the use of linear regression as a forecasting technique, in the context of sales forecasting. The list above would provide a good basis for an answer, but you must always be careful to adapt your discussion to the specific situation given, which in this case was sales forecasting.

8.4 Cost forecasting and changes in prices

TOPIC LINK

Forecasting and indices

Data used in forecasting may need to be adjusted to take account of any movements in prices that may have occurred, usually as a result of **inflation**.

Suppose that cost and volume of output data have been collected for a five-year period during which time inflation has been running at 8% per annum. Even if the volume of output in two of the years is the same, the costs will be different because of inflation. We therefore need to remove the effects of inflation so that the **costs can be compared on a like-for-like basis**, the only factor affecting them being output volume. We do this by adjusting figures to a **common basis** using **index numbers**.

The basic approach is as follows.

Step 1. Remove the effects of price movements by **adjusting the data to a common basis**, usually to the price level of the base period (actual cost × (100/index for the year in question)). This is the reverse of making costs 'more up to date'.

Step 2. Apply the **forecasting technique** to the data produced in step 1.

Step 3. **Adjust** the forecast produced in step 2 to take account of price movements (unadjusted forecast × (index for year in question/100)).

Example: forecasting and price movements

Move Away Ltd's costs for the last three years and an index of the movement in prices over the same period are given below.

Year	*Volume of output*	*Total cost*	*Price level index*
	Units	£	
0	26,000	401,600	100
1	32,000	565,440	120
2	36,000	647,000	125

Prices therefore increased by 20% between Year 0 and Year 1 and by 25% between Year 0 and Year 2. Between Year 1 and Year 2 they increased by ((125 – 120)/120) × 100% = 4.17%. Let's take account of inflation.

Step 1. Adjust the data to a common basis, index level 100.

Year	*Actual cost*	*Cost at price level index = 100*
	£	
0	401,600 × 100/100 =	401,600
1	565,440 × 100/120 =	471,200
2	647,000 × 100/125 =	517,600

The figures in the right hand column represent the costs if there had been no inflation between Year 0 and Year 2.

Step 2. The scattergraph method can now be applied to the costs (at price level index = 100) and it would show that fixed costs are £100,000 and variable cost per unit is £11.60 (in terms of Year 0 prices). If forecast output in Year 4 is 38,500 units, total costs (unadjusted for price movements) are forecast as follows.

	£
Variable costs (Year 0 prices) (£11.60 × 38,500)	446,600
Fixed costs (Year 0 prices)	100,000
Total costs (Year 0 prices)	546,600

Step 3. If the average price level index for Year 4 is estimated to be 137, at Year 4 prices we can calculate total costs as £546,600 × 137/100= £748,842

Data used in time series analysis can be adjusted for price movements in exactly the same way.

Activity 5.19

Using the average price level index, adjust the following costs so that they can be used for forecasting.

Year	*Cost*	*Average price level index*
	£	
0	145,000	100
1	179,200	112
2	209,100	123
3	201,600	144
4	248,000	160

Activity 5.20

The scattergraph method was applied to the data in Activity 5.18 (once the data had been adjusted for price movements). Fixed costs were estimated to be £80,000 and variable cost per unit to be £1 per unit. Forecast the total cost that should be expected in Year 5 if output is 85,000 units and the average price level index is 180.

9 Forecasting problems

All forecasts are subject to error, but the likely errors vary from case to case.

- The **further into the future** the forecast is for, the **more unreliable** it is likely to be.
- The **less data** available on which to base the forecast, the **less reliable** the forecast.
- The **pattern** of trend and seasonal variations **may not continue** in the future.
- **Random variations** may upset the pattern of trend and seasonal variation.

There are a number of changes that also may make it difficult to forecast future events.

Type of change	Examples
Political and economic changes	Changes in interest rates, exchange rates or inflation can mean that future sales and costs are difficult to forecast.
Environmental changes	The building of high-speed rail links might have a considerable impact on some companies' markets.
Technological changes	These may mean that the past is not a reliable indication of likely future events. For example new faster machinery may make it difficult to use current output levels as the basis for forecasting production output.
Technological advances	Advanced manufacturing technology is changing the cost structure of many firms. Direct labour costs are reducing in significance and fixed manufacturing costs are increasing. This causes forecasting difficulties because of the resulting changes in cost behaviour patterns, breakeven points and so on.
Social changes	Alterations in taste, fashion and the social acceptability of products can cause forecasting difficulties.

ATTENTION!

These changes will not be relevant in all scenarios and so don't simply regurgitate them. Read the task data very carefully in the exam, think about what is included in this list and use your common sense. There are often hints in the task data.

IMPORTANT POINT

Note that forecasting may not involve complex techniques like regression analysis and time series analysis. Forecasts can simply be prepared on the basis of somebody's knowledge of a particular environment, industry or organisation. In the June 1998 exam, for example, candidates had to forecast the number of pupils and the income of a school given information provided by the head teacher, such as proportions of parents choosing the school. Candidates therefore simply had to apply basic mathematical techniques such as multiplication.

Key learning points

- ☑ A **time series** is a series of figures or values recorded over time. A graph of a time series is called a **historigram**.
- ☑ There are four components of a time series.
  - The **trend (T)** is the underlying long-term movement over time in the values of the data recorded.
  - **Seasonal variations (S)** are short-term fluctuations due to different circumstances which affect results at different points in time.
  - **Cyclical variations (C)** are medium-term changes in results caused by circumstances which repeat in cycles.
  - **Random variation (I)** can also occur.
- ☑ There are two models of time series, the **additive model (Y = T + S + I)** and the **proportional/ multiplicative model (Y = T × S × I)**.
- ☑ One method of **finding** the **trend** is by the use of **moving averages**. Remember that when finding the moving average of an **even number of results, a second moving average has to be calculated** so that trend values can relate to specific actual figures.
- ☑ **Seasonal variations** are the difference between actual and trend figures. They can be estimated using the **additive model (Y – T)** or **the proportional (multiplicative) model (Y/T)**.
- ☑ **Deseasonalised** or **seasonally-adjusted data** is actual data with seasonal variations removed, to leave a figure representing the trend in the actual data.
- ☑ Forecasts are made using time series analysis as follows.

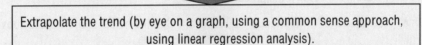

Find a trend by moving averages or seasonally-adjusting a time series.

Extrapolate the trend (by eye on a graph, using a common sense approach, using linear regression analysis).

Adjust the forecast trend values by the appropriate seasonal variations.

- ☑ **Linear regression** equations express the relationship between a dependent variable, y, and an independent variable, x, and can be used to represent the equation of the trend line. When forecasting sales, the independent variable is time.
- ☑ Linear regression can also be used for cost forecasting.
- ☑ Two simple cost forecasting techniques are the **scattergraph method** and the **high-low method**.
- ☑ All forecasts are subject to error, but the likely errors vary from case to case, and there are a number of changes that also make it difficult to forecast future events.
- ☑ Index numbers may need to be used in forecasting data to take account of any movements in prices that have occurred.

Quick quiz

1 What are the four components of a time series?

A Trend, seasonal variations, cyclical variations, relative variations
B Trend, systematic variations, cyclical variations, relative variations
C Trend, systematic variations, seasonal variations, random variations
D Trend, seasonal variations, cyclical variations, random variations

2 The multiplicative model expresses a time series as Y = T + S + R. *True or false?*

3 *Fill in the gaps with the appropriate mathematical symbols.*

Additive model of time series	Y = T......S......R
Seasonal components, S	S = Y ....T
Proportional model of time series	Y = T .....S .....R
Seasonal component, S	S = Y.............T

4 *Choose the correct words from those highlighted.*

The **additive/proportional** model is better than the **additive/proportional** model for forecasting when the trend is increasing or decreasing over time.

5 Which of the following is correct if the additive model of time series analysis is being applied?

A Forecast Y = forecast T × S
B Forecast S = Y × T
C Forecast Y = forecast T + S
D Forecast T/forecast S = forecast Y

6 *Choose the correct word from those highlighted.*

A multiplicative model seasonal component of –25% means that the actual figure is 25% **above/below** the trend.

7 Large residuals suggest that any forecast is likely to be unreliable. *True or false?*

8 What variable is used to signify 'time' in the regression equation y = a + bx when regression analysis is used for forecasting?

A x
B a
C b
D y

9 *Fill in the blank.*

The algebraic approach to the high-low method of cost forecasting involves reviewing records of costs in previous periods and selecting the costs of the periods with the highest and lowest ....

10 *Choose the correct word from those highlighted.*

Interpolation/extrapolation means using a line of best fit to predict a value outside the two extreme points of the observed range of data.

Answers to quick quiz

1 D

2 False. It is $Y = T \times S \times R$

3 Additive model $Y = T + S + R$
$S = Y - T$

Proportional model $Y = T \times S \times R$
$S = Y/T$

4 The proportional model is better than the additive model.

5 C

6 below

7 True

8 A

9 levels of activity

10 Extrapolation

ASSESSMENT KIT ACTIVITIES

The following activities in the BPP Assessment Kit for Units 8 & 9 include topics covered in this chapter.

Activities 7-11, 14, 15, 16, 17, 27, 33, 34 and 37
Lecturers' practice activities 4, 5 and 6

Activity checklist

This checklist shows which performance criteria, range statement or knowledge and understanding point is covered by each activity in this chapter. Tick off each activity as you complete it.

Activity		
5.1	☐	This activity deals with Range Statement 8.1: methods of summarising data (time series), Range Statement 9.1: projections (seasonal variations), Unit 8 Knowledge & Understanding point (3): basic statistical methods (time series analysis), and Unit 9 Knowledge & Understanding point (3): basic statistical methods (time series).
5.2	☐	This activity deals with Range Statement 8.1: methods of summarising data (time series), Range Statement 9.1: projections (trends; seasonal variations), Unit 8 Knowledge & Understanding point (3): basic statistical methods (time series analysis), and Unit 9 Knowledge & Understanding point (3): basic statistical methods (time series).
5.3	☐	This activity deals with Range Statement 8.1: methods of summarising data (time series), Range Statement 9.1: projections (trends), Unit 8 Knowledge & Understanding point (3): basic statistical methods (time series analysis), and Unit 9 Knowledge & Understanding point (3): basic statistical methods (time series).
5.4	☐	This activity deals with Performance Criteria 8.1B regarding the monitoring and analysis of trends.
5.5	☐	This activity deals with Range Statement 8.1: methods of summarising data (time series), Range Statement 9.1: projections (seasonal variations), Unit 8 Knowledge & Understanding point (3): basic statistical methods (time series analysis), and Unit 9 Knowledge & Understanding point (3): basic statistical methods (time series).
5.6	☐	This activity deals with Range Statement 8.1: methods of summarising data (time series), Range Statement 9.1: projections (trends; seasonal variations), Unit 8 Knowledge & Understanding point (3): basic statistical methods (time series analysis), and Unit 9 Knowledge & Understanding point (3): basic statistical methods (time series).
5.7	☐	This activity deals with Range Statement 9.1: forecasts and projections.
5.8	☐	This activity deals with Range Statement 9.1: forecasts and projections.
5.9	☐	This activity deals with Performance criteria 9.1C regarding the preparation of forecasts.

Activity checklist (cont'd)

5.10	☐	This activity deals with Performance Criteria 8.1F regarding the consultation with relevant staff about the analysis of trends, and Performance Criteria 9.1B regarding communication with relevant individuals.
5.11	☐	This activity deals with Range Statement 8.1: methods of summarising data (time series), Range Statement 9.1: forecasts and projections, Unit 8 Knowledge & Understanding point (3): basic statistical methods, and Unit 9 Knowledge & Understanding point (3): basic statistical methods.
5.12	☐	This activity deals with Performance Criteria 8.1B regarding the monitoring and analysis of trends, Performance Criteria 8.1C regarding the comparison of trends with previous experience and the identification of potential implications, Performance Criteria 9.1C regarding the preparation of forecasts, and Performance Criteria 9.1D regarding the review and revision of forecasts.
5.13	☐	This activity deals with Unit 8 Knowledge & Understanding point (3): basic statistical methods, and Unit 9 Knowledge & Understanding point (3): basic statistical methods.
5.14	☐	This activity deals with Range Statement 9.1: forecasts (expenditure).
5.15	☐	This activity deals with Range Statement 9.1: forecasts (expenditure).
5.16	☐	This activity deals with Range Statement 9.1: forecasts (expenditure).
5.17	☐	This activity deals with Performance Criteria 9.1C regarding the preparation of forecasts with explanations of assumptions.
5.18	☐	This activity deals with Range Statement 9.1: forecasts (expenditure), Unit 8 Knowledge & Understanding point (3): basic statistical methods and Unit 9 Knowledge & Understanding point (3): basic statistical methods.
5.19	☐	This activity covers Performance Criteria 9.1C regarding the preparation of forecasts with explanations of adjustments and Performance Criteria 9.1D regarding the review and revision of the validity of forecasts in the light of anticipated changes.
5.20	☐	This activity deals with Range Statement 9.1: forecasts (expenditure).

PROFESSIONAL EDUCATION

PART B

Core theme 1: standard costing

chapter 6

Calculating variances

Contents

1 Introduction
2 Standard costs and standard costing
3 Variances
4 Deriving standard and actual information
5 Material variances
6 Labour variances
7 Fixed overhead variances
8 Graphical calculation of material and labour variances
9 Reconciliation statements

Performance criteria

8.1D Compare standard costs with actual costs and analyse any variances

Range statement

8.1 Variance analysis: material price and usage variances; labour rate and efficiency variances; fixed overhead expenditure, volume, capacity and efficiency variances

Knowledge and understanding

Unit 8 Accounting techniques

7 Standard costing

Unit 8 Accounting principles and theory

8 Marginal and absorption costing

Signpost

The topics covered in this chapter are relevant to **Unit 8** but you do need to be aware of variances for your study of flexible budgeting in **Unit 9** (Chapter 10) and so we recommend that you work through this chapter whichever unit you are studying.

1 Introduction

If you sat Unit 6 under the previous version of the standards, **much** of what we will be looking at in this chapter **will not be new** to you as you will have covered standard costing and variance analysis at an introductory level in your earlier studies.

If you don't remember much of your Unit 6 studies (old version of the standards), however, or if you sat Unit 6 under the new version of the standards, don't worry: we will be **looking at standard costing and variance analysis from scratch** before moving on to some of the slightly **more complicated aspects** of the topic that you might encounter in exam tasks.

In the next chapter we will see how to interpret, analyse and use the variances you have calculated. It is vital that you understand completely both this chapter and the one which follows as the **calculation and interpretation of variances** has **appeared** in **every Unit 8 exam.**

You might find the **fixed overhead variances** covered in Section 7 rather tricky. Don't worry if you do – most students find them **more difficult to grasp initially** than material and labour variances.

2 Standard costs and standard costing

2.1 What is a standard?

A **standard** represents **what we think should happen**. It is our best **'guestimate'** of how long something will take to produce, what quantity of materials it will require, how much it will cost and so on.

The **materials standard for a product** is our **best estimate of how much material is needed to make the product (standard materials usage) multiplied** by our **best estimate of the price** we will have to **pay** for the material **(standard materials price)**. For example, we might think that two square metres of material should be needed to make a curtain and that the material should cost £10 per square metre. The standard material cost of the curtain is therefore 2 × £10 = £20.

Likewise the **labour standard** for a product is an **estimate of how many hours are needed to make the product multiplied by the amount the employee is paid per hour**.

2.2 Standard costs

The **standard cost of a product** or service is made up of a **number of different standards**, **one for each cost element** (direct materials, direct labour, overheads / indirect costs), each of which has to be set by management. Each standard has **two parts** (as we saw in Section 2.1).

- A **monetary or rate** element (price per kg, rate per hour and so on)
- A **resource** element (kgs per unit, hours per unit and so on)

TOPIC LINK

Standards and control systems

Remember the importance of standards in control systems.

2.2.1 Standard cost cards

The standards for each part of the overall standard cost are recorded on a standard cost card, an example of which is given below.

STANDARD COST CARD
Product: the Splodget, No 12345

	Cost	*Requirement*	£	£
Direct materials				
A	£2.00 per kg	6 kgs	12.00	
B	£3.00 per kg	2 kgs	6.00	
C	£4.00 per litre	1 litre	4.00	
Others			2.00	
				24.00
Direct labour				
Grade I	£4.00 per hour	3 hrs	12.00	
Grade II	£5.40 per hour	5 hrs	27.00	
				39.00
Variable production overheads	£1.00 per hour	8 hrs		8.00
Fixed production overheads	£3.00 per hour	8 hrs		24.00
Standard full cost of production				95.00

Standard costs may be used in **both marginal and absorption costing systems**. The card above has been prepared under an absorption costing system, the standard absorption rates being the same as the predetermined overhead absorption rates calculated for an absorption costing system.

Activity 6.1

Kent Ltd makes one product, the JK66. Two types of labour are involved in the preparation of a JK66, skilled and semi-skilled. Skilled labour is paid £10 per hour and semi-skilled £5 per hour. Twice as many skilled labour hours as semi-skilled labour hours are needed to produce a JK66, four semi-skilled labour hours being needed.

A JK66 is made up of three different direct materials. Seven kilograms of direct material D1, four litres of direct material D2 and three metres of direct material D3 are needed. Direct material D1 costs £1 per kilogram, direct material D2 £2 per litre and direct material D3 £3 per metre.

Variable production overheads are incurred at Kent Ltd at the rate of £2.50 per direct labour (skilled) hour.

A system of absorption costing is in operation at Kent Ltd. The basis of absorption is direct labour (skilled) hours. For the forthcoming accounting period, budgeted fixed production overheads are £250,000 and budgeted production of the JK66 is 5,000 units.

Task

Use the above information to draw up a standard cost card for the JK66.

2.3 How standards are set

2.3.1 Standard usage of materials

To ascertain how much material should be used to make a product, technical specifications have to be prepared. This will be done by experts in the **production department**. On the basis of these **technical and engineering specifications** and in the light of **experience**, a bill of materials will be drawn up which lists the quantity of materials required to make a unit of the product. These quantities can include **allowances for wastage** of materials if that is normal and unavoidable.

2.3.2 Standard prices of materials

The proper approach to setting a standard price for a particular material is to **study the market** for that material and become aware of any likely **future trends**. If your company makes apple pies, news of a disastrous apple crop failure clearly has implications for forecasting raw materials prices.

In practice it is not always possible or practicable to acquire full information. In such circumstances it is likely that standard prices would be set on the basis of **current prices** and any **notification from suppliers of changes** (for example a new catalogue or price list).

Sometimes businesses are able to enter into a **contract** stating that an agreed price will be charged for an agreed period. Obviously this **reduces** the **uncertainty** in the standard setting process.

Standards should also take into account any **discount** that may be available for **bulk purchase**. Management will need to consider whether it is economical to buy in sufficiently large quantities to earn the discounts, after considering the costs of holding the stock.

2.3.3 Establishing standard labour costs

In principle it is easy to set standards for labour. You simply need to find out how long it should take to produce a unit and multiply this time by the rate that the person who produces the unit is paid.

In practice, of course, it is **not** this **straightforward**. For example, an **experienced worker** may be able to **do the job in less time than a novice**, and two equally experienced workers may take a different length of time to do the same job. Some time must be spent recording actual performance before a realistic standard can be established.

Example: labour standards

Fix-a-car Ltd employs two female mechanics, Georgina, who is an apprentice, and Clarissa, who has given loyal service for ten years. The accountant is looking through last week's figures and decides to note down the time each mechanic took to perform each of ten MOT tests.

Georgina (minutes)	63	55	50	57	49	52	58	57	70	69
Clarissa (minutes)	30	28	35	25	32	33	29	31	30	27

Georgina is presently paid £4.50 per hour and Clarissa £8 per hour.

Task

Calculate the standard time for performing an MOT test and the standard labour cost for performing an MOT test.

Solution

The total time taken for 20 MOT tests is 880 minutes, an average of 44 minutes per test. Georgina takes a total of 580 minutes and Clarissa 300 minutes. Multiplied by their respective hourly rates the total cost is £83.50 or an average of £4.18 per MOT.

We have therefore calculated a standard time per MOT of 44 minutes and a standard labour cost per MOT test of £4.18.

These figures have considerable **shortcomings** however.

- They take **no account of the time of day** when the work was performed, or the **type** or **age** of **vehicle** concerned.
- We cannot tell to what extent the difference in performance of the two mechanics is due to their **relative experience** and to what extent it is **due to other factors**: possibly Georgina does the more difficult jobs to gain experience, while Clarissa works on cars that she regularly maintains for established customers who ask for her.

On the other hand it is **quite likely** that a **better controlled set** of measurements would **give very similar results** to those obtained using historical figures. In a case like this there is probably very little point in trying to be more scientific and 'accurate'. Even if the garage performed 20 MOTs a day, the first set of figures would have to be quite significantly wrong for a more accurate estimation to make any significant difference to the accuracy of the costing.

If, however, we were dealing with a **high volume business** where, say, 10,000 units were produced an hour, then **small differences** in times and costs per unit (or batch or whatever) would have a **considerable impact** on the accuracy of the costing. In such cases, the taking of more precise measurements in controlled conditions and the use of **sophisticated statistical techniques** would be **worthwhile**.

2.3.4 Behavioural implications of standards

How would these figures affect Georgina and Clarissa if they were used as standards? So far as Georgina is concerned a standard time of 44 minutes is a good target to aim at as she is expected to improve her performance, but she is not expected to be as fast as the more experienced mechanic Clarissa. For Clarissa the standard could be demotivating as she may not work so hard if she knows she has half as long again as she needs to do an MOT.

A 'time saved bonus' for MOT tests taking less than 44 minutes is a good idea in this case: Clarissa will not slack off if she is financially rewarded for her hard work, and Georgina has a further incentive to speed up her own work.

2.3.5 Responsibility for setting standards

The responsibility for setting standards should be shared between the managers who are able to provide the necessary information about expected prices, efficiencies of working and so on.

2.3.6 Updating standard costs

Standard costs are usually revised once a year (to allow for inflation in material prices and wage rates, changes in expected efficiency of material usage and so on). They may be revised more frequently if conditions are changing rapidly, however.

2.4 Performance standards

The **quantity of material and labour time required** will **depend on the level of performance** required by management. Four types of performance standard might be set.

Performance standard	Detail
Ideal	Based on **perfect operating conditions**: no wastage, no spoilage, no inefficiencies, no idle time, no breakdowns. Employees will often feel that the goals are unattainable, become demotivated and not work so hard.
Attainable	Based on the hope that a standard amount of work will be carried out efficiently, machines properly operated or materials properly used. **Some allowance is made for wastage and inefficiencies**. If well-set they provide a useful psychological incentive by giving employees a realistic, but challenging target of efficiency.
Current	Based on **current working conditions** (current wastage, current inefficiencies). They do not attempt to improve on current levels of efficiency.
Basic	**Kept unaltered over a long period of time**, and may be out of date. They are used to show change in efficiency or performance over a long period of time. They are perhaps the least useful and least common type of standard in use.

Ideal standards, attainable standards and current standards each have their supporters and it is by no means clear which of them is preferable.

- Ideal standards may provide an incentive to greater efficiency even though the standard cannot be achieved.
- If ideal standards are used for budgeting, an allowance will have to be included for 'inefficiencies'.
- Current standards or attainable standards are a better basis for budgeting, because they represent the level of productivity which management will wish to plan for.

When setting standards, managers must be aware of the need to establish a useful control measure **and** the need to set a standard which will have the desired motivational effect on employees. These two requirements often conflict, so that the final standard cost might be a compromise between the two.

2.5 What is standard costing?

Standard costing is the **preparation of standard costs for use** in the following situations.

- In costing as a means of **valuing stocks and the cost of production**. It is an alternative method of valuation to methods like FIFO, LIFO or replacement costing.
- In **variance analysis**, which is a means of monitoring and **controlling the performance of the business**.

The main use of standard costs is in **variance analysis.** This involves **comparing standard costs with actual costs** to **derive** a **difference**, or **variance.**

The **identification, analysis** and **reporting** of **variances** enables managers to **monitor whether standard performance is being achieved**. The following types of question can be answered by a detailed analysis of variances.

- Are material prices higher or lower than in the standard cost?
- Is material wastage being kept at standard levels?
- Has it been necessary to pay higher wage rates than expected?

We are going to be looking at variance analysis in the remainder of this chapter and the next.

Activity 6.2

What sort of problems can you envisage arising when setting standards?

3 Variances

The **actual results** achieved by an organisation will more than likely be **different from the expected results** (which are based on standard costs). Such differences may occur between individual items, such as the cost of labour, and between the total expected costs and the total actual costs. These **differences are variances**.

TOPIC LINK

Variances and control systems

We mentioned **variances** in our discussion of control systems in Chapter 1. They represent the **difference between the actual data as recorded by the sensor and the standard or plan**. They therefore enable management to analyse the difference between what the actual output should have cost and what it did cost.

The individual variances (for materials, labour and fixed overheads) that we will be looking at will be brought together at the end of the chapter into a statement that reconciles the actual cost of production to what actual production should have cost (the standard cost of production).

When actual results are better than expected results, we have a **favourable variance (F).** If actual results are worse than expected results, we have an **adverse variance (A).**

3.1 Timing of feedback

Do you think management should know that a certain material, for example, cost more than expected as soon as possible (when it is purchased) or when it is used in production, or even when the goods into which it has been made are sold to customers?

You know from your own experience that the sooner a problem is recognised, the sooner it can be rectified. So it is only sensible that management are aware **as soon as possible**, when the material is purchased, that the actual cost is greater than the expected cost. If the problem is not diagnosed until later, additional material may be purchased at the high price before remedial action is taken.

IMPORTANT POINT

Differences between actual cost and expected cost should be highlighted as soon as possible.

3.2 Variances and exam tasks

Recent exam tasks on standard costing and variance analysis have tended to have three distinct parts.

3.2.1 Part 1

You have to work out various pieces of information needed in subsequent variance calculations from budget data, actual data and notes provided. For example you might need to calculate actual hourly rates of pay, standard fixed overhead per unit and so on.

3.2.2 Part 2

Using the information you have worked out and/or task data provided, you have to perform a number of straightforward variance calculations. You then have to use these variances in a statement reconciling the standard cost of actual production (what the actual production should have cost) with the actual cost of production.

3.2.3 Part 3

The assessor provides you with some additional data and you have to carry out more detailed analysis, often providing your results in a report or memo.

3.2.4 Summary

Of course, there is no guarantee that the assessor will continue to adopt this style and no task will be the same as any which have appeared before. But we can use this outline as the framework for our study of standard costing and variance analysis.

So, in the next section we will see how to deal with Part 1. We will then look in detail at the calculation of material, labour and fixed overhead variances and have a go at reconciliation statements (Part 2). And in the next chapter we will consider how to analyse variances (Part 3).

ATTENTION!

Variance calculations were required in all of the Unit 8 exams under the old version of the standards and it will remain a **very** important topic.

4 Deriving standard and actual information

4.1 Information provided in tasks

Typically you will be provided with either budget or standard cost information, as well as actual data.

4.1.1 Presentation approach 1

You could be given the standard cost of producing/supplying one unit of the product/service in question. Here's an example for Variances Ltd's product W. Assume that Variances Ltd uses marginal costing and so fixed overheads are not included in the standard cost of the W.

Product W: standard cost card

	Standard input	*Standard price per kg/hr*	*Standard cost*
		£	£
Material	9 kgs	18.00	162
Labour	10 hours	12.00	120
Standard cost per W			282
Budgeted production level			510 units

4.1.2 Presentation approach 2

Alternatively information might be presented in budgetary terms. (We look at budgets in detail in Part C. For now, all you need to know is that budgets are plans set to achieve targets.) Here is an example based on the product W information above.

Product W: budgeted production for 20X2		
Budgeted production level		510 units
		£
Material	4,590 kgs	82,620
Labour	5,100 hrs	61,200
		143,820

4.1.3 Points to note

- **Approach 1** shows **unit data**, **approach 2** shows **totals data**.
- **Both approaches** are actually **showing the same data**.
  - Multiply the £162 standard cost of material per W in approach 1 by the budgeted production of 510 units, to give the £82,620 in approach 2.
  - Divide the total budgeted labour cost of £61,200 in approach 2 by the 5,100 hours also in approach 2 to give the standard rate of £12 per hour shown in approach 1. And divide the 5,100 hours of labour shown in approach 2 by the budgeted production of 510 units to give the standard input per W of 10 hours (as shown in approach 1).

4.1.4 Presentation of actual data

Actual data is normally shown in a format similar to approach 2 above, in terms of totals.

Product W: actual production for 20X2		
Actual production level		500 units
		£
Material	5,000 kgs	100,000
Labour	4,500 hrs	45,000
		145,000

4.2 What's next?

Having been given this information, you'll typically be asked to carry out some calculations to derive detailed standard and actual information. The calculations required are extremely straightforward. You simply need to show that you **understand accounting data** and that you can see the **links** between pieces of data. Look back at the 'patterns in numbers' section in Chapter 4 if necessary.

4.2.1 Simple calculations

Using the standard, budget and actual information above, let's take a look at a few simple examples of the types of calculation you could be asked to carry out.

TOPIC LINK

Rearranging equations and efficient calculations

You will need to apply the concepts and ideas covered in this section of Chapter 4.

(a) Actual cost per kg of material

= total actual cost ÷ actual kgs used
= £100,000 ÷ 5,000 kgs = £20 per kg

(b) Actual rate per labour hour

= total actual cost ÷ actual labour hours
= £45,000 ÷ 4,500 hrs = £10 per hour

(c) If you were given unit data using presentation approach 1, you might be asked to calculate the budgeted cost of material.

= standard cost per W × budgeted production
= £162 × 510 = £82,620

(d) Or if you were given total data using presentation approach 2, you might be asked to calculate the standard rate per labour hour.

= total budgeted cost ÷ total budgeted hours
= £61,200 ÷ 5,100 = £12 per hour

IMPORTANT POINT

Standard 'something' for actual output

When you need to find the standard 'something' (usage of material, labour hours worked) for actual output (which simply means the amount of material or labour that should have been used for actual output), you simply multiply together the standard usage (or hours) and the actual level of output.

(e) Standard usage of material for actual output (the amount of material that should have been used for actual output)

= standard input of material per W × actual output
= 9 kgs × 500 = 4,500 kgs

(f) Standard hours for actual output (the number of labour hours that should have been worked for actual output)

= standard input of labour per W × actual output
= 10 hrs × 500 = 5,000 hrs

4.2.2 Calculation of unit and total costs

IMPORTANT POINT

The assessor has confirmed that you need to be able to calculate unit and total costs on marginal costing and absorption costing bases. We covered these costing methods in Chapter 2.

REMEMBER...

Absorption costing and marginal costing

Both standard and actual absorbed costs include fixed overheads. Fixed overheads are absorbed into both using the predetermined overhead absorption rate unless task data indicates otherwise.

Standard and actual marginal costs do not include fixed overheads.

The standard cost card for product W in Section 4.1.1 shows the standard marginal cost of the product. Now let's assume that Variances Ltd uses standard absorption costing.

	Standard input	*Standard price per kg/hr*	*Standard cost*
		£	£
Material	9 kgs	18.00	162
Labour	10 hours	12.00	120
Fixed overheads	10 hours	8.00	80
Standard cost per W			362
Budgeted production level			510 units

Attempt the following activities to make sure that you can calculate unit and total costs correctly.

Activity 6.3

Each unit of product Omega requires 4 metres of material at £5 per metre and 3 hours of labour at £15 per hour.

(a) What is the standard marginal cost of product Omega?

(b) What is the standard absorption cost of product Omega if overheads are absorbed at the rate of £10 per labour hour?

Activity 6.4

The following data relates to production of Ableman Ltd's product during 20X3.

Budget	
Output	5,000 units
Material	20,000 metres at £10 per metre
Labour	15,000 hours at £8 per hour
Fixed overheads	£240,000
Actual	
Output	5,150 units
Material	21,630 metres costing £214,137
Labour	16,480 hours costing £148,320
Fixed overheads	£280,000

Fixed overheads are absorbed on a per unit basis.

Tasks

(a) Calculate the budgeted unit cost and budgeted total cost of production in 20X3 using the following.

  (i) Marginal costing
  (ii) Absorption costing

(b) Perform the same calculations in (a) above but for actual output.

The following example is **based** on a task in the June 1999 exam. It demonstrates more of the sort of calculations you could face.

Example: deriving standard and actual data

Consider the following information about LEFM Ltd's production of product K during control period 2.

LEFM Ltd – Production report for control period 2

		Budgeted output		*Actual output*
Number of product K produced		875		850
Inputs	*Units of input*	*Standard cost per unit of input* £	*Actual cost per unit of input* £	*Actual cost of actual output* £
Material	2.5 litres	200.00	201.00	512,550
Labour	5 hours	30.00	29.50	120,360
Fixed overheads	5 hours	120.00		622,200
				1,255,110

Tasks

Calculate the following.

(a) Actual litres of material used in producing the actual output
(b) Actual hours worked in control period 2
(c) Standard litres of material that should have been used to produce the actual output
(d) Standard hours that should have been worked to produce the actual output
(e) Standard hours of fixed overheads charged to the budgeted output
(f) Standard hours of fixed overheads charged to the actual output

Solution

(a) Actual litres used

= actual material cost of actual output ÷ actual cost per litre
= £512,550 ÷ £201 = 2,550 litres

(b) Actual hours worked

= actual labour cost of actual output ÷ actual cost per hour
= £120,360 ÷ £29.50 = 4,080 hours

(c) Standard usage of material for actual output

= standard input of material × actual output
= 2.5 litres × 850 units = 2,125 litres

(d) Standard hours for actual output

= standard input of labour × actual output
= 5 hrs × 850 units = 4,250 hours

(e) Standard hours of fixed overheads charged to budgeted output

= 5 hrs × 875 units
= 4,375 hours

(f) Standard hours of fixed overheads charged to actual output

= 5 hrs × 850 units
= 4,250 hours

What you are asked to calculate will, of course, depend on the data provided and the variance calculations required later in the task.

4.2.3 Standard and actual cost of actual production

In the next activities, which are also about deriving standard and actual data, you have to do two calculations which you will need when you prepare a reconciliation statement.

We will look at the calculations here and see how to incorporate these into the statement later in the chapter.

IMPORTANT POINT

Standard cost of actual production represents what actual production should have cost in total.

∴ Standard cost of actual production = standard cost per unit × actual production level

Actual cost of actual production = actual cost per unit × actual production
or = total of actual costs

The **standard marginal cost of actual production** for Variances Ltd's product W in 20X2 = £282 × 500 = £141,000, while the **standard absorption cost of actual production** is £362 × 500 = £181,000.

The **actual marginal cost of actual production** of product W during 20X2 = £145,000 (as shown in Section 4.1.4).

If actual fixed overheads were £45,800 (say), the **actual absorption cost of actual production** would have been £145,000 + £45,800 = £190,800.

Activity 6.5

Suppose the standard variable cost per unit of product J is £10. Budgeted production is 4,000 units, actual production is 4,200 units. Budgeted fixed overheads per unit are £2. What is the standard cost of actual production?

Don't forget that if absorption costing is being used, fixed overhead must be included. Task data is likely to set out the absorption basis, as in the activity below.

Activity 6.6

Michael Ltd makes three products, the Harlequin, the Joker and the Jester. All of the products are made using the same material and the same labour.

Standard and budget information

- Standard material cost per kg is £20.
- Standard material requirements per unit

	Kgs
Harlequin	5
Joker	4
Jester	3

- Standard labour cost per hour is £10.
- Standard labour requirements per unit

	Hrs
Harlequin	2
Joker	3
Jester	4

- Budgeted production levels

	Units
Harlequin	500
Joker	1,000
Jester	1,500

- Budgeted fixed factory overheads are £600,000.

Actual information

- 1,260 kgs of material were purchased for £22,050 for production of the Harlequin.
- £5,390 was paid for 550 hours of work on production of the Harlequin.
- Actual production levels

	Units
Harlequin	200
Joker	1,150
Jester	1,700

- Actual fixed factory overheads are £780,000.
- Budgeted and actual fixed factory overheads are absorbed on the basis of budgeted labour hours.

Task

Calculate the following.

(a) Total budgeted labour hours
(b) Standard fixed factory overhead absorption rate
(c) Budgeted fixed factory overhead apportioned to product Harlequin
(d) Actual fixed factory overhead apportioned to product Harlequin
(e) Actual labour rate per hour for production of Harlequin
(f) Actual cost of material per kg for production of Harlequin
(g) Standard absorption cost of actual production of Harlequin
(h) Actual absorption cost of actual production of Harlequin

We are now going to move on to Part 2 as described in Section 3 and look at straightforward variance calculations.

5 Material variances

We know from the information in Section 4.1.4 that the material used to produce the 500 units in 20X2 cost £100,000. But what should it have cost?

Each unit of W should cost £162 in material (see Section 4.1.1), so 500 units should have cost £162 $\times$ 500 = £81,000.

Why might the **actual cost** have been **greater** than the **planned** cost?

- The cost per kg of material could have been greater than planned.
- More material than planned could have been used to make the 500 units of W.
- Both the cost per kg and the material usage could have been greater than planned.

Let's show the data we have about actual and standard material usage and prices **diagrammatically**.

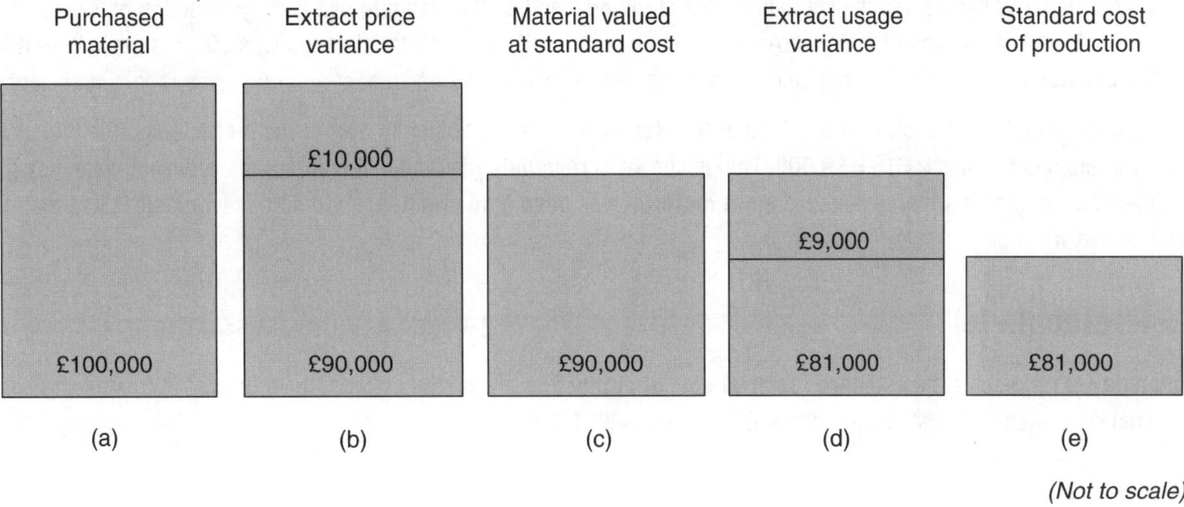

5.1 Rectangle (a)

Rectangle (a) represents the **actual purchase** of 5,000 kgs for £100,000.

We have established that any **difference** between planned cost and actual cost needs to be **highlighted as soon as possible** (when the material is purchased). At the point of purchase we don't yet know whether more material has been used than planned, however, because production has not yet taken place. So any **difference** between the planned and actual cost must therefore be due to the **actual price** per kg being **different** to the **planned or standard price** per kg.

5.2 Rectangle (b)

The 5,000 kgs purchased should have cost 5,000 kgs × £18 = £90,000 and so the difference of £(100,000 – 90,000) = £10,000 must be due to **paying more for the materials** purchased than planned. This price variance of £10,000 is shown in **rectangle (b)** (and is the difference between rectangles (a) and (c)).

Price variances are **adverse** if the material **cost more than planned.** They are **favourable** if it **cost less than planned.**

5.3 Rectangle (c)

Rectangle (c) shows the material **valued** at its 'correct' **(standard)** cost of £90,000, the value at which it is **issued to production** (the price variance having been extracted already, at the point of purchase).

IMPORTANT POINT

When calculating variances, material used in production is valued at standard cost.

5.4 Rectangle (d)

Production of one W should use the standard 9 kgs of material and so the standard usage for production of 500 units of W is 500 × 9 kgs = 4,500 kgs of material. As 5,000 kgs were actually used, material **usage** was 500 kgs **more than it should have been.** It is **inefficient** to use more material than necessary and so a cost must be given to this inefficiency.

The material **issued to production** was valued at the **standard price** of £18 per kg and so the **inefficiency** (the material usage variance) is 500 kgs × £18 = £9,000. This is shown in **rectangle (d)** (and is the difference between rectangles (c) and (e)). The variance is **adverse** because **more material was used than planned**. It would be favourable if less material than planned was used.

5.5 Rectangle (e)

Rectangle (e) represents the **standard material cost of production** – what the material for output of 500 units should have cost. This standard cost is 500 units × £18 × 9 kgs = £81,000.

5.6 Summary

Looking at the diagram it should be clear that the **difference between the planned or standard material cost of production as represented by rectangle (e) (ie what the output should have cost) and the actual cost (what it did cost, the material purchased, as represented by rectangle (a))** is made up of the **price variance** and the **usage variance.**

	£'000	£'000
Standard material cost of production		81
Price variance	10 (A)	
Usage variance	9 (A)	
Total variance		19 (A)
Actual material cost of production		100

If the variances had been favourable, they would be deducted from standard cost of production to reconcile to actual cost of production.

Example: material variances

Overcast Ltd's product X has a standard material cost of 10 kilograms of material Y at £10 per kilogram (= £100 per unit of X). During period 4, 1,000 units of X were manufactured, using 11,700 kilograms of material Y which cost £98,600.

Task

Draw a diagram similar to that at the beginning of Section 5 to illustrate this information and then calculate the following variances.

(a) The material price variance
(b) The material usage variance

Solution

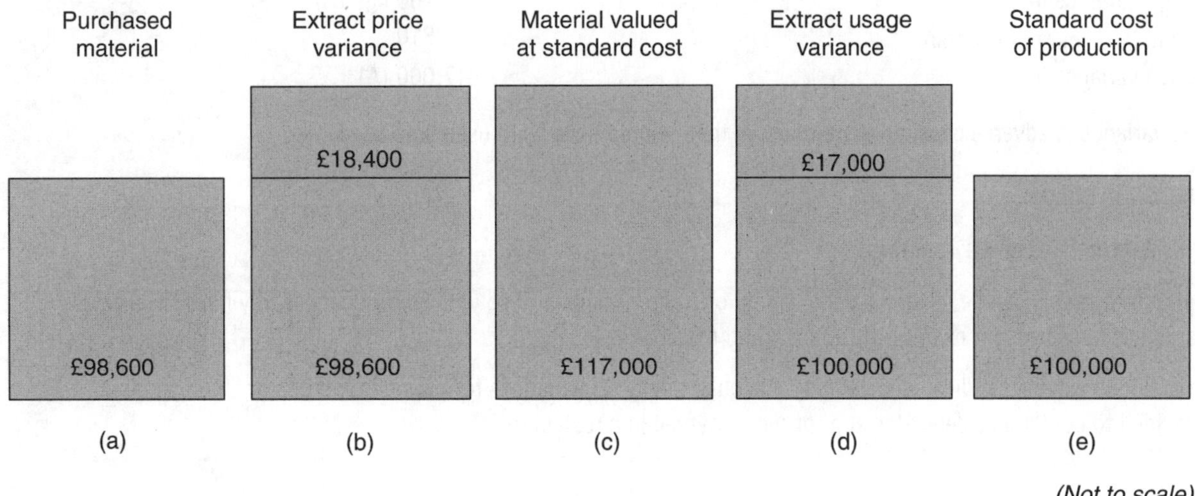

Rectangles (b) and (c)

Material purchased **should have cost** 11,700 kgs × £10 = £117,000, which is **more than the actual cost**. This gives a price variance of £(117,000 – 98,600) = £18,400. Note that the standard cost (what the material should have cost) is greater than the actual cost. The **favourable variance** is therefore **'added on'** to the rectangle representing actual cost of purchases to give a rectangle representing the standard cost of purchases.

Rectangles (d) and (e)

Material used should have cost 1,000 units × 10 kgs × £10 = £100,000. The **standard cost of standard usage** (£100,000) is therefore **less than the standard cost of actual usage** (£117,000) and so the variance of £(117,000 – 100,000) = £17,000 is **adverse**.

The material price variance in more detail

IMPORTANT POINT

The material price variance is identified and extracted before the material is issued to production and so the price variance is based on the actual 11,700 kgs purchased and used.

This is the difference between what 11,700 kgs should have cost (rectangle (c)) and what 11,700 kgs did cost (rectangle (a)).

	£
11,700 kgs of Y should have cost (× £10)	117,000
but did cost	98,600
Material Y price variance	18,400 (F)

The variance is favourable because the material cost less than it should have.

The material usage variance in more detail

This is the difference between how many kilograms of Y should have been used to produce 1,000 units of X (rectangle (e)) and how many kilograms were used (rectangle (c)), valued at the standard cost per kilogram.

1,000 units should have used (× 10 kgs)	10,000 kgs
but did use	11,700 kgs
Usage variance in kgs	1,700 kgs (A)
× standard cost per kilogram	× £10
Usage variance in £	£17,000 (A)

The variance is adverse because more material than should have been used was used.

WATCH OUR FOR...

Non-manufacturing environments

Variance analysis can be used in a wide variety of environments and so you will not necessarily have to calculate variances based on, for example, product X and material Y.

In previous exams, candidates have had to calculate material variances for presentation pen and notepaper sets provided to conference delegates and for meals served in a restaurant.

Activity 6.7

During April 100 units of a product were manufactured. 520 kgs of material were used in the production of the 100 units of the product at a cost of £1,025. The standard cost of the material is £2 per kg and the standard material cost of the product is £10.

Required

Draw a diagram to illustrate the above data and then calculate the following.

(a) The material price variance
(b) The material usage variance

WATCH OUT FOR ...

Calculations involving percentages

In the past the assessor has asked candidates to carry out simple calculations involving percentage increases and decreases.

You might need to work out the standard cost of a kg of material before a 5% increase brings it up to £10.

Answer: £10/1.05 = £9.52

Or you may need to work out a percentage decrease if a standard is changed from 15 litres per unit to 12 litres per unit.

Answer: ((15 – 12)/15) × 100% = 20%

Activity 6.8

(a) A standard cost is £5.80 per unit after an increase of £1.70. What is the percentage increase?
(b) A standard cost of £12.92 is to be increased by 15%. What is the revised standard cost?

6 Labour variances

The calculation of labour variances is very **similar** to the **calculation of material variances**. The calculation of the labour rate variance is similar to that for the material price variance while the calculation of the labour efficiency variance is similar to that for the material usage variance.

Example: a diagram for labour variances

Let's continue with our example about Variances Ltd and product W. (Look back at Sections 4.1.1 and 4.1.4.)

Task

Draw a diagram similar to that at the beginning of Section 5 to highlight labour rate and labour efficiency variances.

Solution

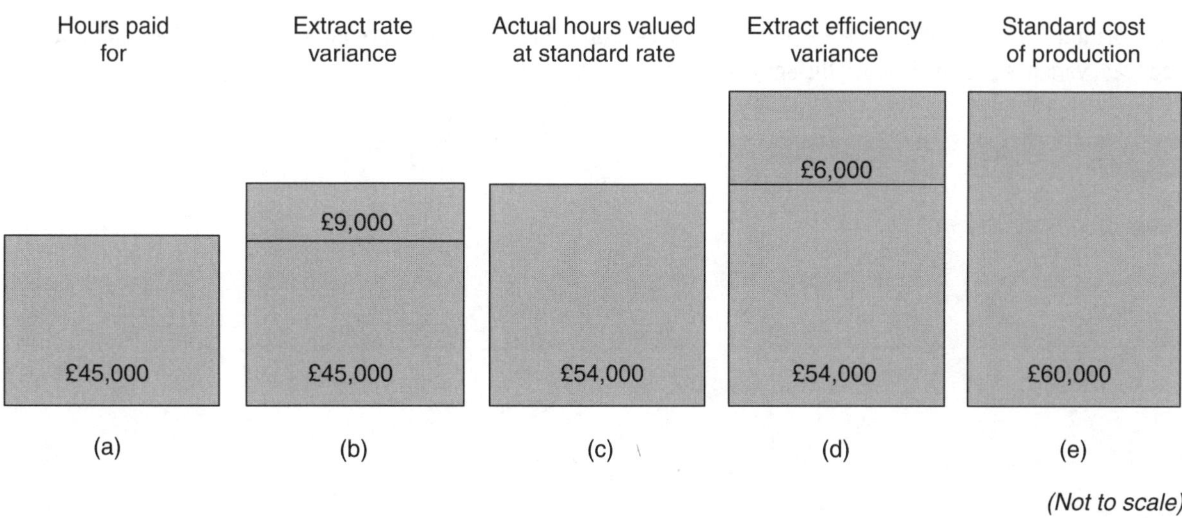

(Not to scale)

Rectangle (a)

Cost of hours worked = £45,000 (4,500 hours × £10 per hour).

Rectangle (b)

Hours worked should have cost 4,500 hours × £12 = £54,000

Rate variance = £(54,000 – 45,000) = £9,000

This variance is **favourable** because the actual cost is less than the standard cost.

Rectangle (c)

This rectangle shows the standard cost of the hours worked.

Rectangle (d)

Production of 500 units should have taken (500 units × 10 hours) 5,000 hours but did take 4,500 hours.

Hours worked on production are valued at the standard rate per hour and so the **labour efficiency variance** = (5,000 – 4,500) hours × £12 = £6,000. This variance is **favourable** because the actual hours were less than the standard hours.

Rectangle (e)

Standard cost of labour for 500 units = 500 units × 10 hours × £12 = £60,000

Example: labour variances

The standard labour cost of Overcast Ltd's product X is 2 hours of grade Z labour at £5 per hour (= £10 per unit of product X).

During period 4, 1,000 units of product X were made, and the labour cost of grade Z labour was £8,900 for 2,300 hours of work.

Task

Draw a diagram similar to that at the beginning of the section to illustrate the above information and then calculate the labour rate variance and the labour efficiency (productivity) variance.

Solution

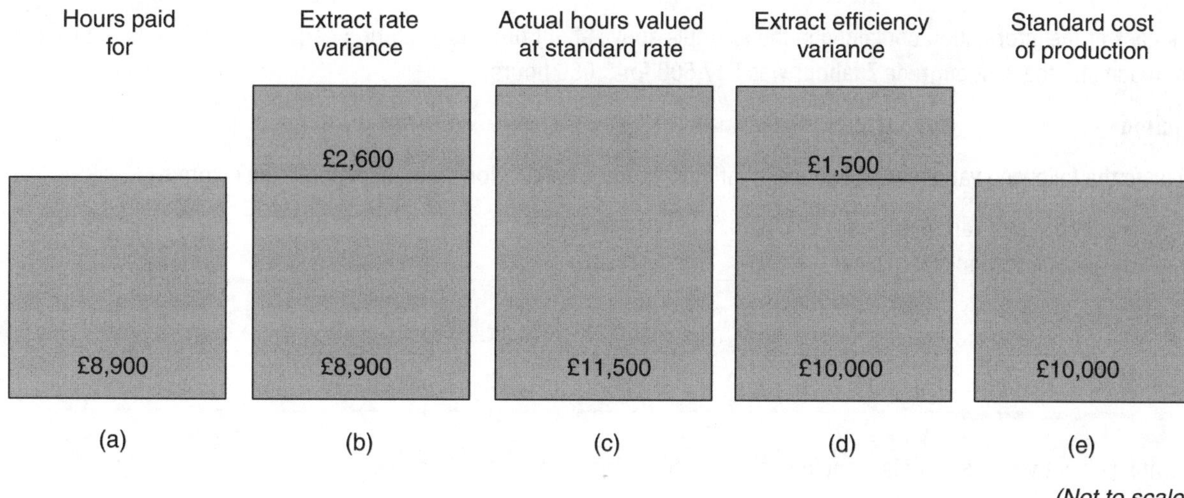

(Not to scale)

Rectangles (b) and (c)

Actual hours should have cost 2,300 hrs × £5 = £11,500

Rectangles (d) and (e)

Standard cost of hours that should have been worked = 1,000 units × 2 hrs × £5 = £10,000

The labour rate variance

This is the difference between what 2,300 hours should have cost (rectangle (c)) and what 2,300 hours did cost (rectangle (a)).

	£
2,300 hours of work should have cost (× £5 per hr)	11,500
but did cost	8,900
Direct labour rate variance	2,600 (F)

The variance is favourable because the labour cost less than it should have cost.

The labour efficiency variance

This is the difference between the number of hours it should have taken to produce 1,000 units of X (rectangle (e)) and how many hours it did take (rectangle (c)), valued at the standard rate per hour.

1,000 units of X should have taken (× 2 hrs)	2,000 hrs
but did take	2,300 hrs
Efficiency variance in hours	300 hrs (A)
× standard rate per hour	× £5
Efficiency variance in £	£1,500 (A)

The variance is adverse because more hours were worked than should have been worked.

Activity 6.9

Look back at the information contained in the example above about product X. During period 5, 1,500 units of product X were made and the cost of grade Z labour was £17,500 for 3,080 hours.

Required

Calculate the following variances. If you feel confident abut the calculations, you could omit the diagram.

(a) The labour rate variance
(b) The labour efficiency variance

Activity 6.10

A company has two departments, shaping and moulding. Budget and standard data for last year was as follows.

	Shaping	**Moulding**
Units of production	8,000	10,000
Standard labour cost per hour	£4.00	£3.50
Standard labour hours per unit	2.0	1.5

The actual results were as follows.

Units of production	7,500	9,000
Labour cost	£70,875	£56,700
Labour hours	16,875	15,750

Task

Calculate labour rate and labour efficiency variances for the two departments.

7 Fixed overhead variances

IMPORTANT POINT

Fixed overhead variances are the same as material and labour variances in that they **measure the difference between what the output should have cost (the planned or standard cost of the actual output) and what it did cost.**

There is a fundamental difference underlying their calculation, however.

Fixed costs do not vary with changes in output (provided output remains within the relevant range). This is a statement of fact since it describes the way in which fixed costs behave. The **budgeted or planned level of fixed costs should therefore be the same whatever the level of output.**

So if an organisation budgets fixed costs to be £5,000 for budgeted output of 100 units, the expected/planned/standard fixed costs if actual output is 120 units should still be £5,000.

IMPORTANT POINT ... (cont'd)

Contrast this with expected/planned/standard material and labour costs, which vary according to the actual level of output (because material and labour costs are variable costs).

In this sense there is no equivalent to a usage or efficiency variance when dealing with fixed overheads.

7.1 Fixed overhead variances and marginal costing

If the **actual fixed** cost **differs** from the **planned fixed cost**, the only reason can be that **expenditure** was **higher or lower than planned**.

The **fixed overhead expenditure variance** is therefore the **difference between planned expenditure and actual expenditure**. This is the only fixed overhead variance which occurs if marginal costing is being used.

7.2 Fixed overhead variances and absorption costing

The situation is slightly more complicated if absorption costing is being used, however. Continuing with our example, suppose now that Variances Ltd's **budgeted and actual fixed overheads** are **£40,800** (£80 per unit (per Section 4.2.2) × 510 units) for 20X2. (Ignore for the moment the £45,800 given for actual fixed overheads in Section 4.2.3.)

The **fixed overhead absorption rate** is therefore £40,800/510 = **£80 per unit.**

Let's see the **impact of an actual production/sales level different to that budgeted**.

Actual production and sales volumes	490	500	510
Budgeted and actual fixed overheads	£40,800	£40,800	£40,800
Fixed overheads charged to (absorbed into) production	490 × £80 = £39,200	500 × £80 = £40,000	510 × £80 = £40,800
Fixed overheads written off to the profit and loss account (under-absorbed overhead)*	£1,600 written off	£800 written off	-

*We know that the **fixed overhead charged to production plus** the **fixed overhead charged to the profit and loss account equals** the **actual overhead** incurred and so the amount written off is the actual overhead minus the amount charged to production.

Now let's see the **impact of a difference between budgeted and actual expenditure**. We stated in Section 4.2.3 that **actual fixed overheads** are greater than budgeted fixed overheads and are **£45,800**.

- The **overhead absorption rate** remains the **same** because it is based on budgeted fixed overheads.
- The amount of **fixed overhead charged to production** is **unchanged** from that in the table above (because the same absorption rate is multiplied by the same production/sales level).

But the fixed overhead charged to production plus the fixed overhead charged to the profit and loss account has to equal the fixed overhead actually incurred.

Actual production and sales volumes	490	500	510
Actual fixed overheads	£45,800	£45,800	£45,800
Fixed overheads charged to (absorbed into) production	490 × £80 = £39,200	500 × £80 = £40,000	510 × £80 = £40,800
Fixed overheads written off to the profit and loss account (under-absorbed overhead)	£6,600 written off	£5,800 written off	£5,000 written off

As you can see, the fixed overhead written off to the profit and loss account has increased by £5,000 compared with when actual fixed overheads were £40,800. The **charge to the profit and loss account** has therefore **increased by the difference between budgeted and actual fixed overheads.**

Two points can be made as a result of these simple examples.

- **Point 1.** The higher the volume of production, the more fixed overheads that are charged to production and the less that has to be written off to the profit and loss account.
- **Point 2.** If actual expenditure is greater than budgeted expenditure, the difference between the two figures has to be charged to the profit and loss account, irrespective of the actual sales and production volumes.

7.2.1 The volume and expenditure variances

Let's now illustrate what we know on a graph.

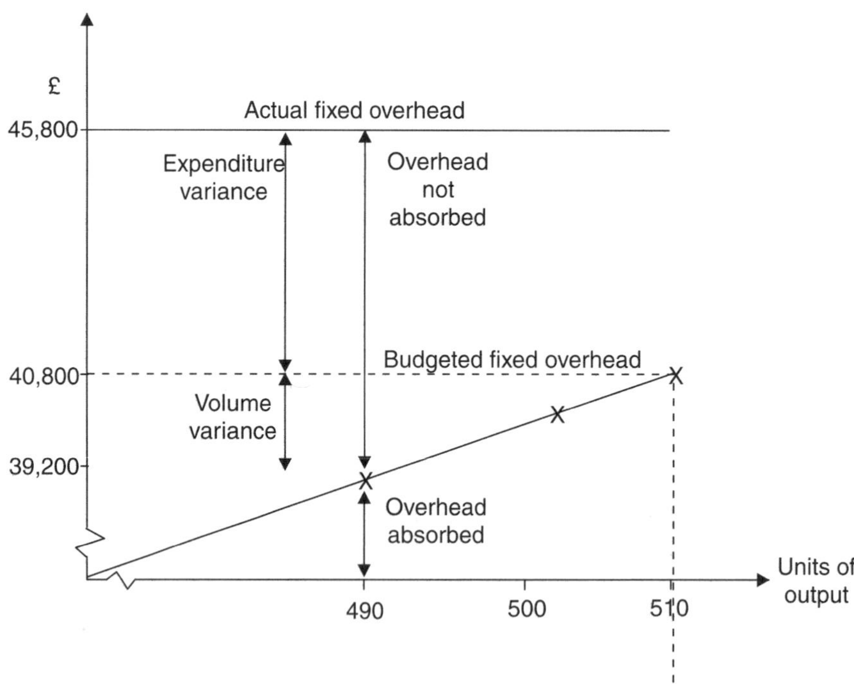

The **overhead not absorbed** into the cost of production because of a difference between budgeted and actual production volumes (£1,600 when output is 490 units in our example above) but **charged instead to the profit and loss account** is known as the fixed overhead **volume variance**.

The **difference between budgeted fixed overhead expenditure and actual expenditure** is the **same irrespective of the actual volume of output** (£5,000 in our example) and this is the fixed overhead **expenditure variance**. Because the actual overhead was greater than the budgeted overhead the variance is adverse.

7.2.2 A more detailed analysis: the efficiency and capacity variances

Let's take the analysis a bit further.

We know that each unit of product W requires ten labour hours. **Two possible overhead absorption rates** can be calculated from this information.

- An overhead absorption rate of £40,800/510 = £80 **per unit**
- A labour hour rate of £40,800/(510 × 10) = £8 **per labour hour**

If 510 units are produced or 5,100 labour hours worked, £40,800 of fixed overheads is charged to, or absorbed into, production. If 470 units are produced or 4,700 labour hours worked, £37,600 of fixed overheads is absorbed. Plotting this information on a graph produces a **line, the slope of which represents the fixed overhead absorption rates** of £80 per unit or £8 per labour hour.

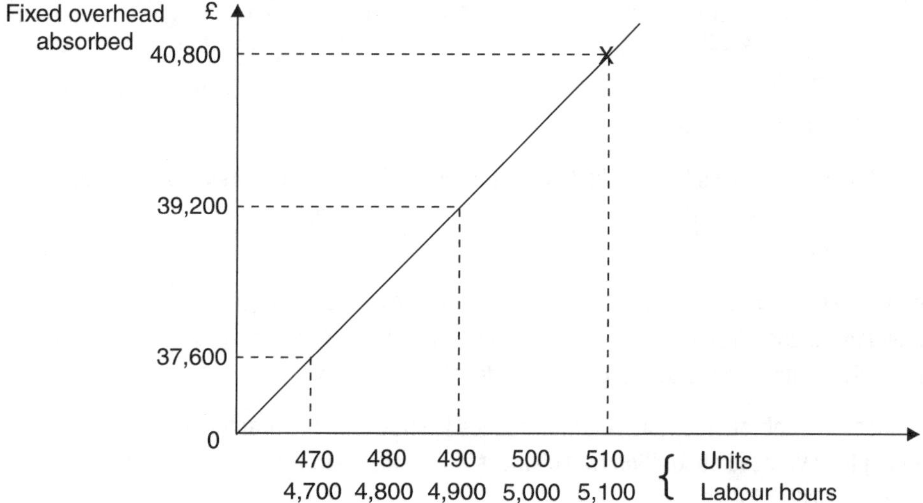

Whichever absorption rate is used, as the activity level increases, the fixed overhead absorbed into production increases.

We know that it takes 4,500 labour hours to produce the 500 units of W actually produced in 20X2 and that actual fixed overheads are £45,800. Let's reflect this information on a graph.

Obviously, **fixed overheads cost £5,000 more than anticipated**. This difference of £5,000 is the **fixed overhead expenditure variance** and, because the expenditure was greater than expected, the variance is **adverse.**

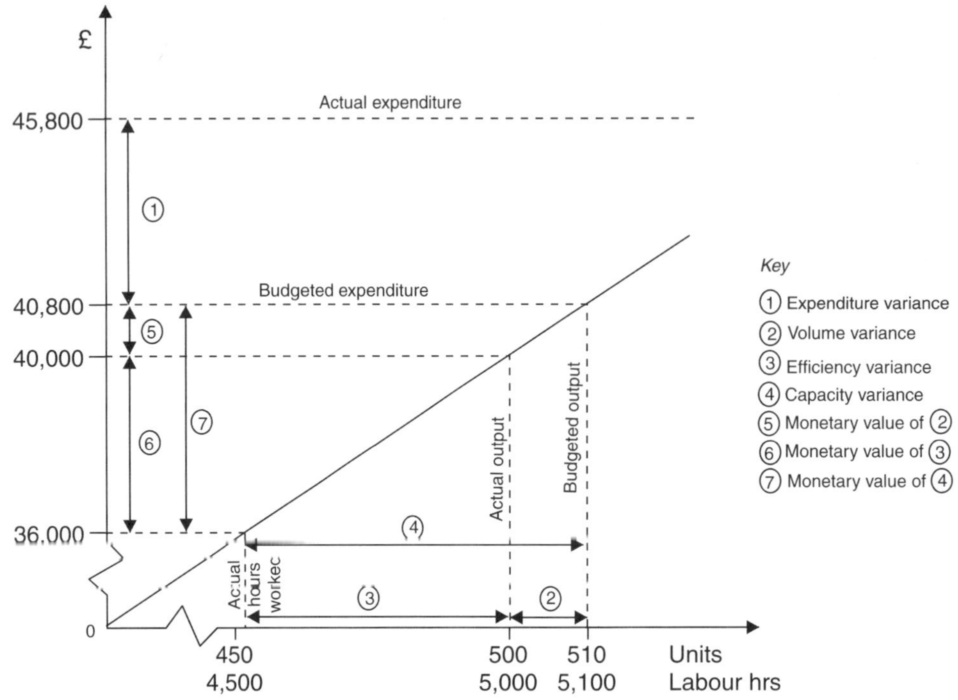

You can see on the vertical axis of the graph (①) that the expenditure variance is the **difference between the budgeted expenditure and the actual expenditure.**

A production level of 500 units means that **production was ten units less than planned,** so the amount of overheads absorbed into production costs was therefore £800 (10 units × £80) less than expected, resulting in an adverse adjustment to the profit and loss account.

This £800 is the **fixed overhead volume variance** we mentioned above and, because it has had a negative impact on profits, it is an **adverse** variance. You can see on the graph (②) that the variance is the **difference between the budgeted production level** (of 510 units) and **the actual production level** (of 500 units).

Look at how the financial implication of this volume variance is shown on the graph (⑤). Can you see that if the slope of the line representing the overhead absorption rate changes, the variance in monetary terms would change. The graph below might make this clearer for you.

Graph of volume variances at various overhead absorption rates

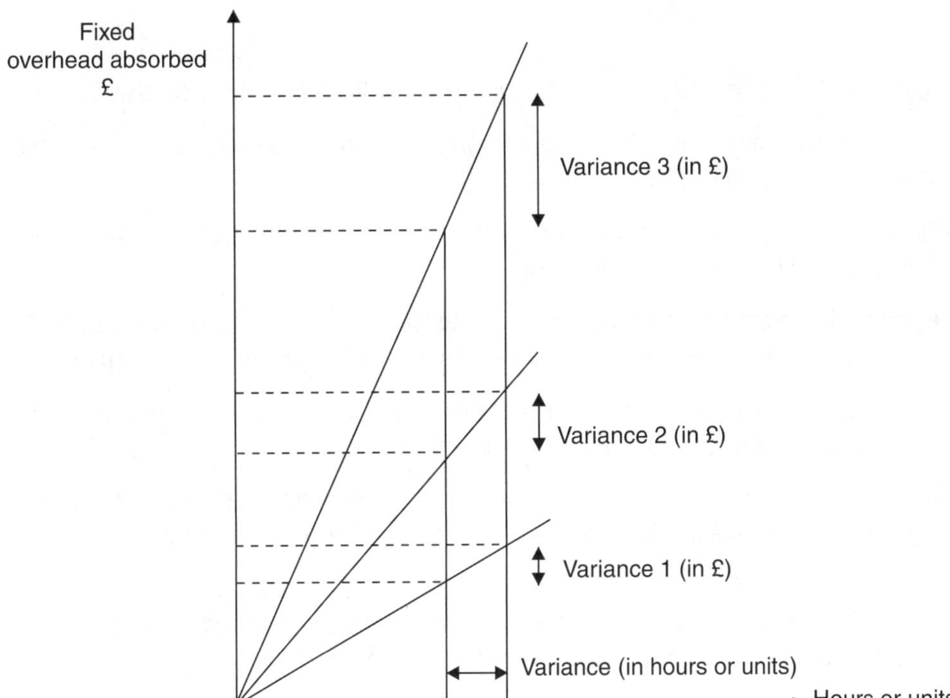

As the absorption rate increases (in other words, as the slope of the line increases), so does the variance in monetary terms, while the variance in hours or units remains the same.

Without worrying too much about the meaning of the term 'efficiency', **4,500 labour hours were worked but 5,000 labour hours of work were produced,** which appears to be quite efficient. In the hours worked (at the budgeted efficiency level), 500 less hours of production should have been produced than actually were produced. This means that 500 × £8 = £4,000 less absorbed fixed overhead should have been charged to the profit and loss account. The 500 hours is a measure of the efficiency with which the workforce were working and so £4,000 must be credited to the profit and loss account because of the efficiency.

This £4,000 is the **(favourable) fixed overhead efficiency variance**, a subdivision of the volume variance. You can see the variance on the graph of the variances (③) as the **difference between the number of hours production that should have been achieved (5,000) and the number of hours that were worked (4,500).**

Although the **budgeted capacity was 510 × 10 = 5,100 hours, the workforce worked for 4,500 hours**. Since we would expect output to be less than budgeted if less hours are worked than budgeted, the financial implications of this difference of 600 hours (600 × £8 = £4,800) must be charged to the profit and loss account.

This £4,800 is known as the **fixed overhead capacity variance** (a subdivision of the volume variance) and, because we would expect output to be less than budgeted, the variance is **adverse**. This is shown on the graph (④) as the **difference between the budgeted number of labour hours and the actual number of labour hours.**

You can see the monetary value of the variances on the vertical axis (⑤, ⑥ and ⑦).

You **do not need to draw your graph to scale**. It can be drawn freehand – you just need to ensure that you have not made any mistakes when calculating the fixed overhead absorption rate and that you have correctly marked on your graph the information provided.

7.2.3 A summary

IMPORTANT POINT

Here's a brief summary of how to use the graphical approach to determine fixed overhead variances.

Step 1. Sketch a graph with units of output and hours of production on the horizontal axis and £ on the vertical axis. This graph DOES NOT HAVE TO BE TO SCALE.

Step 2. Add horizontal lines to show budgeted fixed overhead expenditure and actual fixed overhead expenditure. These lines highlight the expenditure variance.

Step 3. Add a sloping line to show the split between overhead absorbed and overhead not absorbed. This line can be drawn from two points representing the overhead absorbed at two different production levels.

Step 4. Add vertical lines at the points representing budgeted output level, actual output level (which is also standard hours for actual output level) and actual hours worked.

Step 5. The volume variance represents the overhead not absorbed into production because of a difference between budgeted and actual production levels and is based on the difference between budgeted output and actual output.

Step 6. The efficiency variance is a measure of the efficiency of working and is based on the difference between the actual hours worked and the hours that should have been worked (standard hours for actual output).

Step 7. The capacity variance looks at how well available capacity was used and is therefore based on the difference between the available capacity (budgeted hours) and the capacity actually used (actual hours).

Once you understand the 'message' underlying the graphical approach you will no longer need to use it and will be able to calculate the variances without drawing the graph.

Activity 6.11

Chambers Ltd produces and sells one product only, the TN50, the standard cost for one unit being as follows.

	£
Direct material M1 – 10 kilograms at £20 per kg	200
Direct material M2 – 5 litres at £6 per litre	30
Direct wages – 5 hours at £6 per hour	30
Fixed overhead	50
Total standard cost	310

The fixed overhead included in the standard cost is based on an expected monthly output of 900 units. Fixed overhead is absorbed on the basis of direct labour hours.

During April the actual results were as follows.

Production	800 units
Material M1	7,800 kg used, costing £159,900
Material M2	4,300 units used, costing £23,650
Direct wages	4,200 hours worked for £24,150
Fixed overhead	£47,000

Task

(a) Calculate price and usage variances for each material.
(b) Calculate labour rate and efficiency variances.
(c) Using the graphical approach, calculate fixed overhead expenditure, volume, efficiency and capacity variances.

7.3 Alternative non-graphical approach

This is an alternative to the graphical approach we have just worked through. In the exam, invariably the method is left to you.

The fixed overhead total variance may be broken down into two parts as usual.

- An **expenditure variance**
- A **volume variance**. This in turn may be **split into two parts**.
  - An **efficiency variance**
  - A **capacity variance**

In an absorption costing system, **fixed overhead variances** are an attempt to **explain** the **reasons for any under-absorbed or over-absorbed overhead.**

Remember that the absorption rate is calculated as budgeted fixed overhead ÷ budgeted level of activity.

Generally the level of activity used in the overhead absorption rate will be units of production or hours of activity. More often than not, if just one product is being produced, the level of activity is in terms of units produced.

Activity 6.12

The budgeted fixed overheads for 20X7 for Cuthbert's Cups Ltd are £75,000. Budgeted output is 50,000 cups. Each cup is expected to take 15 minutes to manufacture.

Tasks

Calculate the overhead absorption rate per cup and per hour.

You should remember from Chapter 2 that if either the budgeted overhead expenditure or the budgeted activity level or both are incorrect then we will have under-absorbed or over-absorbed overhead.

7.3.1 Expenditure variance

The fixed overhead **expenditure variance** measures the under or over absorption caused by the **actual overhead expenditure being different from budget**.

7.3.2 Volume variance

The fixed overhead **volume variance** measures the under or over absorption caused by the **actual production level being different to the budgeted production level** used in calculating the absorption rate.

IMPORTANT POINT

The **volume variance applies to fixed overhead costs only** and not to variable overheads.

- Variable overheads incurred change with the volume of activity. If the budget is to work for 300 hours and variable overheads are incurred and absorbed at a rate of £6 per hour, the variable overhead budget will be £1,800. If only 200 hours are actually worked, the variable overhead absorbed will be £1,200 and the expected expenditure will also be £1,200, so that there will be no under or over absorption of overhead because of volume changes.
- Fixed overheads are different because the level of expenditure does not change as the number of hours worked varies. If the budget is to work for 300 hours and fixed overheads are budgeted to be £2,400, the fixed overhead absorption rate will be £8 per hour. If actual hours worked are only 200 hours, the fixed overhead absorbed will be £1,600, but expected expenditure will be unchanged at £2,400. There is an under absorption of £800 because of the volume variance of 100 hours shortfall multiplied by the absorption rate of £8 per hour.

7.3.3 Splitting the volume variance

There are two reasons why the actual production or hours of activity may be different from the budgeted production or budgeted number of hours used in calculating the absorption rate.

The first reason is that the **work force or machinery may have been working at a more or less efficient rate than standard** to produce a given output. This is measured by the fixed overhead **(volume) efficiency variance**.

The second reason is that, regardless of the level of efficiency, the **total number of hours worked could have been less or more than was originally budgeted**

- Employees may have worked a lot of overtime.
- There may have been a strike.
- Machinery may have broken down.

Other things being equal, this could lead to under-absorbed or over-absorbed fixed overhead and the effect is measured by the fixed overhead (**volume) capacity variance**.

7.3.4 How to calculate the variances

- **Fixed overhead total variance** is the difference between fixed overhead incurred and fixed overhead absorbed (the under-absorbed or over-absorbed fixed overhead).
- **Fixed overhead expenditure variance** is the difference between the budgeted fixed overhead expenditure and actual fixed overhead expenditure.
- **Fixed overhead volume variance** is the difference between actual and budgeted production/volume multiplied by the standard absorption rate per *unit*.
- **Fixed overhead (volume) efficiency variance** is the difference between the number of hours that actual production should have taken, and the number of hours actually taken (that is, worked) multiplied by the standard absorption rate per *hour*.
- **Fixed overhead (volume) capacity variance** is the difference between budgeted hours of work and the actual hours worked, multiplied by the standard absorption rate per *hour*.

IMPORTANT POINTS

- The **volume variance** is calculated using the standard fixed overhead **per unit**. The **capacity and efficiency variances** use the standard fixed overhead **per hour**.
- Remember the **overheads** are **not always absorbed** on the **basis** of **labour hours**. Machine hours are often used. Previous exam tasks have used operating hours and flights, for example.

You should now be ready to work through an example to demonstrate all of the fixed overhead variances.

Example: fixed overhead variances

Calculate the fixed overhead total variance and its sub-variances for Variances Ltd for 20X2 using the approach set out in Section 7.3.4.

Solution

(a) **Fixed overhead total variance**

	£
Fixed overhead incurred	45,800
Fixed overhead absorbed (500 units × £80 per unit)	40,000
Fixed overhead total variance (= under-/over-absorbed overhead)	5,800 (A)

The variance is adverse because less overheads were absorbed than budgeted.

(b) **Fixed overhead expenditure variance**

	£
Budgeted fixed overhead expenditure	40,800
Actual fixed overhead expenditure	45,800
Fixed overhead expenditure variance	5,000 (A)

The variance is adverse because expenditure was greater than budgeted.

(c) **Fixed overhead volume variance**

The production volume achieved was less than expected. The fixed overhead volume variance measures the difference at the standard rate.

	£
Actual production at standard rate (500 × £80 per unit)	40,000
Budgeted production at standard rate (510 × £80 per unit)	40,800
Fixed overhead volume variance	800 (A)

The variance is adverse because output was less than expected.

(i) The labour force may have worked inefficiently, and produced output at a slower rate than expected. Less overhead will be absorbed if units are produced more slowly. This **efficiency variance** is exactly the same in hours as the direct labour efficiency variance, but is valued in £ at the standard absorption rate for fixed overheads.

(ii) The labour force may have worked fewer hours than budgeted, and therefore produced less output, so there may be a **capacity variance.**

(d) **Fixed overhead efficiency variance**

The efficiency variance is calculated in the same way as the labour efficiency variance.

500 units of product W should take (× 10 hrs)	5,000 hrs
but did take	4,500 hrs
Fixed overhead volume efficiency variance in hours	500 hrs (F)
× standard fixed overhead absorption rate per hour	× £8
Fixed overhead volume efficiency variance in £	£4,000 (F)

The labour force has produced 5,000 standard hours of work in 4,500 actual hours and so output is 500 standard hours higher than budgeted for this reason and the variance is favourable.

(e) **Fixed overhead capacity variance**

The capacity variance is the difference between the budgeted and actual hours of work.

Budgeted hours of work	5,100 hrs
Actual hours of work	4,500 hrs
Fixed overhead volume capacity variance in hours	600 hrs (A)
× standard fixed overhead absorption rate per hour	× £8
Fixed overhead volume capacity variance in £	£4,800 (A)

Since the labour force worked 600 hours less than budgeted, we should expect output to be 600 standard hours less than budgeted and hence the variance is adverse.

WATCH OUT FOR ...

Fixed overhead variances and non-manufacturing environments

Fixed overhead variances do not apply only in a manufacturing context. In the December 1999 exam, candidates were required to calculate the fixed overhead expenditure and volume variances for a hotel complex. The overhead volume variance was based on the number of guest-days. It was not possible to sub-divide the volume variance to determine the capacity and efficiency variances, however, because the activity achieved could not be stated in terms of hours.

8 Graphical calculation of material and labour variances

As well as calculating fixed overhead variances using graphs, it is possible to calculate the variable cost variances in the same way.

We begin by drawing horizontal and vertical axes.

- The **horizontal axis represents quantity** (of hours, kilograms and so on)
- The **vertical axis represents price** (per kg, per hour and so on)

We will show you how to calculate material variances but the same approach can be used for labour variances.

8.1 The standard cost

We know that the standard material cost of Variances Ltd's product W is £162 (9 kgs × £18 per kg) and that, in 20X2, 500 units of product W were made using 5,000 kgs of material which cost £100,000.

To produce 500 units, the standard material usage is 500 × 9 kgs = 4,500 kgs at a standard price of £18 per kg, resulting in a standard cost of 4,500 kgs × £18 = £81,000. We can show the standards (4,500 kgs and £18 per kg) on the axes as follows.

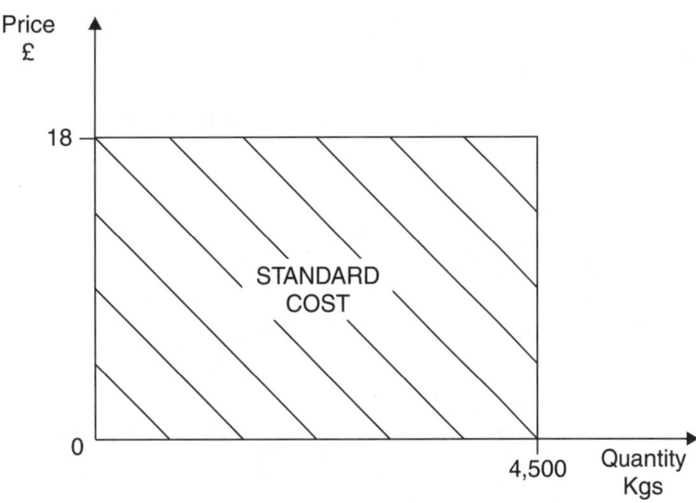

The **area of the rectangle** (4,500 × 18 = 81,000) **represents the standard cost** of £81,000.

8.2 The price variance

The actual price paid for each of the 5,000 kgs was £100,000 ÷ 5,000 = £20 instead of the standard £18. Remember the material **price variance is identified** and **extracted before the stock is issued to production** and so the **price variance** is **based** on the **actual** 5,000 kgs purchased and used. We can therefore represent the **price variance** on the axes as follows.

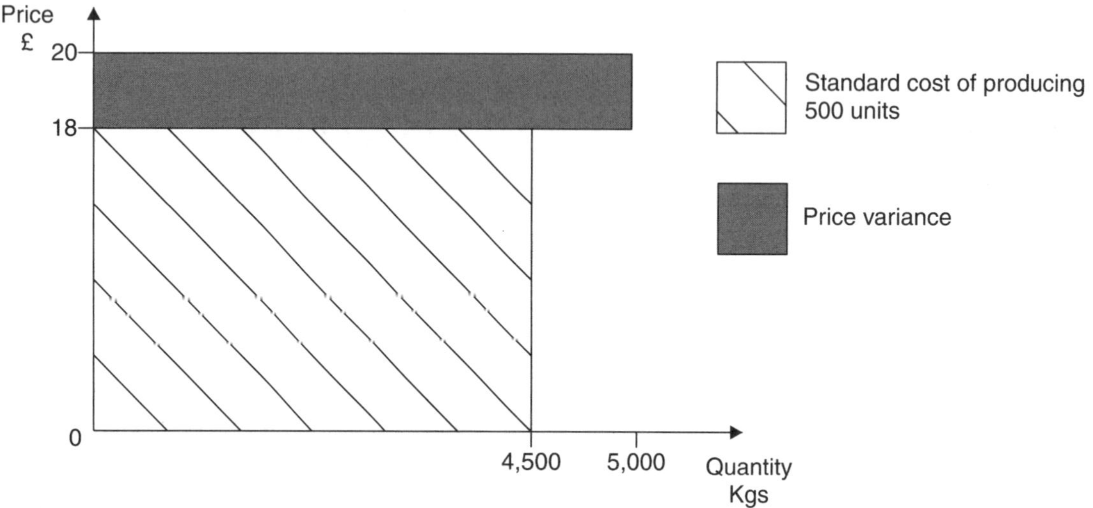

The area of the rectangle representing the price variance is £(20 – 18) × 5,000 = £10,000. We'll just compare this with the variance calculated in the normal way (see Section 5.2) so you can see where the £10,000 comes from.

	£
5,000 kgs should have cost (× £18)	90,000
but did cost	100,000
Price variance	10,000 (A)

8.3 The rate variance

5,000 kgs were actually used instead of the standard 4,500 kgs. This **usage variance** can be shown on the axes as follows.

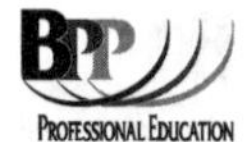

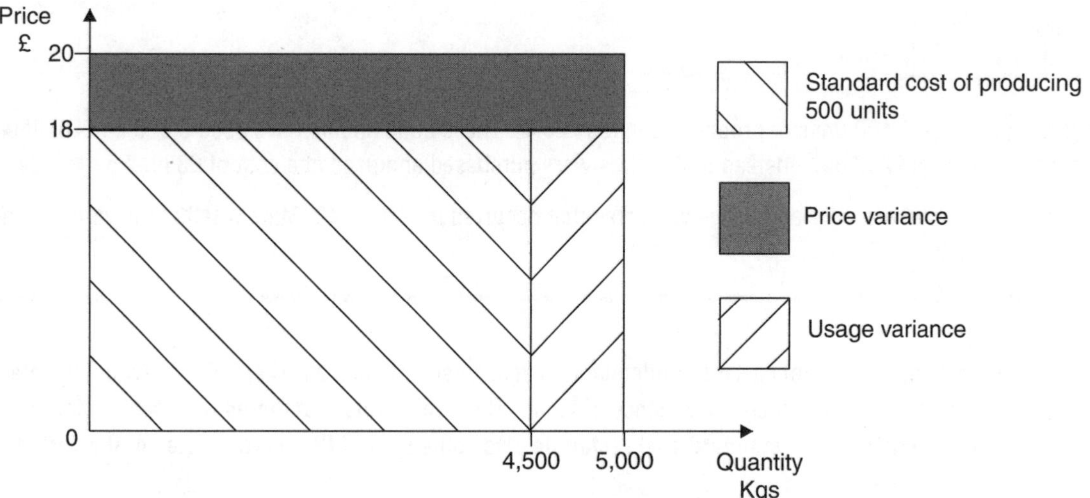

The rectangle representing the usage variance has an area of (5,000 – 4,500) × £18 = £9,000. Let's calculate the usage variance in the usual way just so you can see where the £9,000 comes from.

500 units should have used (× 9 kgs)	4,500 kgs
but did use	5,000 kgs
Usage variance in kgs	500 kgs (A)
× standard price per kg	× £18
Usage variance in £	£9,000 (A)

8.4 Adverse or favourable?

The **rectangle representing the price variance adds to or increases the area of the rectangle representing the standard material cost** and hence the price variance must be **adverse**.

The **rectangle representing the usage variance also adds to the area of the rectangle representing standard material cost** and so the usage variance is also **adverse**.

The variances could have been read off the graphs in a slightly different way.

Price variance:	(£20 × 5,000) – (£18 × 5,000)	= £10,000 (A)
Usage variance:	(£18 × 5,000) – (£18 × 4,500)	= £9,000 (A)

Activity 6.13

Standard labour cost of the Superior version of product Epsilon – 10 hrs at £5 per hour
Actual production in week 52 – 25 units of the Superior version of product Epsilon
Actual hours worked in week 52 – 200
Actual wages paid in week 52 – £900

Draw a diagram representing the rate and efficiency variances which occurred in week 52. State whether the variances are adverse or favourable.

Activity 6.14

Lansdale Ltd produced 1,100 units of product P5 in May 20X2. These units should have used 6,600 litres of liquid L1 which should have cost £237,600. Instead 9,350 litres were purchased and used at a cost of £359,975.

Draw a diagram to show the price and usage variances that occurred in May 20X2. State whether the variances are adverse or favourable.

Some managers may find a diagram easier to understand than a statement such as 'There was a favourable rate variance of £100 and a favourable efficiency variance of £250'. The **sizes of the rectangles** representing the variances and **their position in relation to** the **standard cost rectangle** give some **idea of the relative sizes of the variances and the direction** (adverse or favourable).

IMPORTANT POINT

Note that you do not need to draw these graphs to scale.

9 Reconciliation statements

Now you know how to calculate variances we can move to the final stage of Part 2 of a typical question (see Section 3) and take a look at reconciliation statements, which regularly appear in exam tasks.

9.1 Give us your opinion

What is your opinion of the following reconciliation format?

Statement of budgeted and actual cost of production of product W
20X2

	Actual		*Budget*		*Variance*
Production (units)	500		510		10
	Inputs		*Inputs*		
		£		£	£
Materials	5,000 kgs	100,000	4,590 kgs	82,620	(17,380)
Labour	4,500 hrs	45,000	5,100 hrs	61,200	16,200
Fixed overheads		45,800		40,800	(5,000)
		190,800		184,620	(6,180)

Do you think the statement provides good management information?

- It compares the costs of budgeted output of 510 units with the costs of actual output of 500 units. So it does not compare like with like. The **standard cost of the actual volume of production needs to be reconciled to the actual cost of production.**

- The variances are simply the difference between the budgeted cost and the actual cost. They are not split into price/rate and usage/efficiency variations.

9.2 The correct approach – absorption costing

A **reconciliation** of the difference between the **standard cost of production (what it should have cost) and the actual cost of production** during a period is usually presented as a report to senior management at the end of each control period. The report provides an overview of the divergence between planned costs and actual costs to **different degrees of detail** depending on the organisation. Total cost variances *may* be reported in some organisations whereas, in others, each total variance is broken down into its constituent components.

Let's try and reconcile Variances Ltd's standard cost of actual production in 20X2 with the actual cost, using the variances we have calculated throughout this chapter.

IMPORTANT POINT

The standard cost of production = (standard unit cost) × actual volume of production

VARIANCES LTD – RECONCILIATION STATEMENT 20X2

	£	£	£	
Standard cost of production (500 units × £362)			181,000	
Cost variances	(F)	(A)		
Material price		10,000		
Material usage		9,000		
Labour rate	9,000			
Labour efficiency	6,000			
Fixed overhead expenditure		5,000		
Fixed overhead efficiency	4,000			
Fixed overhead capacity		4,800		
	19,000	28,800	9,800	(A)
Actual cost of production			190,800	

IMPORTANT POINT

Do not include the fixed overhead volume variance as well as the fixed overhead capacity and efficiency variances in a reconciliation statement otherwise you will be double counting (as efficiency variance + capacity variance = volume variance).

Now let's have a look at another example. This will give you a chance to revise the variance calculations we have been looking at and to combine them into a reconciliation statement.

Example: variances and reconciliation statements

Not My Day Ltd manufactures one product (the GLOOM). The company operates a standard costing system and analysis of variances is made every month.

Data for month ended 30 June Year 7

	Actual data	*Budget data*
Production (units)	4,850	5,100
Material	2,300 kgs costing £9,800	2,550 kgs costing £10,200
Labour	8,500 hrs costing £16,800	10,200 hrs costing £20,400
Fixed overheads	£42,300	£37,740

Task

Using the information above, calculate all variances and prepare a reconciliation statement for the month ended 30 June Year 7.

Solution

(a) Standard material cost per kg = £10,200 ÷ 2,550 = £4

	£
2,300 kg of material should cost (× £4)	9,200
but did cost	9,800
Material price variance	600 (A)

(b) Standard material usage per GLOOM = 2,550 kgs ÷ 5,100 = 0.5 kgs

4,850 GLOOMS should use (× 0.5 kgs)	2,425 kg
but did use	2,300 kg
Material usage variance in kgs	125 kg (F)
× standard cost per kg	× £4
Material usage variance in £	£ 500 (F)

(c) Standard labour rate per hour = £20,400 ÷ 10,200 = £2

	£
8,500 hours of labour should cost (× £2)	17,000
but did cost	16,800
Labour rate variance	200 (F)

(d) Standard labour requirement per GLOOM = 10,200 hrs ÷ 5,100 = 2 hrs

4,850 GLOOMS should take (× 2 hrs)	9,700 hrs
but did take	8,500 hrs
Labour efficiency variance in hours	1,200 hrs (F)
× standard cost per hour	× £2
Labour efficiency variance in £	£2,400 (F)

(e) Overhead absorption rate per hr = £37,740/10,200 = £3.70

	£
Budgeted fixed overhead (5,100 units × 2 hrs × £3.70)	37,740
Actual fixed overhead	42,300
Fixed overhead expenditure variance	4,560 (A)

(f)

Labour efficiency variance in hrs	1,200 hrs (F)
× standard absorption rate per hr	× £3.70
Fixed overhead volume efficiency variance	£4,440 (F)

(g)

Budgeted hours of work	10,200 hrs
Actual hours worked	8,500 hrs
Capacity variance in hrs	1,700 hrs (A)
× standard absorption rate per hr	× £3.70
	£6,290 (A)

We need to work out the **standard unit cost**.

	£
Material (0.5 kgs × £4)	2.00
Labour (2 hrs × £2)	4.00
Overheads (2 hrs × £3.70)	7.40
	13.40

NOT MY DAY LTD – RECONCILIATION STATEMENT JUNE YEAR 7

	£	£	£
Standard cost of production (4,850 units × £13.40)			64,990
Cost variances	(F)	(A)	
Material price		600	
Material usage	500		
Labour rate	200		
Labour efficiency	2,400		
Fixed overhead expenditure		4,560	
Fixed overhead volume efficiency	4,440		
Fixed overhead volume capacity		6,290	
	7,540	11,450	3,910 (A)
Actual cost, June Year 7			68,900

Check	£
Materials	9,800
Labour	16,800
Fixed overhead	42,300
Actual costs of production	68,900

9.3 The correct approach – marginal costing

How would we prepare a reconciliation statement if standard marginal costing was in use?

Let's return to our Variances Ltd example.

- If Variances Ltd uses standard marginal costing instead of standard absorption costing there will be no fixed overhead volume variance

- We need to reconcile the standard **variable** cost of production and the actual **full** cost of production. The standard variable unit cost of production is £(362 – 80) = £282 (the total of standard material and labour costs per unit).
- The other variances are unchanged.

A reconciliation statement might therefore appear as follows.

VARIANCES LTD – RECONCILIATION STATEMENT 20X2

	£	£	£
Standard variable cost of production (500 units × £282)			141,000
Cost variances	(F)	(A)	
Material price		10,000	
Material usage		9,000	
Labour rate	9,000		
Labour efficiency	6,000		
	15,000	19,000	4,000 (A)
Actual variable cost of production			145,000
Budgeted fixed overhead		40,800	
Expenditure variance		(5,000) (A)	
Actual fixed overhead			45,800
Actual cost of production			190,800

Example: marginal costing reconciliation statements

And here is the marginal costing statement for Not My Day Ltd from our earlier example.

NOT MY DAY LTD – RECONCILIATION STATEMENT JUNE YEAR 7

	£	£	£
	(F)	(A)	
Standard variable cost of production (4,850 units × £6)			29,100
Variable cost variances			
Material price		600	
Material usage	500		
Labour rate	200		
Labour efficiency	2,400		
	3,100	600	2,500 (F)
Actual variable cost of production			26,600
Budgeted fixed overhead		37,740	
Expenditure variance		4,560 (A)	
Actual fixed overhead			42,300
Actual cost of production			68,900

9.4 Advantages of this format

As you can see, the revised statements in the two examples provide more meaningful information than the statement we asked you to give your opinion on.

- They **compare like with like**, based on the actual production achieved.
- They **highlight** the **areas** giving rise to any **differences** between planned and actual cost.
- They allow **management by exception**.

By **splitting variances** into components in the statements we can see what part of the total material variance (say) is the **responsibility** of the purchasing manager (price variance) and what part is the responsibility of the production manager (usage variance).

We return to the issue of responsibility in the next chapter.

Another advantage of the format above is that it **avoids** the use of **under/over absorption** of fixed overhead. Knowing what students think of that particular bookkeeping exercise, you're probably very pleased!

Activity 6.15

Sure Fire Shoes Ltd manufacture shoes. One of their products, a leather shoe style 'Delilah', has the following standard unit cost and selling price.

		£	£
Direct materials			
Leather	3 units at £5 per unit	15	
Other materials		3	
			18
Direct labour	$1\frac{1}{2}$ hours at £4 per hour		6
Fixed overheads	$1\frac{1}{2}$ hours at £6 per hour		9
Standard cost			33

Budgeted production for period 7 was 3,000 shoes (Delilah style).

During period 7, 3,200 shoes (Delilah style) were produced and results were as follows.

Leather purchased and used:	quantity	9,750 units
	cost	£45,400
Other materials purchased and used		£9,500
Direct labour:	hours worked and paid for	5,850 hours
	labour cost	£24,100
Fixed overheads		£31,500

Task

Prepare a reconciliation statement for period 7 reconciling budgeted and actual costs and specifying all the relevant variances.

Activity 6.16

You have been asked to examine the performance of a furniture company for May Year 1. The standard cost of one unit of a particular product for May was as follows.

		£
Direct material	5 kilos at £4 per kilo	20
Direct labour	4 hours at £6 per hour	24
Overheads (based upon an overhead absorption rate of £4 per labour hour)		16
		60

Budgeted output in May was 1,200 units and the results were as follows.

(a) 1,300 units were made.
(b) Direct material used was 6,600 kilos at a total cost of £25,080.
(c) Direct labour was 5,330 hours at a cost of £32,513
(d) Actual fixed overheads were £22,000.

Tasks

(a) Calculate the following.

(i) Material price variance
(ii) Material usage variance
(iii) Labour rate variance
(iv) Labour efficiency variance
(v) Fixed overhead expenditure variance
(vi) Fixed overhead efficiency variance
(vii) Fixed overhead capacity variance

(b) For May Year 1 reconcile the standard costs for actual production with actual costs, clearly showing the total variance for each element of cost. (*Note*. Sub-variances are not required.)

Activity 6.17

You work as assistant accountant for Leytoss Pumps Ltd. The company manufactures a single type of pump and uses a standard costing system to monitor and control costs.

Standard and actual cost data for direct costs for the month of June are shown below.

Standard costs

	£ per unit
Direct material: 4.3 kg × £8 per kg	34.40
Direct labour: 1.5 hrs × £4 per hr	6.00
Total direct costs	40.40

Actual results

Direct material purchased and used = 19,500 kg at £8.50 per kg
Direct labour costs incurred = £26,286 paid for 6,740 hours
Number of pumps produced in June = 4,500

Tasks

(a) Calculate the direct cost variances for June.

(b) Present the variances in a statement which reconciles the standard direct cost of production with the actual direct cost for June, using the following format.

Reconciliation of standard direct cost of production with actual direct cost for June

	£	£
Standard direct cost of production = 4,500 × £40.40		181,800
Direct cost variances		
Direct material price		
Direct material usage		
Direct labour rate		
Direct labour efficiency		
Actual direct cost of production		

ATTENTION!

Beware of giving almost perfect answers to tasks set in *previous* exams when facing your exams. Although this demonstrates remarkable memory skills, it won't demonstrate that you are competent! Answer the actual tasks set, not those you have worked through in the run up to the exam.

Activity 6.18

Cavanagh Ltd operates a standard costing system. The company manufactures a single product from raw material Theta. During the four-week period ended 26 May the following costs were recorded.

	Standard	*Actual*
	£	£
Raw material Theta	75,000	76,570
Direct wages	125,000	110,295
Fixed overhead	34,000	32,762

The following additional information is applicable.

(a) The standard material cost of each unit produced is 25 kg at 30 pence per kg; actual costs were 26 kg at 31 pence per kg.

(b) The standard wages cost per unit is 2.5 labour hours at £5.00 per hour; actual wages cost was 2.25 hours at £5.16 per hour.

(c) 9,500 units were produced. Budgeted production was 10,000 units.

(d) 20,250 hours were worked.

Task

Prepare a statement of variances reconciling the standard costs for actual production for the period with the actual costs incurred.

ATTENTION!

The assessor has stressed the importance of showing your workings to calculations: 'Simply writing the answer is a high-risk strategy. One silly error and you might appear to have a totally different answer to the correct one. Without workings, no credit can be given. With workings, however, the examiner can see your logic and give you credit for the correct process.'

Key learning points

- ☑ A **standard** represents what we think should happen, a best 'guestimate'.
- ☑ The **standard cost** of a product is made up of a number of different standards, one for each cost element. Each standard has two parts.
  - A monetary/rate element
  - A resource element
- ☑ Make sure that you have an understanding of how standards are set.
- ☑ The responsibility for setting standards should be shared between the managers who are able to provide the necessary information about expected prices, efficiencies of working and so on.
- ☑ Standard costs are usually revised once a year (to allow for inflation in material prices and wage rates, changes in expected efficiency of material usage and so on). They may be revised more frequently if conditions are changing rapidly, however.
- ☑ **Performance standards** are used to set targets for material usage and labour efficiency. There are four types: **attainable, ideal, current** and **basic**.
- ☑ **Variances** measure the difference between actual results and expected results.
- ☑ When actual results are better than expected results, we have a **favourable variance (F).** If actual results are worse than expected results, we have an **adverse variance (A).**
- ☑ Differences between actual results and expected results should be brought to the attention of management as soon as possible.
- ☑ The first section of exam tasks on standard costing has required candidates to derive standard and actual data. You need to be able to see **patterns in numbers, rearrange equations** and carry out **efficient calculations.**
- ☑ Here is an example showing how to establish material variances.

☑ And here is one depicting labour variances.

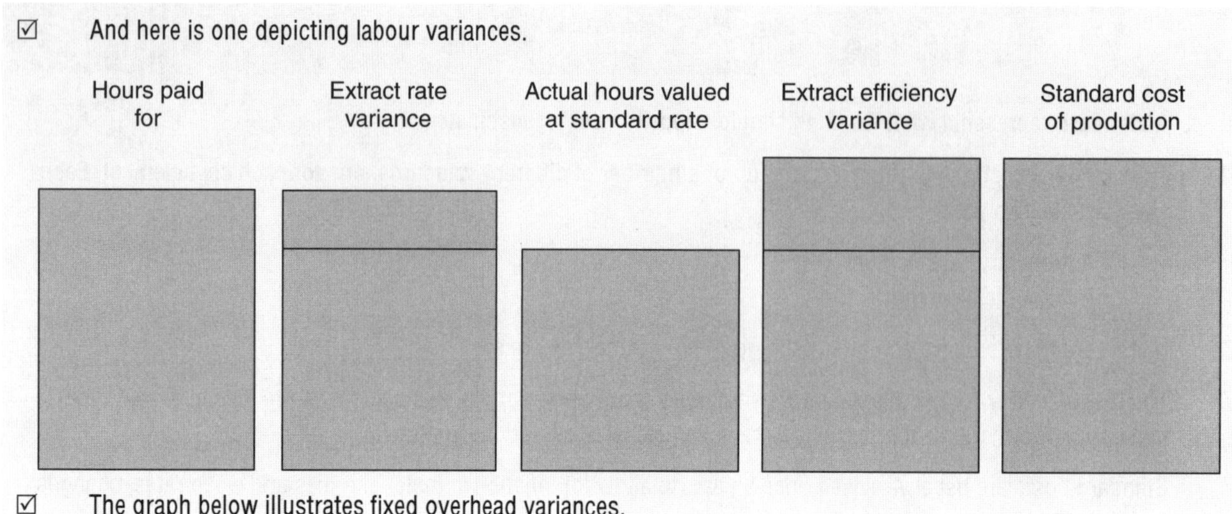

☑ The graph below illustrates fixed overhead variances.

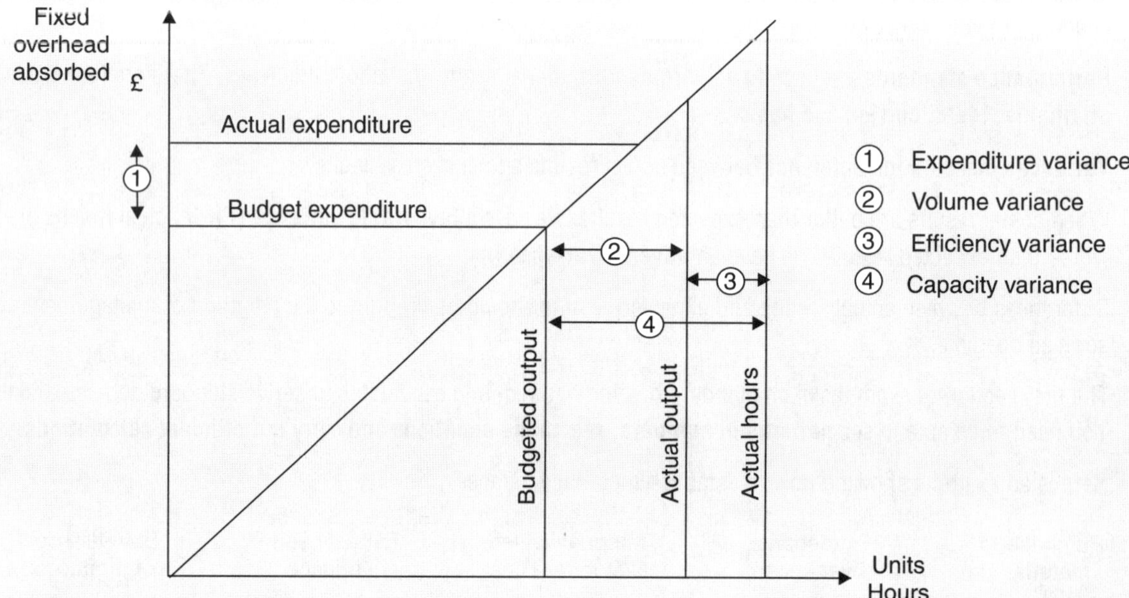

☑ The **expenditure variance** represents the overhead not absorbed into the cost of production because of a difference between budgeted and actual expenditures.

☑ The **volume variance** represents the overhead not absorbed into the cost of production because of a difference between budgeted and actual production levels. It is based on the difference between budgeted output and actual output.

☑ The **efficiency variance** is a measure of the efficiency of working and is based on the difference between the actual hours worked and the hours that should have been worked (standard hours for actual output).

☑ The **capacity variance** looks at how well available capacity was used and is therefore based on the difference between the available capacity (budgeted hours) and the capacity actually used (actual hours).

☑ Material and labour variances can also be calculated using **graphs**.

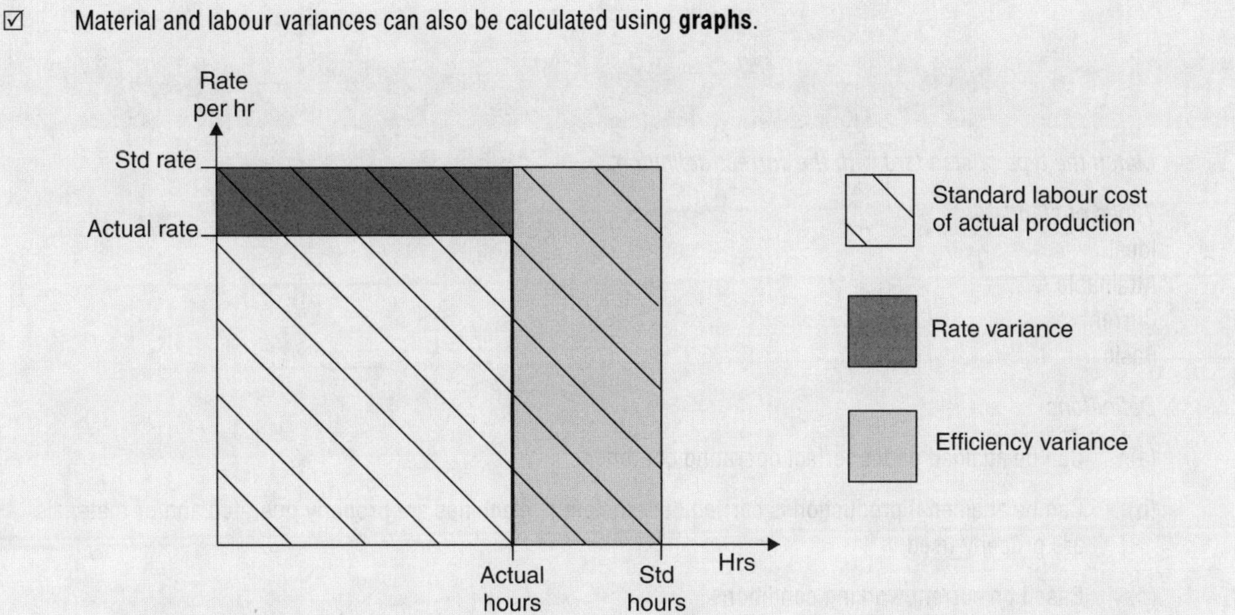

☑ A **reconciliation statement** provides a reconciliation between the standard cost of actual production and the actual cost of production using variances.

Quick quiz

1 *Match the type of standard with the correct definition.*

Types of standard
Ideal
Attainable
Current
Basic

Definitions

(a) Can be attained under perfect operating conditions

(b) Can be attained if production is carried out efficiently, machines are properly operated and/or materials are properly used

(c) Based on current working conditions

(d) Remains unchanged over the years and is used to show trends

2 *Fill in the blanks in the diagram with the names of variances.*

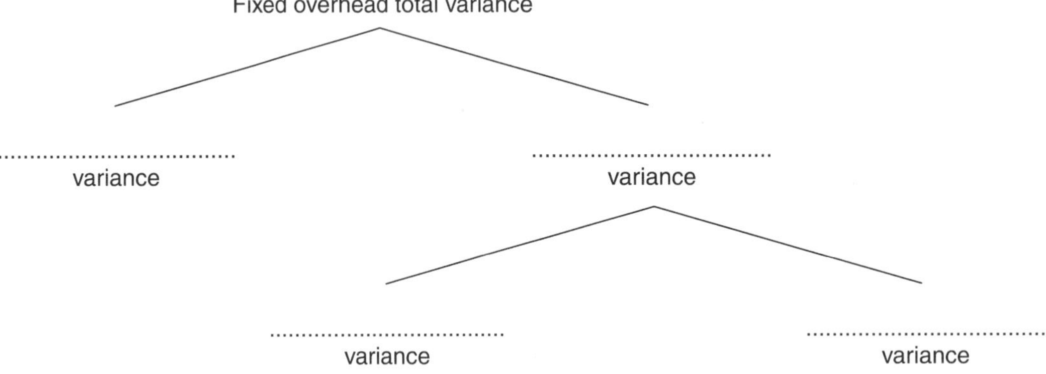

3 *Choose the appropriate word from those highlighted.*

Actual labour hours worked were higher than the budgeted labour hours for the period. The fixed overhead capacity variance will therefore be **adverse/favourable.**

4 Which of the following statements about the fixed overhead volume variance is true?

A It is the same whether marginal costing or absorption costing is used.
B It does not exist if absorption costing is used.
C It dos not exist if marginal costing is used.
D It is made up of an expenditure variance and an efficiency variance.

5 *Choose the correct words and symbol from those highlighted.*

Standard labour hours for actual output = **standard/actual** labour hours per unit ×/÷ **standard/actual** number of units

6 In the following diagrammatic presentation of the purchase and use in production of some material, what type of variances have arisen?

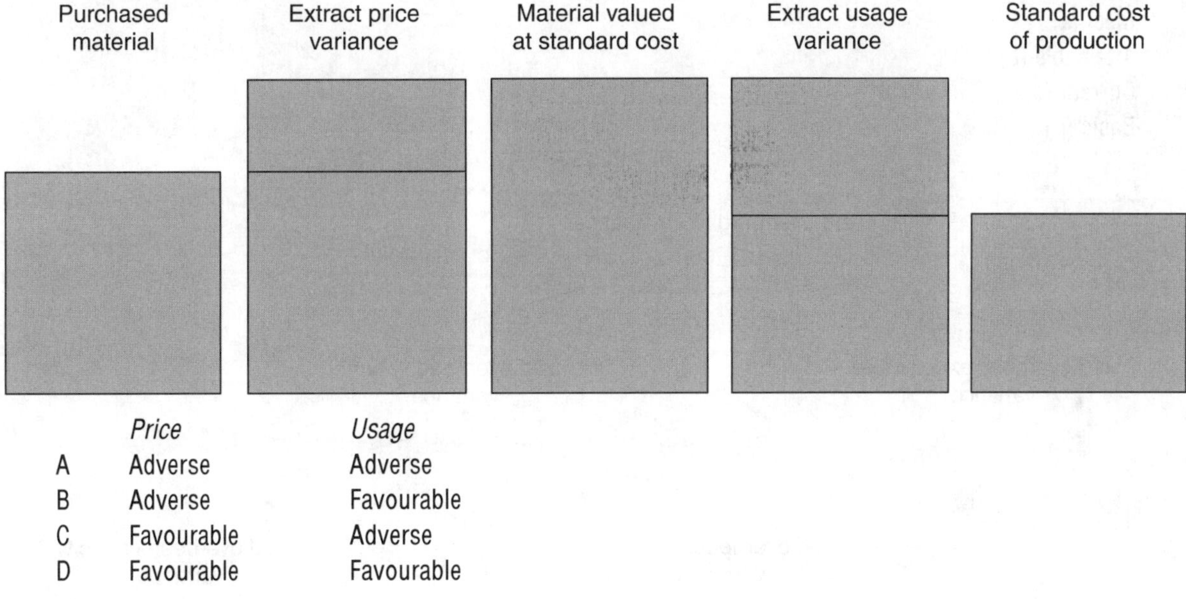

	Price	*Usage*
A	Adverse	Adverse
B	Adverse	Favourable
C	Favourable	Adverse
D	Favourable	Favourable

7 *Fill in the blanks.*

The difference between the labour hours that should have been worked to produce the actual production, and the hours that were worked, valued at the standard labour rate per hour, is the .... variance.

8 In the diagram below, what type of variances have arisen?

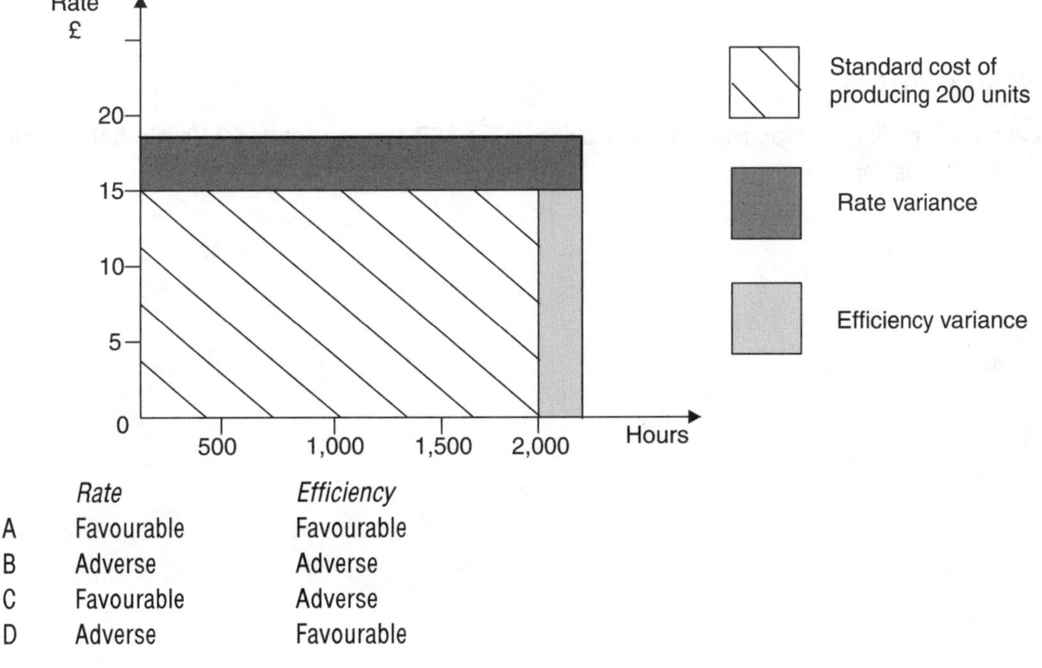

	Rate	*Efficiency*
A	Favourable	Favourable
B	Adverse	Adverse
C	Favourable	Adverse
D	Adverse	Favourable

Answers to quick quiz

1 Ideal (a)
Attainable (b)
Current (c)
Basic (d)

2

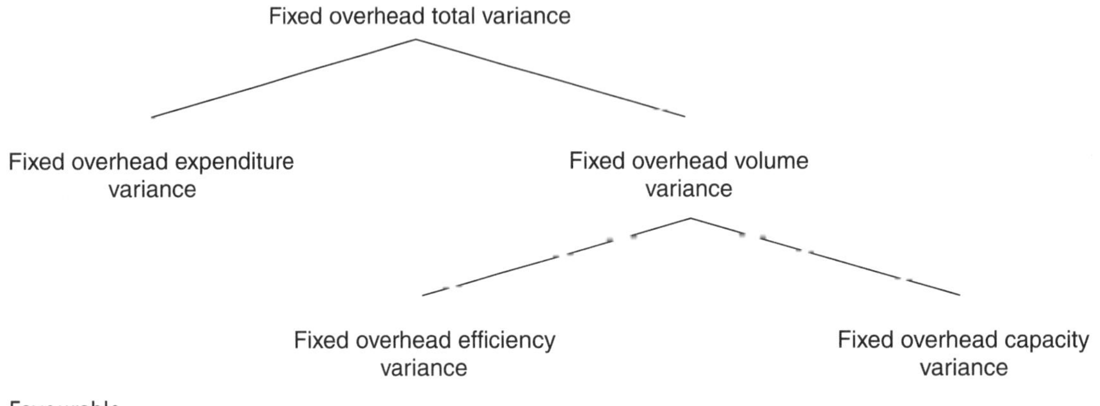

3 Favourable

4 C

5 Standard labour hours for actual output = standard labour hours per unit × actual number of units

6 C

7 Labour efficiency variance

8 B

ASSESSMENT KIT ACTIVITIES

See the box at the end of Chapter 7 for details of the activities in the BPP Assessment Kit for Units 8 & 9 which include topics covered in this chapter.

Activity checklist

This checklist shows which performance criteria, range statement or knowledge and understanding point is covered by each activity in this chapter. Tick off each activity as you complete it.

Activity		
6.1	☐	This activity deals with Unit 8 Knowledge & Understanding point (7): standard costing.
6.2	☐	This activity deals with Unit 8 Knowledge & Understanding point (7): standard costing.
6.3	☐	This activity deals with Unit 8 Knowledge & Understanding points (7): standard costing and (8): marginal and absorption costing.
6.4	☐	This activity deals with Unit 8 Knowledge & Understanding point (8): marginal and absorption costing.
6.5	☐	This activity deals with Unit 8 Knowledge & Understanding points (7): standard costing and (8): marginal and absorption costing.
6.6	☐	This activity deals with Unit 8 Knowledge & Understanding points (7): standard costing and (8): marginal and absorption costing.
6.7	☐	This activity deals with Performance Criteria 8.1D regarding the comparison of standard costs with actual costs and the analysis of any variances, and Range Statement 8.1: variance analysis (material price and usage variances).
6.8	☐	This activity deals with Unit 8 Knowledge & Understanding point (7): standard costing.
6.9	☐	This activity deals with Performance Criteria 8.1D regarding the comparison of standard costs with actual costs and the analysis of any variances, and Range Statement 8.1: variance analysis (labour rate and efficiency variances).
6.10	☐	This activity deals with Performance Criteria 8.1D regarding the comparison of standard costs with actual costs and the analysis of any variances, and Range Statement 8.1: variance analysis (labour rate and efficiency variances).
6.11	☐	This activity deals with Performance Criteria 8.1D regarding the comparison of standard costs with actual costs and the analysis of any variances, and Range Statement 8.1: variance analysis (material price and usage variances; labour rate and efficiency variances; fixed overhead expenditure, volume, capacity and efficiency variances).
6.12	☐	This activity deals with Unit 8 Knowledge & Understanding point (8): marginal and absorption costing.

Activity checklist (cont'd)

6.13	☐	This activity deals with Performance Criteria 8.1D regarding the comparison of standard costs with actual costs and the analysis of any variances, and Range Statement 8.1: variance analysis (labour rate and efficiency variances).
6.14	☐	This activity deals with Performance Criteria 8.1D regarding the comparison of standard costs with actual costs and the analysis of any variances, and Range Statement 8.1: variance analysis (material price and usage variances).
6.15	☐	This activity deals with Performance Criteria 8.1D regarding the comparison of standard costs with actual costs and the analysis of any variances, and Range Statement 8.1: variance analysis (material price and usage variances; labour rate and efficiency variances; fixed overhead expenditure, volume, capacity and efficiency variances).
6.16	☐	This activity deals with Performance Criteria 8.1D regarding the comparison of standard costs with actual costs and the analysis of any variances, and Range Statement 8.1: variance analysis (material price and usage variances; labour rate and efficiency variances; fixed overhead expenditure, volume, capacity and efficiency variances).
6.17	☐	This activity deals with Performance Criteria 8.1D regarding the comparison of standard costs with actual costs and the analysis of any variances, and Range Statement 8.1: variance analysis (material price and usage variances; labour rate and efficiency variances).
6.18	☐	This activity deals with Performance Criteria 8.1D regarding the comparison of standard costs with actual costs and the analysis of any variances, and Range Statement 8.1: variance analysis (material price and usage variances; labour rate and efficiency variances; fixed overhead expenditure, volume, capacity and efficiency variances).

chapter 7

Analysing variances

Contents

1 Introduction
2 Causes of variances
3 Investigation of variances
4 Management control action
5 Variance analysis reports
6 Subdivision of variances
7 The impact of price changes on reported variances
8 Spreadsheets

Performance criteria

8.1D Compare standard costs with actual costs and analyse any variances

Range statement

8.1 Variance analysis: material price and usage variances; labour rate and efficiency variances; fixed overhead expenditure, volume, capacity and efficiency variances; subdivision of variances

Knowledge and understanding

Unit 8 Accounting techniques

3 Basic statistical methods: index numbers

4 Use of relevant computer packages

Signpost

This chapter is relevant whether you are studying **Unit 8** or **Unit 9**. Spreadsheets, which are covered in Section 8, are an important area of knowledge and understanding for both units, and you need to be aware of variances for your study of flexible budgeting in Unit 9 (Chapter 10). You must therefore work through this chapter whichever unit you are studying.

1 Introduction

This chapter builds on what was covered in the previous chapter and looks at what must be done with the variances once they have been calculated. It therefore considers the stages of the control system model in Chapter 1 that are concerned with **analysing variances** and **deciding on appropriate control action**.

We will also study examples of the **more complex variance calculations** that might appear in exam tasks. These invariably involve the **subdivision of variances** and interpretation of resulting information.

Most of what is covered in this chapter relates to Part 3 of the typical exam task on standard costing. Look back to Chapter 6 Section 3.2.3 if you need reminding about this.

2 Causes of variances

2.1 Material price variances

An **adverse** price variance would suggest that the **managers responsible for buying decisions have paid too much for the materials**, and should be more careful in future. There are **reasons** why a large adverse or favourable price variance might occur, however, which are **outside the buying management's control**.

2.1.1 Inflation

This is discussed more fully later.

2.1.2 Seasonal variations in prices

If material prices fluctuate seasonally, the standard price might be an average price for the year as a whole, on the assumption that it is impractical to buy a whole year's supply in the cheap season and store it until needed. In such a situation, price variances should be favourable for purchases in the cheap season and adverse for purchases in the more expensive season.

2.1.3 Rush orders

If buying managers are asked to make an order for immediate delivery, they might have to forgo a bulk purchase discount, or pay more for the quick supply lead time. The responsibility for the resulting adverse price variance should therefore belong to whoever made the rush order necessary in the first place.

2.2 Materials usage variances

A materials usage variance indicates that the quantity of materials consumed was larger or smaller than standard. It could indicate that materials **wastage** was higher or lower than it should have been or that the quantity of **rejects** was above or below standard. Wastage costs money, and should be kept to a minimum.

The size of a materials usage variance, however, just like the size of a labour efficiency variance, **depends on the standard rate of usage** (or efficiency) and **whether the standard was attainable or ideal.**

2.3 Labour rate variances

You might think that the rate variance is something that operational managers can do little about, since rates of pay will be agreed at a senior level between the board of directors and trade union officials. A rate variance might be due to **unexpected overtime working** (with overtime paid at a premium rate), however, or **productivity bonuses** added on to basic rates. To some extent, these should be **controllable by operational managers.**

2.4 Labour efficiency variances

A standard time for labour to produce an item of work will normally take into account contingency allowances for down time and rest periods. In a production industry based on batch production or jobbing work, the standard time will include an allowance for setting up times and clearing up times for each batch or job finished.

An **adverse** labour efficiency variance might indicate **poor labour productivity** in a period, for which a badly-motivated workforce or weak supervision might be to blame, but here are some other causes of a variance.

- Excessively **high down times**, due to a serious machine break down, or a bottleneck in production which left many of the workforce idle and waiting for work.
- **Shorter batch runs** than expected, which increase the amount of setting up time and cleaning up time between batches, when no physical output is being produced.

2.5 Overhead variances

Variances are supposed to provide management with control information. For example, an adverse material price variance of £100 tells management that the material used cost £100 more than it should have cost. But what about information provided by overhead variances? What control information is provided by an adverse fixed overhead capacity variance of £450 or a favourable fixed overhead efficiency variance of £690? Why is the information not as clear or easy to understand as that provided by labour and material variances?

2.5.1 Fixed overhead volume variance

Unlike material and labour variances, or the fixed overhead expenditure variance, the fixed overhead volume variance and its sub-divisions are **not a true reflection of extra or lower cash spending** by an organisation. This is because the variances are valued in terms of overhead absorption rates; the estimates used in the calculation of these rates are often quite arbitrary but it is these absorption rates which determine the values assigned to the overhead variances.

With the expenditure variance, the fixed overhead volume variance shows the under-absorbed or over-absorbed fixed overhead. But **under/over absorption is simply a book balancing exercise** caused by using absorption costing, and the level of under-/over-absorbed overhead depends on the accuracy of the original estimates used in calculating the absorption rates. Under/over absorption is not control information, it is simply a figure used to balance the books.

The non-monetary values of the fixed overhead efficiency and capacity variances are of **some relevance for control, however**. They **provide a measure of the difference between budgeted production volume and actual production volume,** and management should obviously be interested in whether budgeted output was achieved, and if not, why not.

The fixed overhead volume variance can therefore be important; it is only the monetary value given to the variance that can be misleading to managers.

2.5.2 Fixed overhead expenditure variance

This fixed overhead variance probably provides the most useful management information as the size of the variance can be said to be controllable. It is made up of a price component and a usage component. It can therefore vary if there are changes in charges (for example salary increases) or if quantities changes (for example if more staff are taken on).

For such variances **to have any practical value as a control measure, the variances for each cost centre need to be calculated, and reported to the managers responsible.**

2.6 A summary

There are many possible reasons for variances arising, including efficiencies and inefficiencies of operations, errors in standard setting and changes in exchange rates. We have provided a brief summary of causes of variances below. This is not an exhaustive list and in an exam you should review the scenario data given and use your imagination and common sense to suggest possible reasons for variances.

ATTENTION!

There is no need to memorise a long list of possible reasons for variances – the assessor has stated that credit is rarely given for such regurgitation. Instead, using the information we have provided here in this chapter as a springboard for ideas, **search the task data for possible causes of variances**. This will ensure that your answers are consistent with task data.

In the Unit 8 December 2000 exam, for example, an adverse labour efficiency variance was entirely due to ferries taking longer to undertake a sea crossing as a result of adverse weather conditions. Unfortunately some candidates searched their memorised lists and suggested that employees had misused their time. In the same exam, inappropriate reasons provided for an adverse fuel (or material) usage variance included pilferage and poor quality materials.

Variance	Favourable	Adverse
Material price	Unforeseen discounts received Greater care in purchasing Change in material standard	Price increase Careless purchasing Change in material standard
Material usage	Material used of higher quality than standard More effective use made of material Errors in allocating material to jobs	Defective material Excessive waste Theft Stricter quality control Errors in allocating material to jobs
Labour rate	Use of workers at a rate of pay lower than standard	Wage rate increase
Labour efficiency	Output produced more quickly than expected because of work motivation, better quality of equipment or materials Errors in allocating time to jobs	Lost time in excess of standard allowed Output lower than standard because of lack of training, sub-standard material etc Errors in allocating time to jobs
Overhead expenditure	Savings in costs incurred More economical use of services	Increase in cost of services Excessive use of services Change in type of services
Overhead volume	Production or level of activity greater than budgeted	Production or level of activity less than budgeted

Activity 7.1

Abacus Ltd's usual supplier of material ND7, Counter Ltd, is having distribution difficulties. The purchasing department have located another supplier of material ND7 (Bean Ltd) but the price per litre will be slightly higher than that charged by Counter Ltd. What type of variance is likely to occur as a result of using Bean Ltd to supply material ND7?

2.7 Interrelationships between variances

Individual variances should not be looked at in isolation. One variance might be interrelated with another, and much of it might have occurred only because the other variance occurred too. **When two variances are interdependent (interrelated) one will usually be adverse and the other favourable**. Here are some examples.

Interrelated variances	Explanation
Materials price and materials usage	If cheaper materials are purchased in order to obtain a favourable price variance, materials wastage might be higher and an adverse usage variance may occur. If the cheaper material is more difficult to handle, there might be an adverse labour efficiency variance too. If more expensive material is purchased, however, the price variance will be adverse but the usage variance might be favourable if the material is easier to use or a higher quality.
Labour rate and labour efficiency/ material usage	If employees are paid higher rates for experience and skill, using a highly skilled team might lead to an adverse rate variance and a favourable efficiency variance and possibly a favourable material usage variance (experienced staff are less likely to waste material, for example). In contrast, a favourable rate variance might indicate a larger-than-expected proportion of inexperienced workers, which could result in an adverse labour efficiency variance, and perhaps poor materials handling and high rates of rejects and hence an adverse materials usage variance.
Fixed overhead efficiency variance and other variances	If overheads are absorbed on the basis of labour hours, the fixed overhead efficiency variance will be the same, in hours, as the labour efficiency variance. Any interrelationships between other variances and the labour efficiency variance will therefore apply equally to the fixed overhead efficiency variance.

Activity 7.2

Look back at Activity 7.1. What other variances could occur given that a higher price is being charged by Bean Ltd for material ND7?

3 Investigation of variances

TOPIC LINK

We touched on these ideas back in Chapter 1.

Every variance is potentially worthy of investigation. It might seem unnecessary to investigate favourable variances, since they improve profitability and should therefore be encouraged. **Favourable variances** may be just as **worthy of investigation** as adverse variances, however.

- Favourable variances in one area may cause adverse variances in another area.
- Unrealistic standard costs causing favourable variances need to be identified so that planning and control will be improved in future.
- The variance may be caused by data recording errors which means that management is working with inaccurate information.

3.1 Factors to consider before investigation

Here are some factors management should consider before deciding whether or not to investigate the reasons for the occurrence of a particular variance.

3.1.1 Materiality

A standard cost is really only an **average** expected cost, so **small variations** in a single period between actual and standard are bound to occur and are unlikely to be significant. Obtaining an 'explanation' of the reasons why they occurred is likely to be time-consuming and irritating for the manager concerned. The explanation will often be 'chance', which is not, in any case, particularly helpful. For such variations **further investigation is not worthwhile** since such variances are not controllable.

3.1.2 Controllability

If there is a general worldwide price increase in the price of an important raw material there is nothing that can be done internally to control the effect of this. If a central decision is made to award all employees a 10% increase in salary, staff costs in division A will increase by this amount and the variance is not controllable by division A's manager. **Uncontrollable variances call for a change in the standard, not an investigation into the past.**

3.1.3 Variance trend

Although small variations in a single period are unlikely to be significant, small variations that occur consistently may need more attention. Variance trend is probably more important than a single set of variances for one accounting period. The trend **provides an indication of whether the variance is fluctuating within acceptable control limits or becoming out of control.**

- If, say, an efficiency variance is £1,000 adverse in month 1, the obvious conclusion is that there is a problem and that corrective action must be taken. This may be correct, but what if the same variance is £1,000 adverse every month? The *trend* indicates that the standard has been wrongly set.
- Suppose that the same variance is £1,000 adverse for each of the first six months of the year but that production has steadily fallen from 100 units in month 1 to 65 units by month 6. The variance trend in absolute terms is constant, but relative to the number of units produced, efficiency has got steadily worse.

Individual variances should therefore not be looked at in isolation; variances should be scrutinised for a number of successive periods if their full significance is to be appreciated.

4 Management control action

The **action which management may take in response to a variance will depend on the reason why the variance occurred.**

ATTENTION!

You must refer to the scenario details if asked to recommend appropriate management action. The assessor has stated that there will often be clues within the data. In the June 1997 exam, for example, a special order agreed at *short notice* caused a number of variances. So appropriate action might have been to meet special orders at short notice only if the extra costs incurred are recovered by charging a higher sales price.

We looked at appropriate management action in response to reported variances in Chapter 1, so attempt the following activity to check that you can remember the issues covered.

Activity 7.3

Suggest appropriate management control action when variances are due to the following.

(a) Measurement errors
(b) Out of date standards
(c) Efficient or inefficient operations
(d) Random or chance fluctuations

Activity 7.4

Prady Pots Ltd operates a standard marginal costing system. It makes a single product, a large decorative flower pot, using a particular type of clay. Standard costs relating to the flower pot have been calculated as follows.

Standard cost schedule

	£ per unit
Direct material, 10 kg @ £15 per kg	150
Direct labour, 5 hours @ £9 per hour	45
	195

During the week ending 9 November Year 1, 1,000 pots were produced. The relevant information regarding actual performance is as follows.

Direct material. 4,000 kg were in opening stock. 10,000 kg were purchased during the week, the actual cost being £144,000. 3,000 kg were in closing stock. Stocks of the material are valued at the standard price of £15 per kg.

Direct labour. 5,200 hours were worked during the week, total wages being £48,360.

A purchasing manger has been hired recently and has used an alternative supplier of the material, claiming that the previous holder of the position has been paying too high a price per kg.

High rates of absenteeism due to sickness were reported among the workforce during the week and temporary workers had to be employed.

Tasks

(a) Compute the following cost variances for the week ending 9 November Year 1.

  (i) Variable production cost variance
  (ii) Direct wages cost variance, also analysed into rate and efficiency variances
  (iii) Direct material cost variance, also analysed into price and usage variances

(b) Prepare a commentary on the variances for the production manager, indicating any additional information which might prove useful in explaining them.

5 Variance analysis reports

Cast your mind back to the framework of typical variance analysis tasks described in the previous chapter. The **third part** usually requires you to provide a **report or memo** in which you **detail additional analysis or interpretation**. The exact requirements will vary from exam to exam. This section provides you with an example of such a report and shows you how to set out reasons for the variances, possible management action and other points of interpretation.

Remember that we provided more general information about report writing back in Chapter 4.

ATTENTION!

In particular, the assessor has highlighted **poor presentation** of data as a **reason** why some candidates are **assessed as not yet competent.** Specific areas of weakness are as follows.

- Lack of headings
- Single paragraphs in excess of one page
- Failure to identify/relate answers to specific parts of tasks
- No workings or unclear workings

As well as studying the content of our answers in the exam Kit, take a look at how we have set them out. Notice how we have used headings, emboldening (you can underline) and short paragraphs. Our answers are clearly related to particular tasks and we have provided workings, referenced to answers where necessary.

Example: variance reports

Searcher Ltd, a manufacturing firm, operates a standard marginal costing system. It makes a single product, the SE, using a single raw material, EKS. Standard costs relating to the SE have been calculated as follows.

Standard cost schedule – SE

	£ per unit
Direct material EKS, 11 kg at £20 per kg	220
Direct labour, 7 hours at £6 per hour	42
	262

Budgeted fixed overheads per control period are £25,000.

During control period 13, although budgeted production was 950 units, 1,000 units were produced. Other information regarding actual performance during control period 13 is as follows.

Direct material EKS. 10,000 kg were purchased during the period, actual cost being £210,000. There were no opening or closing stocks of raw material EKS.

Direct labour. 6,800 hours were worked during the period, total wages being £42,840.

Fixed overheads. The actual cost for the period was £30,000.

Task

Produce a report for management which includes a statement reconciling budgeted and actual costs and which explains the key features of the variances and makes recommendations for management action.

Solution

REPORT

To: Managers of Searcher Ltd
From: A Student
Date: 13 November Year 7
Subject: **Variance Report – control period 13**

This report contains a statement showing a reconciliation of budgeted and actual costs for control period 13. Key features of the statement are explained and recommendations for management action are provided.

The calculation of the reconciliation statement variances are contained in the appendix to this report.

Reconciliation statement for control period 13

	£ (F)	£ (A)	£
Standard variable cost of production (1,000 units × £262)			262,000
Variances			
Direct labour rate		2,040	
Direct labour efficiency	1,200		
Direct material price		10,000	
Direct material usage	20,000		
	21,200	12,040	9,160 (F)
Actual variable cost of production			252,840
Budgeted fixed overhead	25,000		
Expenditure variance	5,000 (A)		
Actual fixed overhead			30,000
Actual cost of production			282,840

Explanation of variances and recommendations for management action

Direct labour rate variance. An adverse variance arises because the labour force were paid an average of (£42,840/6,800) = £6.30 per hour instead of the standard cost of £6 per hour. If this is a new agreed rate the standard should be revised. It may, however, be due to a short-term need to recruit temporary labour at rates more expensive than standard or to overtime working or bonus payments. The production manager and/or the personnel department should be contacted for further information.

Direct labour efficiency variance. A favourable variance of £1,200 has arisen because the labour force took 200 hours less to produce 1,000 units than the standard allowance. The production manager should be asked to explain the variance. It may be linked to the adverse labour rate variance and the use of more skilled, and hence more expensive labour, who are able to work more efficiently.

Material price variance. Materials were purchased for £21.00 per kg in the period (a price £1.00 more than standard) giving rise to an adverse price variance of £10,000. The purchasing manager should be asked to explain why the more expensive materials were purchased. To judge from the usage variance, the additional expense may have resulted in higher quality materials.

Material usage variance. 1,000 kgs less than standard were used to make 1,000 units. This seems most likely to be because more expensive, higher quality materials were purchased, probably resulting in less waste than standard. It is possible that the need for less rectification work due to higher quality materials also explains why the labour force was more efficient than standard.

Fixed overhead variance. Fixed overheads in the period were £30,000, representing an increase of 20% over the budgeted figures of £25,000. A breakdown of the total figure is needed before control action can be recommended.

Appendix

Calculation of variances

	£
6,800 hours should cost (× £6)	40,800
but did cost	42,840
Direct labour rate variance	2,040 (A)

1,000 units should take (× 7 hours)	7,000 hrs
but did take	6,800 hrs
Direct labour efficiency variance in hrs	200 hrs (F)
× standard rate per hour	× £6
Direct labour efficiency variance in £	£1,200 (F)

	£
10,000 kg should cost (× £20)	200,000
but did cost	210,000
Direct materials price variance	10,000 (A)

1,000 units should use (× 11 kgs)	11,000 kgs
but did use	10,000 kgs
Direct materials usage variance in kgs	1,000 kgs (F)
× standard cost per kg	× £20
Direct materials usage variance in £	£20,000 (F)

	£
Budgeted fixed overhead expenditure	25,000
Actual fixed overhead expenditure	30,000
Fixed overhead variance	5,000 (A)

ATTENTION!

At Technician/NVQ and SVQ Level 4 you need to do more than acquire knowledge and show evidence of comprehension. You must be able to **apply** your knowledge, **analyse** information and **evaluate** results. The activities which follow provide you with an opportunity of practising your application, analysis and evaluation skills. Spend about 70 minutes on Activity 7.5 and 25 minutes on Activity 7.6.

Activity 7.5

Linney Limited uses a standard costing system which produces monthly control statements to monitor and control costs. One of its products is product T/5. To manufacture product T/5, a perishable, high quality raw material is carefully weighed by direct employees. Some wastage and quality control rejects occur at this stage. The employees then compress the material to change its shape and create product T/5. All direct employees are paid a basic hourly rate appropriate to their individual skill level, and a bonus scheme is in operation. Bonuses are paid according to the daily rate of output achieved by each individual.

A standard allowance for all of the above operational factors is included in the standard cost of product T/5. Standard cost data for one unit of product T/5 is as follows.

		Standard cost £ per unit
Direct material	4.5 kg × £4.90 per kg	22.05
Direct labour	10.3 hours × £3.50 per hour	36.05
Standard direct cost		58.10

During November, the following costs were incurred producing 400 units of product T/5.

		Actual costs
		£
Direct material	2,100 kg	9,660
Direct labour	4,000 hours	16,000
Actual direct cost		25,660

Tasks

(a) Calculate the following direct cost variances for product T/5 for November.

- (i) Direct material price
- (ii) Direct material usage
- (iii) Direct labour rate
- (iv) Direct labour efficiency

(b) Present the variances in a statement which reconciles the total standard direct cost of production with the actual direct cost for product T/5 in November.

(c) The production manager receives a copy of the standard costing control statement for product T/5 every month. However, he has recently confessed to you that he does not really have a clear understanding of the meaning of the variances. He has also been baffled by the following statement made by the finance director at a recent meeting of senior managers.

'Assigning responsibility for variances can be complicated if the variances are interdependent, for example if an adverse variance in one part of the organisation is caused by a favourable variance elsewhere.'

As assistant accountant for Linney Limited, you are asked to write a memo to the production manager which explains the following.

- (i) The meaning of each of the direct cost variances calculated for product T/5.
- (ii) Two possible causes of each of the variances which you have calculated for product T/5.
- (iii) Two examples of interdependence which may be present in the variances which you have calculated. Explain clearly why the variances may be interdependent, so that the manager can better understand the meaning of the finance director's statement.

(d) The production manager has now approached you for further explanations concerning the standard costing control system. He is particularly interested in understanding how the standard price is set per kg of material used. Write a second memo to the production manager, explaining the following.

- (i) The information that would be needed to determine the standard price per kg of the material used
- (ii) The possible sources from which this information might be obtained

Activity 7.6

As the management accountant of the Hamilton Manufacturing Co Ltd you have prepared the following variance report for the general manager.

VARIANCE REPORT: SEPTEMBER YEAR 5

	Variance (Adverse)	*Variance (Favourable)*	*Total variance*
	£	£	£
Material:			–2,000
usage	5,500		
price		3,500	
Labour:			–1,500
efficiency	3,000		
rate		1,500	
Fixed overhead:			–500
expenditure		4,500	
efficiency	2,000		
capacity	3,000		

Actual costs for September Year 5 were as follows.

	£
Materials	100,000
Labour	80,000
Fixed overheads	75,000
Total	255,000

The general manager tells you that he is quite satisfied with this result because the total adverse variance of £4,000 is only 1.57% of total costs.

Task

Write a brief report to the General Manager giving *your own* interpretation of the month's results.

6 Subdivision of variances

The assessor tends to get you to do some slightly **more complex variance calculations** in the **third part** of variance analysis tasks. And often you need to incorporate these calculations into a **report**.

Quite often, these more complex calculations involve splitting a variance into two parts.

- **One part** will be caused by a **situation that is known to exist**. This part of the variance is therefore **predictable** to an extent. Examples of predictable causes include **inflation** and **currency fluctuations**.
- The **other part** will be caused by **unknown unpredictable factors.**

The price variance due to other factors is shown by ■ on th

- Price variance due to inflation + price variance

  ∴ Price variance due to other factor

- 200 kgs should have c
  bu

Ac

Activi

By now you should not need to use graphs to subdivide variances, so the remainder of this section adopts our normal approach to variance analysis. Refer back to our two graphs if you get confused, however.

Activity 7.7

During control period 5, 300 labour hours costing £7,500 were worked in production department 1 at Sutton Ltd. An index of labour rates stood at 75 when the standard labour rate of £20 per hour was set in 20X0. It now stands at 105.

Task

Calculate the following.

(a) The rate variance due to updating the standard
(b) The rate variance due to other reasons
(c) The total rate variance

Activity 7.8

Holloway Ltd uses a particular metal in its factory to produce one of its products. The standard cost per kg of the metal is £10. During Year 7, 2,000 kgs were purchased at a cost of £18,000. The index of material prices stood at 350.0 when the standard was set but at 315.81 when the material was purchased.

Task

Subdivide the material price variance arising on the purchase of the metal into the part due to the change in the index and the part arising for other reasons.

Activity 7.9

Pitcher Ltd contracted to buy a quantity of material for $10 per metre when the rate of exchange between the UK pound and the US dollar was $1.60. In April 20X1, when the exchange rate was $1.68, the company paid for 1,600 metres.

Task

Calculate the price variance due to exchange rate movements.

You will not always have to use indices when subdividing variances, however. You might have to subdivide a material usage variance into that part due to the efficiency of the labour force and that part due to other reasons. Or you might have to subdivide a material price variance into the part due to a contract price and the part due to other reasons.

The approach is very similar to the one we looked at above, when we subdivided variances using indices. Take a look through the following example.

Example: subdividing variances

Malvern Ltd produces product N. Budgeted production for quarter 3 was 10,000 units but actual production was 12,000 units because an additional 2,000 units were manufactured to meet a special order agreed at short notice by Malvern Ltd's marketing manager.

Each unit of product N requires 5 kgs of material at a price of £10 per kg. During quarter 3, 70,000 kgs of material were used, costing £740,000.

The normal supplier of the material was unable to meet the extra demand for the special order and so additional materials had to be acquired from another supplier at a price per kg of £10.50. This extra material was not up to the normal specification and so 20% of it had to be scrapped *prior* to being issued to production.

An index measuring material prices stood at 197.6 for quarter 3 but at 190.0 when the material price standard was set.

Tasks

(a) Calculate the amount of the material price variance which arose from producing the special order.

(b) Estimate the revised standard price for materials based on the change in the material price index.

(c) For the 10,000 units of normal production, estimate how much of the price variance was caused by the general change in prices.

(d) Specify how much of the total material price variance is controllable by Malvern Ltd's management, and how much is outside their control.

Solution

(a) Since 20% of the special purchase was scrapped *prior* to being issued to production, only 80% of the material purchased was issued to production (ie 80% × purchase quantity = production quantity). Therefore purchase quantity = production quantity/80% = purchase quantity/0.8, and so the amount of material purchased to make the 2,000 units = (2,000 × 5 kgs)/0.8 = 12,500 kgs.

	£
12,500 kgs should have cost (× £10)	125,000
but did cost (× £10.50)	131,250
Material price variance due to special order	6,250 (A)

(b) Revised standard price = £10 × 197.6/190.0 = £10.40

(c)

Total material used for 12,000 units	70,000 kgs
Less: material used for special order	12,500 kgs
	57,500 kgs
× price increase (£(10.40 – 10.00))	× £0.40
	£23,000 (A)

(d)

	£
Total variance (see working)	40,000
Variance due to inflation	(23,000)
Variance due to special order	(6,250)
Variance controllable by management	10,750

Working

	£
70,000 kgs should have cost (× £10)	700,000
but did cost	740,000
Variance	40,000 (A)

Activity 7.10

PopCo Ltd produces a fizzy drink, the 'secret ingredient' of which is a liquid called Zap. The standard price per litre of Zap is £12. There is a world shortage of Zap and so the purchasing manager has entered into a 12-month contract with a supplier in order to guarantee supplies. The contract price per litre is £13.

During control period 7, PopCo Ltd produced 750 crates of the drink using 1,725 litres of Zap. If it were not for the contract, this Zap would have had to be purchased at the market price of £16.20 per litre.

Task

Calculate the part of the material price variance due to the contract (and the purchasing manager's efficiency) and the part due to the standard being out of date.

7 The impact of price changes on reported variances

Standard costs are usually based on either expected average price levels for the period in question (normally one year) or current price levels. If there is no inflation they should be the same but problems arise when there is price or wage rate inflation.

Suppose that a material currently costs £10 per kilogram but during the course of the next twelve months it is expected to go up in price by 20% to £12 per kilogram. What standard price should be selected?

- The **current** price of £10 per kilogram
- The **average expected** price for the year, which might be, for example, £11 per kilogram

Either would be possible but neither would be entirely satisfactory.

If expected average price levels are applied, actual prices at the beginning of the year will be below standard prices, so that favourable price variances will be reported in the first few control periods (months) of the year. Eventually, as inflation pushes up actual prices to higher than standard prices, adverse price variances will be reported. The changeover from favourable to adverse variances should occur around the middle of the year. **Average price levels might therefore be used for material costs in a period of fairly high inflation.**

If the **standard cost is based on current price levels**, the effect of inflation on actual prices will be to create **ever-increasing adverse price variances** as inflation progresses over time. The **use** of current price levels **might be prudent** for the certain items, however.

- **Labour rates, where management is uncertain about the size of future pay settlements** during the year. When new wages and salary levels are agreed, the size of the expected monthly labour rate variance can be measured (or alternatively, the standard cost could be revised) so that management is made aware of how much of the total rate variance is due to the pay settlements and how much to other causes.

- **Materials prices in a period of fairly low inflation**. The adverse price variances which occur due to inflation ought to remain within a tolerance limit which is fairly close to the standard price; otherwise they might warrant investigation.

Standard costing is very difficult in times of inflation but it is still worthwhile.

- Usage and efficiency variances will still be meaningful.
- Inflation is measurable: there is no reason why its effects cannot be removed from the variances reported. In fact, candidates have been asked to do this in exams (see Section 6).
- Standard costs can be revised so long as this is not done too frequently.

8 Spreadsheets

Variance analysis is often performed using spreadsheets. You should be able to apply the spreadsheet skills covered in other BPP Texts/Kits (eg Unit 4 and Unit 7) to variance analysis. You should therefore be competent in the use of basic spreadsheet functions and **formulae**.

8.1 Spreadsheet formulae

A spreadsheet cell may contain text, a value, or a formula.

(a) **Text**. A text cell usually contains **words**. Numbers that do not represent numeric values for calculation purposes (eg a Part Number) may be entered in a way that tells the spreadsheet package (such as Excel) to treat the cell contents as text. To do this, enter an apostrophe before the number eg '451.

(b) **Values**. A value is a **number** that can be used in a calculation.

(c) **Formulae**. A formula **refers to other cells** in the spreadsheet, and performs some sort of computation with them. For example, if cell C1 contains the formula =A1–B1, cell C1 will display the result of the calculation subtracting the contents of cell B1 from the contents of cell A1. In Excel, a formula always begins with an equals sign: = . There are a wide range of formulae and function available.

Formulae in Microsoft Excel follow a specific syntax (how the formula is written) that includes an equal sign (=) followed by the elements to be calculated (the operands) and the calculation operators. Each operand can be a value that does not change (a constant value), a cell or range reference, a label, a name, or a worksheet function.

Formulae can be used to perform a variety of calculations. Here are some examples.

(a) =C4*5. This formula **multiplies** the value in C4 by 5. The result will appear in the cell holding the formula.

(b) =C4*B10. This **multiplies** the value in C4 by the value in B10.

(c) =C4/E5. This **divides** the value in C4 by the value in E5. (* means multiply and / means divide by.)

(d) =C4*B10–D1. This **multiplies** the value in C4 by that in B10 and then subtracts the value in D1 from the result. Note that generally Excel will perform multiplication and division before addition or subtraction. If in any doubt, use brackets (parentheses): =(C4*B10)–D1.

(e) =C4*117.5%. This **adds** 17.5% to the value in C4. It could be used to calculate a price including 17.5% VAT.

(f) =(C4+C5+C6)/3. Note that the **brackets** mean Excel would perform the addition first. Without the brackets, Excel would first divide the value in C6 by 3 and then add the result to the total of the values in C4 and C5.

(g) = 2^2 gives you 2 **to the power** of 2, in other words 2^2 (or 2 × 2). Likewise = 2^3 gives you 2 cubed (2 × 2 × 2) and so on.

(h) = 4^ (1/2) gives you the **square root** of 4. Likewise 27^(1/3) gives you the cube root of 27 and so on.

Excel calculates a formula from left to right, starting with the equals. You can control how the calculation is performed by changing the syntax of the formula. For example, the formula =5+2*3 gives a result of 11 because Excel calculates multiplication before addition. Excel would multiply 2 by 3 (resulting in 6) and would then add 5.

You may use parentheses to change the order of operations. For example =(5+2)*3 would result in Excel firstly adding the 5 and 2 together, then multiplying that result by 3 to give 21.

Activity 7.11

A spreadsheet has been set up as shown below. The spreadsheet calculates the difference between actual sales and budgeted sales, and expresses the difference as a percentage.

	A	B	C	D	E	F
1	*Sales team comparison of actual against budget sales*					
2	Name	Sales (Budget)	Sales (Actual)	Difference	% of budget	
3		£	£	£	£	
4	Northington	275,000	284,000	9,000	3.27	
5	Souther	200,000	193,000	(7,000)	(3.50)	
6	Weston	10,000	12,000	2,000	20.00	
7	Easterman	153,000	152,000	(1,000)	(0.65)	
8						
9	Total	638,000	641,000	3,000	0.47	
10						

Task

Give a suitable formula for each of the following cells.

(a) Cell D4
(b) Cell E6
(c) Cell E9

ATTENTION!

If you require practice in spreadsheet construction and use, practical, hands-on examples are available in the BPP Publication *Excel Exercises for Technician*. The book is accompanied by a CD containing Excel spreadsheets.

Note that *Excel Exercises for Technician* assumes you already have basic Excel skills (to AAT Foundation Level).

Key learning points

- ☑ **Variances** can be caused by a wide range of factors including the use of higher quality material (causing a favourable material usage variance) or a wage rate increase (causing an adverse material rate variance). In an exam, you should review the scenario data provided and use your knowledge, imagination and common sense to suggest possible reasons for variances.
- ☑ The control information provided by **fixed overhead variances** is not as clear or easily understandable as that provided by material and labour variances.
- ☑ Two variances are **interdependent** (interrelated) if much of one occurred because the other occurred. When two variances are interdependent, one will usually be adverse and one favourable.
- ☑ **Materiality**, **controllability** and **variance trend** should be considered before a decision about whether or not to investigate a variance is taken.
- ☑ **Management action** required in response to a reported variance will depend on the reason why the variance occurred.
- ☑ Remember to adopt the features of **good report writing**.
- ☑ The assessor could well ask you to **subdivide** a **variance** into two parts, perhaps using **indices**.
  - One part will be caused by a situation that is known to exist and is therefore predictable to an extent (eg inflation).
  - The other part will be caused by unknown, unpredictable factors. It is this part upon which management will wish to concentrate.
- ☑ In a period of **inflation**, if expected average price levels are used in the standard cost, favourable price variances will be reported at the beginning of the control period and adverse price variances at the end. If the standard cost is based on current price levels, the effect of inflation on actual prices will be to create ever-increasing adverse price variances as inflation progresses over time.
- ☑ Spreadsheets may be used to perform variance analysis. Ensure you are familiar with spreadsheet formulae.

Quick quiz

1 Favourable variances are never worthy of investigation. *True or false?*

2 Which of the following is not a reason why actual and standard performance might differ?

A Measurement errors
B Realistic standards
C Efficient or inefficient operations
D Random or chance fluctuations

3 *Match the following causes of variances to the appropriate variance*

Variances	Causes
(a) Favourable labour efficiency (b) Adverse material price (c) Adverse fixed overhead volume	(1) Inexperienced staff in the purchasing department (2) Materials of higher quality than standard (3) Production difficulties (4) Strike (5) Poor machine maintenance

4 *Match the two pairs of interrelated variances*

(a) Favourable labour rate
(b) Adverse materials usage
(c) Favourable fixed overhead expenditure
(d) Adverse materials price
(e) Favourable materials usage

5 *Fill in the blanks.*

Before management decide whether or not to investigate the reasons for the occurrence of a particular variance, they should consider three factors: ...., ... and ....

6 *Choose the correct words from those highlighted.*

The standard price of a material is to be updated following a change in a material price index. The material price variance caused by inflation is calculated as the difference between the cost of actual purchases at the **original/revised** standard price and the cost of **standard/actual** purchases at the revised **standard/actual** price.

Answers to quick quiz

1 False

2 B

3 (a) (2)
(b) (1), (2)
(c) (3), (4) or (5)

4 (a) and (b)
(d) and (e)

5 materiality, controllability and variance trend

6 It is calculated as the difference between the cost of actual purchases at the original standard price and the cost of actual purchases at the revised standard price.

ASSESSMENT KIT ACTIVITIES

The following activities in the BPP Assessment Kit for Units 8 and 9 include topics covered both in this chapter and Chapter 6.

Activities 12 to 21
Lecturers' practice activities 7 to 11

Activity checklist

This checklist shows which performance criteria, range statement or knowledge and understanding point is covered by each activity in this chapter. Tick off each activity as you complete it.

Activity		
7.1	☐	This activity deals with Performance Criteria 8.1D regarding the comparison of standard costs with actual costs and the analysis of any variances and Range Statement 8.1: variance analysis (material price and usage variances).
7.2	☐	This activity deals with Performance Criteria 8.1D regarding the comparison of standard costs with actual costs and the analysis of any variances and Range Statement 8.1: variance analysis (material price and usage variances).
7.3	☐	This activity deals with Performance Criteria 8.1D regarding the analysis of variances.
7.4	☐	This activity deals with Performance Criteria 8.1D regarding the comparison of standard costs with actual costs and the analysis of any variances and Range Statement 8.1: variance analysis (material price and usage variances; labour rate and efficiency variances).
7.5	☐	This activity deals with Performance Criteria 8.1D regarding the comparison of standard costs with actual costs and the analysis of any variances and Range Statement 8.1: variance analysis (material price and usage variances; labour rate and efficiency variances; fixed overhead variances).
7.6	☐	This activity deals with Performance Criteria 8.1D regarding the analysis of any variances and Range Statement 8.1: variance analysis (material price and usage variances; labour rate and efficiency variances; fixed overhead variances).
7.7	☐	This activity deals with Performance Criteria 8.1D regarding the comparison of standard costs with actual costs and the analysis of any variances, Range Statement 8.1: variance analysis (labour rate and efficiency variances), and Unit 8 Knowledge & Understanding point (3): basic statistical methods (index numbers).
7.8	☐	This activity deals with Performance Criteria 8.1D regarding the comparison of standard costs with actual costs and the analysis of any variances, Range Statement 8.1: variance analysis (material price and usage variances) and Unit 8 Knowledge & Understanding point (3): basic statistical methods (index numbers).
7.9	☐	This activity deals with Performance Criteria 8.1D regarding the comparison of standard costs with actual costs and the analysis of any variances, Range Statement 8.1: variance analysis (material price and usage variances) and Unit 8 Knowledge & Understanding point (3): basic statistical methods (index numbers).
7.10	☐	This activity deals with Performance Criteria 8.1D regarding the comparison of standard costs with actual costs and the analysis of any variances and Range Statement 8.1: variance analysis (material price and usage variances).
7.11	☐	This activity deals with Unit 8 Knowledge & Understanding point (4): use of relevant computer packages.

PART C

Core theme 2: budgeting

chapter 8

Budgeting

Contents

1 Introduction
2 Planning
3 The decision-making framework
4 The budget preparation timetable
5 Forecasting and budgeting

Performance criteria

9.1A Identify relevant data for projecting forecasts from internal and external sources

Range statement

9.1 Data: information about customers and markets; general economic information

9.1 Forecasts: income; expenditure

9.1 Projections: trends; seasonal variations; market research

9.2 Data: market information; general economic information; strategic plans

Knowledge and understanding

Unit 9 The business environment

1 External sources of information on costs, prices, demand and availability of resources

2 General economic environment

Unit 9 Accounting techniques

6 Co-ordination of the budget system

Knowledge and understanding (cont'd)

Unit 9 Accounting principles and theory

13 Uses of budgetary control: planning, co-ordinating, authorising, cost control

14 Relationship between budgets, forecasts and planning and product-life cycles

Signpost

The topics covered in this chapter are relevant to **Unit 9.** They form an introduction to, and framework for, the remaining chapters in this part of the text.

1 Introduction

This chapter provides an introduction to the chapters in the text dedicated solely to Unit 9 (Chapters 8 to 11).

Sections 2 and 3 provide **background** material and are not core. **Sections 4 and 5**, however, cover **key topics** in your study of Unit 9.

The point to take away from Section 4 is the **importance of co-ordination** of the budget system. This will be reiterated in the next chapter when we look at how budgets are actually prepared.

We covered key forecasting techniques applicable to both Unit 8 and Unit 9 in Chapter 5. In Section 5 of this chapter we cover some forecasting issues of particular relevance to budgets.

2 Planning

An organisation should never be surprised by developments which occur gradually over a period of time because the organisation should have a planning process which forces management to think ahead systematically in both the short term and the long term.

2.1 Long-term planning

Long-term planning, also known as **corporate planning**, involves selecting appropriate strategies so as to prepare a long-term plan to attain the organisation's objectives. (Remember we looked at objectives in Chapter 1.) The time span covered by a long-term plan depends on the organisation, the industry in which it operates and the particular environment involved. Typical periods are 2, 5, 7 or 10 years. Long-term planning is a detailed, lengthy process.

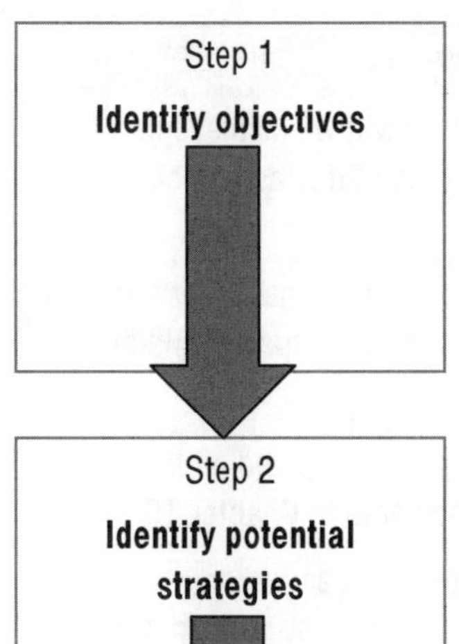

Objectives establish the direction in which the management of the organisation wish it to be heading. Typical objectives include the following.

- To maximise profits
- To increase market share
- To produce a better quality product than anyone else

Objectives answer the question: **'where do we want to be?'**.

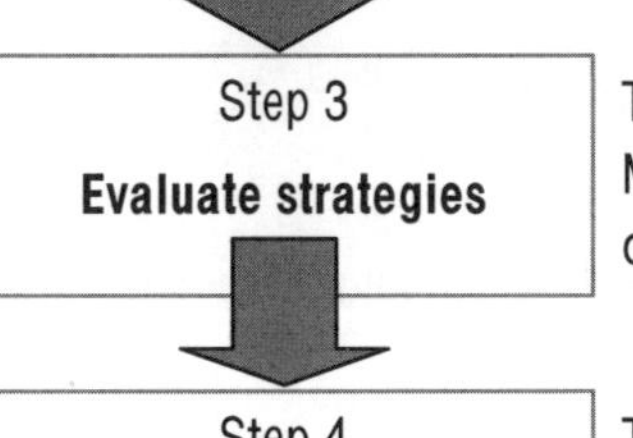

Once an organisation has decided 'where it wants to be', the next step is to identify a range of possible courses of action or **strategies that might enable the organisation to get there.**

An organisation might decide to be the lowest cost producer in the industry, perhaps by withdrawing from some markets or developing new products for sale in existing markets. This might involve internal development or some kind of joint venture.

Step 3
Evaluate strategies

The strategies must then be evaluated **in terms of suitability, feasibility and acceptability**. Management should select those strategies that have the greatest potential for achieving the organisation's objectives. One strategy may be chosen or several.

Step 4
Choose alternative courses of action

The next step in the process is to collect the **chosen strategies** together and **co-ordinate them into a long-term financial plan.** Typically this would show the following.

- Projected cash flows
- Capital expenditure plans
- Projected long-term profits
- Balance sheet forecasts
- A description of the long-term objectives and strategies in words

2.2 Short-term planning

The long-term corporate plan serves as the long-term framework for the organisation as a whole but for operational purposes it is necessary to **convert the corporate plan into a series of short-term plans** (or **budgets**), usually covering one year, which relate to sections, functions or departments.

The annual process of short-term planning should be seen as a means of fulfilling the corporate plan over time. Each short-term plan should steer the organisation towards its long-term objectives.

2.3 Budgets

A budget is basically an **organisation's plan for the forthcoming period**, expressed in **money terms**. It provides a **link** between where the organisation is **now** and where it **wants to be**.

Although budgets are prepared for a wide variety of reasons, we are particularly interested in the following uses.

Use	Detail
Planning	The preparation of a budget forces management to look ahead, to plan how it will achieve its targets and the resources it needs to enable it to do so. We will be looking at this aspect of budgeting in the next chapter.
Communication and coordination	The budget is a means of communicating to each person affected by the plans what he or she is supposed to be doing to ensure the plans are achieved. It also ensures that all departments are working towards the same goals. This is covered in Chapter 9.
Control	Actual results are compared against the budget, departures from budget investigated and management control action taken as necessary. This procedure is considered in Chapter 10.
Motivation	Depending on how it is agreed and set and the degree to which it is perceived as fair and achievable, the budget can motivate management to achieve the organisation's objectives. We return to this point in Chapter 11.

3 The decision-making framework

It has been suggested that the information used at different management levels should be classified into three tiers: strategic planning, management control and operational control.

3.1 Strategic planning

Strategic planning is the process of **deciding on the organisation's objectives**, on **changes in these objectives**, on the **resources needed to attain these objectives**, and on the **policies for acquiring, using and disposing of these resources**.

The strategic planning **process is long-term** in nature and covers such matters as the selection of products to make and markets to sell them to, the required levels of company profitability, the purchase and disposal of subsidiary companies and so on.

Notable **characteristics** of strategic planning are as follows.

- Qualitative or quantitative information often obtained from outside the organisation
- Generally **formulated in writing** (only after discussion by committee (the **Board**))
- **Circulated** to all interested parties within the organisation
- Results in a series of **lesser plans** for sales, production and so on

Strategic planning is therefore the **long-term planning** described in the previous section. **Capital budgeting**, covered in the next chapter, is **part of this long-term planning process.**

3.2 Operational control

Operational control (or **operational planning**) works **out what specific tasks need to be carried out in order to achieve the strategic plan**. For example a strategy may be to increase sales by 5% per annum for at least five years, and an operational plan to achieve this would be sales reps' weekly sales targets.

Notable characteristics of operational planning are the **speed of response** to changing conditions, and the use and understanding of **non-financial information** such as data about customer orders or raw material input.

3.3 Management control: co-ordinating the strategic and operational levels

Management control (or **tactics** or **tactical planning**) is **short term** in nature and sits between strategy and operations. It tries to **ensure that resources are obtained** and **used effectively** and **efficiently** in order to **achieve** the organisation's objective.

For example, management control associated with the strategy to increase sales by 5% per annum for at least five years (see Section 3.2) will involve senior sales managers making plans to increase sales by 5% in the next year, with some provisional planning for future years. This might involve planning direct sales resources, advertising and so on. Management control activities include preparing budgets for the next year for sales, production, stock levels and purchasing, and establishing measures of performance by which profit centres or departmental results can be gauged.

Notable characteristics of management control are that it is **concerned with efficient and effective use of resources.** Management control **information** is often **quantitative** and is commonly expressed in **financial** terms.

Management control and **operational control** are therefore **short-term** in nature, and so are **used in conjunction with short-term planning** described in the previous section.

4 The budget preparation timetable

Let us now look at the steps involved in the preparation of a budget. The procedures will differ from organisation to organisation, but the step-by-step approach described here is indicative of the steps followed by many organisations. The preparation of a budget may take weeks or months and management may meet several times before an organisation's budget is finally agreed.

4.1 *Step 1.* Communicating details of the budget policy and budget guidelines

The long-term plan is the starting point for the preparation of the annual budget. For example, if the long-term plan calls for a more aggressive pricing policy, the budget must take this into account. Managers should also be provided with important guidelines for wage rate increases, changes in productivity and so on, as well as information about industry demand and output.

4.2 *Step 2.* Determining the factor that restricts output

This is known as the **principal budget factor** (or **key budget factor** or **limiting budget factor)** and it is often the starting point for budget preparation.

For example, a sales department might estimate that it could sell 1,000 units of product X, which would require 5,000 hours of grade A labour. If there are no units of product X already in stock, and only 4,000 hours of grade A labour available in the period, the company would be unable to sell 1,000 units of X because of the shortage of labour hours. Grade A labour would be a limiting budget factor, and management must choose one of the following options.

- Reduce budgeted sales by 20%.
- Try to increase the availability of grade A labour by 1,000 hours (25%) by recruitment or overtime working.
- Try to sub-contract the production of 1,000 units to another manufacturer, but still profit on the transaction.

In most organisations the principal budget factor is sales demand: a company is usually restricted from making and selling more of its products because there would be no sales demand for the increased output at a price which would be acceptable to the company. The principal budget factor may also be machine capacity, distribution and selling resources or the availability of key raw materials or cash. Once this factor is defined then the rest of the budget can be prepared. For example, if sales are the principal budget factor then the production manager can only prepare his budget after the sales budget is complete.

Management may not know what the limiting budget factor is until a draft budget has been attempted. The first draft budget will therefore usually begin with the preparation of a draft sales budget.

If an organisation produces **two or more products** and the **principal budget factor is *not* sales demand**, a technique known as **limiting factor analysis** must be used to determine the most profitable production plan. We will be looking at limiting factors in the next chapter.

4.3 *Step 3.* Preparation of the sales budget

We have already established that, for many organisations, the principal budget factor is sales volume. The sales budget is therefore often the primary budget from which the majority of the other budgets are derived, and is **based on the sales forecast and the production capacity of the organisation**. (We looked at sales forecasting techniques in Chapter 5 and return to the issue in the next section.) The sales budget may be subdivided, possible subdivisions being by product, by sales area, by management responsibility and so on.

4.4 *Step 4.* Initial preparation of budgets

We will look at the way in which budgets are prepared in the next chapter.

4.5 *Step 5.* Negotiation of budgets with superiors

Once a manager has prepared his draft budget he should submit it to his superior for approval. The superior should then incorporate this budget with the others for which he or she is responsible and then submit this budget for approval to his or her superior. This process continues until the final budget is presented to senior management for approval.

4.6 *Step 6.* Co-ordination of budgets

Remember that it is unlikely that performance of the above steps will be problem-free. The budgets must be reviewed in relation to one another. Such a **review may indicate that some budgets are out of balance with others and need modifying** so that they will be compatible. The **revision of one budget may lead to the revision of all budgets**.

4.7 *Step 7.* Final acceptance of the budgets

When all the budgets are in harmony with one another they are summarised into an overall budget.

4.8 *Step 8.* Communication of the budgets

It is vital to the success of the budgets that, once approved, they are communicated to all those in the organisation who need to know what they have to achieve. This should be done in good time for the start of the new budget period. The employees who have to deliver individual sections of the budget need to know what is expected of them.

4.9 *Step 9.* Budget review

The budgeting process does not stop once the budgets have been agreed. Actual results should be compared on a regular basis with the budgeted results. Management should receive a report detailing the differences and should investigate the reasons for the differences. **If the differences are within the control of management, corrective action should be taken** to ensure that such inefficiencies do not occur in the future.

The **differences may have occurred, however, because the budget was unrealistic to begin with or because the actual conditions did not reflect those anticipated (or could have possibly been anticipated).** This would therefore invalidate the remainder of the budget.

Senior management should meet periodically to evaluate the organisation's actual performance, and **may need to reappraise the organisation's future plans in the light of changes to anticipated conditions and to adjust the budget to take account of such changes**.

The important point to note is that the budgeting process does not end for the current year once the budget period has begun: budgeting should be seen as a **continuous** and **dynamic** process.

5 Forecasting and budgeting

It has been said that budgeting is more a test of forecasting skill than anything else and there is a certain amount of truth in such a comment. Forecasts need to be made of sales volumes and prices, wage rates and earnings, material availability and prices, rates of inflation and the cost of overhead items such as power. It is *not* sufficient to simply add a percentage of last year's budget in the hope of achieving realistic forecasts.

A **forecast** is an **estimate of what might happen in the future**. It is a **best estimate**, based on certain **assumptions** about what is expected to happen.

A **budget** is not the same as a forecast. It is a **plan of what the organisation is aiming to achieve and what it has set as a target**. A budget should be **realistic** and so it will be based to some extent on forecasts prepared. In preparing a budget, however, management will be trying to **establish some control** over the conditions that will apply in the future.

When a budget is set it will for a **short time be the same as the forecast**. As actual events progress and the situation develops and changes, however, **new forecasts might be prepared that differ from the budget targets**. Management might be able to **take control action** to bring forecasts back into line with the budget; **alternatively**, management will

have to **accept that the budget will not be achieved, or it will be exceeded**, depending on what the current forecasts indicate.

5.1 Sales forecasting for budgets

The sales budget is frequently the **first budget prepared** since sales is usually the **principal budget factor** but before the sales budget can be prepared a sales or revenue forecast has to be made.

5.1.1 Factors to consider

Sales forecasting is complex and difficult and a number of factors have to be considered.

- Past sales patterns
- The economic environment
- Results of market research
- Anticipated advertising
- Competition
- Changing consumer taste
- New and existing legislation
- Distribution
- Pricing policies and discounts offered
- Environmental factors

5.1.2 Forecasting methods

As well as bearing in mind the above factors, management can also use a number of forecasting methods, often using more than one of them at a time in an attempt to reduce the level of uncertainty.

- Ask **sales personnel** to provide **estimates**. The sales team will have up-to-date first hand knowledge of current sales patterns and will have a 'feel for the market'. They will know how well current products are selling and how many orders there are on the order books.
- Use **survey/market research** methods (especially if an organisation is considering introducing a new product or service). Statistical error and inaccurate responses might limit these methods' usefulness, however. We covered this in Chapter 3.
- Investigate **secondary sources** of data for the industry, although these will have been collected for another purpose and so their limitations will not be known. Again, this is covered in Chapter 3.
- Although the information received may not be accurate, consult **customers** about their future requirements. This can be particularly helpful if an organisation has a small number of customers with whom long-term relationships have been developed and/or you want to increase sales to existing customers. This was also covered in Chapter 3.
- Use **mathematical techniques** to estimate sales levels. These include time series analysis and linear regression analysis, which we looked at in Chapter 5. They will not necessarily provide accurate forecasts, but on the whole they are likely to provide more reliable estimates than guesswork.
- Study the **general economic climate**, although you need to make the major assumption that past patterns will repeat in the future.

5.1.3 Product life cycle

Forecasts can also be **based on established patterns of behaviour**. **One model of behaviour** is the **product life cycle**.

The sales volume and profitability of a product can be expected to change over time. The product life cycle is an attempt to **recognise distinct stages in a product's sales history.**

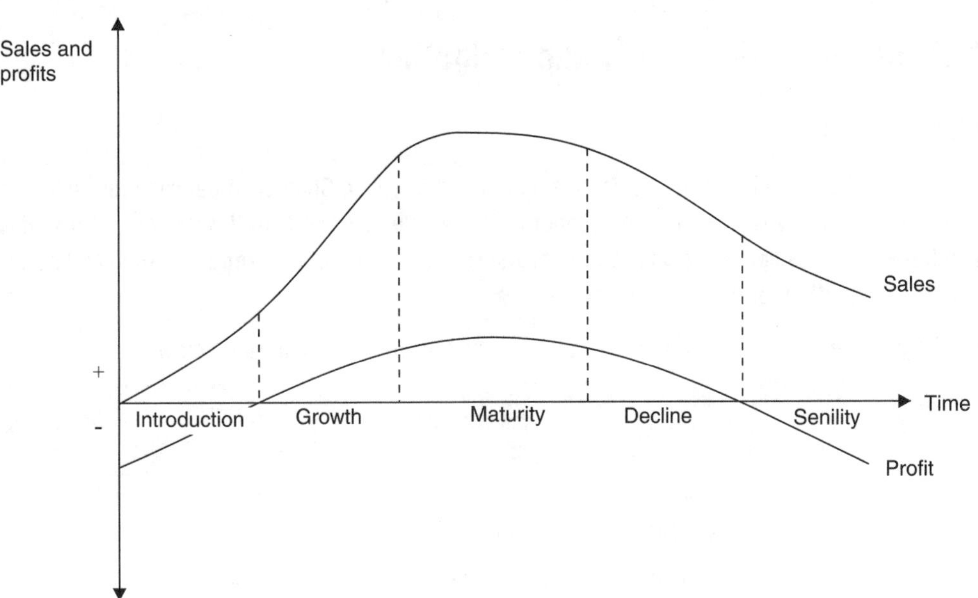

Phase	Detail
Introduction	The product is introduced to the market. Heavy capital expenditure will be incurred on product development and perhaps on the purchase of new fixed assets and building up stocks for sale. The product will begin to earn revenue, but initially demand is likely to be small. The organisation may have to spend on further advertising to bring the product or service to the market's attention.
Growth	The product gains a bigger market as demand builds up. Sales revenues increase and the product begins to make a profit. The initial costs of the investment in the new product are gradually recovered.
Maturity	Eventually, the growth in demand will slow down and the product will enter a period of relative maturity. It will continue to be profitable but may be modified or improved, as a means of sustaining its demand.
Saturation and decline	At some stage, the market will have bought enough of the product and it will therefore reach 'saturation point'. Demand will start to fall. For a while, the product will still be profitable in spite of declining sales, but eventually it will become a loss-maker and this is the time when the organisation should decide to stop selling the product or service.

Information about the stage a product has reached in its life cycle may provide an important indicator of its likely future sales volume and so provide invaluable information for forecasting. If a product is in its growth stage, volumes are likely to increase whereas if it is in decline, volumes are obviously likely to fall.

5.1.4 Market considerations

The market in which a product is being sold will also impact on forecasting. In a declining market, sales volumes are likely to drop in the future, volumes in new markets are likely to increase whereas volumes in established markets may well remain fairly constant.

5.2 Analysis of economic activity and budgeting

5.2.1 The trade cycle

The cyclical variations of economic activity (which we mentioned briefly in Chapter 5) between recession and economic boom affect individual businesses as well as the economy as a whole. **Economic indicators are a form of external information which a business can make use of in appraising the market for its products.** Such an appraisal can provide invaluable **information** for budgeting purposes.

There are four main phases in the trade (or business) cycle, as shown on the diagram below.

Phase	Point on diagram below	What occurs
Recession	A	Many investments suddenly become unprofitable and so consumption, new investment, production and employment all fall Profits fall and some businesses fail Recession can turn into severe depression (point B)
Depression	B	Heavy unemployment and low consumer demand Over-capacity (unused capacity) in production Prices stable, or even falling Business profits low, business confidence in the future low
Recovery	C	Investment picks up and employment rises Consumer spending rises and profits rise Business confidence grows and prices stable, or slowly rising
Boom	D	Consumer spending rising fast Output capacity reached: labour shortages occur Output can only be increased by new labour-saving investment Investment spending high Increases in demand now stimulate prices rises Business profits high

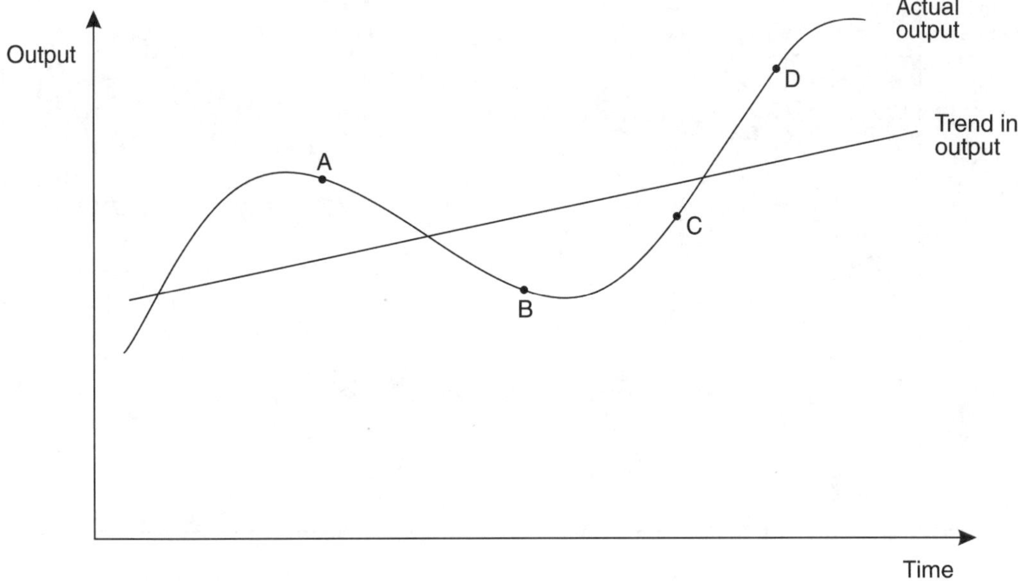

5.2.2 Economic indicators

Gross domestic product (GDP) (indexed to remove the effects of inflation) is generally seen as one of the best indicators of a nation's economic well-being but there is a wide variety of other items of information which are collected over time. To see how we might use other time series data as a way of assessing or forecasting the level of economic activity or GDP, we need to look at the concepts of leading, coincident and lagging indicators.

- A **leading indicator** is an indicator which anticipates the trend of the main series of data.
- A **coincident indicator** is an indicator which follows the main trend.
- A **lagging indicator** is an indicator which follows the main trend after some delay ('lagging behind' the main trend).

Suppose that the graph below plots economic data for a country. The dotted line AA shows the trend in economic output: the value of everything which is produced in the economy in a period of time. We can then consider the other series of data represented by lines BB, CC and DD.

- Line BB reaches its peaks (high points) and its trough (low point) at the same time as line AA: it falls when AA is falling and rises when AA is rising. BB is a *coincident* indicator for AA, the trend in economic output.
- Line CC reaches its high points and its low point some time before line AA does so. It follows a pattern of rising and falling similar to AA, but ahead of AA. CC is a *leading* indicator of economic activity.
- Line DD follows a similar pattern to line AA but only after some delay. DD is a *lagging* indicator of economic activity.

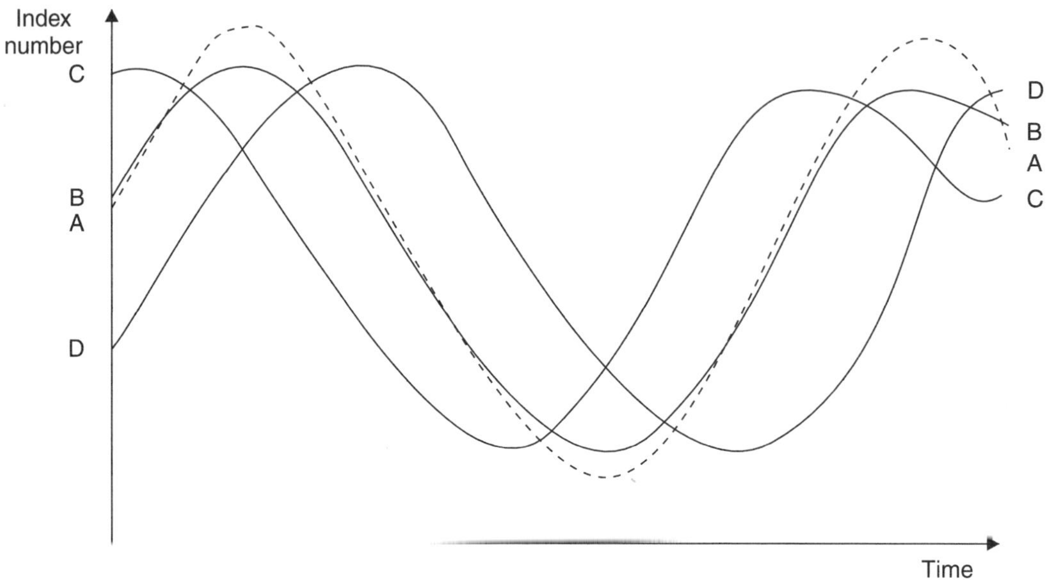

You need to be aware of the meaning of the terms leading, coincident and lagging indicators so that you can make use of the concepts in appraising economic or other information from outside an organisation.

The statistical techniques involved in establishing the degree to which economic indicators lead or lag behind the trend in GDP are complex. Here are some examples for the UK economy, as stated in a UK government publication.

Timing of some cyclical economic indicators	Lead (–)/lag (+) Months
Longer leading indicators	
Total houses started, Great Britain	–12
CBI quarterly survey: change in optimism (percentage balance)	–9
Financial Times – Actuaries 500 share index	–7
Shorter leading indicators	
New car registrations	–6
Change in total consumer credit	–6
Coincident indicators	
Volume of retail sales	–1
Gross domestic product at constant prices	0
CBI quarterly survey: change in stocks of raw materials (percentage balance)	2
Lagging indicators	
Adult unemployment	6
Engineering industries, total value of orders on hand	12

You should be able to see that if we want to **forecast the pattern of economic output** over short-term future periods, then we can do so **by following what is happening to leading indicators**. As you should be able to see from the above table, if after a period of falling levels of new car registrations, there is now a rise, this could indicate a recovery in activity in the economy as a whole (measured by GDP) in six months' time.

Activity 8.1

You are employed by a medium-sized company in the construction industry which builds low-cost houses for sale mainly to 'first-time buyers'. The business has been suffering badly during a recession and the directors of the company are very anxious about future trends in the industry. They have asked you to collect as much relevant information as you can from published statistics and other sources as a first step towards undertaking an appraisal of the company's 'external environment'. So far you have been able to locate the following.

(a) Official statistics relating to employment, unemployment and labour rates

(b) Information on 'new housing starts'

(c) Retail and wholesale price indices

(d) Information published by building societies on the prices of houses of different types in different parts of the country and the value of mortgages granted

(e) Population statistics

(f) Figures of average costs of construction firms published by the trade association

(g) Special surveys of the construction industry in the financial press

Tasks

(a) Write a report to the Managing Director explaining how information from *any four* of the sources listed above might be of value in assessing future trends for the company. Remember that you need to bear in mind the particular situation of the company when analysing the detailed information. Comment on the relevance, reliability and timeliness of the information.

(b) The Managing Director has been reading a statistical report published by the trade association on general trends in the construction industry. He has highlighted certain phrases in the report as follows and has asked you to explain each of them briefly in non-technical language:

It is difficult to *extrapolate* a trend line because the industry is subject to pronounced *cyclical fluctuations*.... The wide *seasonal variations* which are experienced in the industry can be eliminated by using *moving averages*.... Experience has shown that expenditure on capital equipment by the industry is a fairly weak *leading indicator* for trends in the industry as a whole.'

Briefly explain each phrase printed in italics above.

ATTENTION!

You will have to attempt **all** the tasks in the exam – there is no 'choice'. So you cannot avoid a topic because you do not like it or because you think it is difficult. You have got to be able to **demonstrate competence in all areas.**

Key learning points

- ☑ **Planning** must cover both the **long term** and the **short term**.
- ☑ **Long-term planning** involves four steps.

Step 1
Identify objectives
▼
Step 2
Identify potential strategies
▼
Step 3
Evaluate strategies

Step 4
Choose alternative courses of action

- ☑ **Strategic planning** is long term. **Management control** and **operational control** are short term.
- ☑ A budget is a **quantified plan of action** for a forthcoming accounting period. It can be used for **planning**, **communicating** and **coordinating**, **control** and **motivation**.
- ☑ The **budget preparation process** is as follows.
  - Communicating details of the budget policy and budget guidelines
  - Determining the factor that restricts output
  - Preparation of the sales budget
  - Initial preparation of budgets
  - Negotiation of budgets with superiors
  - Co-ordination of budgets
  - Final acceptance of the budgets
  - Communication of the budgets
  - Budget review
- ☑ The **principal budget factor** should be identified at the beginning of the budgetary process, and the budget for this is prepared before all the others.
- ☑ **Sales forecasting** needs to take into account factors such as the economic environment, new technology and the **product life cycle.** The product life cycle has four stages.
  - Introduction
  - Growth
  - Maturity
  - Saturation and decline
- ☑ Methods of forecasting include using **sales personnel's estimates**, **market research**, **mathematical models** and **mathematical techniques**.
- ☑ There are four main phases of the **trade/business cycle** (recession, depression, recovery, boom).
- ☑ Economic indicators include **leading, lagging** and **coincident indicators.**

Quick quiz

1 *Choose the correct word from those highlighted.*

Objectives/strategies establish the direction in which the management of the organisation wish it to be heading.

2 Which of the following statements is true?

A Management control sits between strategy and operations.
B Strategic planning sits between operations and management control.
C Operational control sits between strategy and management control.
D Strategic planning, management control and operational control all operate at the same level.

3 *Put the following stages in the preparation of the budget in the correct order.*

(a) Preparation of the sales budget
(b) Determining the factor that restricts output
(c) Budget review
(d) Communication of the budgets
(e) Communication of details of budget policy and budget guidelines
(f) Initial preparation of budgets
(g) Co-ordination of budgets
(h) Negotiation of budgets with superiors
(i) Final acceptance of the budgets

4 *Choose the correct words from those highlighted.*

A **forecast/budget** is an estimate of what might happen in the future. It is a best estimate, based on certain assumptions about the conditions that are expected to apply. A **budget/forecast**, in contrast, is a plan of what the organisation is aiming to achieve and what it has set as a target.

5 What are the four stages of the product life cycle?

A Start, mid years, saturation, decline
B Introduction, adolescence, dotage, death
C Birth, growth, old age, decline
D Introduction, growth, maturity, saturation and decline

6 Noted below are the four main phases of the trade/business cycle. Match these phases to points A-D on the diagram.

Phases: depression, recession, boom, recovery

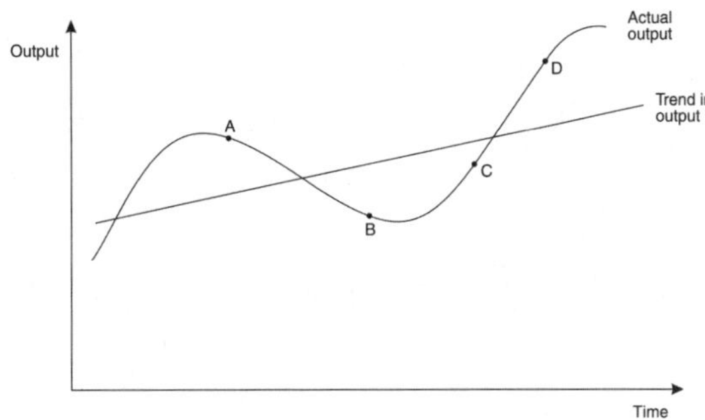

Answers to quick quiz

1. Objectives
2. A
3. (e), (b), (a), (f), (h), (g), (i), (d), (c)
4. A **forecast** in an estimate, a **budget** is a plan.
5. D
6. A Recession
   B Depression
   C Recovery
   D Boom

ASSESSMENT KIT ACTIVITIES

The topics covered in this chapter tend to provide the background to exam tasks and hence are not covered by specific activities in the BPP Exam Kit for Units 8 & 9.

Activity checklist

This checklist shows which performance criteria, range statement or knowledge and understanding point is covered by the activity in this chapter. Tick off the activity as you complete it.

Activity		
8.1	☐	This activity deals with Performance Criteria 9.1A regarding the identification of relevant data for projecting forecasts from internal and external sources.

chapter 9

Budget preparation

Contents

1 Introduction
2 Sales budgets
3 Production budgets
4 Resource budgets
5 Budgets covering more than one period
6 Budgeted profit and loss account
7 Capital expenditure budgets
8 Other aspects of budget preparation
9 Accounting for waste, rejects and inefficiency
10 Limiting factors

Performance criteria

9.2A Present to management draft budget proposals in a clear and appropriate format and on schedule

9.2B Verify that draft budget proposals are consistent with organisational objectives and include all relevant data and assumptions

9.2C Break down budgets into periods appropriate to the organisation

9.2D Communicate with budget holders in a manner which maintains goodwill and ensure budget proposals are agreed with budget holders

Range statement

9.2 Types of budgets: budgets for income and expenditure; resource budgets (production budget, material budget, labour budget, fixed overhead budget); capital budgets

9.2 Data: accounting information; wage and salary information; market information

Knowledge and understanding

Unit 9 Accounting techniques

3 Basic statistical methods: index numbers

5 Development of production, resource and revenue budgets from forecast sales data

6 Coordination of the budget system

Knowledge and understanding (cont'd)

Unit 9 Accounting techniques

7 The effect of capacity constraints, other production constraints and sales constraints on budgets; limiting (key or budget) factor

Unit 9 Accounting principles and theory

15 Different types of budgets: budgets for income and expenditure; resource budgets (production, material, labour and other resource budgets); capital budgets

Signpost

The topics covered in this chapter are relevant to **Unit 9**.

1 Introduction

This is a very **important** chapter. **Core** topics are covered and you will definitely need to apply at least some of what you study in this chapter in the exam.

Sections 2 to 5 take you through the preparation of **budgets for sales, production, labour and material,** which are the ones you are most likely to encounter in the exam. In sections 8 to 10 we look at some of the **complications** that the assessor might introduce into a budget preparation task.

Make sure that you attempt all of the activities in this chapter as they provide vital practice on key skills you will require in the exam.

2 Sales budgets

As you now know, for most organisations the **principal budget factor** is **sales** and so the sales budget is the **first to be prepared**.

The sales forecast may not necessarily be the same as the **budgeted sales volume**.

- The budgeted volume might be **more** than the forecast volume in order to **provide managers with a target** for achievement.
- On the other hand, the budgeted volume might be **less** than the forecast volume because there is a **limit on the organisation's output**, such as limited production capacity or a shortage of a resource (such as labour or raw materials).

Budgeted sales revenue is easy to calculate: budgeted sales volume × selling price per product. You will see in later activities and examples in this chapter how such calculations are integrated into exam tasks.

3 Production budgets

Once the sales budget is prepared, an organisation knows how many **units** it plans to **sell**. This is **unlikely to be the same as the number it will produce**, however.

- The organisation might be intending to change the amount of finished goods it holds in **stock**.
- Some of the units produced might be **rejected**.

We will look at how to deal with the problem of rejected units later in the chapter. Let's see now how to **take into account changes in finished goods stock**.

If the number of **units in opening and closing stocks** is to be the **same**, the number of units produced is the same as the number of units sold.

∴ **Production = sales**

Now suppose there are **no opening stocks** but at the end of the period a certain level of **closing stocks** is **required**. The number of units produced must cover the number of units being sold plus the number of units that are required for closing stock

∴ **Production = sales + closing stock**

Finally suppose that there were **some units in opening stock**. These units could be sold or could become part of closing stock and so the number of units that needs to be produced to cover sales and closing stock can be reduced by the number of units in opening stock.

∴ **Production = sales + closing stock – opening stock**

Rather than deriving this formula from scratch you could take an alternative approach. You may remember from your **financial accounting studies** that:

Opening stock + production – closing stock = sales

Rearranging this equation (look back at Section 2 of Chapter 4 on rearranging equations if you need to), we get:

Production = sales + closing stock – opening stock

IMPORTANT POINT

Always check your answers for **reasonableness**. If stock levels are going to fall, production volume will be less than sales volume because some of the units that were in stock can be sold.

On the other hand, if stock levels are going to rise, production volume must be greater than sales volume because as well as producing the units that are to be sold, some additional units must be produced for closing stock.

Tasks requiring you to produce a production budget will usually give you information about sales levels and opening and closing stock. By applying the **formula** above the **production budget** can be **derived** very easily. Let's have a look at an example.

Example: the preparation of the production budget

Pearson Ltd manufactures two products, P and L, and is preparing its budget for Year 3. The company currently holds 800 units of P and 1,200 units of L in stock, but 250 of these units of L have just been discovered to have deteriorated in quality, and must therefore be scrapped. Budgeted sales of P are 3,000 units and of L 4,000 units, provided that the company maintains finished goods stocks at a level equal to three months' sales.

Task

Prepare the production budget for Year 3.

Solution

Either by rearranging the formula from your financial accounting studies or deriving the formula from scratch, you need to work with production = sales + closing stock – opening stock.

	Product P		*Product L*	
	Units	Units	Units	Units
Budgeted sales		3,000		4,000
Closing stocks (3/12 of 3,000/4,000)	750		1,000	
Opening stocks (minus stocks scrapped)	800		950	
(Decrease)/increase in stocks		(50)		50
Production		2,950		4,050

The layout of this answer shows that stocks of product P have decreased, while those of product L have increased. A reasonableness check on an answer would therefore require production of P to be less than sales, but production of L to be greater than sales.

WATCH OUT FOR ...

Different ways of describing stock levels

Opening and closing stock levels may be given in terms of units, kgs, litres and so on.

Finished goods stock could be given in terms of **number of days' sales.**

Raw materials stock could be given in terms of **number of days' production**.

For example, suppose control period 4 is four weeks long. Production is carried out for five days a week. Budgeted production in control period 4 is 1,500 units. Opening stock of raw material J should be sufficient for two days' production.

∴ Opening stock = (two days/(four weeks × five days)) × 1,500 units = 150 units.

Beware of making **two common errors** in this area.

Error 1. Making your own assumptions about the number of days in the period. If the task specifies 30 days per period and supply sufficient for five days is needed, the correct fraction is 5/30 (not 5/6 or 5/28).

Error 2. Using the incorrect base. If the task specifies that closing stock should be sufficient for four days' sales in the following period, credit will be lost for sales in the current period or production in the current/next period.

The overall message is **read the task data carefully.**

4 Resource budgets

4.1 Materials usage and labour utilisation budgets

Once the production budget in units has been set, the labour and material that is needed to produce the budgeted production level can be calculated.

The materials usage and labour utilisation budgets can be drawn up in quantities and hours and then converted into monetary figures if necessary.

IMPORTANT POINT

If a task specifies that there is a **guaranteed weekly wage**, do not calculate an hourly rate – it's a complete waste of time! The guaranteed weekly wage must be **paid irrespective of the volume of output**.

The activity below requires you to draw up very simple materials usage and labour utilisation budgets. **Aim to get the correct numbers.** Don't worry too much at this stage what your budget looks like. The layout of your budgets will improve with practice.

Activity 9.1

Bertram Manufacturing Ltd produces a single product.

Sales of the product in the next four week period are expected to be 280 units. At the beginning of the period a stock of 30 units is expected, although the budgeted closing stock is 5 units.

Each unit of the product requires two hours of grade O labour and three hours of grade R labour. Grade O labour is paid £15 per hour, whereas grade R labour receive a guaranteed weekly wage of £280. Sixteen members of the workforce of twenty are paid the guaranteed weekly wage.

Just one raw material is used in production of the product. A unit of the product requires 7 kg of raw material. The expected price per kg of the raw material is £50.

Task

On the basis of the information above prepare the following budgets for the four-week period.

(a) Production budget
(b) Materials usage budget (in kgs and £)
(c) Labour utilisation budget (in £)

4.2 Materials purchases budget

Once the materials usage budget has been set, the materials purchases budget can be established. Although in theory the materials purchased could be the same as the materials used, this is unlikely to be the case.

- The organisation might be planning to change the level of raw materials it holds in **stock**.
- There might be **wastage** or **loss** of raw materials.

We will look at how to deal with wastage or loss later in the chapter. Here we consider **changes in raw materials stock levels**.

The approach is very similar to that required to determine production.

If there are **no planned changes** between opening and closing **stock levels** of raw materials, raw materials purchases will be the same as raw materials usage.

Materials purchases = materials used in production

Now suppose that there are **no opening stocks** of raw materials but at the end of the period a certain level of raw materials is required in **closing stock**. The materials purchased must cover the materials needed for production plus the quantity required for closing stock.

Materials purchases = materials used in production + closing stock

Finally suppose that there were some raw materials in **opening stock**. These raw materials could be used in production or could become part of closing stock. The materials purchased to cover production and closing stock can therefore be reduced by the raw materials in opening stock.

Materials purchases = materials used in production + closing stock – opening stock

Again, rather than deriving this formula from scratch you can use a formula from your **financial accounting studies**.

Opening stock + purchases – closing stock = materials used in production

Rearranging this formula we get

Materials purchases = materials used in production + closing stock – opening stock

IMPORTANT POINT

You can apply the same **reasonableness** check here as that used for the production budget. If stock levels are going to fall, purchases will be less than usage because some of the material that was in stock can be used in production.

On the other hand, if stock levels are going to rise, purchases will be greater than usage because as well as being used in production, some material must be purchased for stock.

Activity 9.2

Given the information below, establish the materials purchases budget.

	Superior model	*Standard model*
Forecast sales (units)	1,500	2,200
Budgeted opening finished stock (units)	150	200
Budgeted closing finished stock (units)	200	250
Material per unit	5 kgs	4 kgs

Budgeted opening materials stock	800 kgs
Budgeted closing materials stock	1,500 kgs

Activity 9.3

Furniture Creations Ltd produces two pieces of furniture, a large chest and a wardrobe, from the same type of wood. The data below relates to period 1.

(a)	Budgeted production	Chest	450 units
		Wardrobe	710 units
(b)	Materials requirements	Chest	25 kgs
		Wardrobe	40 kgs
(c)	Opening stock of wood	40,000 kgs	
(d)	Closing stock of wood	sufficient for 15 days' production	
(e)	Length of each period	25 days	

Task

If production levels in period 2 are expected to be 15% higher than those in period 1, calculate the purchases budget (in kgs) for period 1.

WATCH OUT FOR...

Ways to save yourself extra work

Look back at your answers to the activities above. Did you try to derive the purchases required for each product by dividing in some way the opening and closing materials stocks? Although not wrong this is unnecessary – as our answers show you simply need **one budget.**

Activity 9.4

Frinton Foods Ltd manufactures two milk based drinks, Frothy Fruit and Fruit Smoothie, which use the same raw materials, milk and fresh fruit. One unit of Frothy Fruit uses 3 litres of milk and 4 kilograms of fresh fruit. One unit of Fruit Smoothie uses 5 litres of milk and 2 kilograms of fresh fruit. A litre of milk is expected to cost £0.30 and a kilogram of fresh fruit £0.70.

Budgeted sales for Year 2 are 8,000 units of Frothy Fruit and 6,000 units of Fruit Smoothie; finished goods in stock at 1 January Year 2 are 1,500 units of Frothy Fruit and 300 units of Fruit Smoothie, and the company plans to hold stocks of 600 units of each product at 31 December Year 2.

Stocks of raw material are 6,000 litres of milk and 2,800 kilograms of fresh fruit at 1 January, and the company plans to hold 5,000 litres and 3,500 kilograms respectively at 31 December Year 2.

The warehouse and stores managers have suggested that a provision should be made for damages and deterioration of items held in store, as follows.

Frothy Fruit:	loss of 50 units	Milk:	loss of 500 litres
Fruit Smoothie:	loss of 100 units	Fresh fruit:	loss of 200 kilograms

Task

Prepare a material purchases budget for Year 2.

4.3 Co-ordination of the budget system

IMPORTANT POINT

You should now realise the **importance of coordination** in budget preparation. The production and resource budgets must be set so that there are the necessary resources to enable the sales budget to be met. And there is little point in the materials usage budget being based on a budgeted production level of 10,000 units if the budgeted production level in the production budget has been changed to 15,000 units.

4.4 Cost of production budgets

Once you have established budgets for the cost of material and the cost of labour, you can easily draw up budgets for the cost of production (as opposed to the level of production, covered in Section 3).

A **cost of production budget** is simply the **sum** of **budgets for the cost of material usage and the cost of labour**.

IMPORTANT POINT

The cost of production includes the cost of material usage rather than the cost of material purchases as some material may be purchased and then held in stock rather than used in production.

Labour hours worked cannot be stored to be used later, however, and so the cost of labour budget is included in the cost of production budget.

4.5 Cost of sales budgets

You should be aware from your financial accounting studies that the cost of sales is the cost of production adjusted by opening and closing stock values.

Cost of sales = opening stock + cost of production – closing stock

A cost of sales budget is therefore based on the cost of production budget, but adjusted by opening and closing stock values of finished goods.

Activity 9.5

An organisation is constructing its budget for the coming year. It makes three products, X, Y and Z. Sales forecasts for the year are as follows.

	X	*Y*	*Z*
Sales team 1 (in units)	3,000	5,000	4,000
Sales team 2 (in units)	5,000	7,000	6,000
	8,000	12,000	10,000

Budgeted selling prices are X – £60, Y – £110, Z – £90.

You are given the following unit standard cost data.

	X	*Y*	*Z*
Plastic (type B15) (in kilos)	2.00	3.00	2.5
Metal (type 1/37-D) in kilos)	3.00	4.00	1.5
Labour hours – Department 1	0.75	1.25	2.0
– Department 2	1.50	2.00	2.5

Plastic costs £3 per kg, while metal costs £2 per kg. The labour rate in department 1 is £4 per hour, while in department 2 it is £3 per hour.

Opening and closing stocks are budgeted as follows.

	In units			*In kilos*	
	X	*Y*	*Z*	*Plastic*	*Metal*
Opening stock	1,000	1,200	1,500	5,000	7,500
Closing stock	1,200	1,000	1,800	8,000	10,000

Task

Prepare the following budgets.

(a) Sales budget in revenue
(b) Production budget in units for each product
(c) Material purchases budget in kgs and in £
(d) Departmental labour cost budgets in hours and in £
(e) Cost of production budgets for each product

5 Budgets covering more than one period

The budgets we have looked at **so far** have been for **more than one product** but have **covered just one period**. This is one of the types of budget that you will encounter in the exam. **Below** is an example of a budget for **just one** product covering **more than one period**. This is the other type of budget that you are likely to encounter.

IMPORTANT POINT

The link between opening stock and closing stock

In many single product/multi-period budget preparation tasks you are not given information about opening stock each period, only closing stock.

Closing stock at the end of one period is the opening stock of the next and so if you know that closing stock of period 1 is 500 units valued at £1,000, opening stock of period 2 is the same 500 units valued at £1,000.

Look out for this in the example and activity below.

Example: multi-period/single product budget

Holloway Ltd is preparing its annual budgets for the year to 31 December 20X4. It manufactures and sells one product, which has a selling price of £150. The marketing director believes that the price can be increased to £160 with effect from 1 July 20X4 and that at this price the sales volume for each quarter of 20X4 will be as follows.

	Sales volume
Quarter 1	40,000
Quarter 2	50,000
Quarter 3	30,000
Quarter 4	45,000

Sales for each quarter of 20X5 are expected to be 40,000 units.

Each unit of the finished product which is manufactured requires four units of component R and three units of component T, together with a body shell S. These items are purchased from an outside supplier. Currently prices are:

Component R	£8.00 each
Component T	£5.00 each
Shell S	£30.00 each

The components are expected to increase in price by 10% with effect from 1 April 20X4; no change is expected in the price of the shell.

Assembly of the shell and components into the finished product requires 6 labour hours: labour is currently paid £5.00 per hour. A 4% increase in wage costs is anticipated to take effect from 1 October 20X4.

Stocks on 31 December 20X3 are expected to be as follows.

Finished units	9,000 units
Component R	3,000 units
Component T	5,500 units
Shell S	500 units

Closing stocks at the end of each quarter are to be as follows.

Finished units	10% of next quarter's sales
Component R	20% of next quarter's production requirements
Component T	15% of next quarter's production requirements
Shell S	10% of next quarter's production requirements

Tasks

Prepare the following budgets of Holloway Ltd for the year ending 31 December 20X4, showing values for each quarter and the year in total.

(a) Sales budget (in £s and units)
(b) Production budget (in units)
(c) Material usage budget (in units)
(d) Material purchases budget for component R (in units)
(e) Labour cost budget (in £s)

Solution

(a) **Sales budget**

	Quarter 1	*Quarter 2*	*Quarter 3*	*Quarter 4*	*Total*
Units	40,000	50,000	30,000	45,000	165,000
Unit price	£150	£150	£160	£160	
Sales revenue	£6,000,000	£7,500,000	£4,800,000	£7,200,000	£25,500,000

(b) **Production budget (in units)**

Remember that production = sales + closing stock – opening stock

	Quarter 1	*Quarter 2*	*Quarter 3*	*Quarter 4*	*Total*
Opening stock	(9,000)	(5,000)	(3,000)	(4,500)	
Sales	40,000	50,000	30,000	45,000	
Closing stock (10% of next quarter's sales)	5,000	3,000	4,500	4,000	
Production	36,000	48,000	31,500	44,500	160,000

(c) **Material usage budget (in units)**

	Quarter 1	*Quarter 2*	*Quarter 3*	*Quarter 4*	*Total*
Component R (production × 4)	144,000	192,000	126,000	178,000	640,000
Component T (production × 3)	108,000	144,000	94,500	133,500	480,000
Shell S	36,000	48,000	31,500	44,500	160,000

(d) **Materials purchases budget for component R (in units)**

Use material purchases = materials used in production + closing stock – closing stock

	Quarter 1	*Quarter 2*	*Quarter 3*	*Quarter 4*	*Total*
Used in production (from (c))	144,000	192,000	126,000	178,000	640,000
Closing stock (20% of next qtr's production requirements)	38,400	25,200	35,600	32,000 (W)	32,000
Opening stock	(3,000)	(38,400)	(25,200)	(35,600)	(3,000)
	179,400	178,800	136,400	174,400	669,000

Working

Production in quarter 5 = sales + closing stock – opening stock
= 40,000 + 4,000 – 4,000
= 40,000

Component R required for production = 4 × 40,000
= 160,000

∴ Closing stock = 20% × 160,000 = 32,000

(e) **Labour cost budget**

	Quarter 1	*Quarter 2*	*Quarter 3*	*Quarter 4*	*Total*
	£	£	£	£	£
Production × 6 hours × rate	1,080,000	1,440,000	945,000	1,388,400	4,853,400

IMPORTANT POINT

You may be surprised to know that for budgeting you require **no new knowledge**. You have just got to look at the process of developing a budget from a **different perspective** to that adopted when drawing up financial statements.

When recording historical data for use in financial accounts, the results of month 1 feed into month 2. Planning and budgeting often requires estimates to be made for month 2 in order to establish what would happen in month 1. For example, if goods have to be made the month before they are sold, you need to know the planned sales in month 2 in order to be able to determine the production data for month 1.

Activity 9.6

A product manager for J&L Ltd has responsibility for a single product and is in the process of submitting data to be compiled into budgets for 20X9.

Shown below are the agreed budgeted sales for the product for December 20X8 to May 20X9.

	Dec	*Jan*	*Feb*	*Mar*	*Apr*	*May*
Units	14,000	16,000	22,000	17,000	20,000	24,000

The company policy is that, at each month end, the closing stock of finished goods should be 25% of the following month's forecast sales and the stock of raw material should be sufficient for 10% of the following month's production. Stock levels currently conform to this policy. One unit of raw material makes one unit of finished stock, there is no wastage.

Task

Compute the budgeted monthly production in units and material purchases in units from January to March 20X9.

6 Budgeted profit and loss account

A business might want to estimate its profitability for a coming period. This involves the preparation of a budgeted profit and loss account.

It is important that you remember that, just like historical financial statements, **budgeted profit and loss accounts are based on the accruals concept**. Budget questions may be accompanied by a large amount of sometimes confusing detail. This should not blind you to the fact that **many figures can be entered very simply from the logic of the trading situation described**.

For example, you may be given a simple statement that a business pays rates at £1,500 a year, followed by a lot of detail to enable you to calculate a prepayment at the beginning and end of the year. If you are preparing a budgeted profit and loss account for the year do not lose sight of the fact that the rates expense can be entered as £1,500 without any calculation at all.

Example: a budgeted P&L account

ABC Manufacturing Limited produces two products, Alphas and Betas. The budget for the forthcoming year to 31 March Year 8 is to be prepared. Expectations for the forthcoming year include the following.

(a) **Finished products**

The sales director has estimated the following.

		Alpha	*Beta*
(i)	Demand for the company's products	4,500 units	4,000 units
(ii)	Selling price per unit	£32	£44
(iii)	Closing stock of finished products at 31 March Year 8	400 units	1,200 units
(iv)	Opening stock of finished products at 1 April Year 7	900 units	200 units
(v)	Unit cost of this opening stock	£20	£28
(vi)	Amount of plant capacity required for each unit of product		
	Machining	15 mins	24 mins
	Assembling	12 mins	18 mins
(vii)	Raw material content per unit of each product		
	Material M1	1.5 kilos	0.5 kilos
	Material M2	2.0 kilos	4.0 kilos
(viii)	Direct labour hours required per unit of each product	6 hours	9 hours

Finished goods are valued on a FIFO basis at full production cost.

(b) **Raw materials**

		Material M1	*Material M2*
(i)	Closing stock requirement in kilos at 31 March Year 8	600	1,000
(ii)	Opening stock at 1 April Year 7 in kilos	1,100	6,000
(iii)	Budgeted cost of raw materials per kilo	£1.50	£1.00

Actual costs per kilo of opening stocks are as budgeted cost for the coming year.

(c) **Direct labour**

The standard wage rate of direct labour is £1.60 per hour.

(d) **Production overhead**

Production overhead is absorbed on the basis of machining hours, with separate absorption rates for each department. Overheads in the machining department are anticipated to be £39,500, while in the assembling department they are anticipated to be £18,650.

Depreciation is taken at 5% straight line on plant and equipment. A machine costing the company £20,000 is due to be installed on 1 October Year 7 in the machining department, which already has machinery installed to the value of £100,000 (at cost). The total cost of plant and equipment is £187,000. Land worth £180,000 is to be acquired in December Year 7.

(e) Selling and administration expenses are expected to be £30,400.

(f) There is no opening or closing work in progress and inflation should be ignored.

Task

Prepare the following for the year ended 31 March Year 8 for ABC Manufacturing Ltd.

(a) Sales budget
(b) Production budget (in quantities)
(c) Plant utilisation budget
(d) Direct materials usage budget
(e) Direct labour budget
(f) Production overhead budget
(g) Computation of the factory cost per unit for each product
(h) Direct materials purchases budget
(i) Cost of sales budget
(j) A budgeted profit and loss account

Solution

(a) **Sales budget**

	Market demand	*Selling price*	*Sales value*
	Units	£	£
Alpha	4,500	32.00	144,000
Beta	4,000	44.00	176,000
			320,000

(b) **Production budget**

	Alpha	*Beta*
	Units	Units
Sales requirement	4,500	4,000
(Decrease)/increase in finished goods stock	(500)	1,000
Production requirement	4,000	5,000

(c) **Plant utilisation budget**

Product		*Machining*		*Assembling*	
	Units	Hours per unit	Total hours	Hours per unit	Total hours
Alpha	4,000	0.25	1,000	0.20	800
Beta	5,000	0.40	2,000	0.30	1,500
			3,000		2,300

(d) **Direct materials usage budget**

		Material M1	*Material M2*
		kg	kg
Required for production:			
Alpha:	4,000 × 1.5 kilos	6,000	-
	4,000 × 2.0 kilos	-	8,000
Beta:	5,000 × 0.5 kilos	2,500	-
	5,000 × 4.0 kilos	–	20,000
Material usage		8,500	28,000
Unit cost		£1.50 per kilo	£1.00 per kilo
Cost of materials used		£12,750	£28,000

(e) **Direct labour budget**

Product	*Production* Units	*Hours required per unit*	Total hours	*Rate per hour* £	*Cost* £
Alpha	4,000	6	24,000	1.60	38,400
Beta	5,000	9	45,000	1.60	72,000
			Total direct wages		110,400

(f) **Production overhead budget**

			Machining dept	*Assembling dept*
			£	£
Production overhead allocated and apportioned (excluding depreciation)			39,500	18,650
Depreciation costs				
(i)	Existing plant:	(5% of £100,000 in machining)	5,000	
		(5% of £87,000 in assembly)		4,350
(ii)	Proposed plant:	(5% of 6/12 × £20,000)	500	
Total production overhead			45,000	23,000
Total machine hours (see (c))			3,000 hrs	2,300 hrs
Absorption rate per machine hour			£15	£10

(g) **Cost of finished goods**

			Alpha		**Beta**
			£		£
Direct material	M1	1.5 kg × £1.50	2.25	0.5 kg × £1.50	0.75
	M2	2.0 kg × £1.00	2.00	4.0 kg × £1.00	4.00
Direct labour		6 hrs × £1.60	9.60	9 hrs × £1.60	14.40
Production overhead					
Machining department		15 mins at £15 per hr	3.75	24 mins at £15 per hr	6.00
Assembling department		12 mins at £10 per hr	2.00	18 mins at £10 per hr	3.00
Production cost per unit			19.60		28.15

(h) **Direct material purchases budget**

	M1	*M2*
	kg	kg
Closing stock required	600	1,000
Production requirements	8,500	28,000
	9,100	29,000
Less opening stock	1,100	6,000
Purchase requirements	8,000	23,000
Cost per unit	£1.50	£1.00
Purchase costs	£12,000	£23,000

(i) **Cost of sales budget (Using FIFO)**

	Alpha			*Beta*		
	Units		£	Units		£
Opening stocks	900	(× £20.00)	18,000	200	(× £28.00)	5,600
Cost of production	4,000	(× £19.60)	78,400	5,000	(× £28.15)	140,750
	4,900		96,400	5,200		146,350
Less closing stocks	400	(× £19.60)	7,840	1,200	(× £28.15)	33,780
Cost of sales	4,500		88,560	4,000		112,570

Notes

(i) The cost of sales of Alpha = 900 units at £20 each plus 3,600 units at £19.60 each.

(ii) The cost of sales of Beta = 200 units at £28 each plus 3,800 units at £28.15 each.

(j) **Budgeted profit and loss account for year to 31 March Year 8**

	Alpha	*Beta*	*Total*
	£	£	£
Sales	144,000	176,000	320,000
Less cost of sales	88,560	112,570	201,130
Gross profit	55,440	63,430	118,870
Less selling and administration			30,400
Net profit			88,470

Note. There will be no under-/over-absorbed production overhead in the budgeted profit and loss account.

7 Capital expenditure budgets

Because of the monetary amounts involved in capital expenditure, the **capital expenditure budget is an important budget**. The steps in the preparation of such a budget are as follows.

An accountant or **budget officer responsible** for the capital expenditure budget should communicate between interested parties, provide necessary data to assist in budget preparation, draw up a timetable to ensure that proper consultation takes place and so on.

↓

A detailed capital expenditure budget should be prepared for the budget period (usually 12 months) but additional **budgets should be drawn up for both the medium and long term** (which requires consideration of the organisation's requirements for land, buildings, plant, machinery, vehicles, fixtures and fittings and so on for the short, medium and long term).

↓

The annual **budget** should be **broken down into monthly or quarterly spending**, the details of which can be incorporated into a cash budget (not assessable in Unit 9).

↓

Suitable **financing** must be arranged as necessary.

↓

The capital expenditure budget should **take account of the principal budget factor**. If available funds are limiting the organisation's activities then it will more than likely limit capital expenditure.

↓

As part of the overall **budget coordination** process, the capital expenditure budget must be reviewed in relation to the other budgets. Proposed expansion of production may require significant fixed assets expenditure which should be reflected in the budget.

↓

The capital expenditure budget should be **updated** on a regular basis since both the timing and amount of expenditure can change at short notice.

8 Other aspects of budget preparation

8.1 Budgets for departments not involved in manufacturing

Budgets are also prepared for those departments and functions not involved in manufacturing. An organisation may therefore also prepare an administration budget, a marketing budget, a research and development budget and so on.

Such budgets **do *not* take as their starting point the sales budget** (if sales are the principal budget factor) because the level of administration costs, say, is unlikely to vary in proportion to the level of sales. Instead the administration cost budget will be drawn up following meetings between the management accountant and various members of staff ranging from the managing director down to office managers and supervisors.

In Chapter 11, we will be examining a method of budgeting called zero based budgeting, which is ideal for budgeting in such cases.

8.2 Non-manufacturing scenarios

Although a task might be based on data about a manufacturing organisation, the scenario could well describe some sort of service organisation. Remember that the management accounting information should **help** managers and so you need to **apply** the general knowledge you gain from this text to the scenario in question.

A budget in a university, for example, needs to include teaching and non-teaching costs, rather than direct labour and indirect labour costs. And instead of products X, Y and Z, the budget may need to be based around the different degree courses offered by the university.

Activity 9.7

ND Consultancy Ltd is a service-based business offering four different services to clients. You ascertain the following information for the coming year.

	Service 1	*Service 2*	*Service 3*	*Service 4*
Charge per hour to clients	£20	£25	£30	£40
Budgeted chargeable hours	10,584	6,804	5,292	7,560
Payment per hour to employee	£8	£10	£11	£14

Staff are expected to work a 35 hour week for 48 weeks per year. 10% of their time is non-chargeable. Other costs include office administration (£185,000), marketing and selling expenses (£75,000) and rental (£160,000). It is company policy to employ part-time as well as full-time staff.

Tasks

Calculate the following.

(a) Revenue budget by service
(b) Number of employees in total and by service
(c) Direct wages budget

8.3 Indices and budgets

TOPIC LINK

Indices and budgets

Suppose that the standard or budgeted price for a kg of material or an hour of labour time requires updating. You can use indices to increase/decrease prices and rates so that budgets are prepared on the basis of current information.

You should know how to do this by now, so have a go at the following activity!

Activity 9.8

The current standard price per litre of a particular chemical of £10 was set when an index of material prices stood at 150. Given that this index now stands at 190, what price should be used for preparing the annual budget?

9 Accounting for waste, rejects and inefficiency

In many exam tasks, you are asked to deal with a situation in which **not all resources** are actually **used to make saleable products.**

9.1 Rejects

Some finished goods may not be saleable, perhaps because of a problem with the production process or exceptionally high quality control procedures, and so have to be scrapped. The **budgeted production level** must therefore be **higher** than the **budgeted sales level** so as to allow for the expected level of rejects.

Reject units require an **adjustment** to the **production budget**.

Note, however, that if the production budget is adjusted there will be a knock-on effect on the labour and materials usage budget.

9.2 Wastage

The amount of **raw material used to meet the budgeted production level** might be **less** than the **amount of raw material contained in the finished products** for a number of reasons.

- Evaporation
- Spillage
- Natural wastage (such as the skin of fruit used to make fruit juice)

If this **wastage occurs before production** commences, the **materials purchases budget** must be **adjusted** to ensure that sufficient material is available to meet the materials usage budget.

If this **wastage occurs during production**, the **materials usage budget** must be **adjusted** to ensure that sufficient material is available to meet the production budget.

9.3 Inefficiency

A workforce that is expected to work at a particular level of efficiency may not always be able to achieve this.

- If it is known in advance that the workforce will be **inefficient** (perhaps because of technical difficulties with machinery so that idle time occurs), **additional hours** over and above the standard budgeted hours will be required to meet budgeted production.
- On the other hand, if it is known that the workforce should work at **above standard levels of efficiency, fewer hours** will be required.

In both situations, **adjustments** must be made to the **labour budget**.

9.4 The required approach

The approach to dealing with all three problems is very similar. Here we will look at how to deal with rejected units.

The principal point to grasp is that only good production can be sold and so if any units are faulty, **gross production** must be **greater** than **good production**.

Good production + faulty production = gross production

Let's say that gross production represents 100% of total production.

Good production (as a % of gross production) + faulty production (as a % of gross production) = gross production (100%)

Manipulation of this formula (look back to Chapter 4 if necessary) will then allow you to deal with any variation in the way in which task data about reject units is provided.

For example, suppose that 2% of gross production is rejected at the end of production.

Faulty production = 2% (or 2/100) of gross production

$\therefore$ 100/2 × faulty production = gross production (1)

Given a 2% reject rate, (100% – 2%) 98% of gross production is good.

Good production = 98% (or 98/100) of gross production
$\therefore$ 100/98 × good production = gross production (2)

By equating (1) and (2):

100/2 × faulty production = 100/98 × good production
Faulty production = (2/100) × (100/98) × good production
$\therefore$ Faulty production = 2/98 × good production

Likewise, suppose a reject rate was 7% of gross production.

100/93 × good production = gross production
7/93 × good production = faulty production

What about taking account of **inefficiency due to idle time**?

For example, suppose production of a product requires 1,000 hours and, of the total hours paid for, it is anticipated that 1% will be idle time. How many hours need to be worked?

Good (or productive) hours = 99% (or 99/100) of gross hours

$\therefore$ 1,000 = 99/100 × gross hours
$\therefore$ 1,000 × 100/99 = gross hours
$\therefore$ 1,010 hours = gross hours

Try the activity below to check your understanding of how to deal with faulty production. Activities 9.9 and 9.10 incorporate raw material wastage while the example following Activity 9.9 requires the labour budget to be adjusted for inefficiency.

Activity 9.9

(a) The budgeted good production of XY Ltd in April 20X3 is 810 units. 10% of production is expected to be faulty.

- (i) What is gross production?
- (ii) How many units will be faulty?

(b) 475 units of production are required to enable AB Ltd's sales demand for quarter 3 of 20X3 to be met. 5% of units produced are likely to be scrapped. How many units need to be produced to enable sales demand to be met?

Example: scrap and inefficiency

Mowbray Ltd manufactures a single product with a single grade of labour. Its sales budget and finished goods stock budget for period 3 of Year 6 are as follows.

Sales	700 units
Opening stocks, finished goods	50 units

Closing stocks of finished goods must be sufficient for two days' sales, based on the activity for period 3

The goods are inspected only when production work is completed, and it is budgeted that 10% of total finished work will be scrapped. The standard direct labour hour content of the product is three hours. The budgeted productivity ratio for direct labour is only 80% (which means that labour is only working at 80% efficiency). The company employs 18 direct operatives, who are expected to average 144 working hours each in period 3. The sales activity is budgeted to take place over 20 days in period 3.

Tasks

- (a) Prepare a production budget.
- (b) Prepare a direct labour budget.
- (c) Comment on the problem that your direct labour budget reveals, and suggest how this problem might be overcome.

Solution

(a) **Production budget**

Remember production = sales + closing stock – opening stock.

	Units
Sales	700
Add closing stock (700 units/20 days × 2 days' stock)	70
	770
Less opening stock	50
Production required of 'good' output	720

Total production required (ie gross production) = 100/90 × 720 = 800 units

(b) Now we can prepare the direct labour budget. Note that we take account of the efficiency rate of 80% in exactly the same way as we did for faulty production.

Standard hours per unit	3
Total standard hours required = 800 units × 3 hours	2,400 hours
Productivity ratio	80%

Gross hours required = 100/80 × productive hours = 100/80 × 2,400 = 3,000 hours

(c) If we look at the direct labour budget against the information provided, we can identify the problem.

	Hours
Budgeted hours available (18 operatives × 144 hours)	2,592
Actual hours required	3,000
Shortfall in labour hours	408

The (draft) budget indicates that there will not be enough direct labour hours to meet the production requirements. This problem might be overcome in one, or a combination, of the following ways.

- Reduce the closing stock requirement below 70 units. This would reduce the number of production units required.
- Persuade the workforce to do some overtime working.
- Perhaps recruit more direct labour if long-term prospects are for higher production volumes.
- Discuss with the workforce (or their union representatives) the following possibilities.
  - Improve the productivity ratio, and so reduce the number of hours required to produce the output.
  - If possible, reduce the wastage rate below 10%.

We return to the problem of a shortage of resources in the next section.

Activity 9.10

Sulgrave Ltd has recently completed its sales forecasts for the year to 31 December Year 4. It expects to sell two products – P1 and P2 – at prices of £135 and £145 each respectively. Sales demand is expected to be 10,000 units of P1 and 6,000 units of P2.

Both products use the same raw materials and skilled labour but in different quantities per unit:

	P1	*P2*
Material M1	10 kgs	6 kgs
Material M2	4 litres	8 litres
Skilled labour	6 hours	4 hours

The prices expected during Year 4 for the raw materials are £1.50 per kg of material M1 and £4 per litre of material M2. The skilled labour rate is expected to be £6.00 per hour.

Stocks of raw materials and finished goods on 1 January Year 4 are expected to be:

Material M1	400 kgs	@ £1.20 per kg
Material M2	200 litres	@ £3.00 per kg
P1	600 units	@ £70.00 each
P2	800 units	@ £60.00 each

All stocks are to be reduced by 15% from their opening levels by the end of Year 4 and are valued using the FIFO method.

On average, 3% of the total input of material M2 is spilt during production.

The company uses absorption costing. Variable production overhead costs are expected to be £2 per skilled labour hour. Fixed production overhead costs are expected to be £315,900 per annum.

Tasks

Prepare for the year to 31 December Year 4 Sulgrave Ltd's:

(a) Production budget (in units)
(b) Raw material purchases budget (in units and £)
(c) Production cost budget

10 Limiting factors

A **scarce resource** that **limits an organisation's ability to meet potential sales demand** is known as a **limiting (key** or **budget) factor**.

So if potential maximum sales demand is 1,000 units but there is only enough material to produce 800 units, material is a limiting factor.

In the exam you could encounter limiting factors in two different types of scenario. Both require you to carry out a **rescheduling** exercise. Rescheduling is a matter of **co-ordination**, but it is more than arranging for resources to be available when required (which is what we are doing when developing production and resource budgets which ensure that the sales budget can be met). Rescheduling is also concerned with co-ordination for **efficiency**.

In terms of the exam, this means that you could be provided with additional information which indicates that there could be cost savings from revising the original production and resource budgets you prepared to ensure budgeted sales demands could be met.

Exactly how those cost savings can be achieved will depend on the task data with which you are provided.

10.1 Multi-product/single period budget task

In this scenario, an organisation might sell one of its products (say product X) under a **long-term contract**, the terms of which **cannot be amended**. Rescheduling will involve **diverting production facilities** from one product to another. The **scarce resource** must therefore be **used first** to **produce** the **volume** of product X **specified in the contract**. The remaining resource can then be used to produce units of the other product (say product Y). Maximum sales demand for product Y may not be met.

Example: limiting factors

Southcott Ltd makes two products, one for the home market (H) and one for export (E). H is sold under a long-term contract to a large retail company only. The contract specifies the volume of deliveries each week. Because of penalty clauses in the contract it is not possible to reduce the sales volume of the H.

The budgeted weekly demand for H is 500 units, that for E is 400 units.

Each unit of H requires 10 kgs of sugar, while each unit of E requires 12 kgs of sugar. Sugar available for production in November 20X1 is expected to total 9,440 kgs.

Task

On the basis of the information above, determine the budgeted production level of the two products.

Solution

	Kgs
Sugar available	9,440
Sugar used in production of H to meet contract (500 × 10 kgs)	5,000
Sugar remaining for production of E	4,440

With 4,440 kgs of sugar, 4,440/12 = 370 units of E can be manufactured.

Budgeted production levels

Product H	500 units
Product E	370 units

Activity 9.11

Alexandra Ltd produces two products, the S and the R. Alexandra Ltd is contracted to supply 1,800 units of S a month to Derwent plc under a non-negotiable contract. Estimated monthly demand for R is 3,500 units.

During December 20X3, a large proportion of the workforce are attending a training programme and so labour hours available will be insufficient to meet sales demand for the two products.

Task

If each unit of S requires half an hour of labour time and each unit of R requires ten minutes, calculate budgeted production levels if the budgeted labour hours available in December 20X3 are 1,400.

10.1.1 Contribution per unit of limiting factor

ATTENTION!

The AAT has confirmed that contribution per unit of limiting factor will **not** be assessed during the changeover between the old and the revised versions of the standards. The first time the technique could possibly be assessed is therefore in the June 2005 exam. You therefore only need to read this section if you are sitting a 2005 exam.

Instead of a scenario in which production/sales of one product cannot be reduced because of penalty clauses in a contract, you may first have to identify the product that will have the least effect on contribution (and hence profit) if its production and sales levels were to be reduced.

The technique used to identify the product is known as contribution per unit of limiting factor (or limiting factor analysis). It is based on the marginal costing principles that profit is maximised when contribution is maximised, and that fixed costs in the period will be the same regardless of the products manufactured.

Contribution will be maximised by earning the biggest possible contribution from each unit of limiting factor. Thus if grade A labour is the limiting factor, contribution will be maximised by earning the biggest contribution from each hour of grade A labour worked. Similarly, if machine time is in short supply, profit will be maximised by earning the biggest contribution from each machine hour worked.

You therefore need to **determine the contribution earned by each different product from each unit of the limiting factor**. This sounds far more complicated than it actually is, so let's have a look at an example.

Example: contribution per unit of limiting factor

AB Ltd makes two products, the Ay and the Be. Unit variable costs are as follows.

	Ay	*Be*
	£	£
Direct materials	1	3
Direct labour (£3 per hour)	6	3
Variable overhead	1	1
	8	7

The sales price per unit is £14 per Ay and £11 per Be. During July the available direct labour is limited to 8,000 hours. Sales demand in July is expected to be 3,000 units for Ays and 5,000 units for Bes.

Task

Determine the profit-maximising production mix to include in the budget, assuming opening stocks of finished goods and work in progress are budgeted to be nil.

Solution

Confirm that the limiting factor is something other than sales demand.

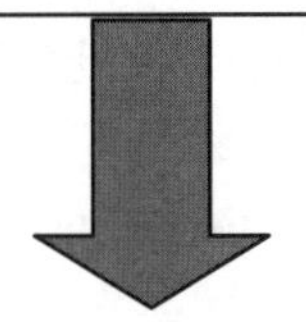

	Ays	*Bes*	*Total*
Labour hours per unit	2 hrs	1 hr	
Sales demand	3,000 units	5,000 units	
Labour hours needed	6,000 hrs	5,000 hrs	11,000 hrs
Labour hours available			8,000 hrs
Shortfall			3,000 hrs

Labour is the limiting factor on production.

Identify the contribution earned by each product per unit of limiting factor, that is per labour hour worked.

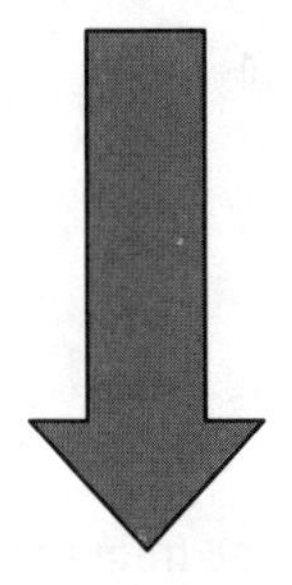

	Ays	*Bes*
	£	£
Sales price	14	11
Variable cost	8	7
Unit contribution	6	4
Labour hours per unit	2 hrs	1 hr
Contribution per labour hour (= unit of limiting factor)	£3	£4

Although Ays have a higher unit contribution than Bes, two Bes can be made in the time it takes to make one Ay. Because labour is in short supply it is more profitable to make Bes than Ays.

Work out the budgeted production and sales mix.

Sufficient Bes will be made to meet the full sales demand, and the remaining labour hours available will then be used to make Ays.

Product	*Demand*	*Hours required*	*Hours available*	*Priority of manu-facture*	*Units manu-factured*
Bes	5,000	5,000	5,000	1st	5,000
Ays	3,000	6,000	3,000 (bal)	2nd	1,500
		11,000	8,000		

Sales and production of Ays should therefore be reduced to below maximum demand as this will have a less adverse affect on profit than reducing sales/ production of Bes.

IMPORTANT POINT

Note that it is *not* more profitable to begin by making as many units as possible with the bigger unit contribution. We could make 3,000 units of Ay in 6,000 hours and 2,000 units of Be in the remaining 2,000 hours but profit would be only £6,000. Unit contribution is not the correct way to decide priorities, because it takes two hours to earn £6 from a Ay and one hour to earn £4 from a Be. Bes make more profitable use of the scarce resource, labour hours.

10.1.2 Contribution per unit of limiting factor and penalty clauses in contracts

Continuing with our example about AB Ltd above, let's now suppose that you are informed that the company has entered into a long-term contract to sell 1,800 Ays per month to a particular customer. Penalty clauses in the contract make it impossible for AB Ltd to break the terms of the contract.

The budgeted production and sales mix will therefore have to be amended so that these 1,800 Ays are produced before any other products.

Product	*Demand*	*Hrs required*	*Hrs available*	*Priority for manufacture*	*Units manufactured*
Ays	1,800	3,600	3,600	1st	1,800
Bes	5,000	5,000	4,400 (bal)	2nd	4,400
Ays	1,200*	2,400	–	–	–
		11,000	8,000		

* 3,000 – 1,800 for contract

The sales/production mix has now changed to 1,800 Ays and 4,400 Bes.

10.2 Single product/multi-period budget task

In tasks concerned with just **one product**, limiting factors may require production to be **rescheduled** from one **period when there is excess demand** (because there is a shortage of a resource such as raw material or labour) **to earlier periods** when there is **surplus production capacity.**

If there is a **finance charge** associated with this, maximum use should be made of any surplus in the periods closest to the period in which there is excess demand.

Consider the following single product/multi-period example.

Month	*1*	*2*	*3*
	Units	Units	Units
Maximum capacity	3,000	3,000	3,000
Planned production (for immediate sale)	2,800	2,750	3,300
Surplus/(deficit)	200	250	(300)
Change in planned production	50	250	(300)
Revised production	2,850	3,000	3,000

If any units made earlier than one month before being sold incur financing costs of £1 per unit per month, the additional costs would be (50 units × £1 × 2 months) + (250 units × £1 × 1 month) = £350.

WATCH OUT FOR...

Efficient calculations

Let's continue with the rescheduling illustration above. Suppose that the initial planned production schedule can only be met by overtime working because of a shortage of labour, which increases the cost per unit from £20 to £30.

How would you calculate the cost saving associated with the revised production schedule?

Do not calculate the total production cost over the three months of the original production schedule, the total production cost over the three months of the revised production schedule, deducting the latter from the former to get the cost saving.

Instead you need to realise that the **saving** is **solely associated** with the **300 units** produced during months 1 and 2 instead of during month 3 and that the **saving per unit** is £(30 – 20). The total cost saving is therefore 300 x £(30 – 20) = £3,000.

This figure would need to be reduced by any financing costs of rescheduling.

Alternatively:

- Scenario details might state that there is a maximum amount of labour hours available per period before overtime is incurred. A review of your original budget could indicate that although you will have to pay overtime in some periods, in others there may be surplus labour hours. The task might then ask you to identify and quantify the possible cost savings from rescheduling to reduce the overtime payments.
- Or you might be told that there is a limited amount of material available from an existing supplier, a problem that can only be overcome by purchasing elsewhere at a higher price, in certain periods. In other periods less than the maximum amount of available material may be required, however. The task might then ask you to identify and quantify the possible cost savings from rescheduling to reduce the expensive purchases.

You've already seen an example of rescheduling production so have a go at the following activities which require you to reschedule material purchases and labour hours worked.

Activity 9.12

You have been provided with the following information about Coombe Ltd.

(a) Budgeted production of component CX1 for the four control periods of 20X0

Control period 1	400 units
Control period 2	560 units
Control period 3	350 units
Control period 4	890 units

(b) Each unit of component CX1 requires 8 kgs of material.

(c) The material is currently supplied under long-term contract by Little Ltd. Little Ltd can supply a maximum of 4,000 kgs per control period.

(d) Given the perishable nature of the material it has to be used in the same control period in which it is purchased.

(e) Should Coombe Ltd require more than 4,000 kgs per control period, Little Ltd can produce additional material in the preceding control period and store it in a controlled environment, providing it has spare capacity.

Task

Determine whether Coombe Ltd will be unable to meet budgeted production in any control period of 20X0 because of a shortage of material.

Activity 9.13

The budgeted production levels for one of Hibbert Ltd's products during the first three control periods of 20X2 are as follows.

Period 1	7,000 units
Period 2	5,600 units
Period 3	9,100 units

Each unit requires two labour hours. Hibbert Ltd employees 100 workers who each work 140 hours per control period. Each employee is paid a guaranteed wage of £1,120 per period. The cost of any overtime is £10 per hour.

Task

Given that it is Hibbert Ltd's policy to keep overtime payments to a minimum, calculate the value of possible overtime savings if production can be rescheduled.

10.3 How to alleviate a limiting factor

You could be asked to recommend action that might go some way to alleviating a limiting factor. A shortfall in labour is normally a short-term problem as paying a higher rate and/or training should increase availability. We looked at possible ways to deal with a labour shortage in Section 9. The appropriate course of action will very much depend on the task data.

IMPORTANT POINT

Remember that the advice you give in an exam must be tailored to the task data. Don't recommend buying in finished goods if the organisation in question is the sole producer of the product.

Activity 9.14

How might management find their way round a limiting factor of raw materials?

We'll finish this chapter with an activity taken from the December 1997 exam. It covers a wide range of topics and tests your understanding of many of the main points we have covered in this chapter.

Activity 9.15

(a) George Phillips makes and sells two types of garden ornament, the Alpha and the Beta. George prepared his 20X8 budget several months ago but since then he has discovered that there is a shortage of raw material used for making the ornaments. As a result, he will only be able to acquire 20,000 kilograms of the raw material for the first 13 weeks of 20X8.

An extract from his original budget is reproduced below.

Sales budget

	Units	*Selling price*	*Turnover*
		£	£
Alpha	6,500	36.00	234,000
Beta	7,800	39.00	304,200

Extract from the production budget

	Units produced	*Material per unit*	*Total material*
		kg	kg
Alpha	6,900	2.0	13,800
Beta	9,000	1.5	13,500
Materials issued to production			27,300

Purchases budget

	Kilograms	*Price per kilogram*	*Total cost*
		£	£
Materials issued to production	27,300	5.00	136,500
Opening stock	(6,000)	5.00	(30,000)
Closing stock	6,600	5.00	33,000
Purchases	27,900		139,500

Labour budget

	Units produced	*Labour hours per unit*	*Total hours*
Alpha	6,900	2.500	17,250
Beta	9,000	2.785	25,065
Labour hours			42,315
Labour cost			£169,260

George also provides you with the following additional information.

- The budget is based on a 13-week period.
- Employees work a 35-hour week.
- The closing stocks of materials and finished products must be kept to the figures in the original budget.
- The original sales budget represents the maximum demand for the Alpha and the Beta in a 13-week period.

Task

You are the recently appointed accounting trainee at the company. George Phillips asks you to revise his budget for the first 13 weeks of 20X8 to take account of the shortage of the raw materials. You should prepare the following budgets.

(i) Materials purchases
(ii) Materials issued to production
(iii) Sales volume and turnover
(iv) Labour hours and cost
(v) The number of employees required

(b) On reviewing the revised figures George realises that there are too many employees and he calls a meeting of the managers of the business. During the meeting two issues are raised.

(i) The production manager does not wish to reduce the number of employees as he will lose key trained staff who may not wish to be re-employed later. He argues that the labour costs are fixed as the employees are not employed on a piece work basis.

(ii) In preparing the original budget George had been advised by one of the partners at the firm's auditors that the key factor should be identified before the budget was prepared. He had assumed that sales would be a key factor and therefore the budget had been based on sales; this was invalid since materials are now the limiting factor.

Task

You have been requested to prepare a report covering the issues raised by George Phillips and his managers at the meeting.

Key learning points

- ☑ The **production budget** is based on the following formula:

  Production = sales + closing stock – opening stock

- ☑ The **materials usage** and **labour utilisation budget** can be prepared once the production budget has been set.

- ☑ The **materials purchases budget** can then be drawn up. It is based on the following equation:

  Materials purchases = materials used in production + closing stock – opening stock

- ☑ Watch out for the different ways of **describing stock levels.**

- ☑ Exam tasks will **either** involve **multi-product/single period** budgets or **single product/multi-period** budgets.

- ☑ Watch out for the **link between opening and closing stock** in multi-period budgets, for non-manufacturing scenarios and for the use of **indices.**

- ☑ Exam tasks often require you to account for **waste, rejects and inefficiency**. You need to be able to manipulate the following formulae (or versions of them, depending on the problem):

  Good production = ((100 – reject%)/100) × gross production
  Rejected units = (reject%/100) × gross production

- ☑ A scarce resource that limits an organisation's ability to meet potential sales demand is known as a **limiting** (or **key** or **budget) factor**.

- ☑ The occurrence of a limiting factor will require you to carry out some form of **rescheduling**.

- ☑ In a **multi-product/single period** task, rescheduling will involve diverting production facilities from one product to another.

- ☑ **Contribution per unit of limiting factor technique** is required if you need to identify the priority for production of a number of different products and contribution (and hence profit) is to be maximised.

- ☑ In a **single product/multi-period** task, rescheduling may involve diverting production from one period when there is excess demand (because of a resource shortage) to earlier periods when there is surplus production capacity.

- ☑ Alternatively, you may need to reschedule in order to save overtime costs or the costs of using more expensive suppliers.

Quick quiz

1 *Choose the correct words from those highlighted.*

If closing stock is greater than opening stock, production will be **greater than/less than** sales.

2 *Complete the following equation which is useful when preparing a materials purchases budget.*

Material purchases = ... + ... – ....

3 What two types of budget could you encounter in an exam?

I Single period/multi-product
II Single period/single product
III Multi-period/multi-product
IV Multi-period/single product

A I and IV
B II and III
C I and III
D III and IV

4 A standard labour rate of £20 per hour was set when the index of labour costs stood at 290. It now stands are 380. What labour rate should be used in the budget currently being prepared?

5 If wastage of materials occurs during production, the materials usage budget should be adjusted. *True or false?*

6 Suppose 3% of finished units are rejected at the end of production. How many units must be produced if 1,200 good units are required?

Answers to quick quiz

1 Greater than

2 Materials purchases = materials used in production + closing stock – opening stock

3 A

4 £20 × 380/290 = £26.21 per hour

5 True

6 97% of production is good

∴ Good production = 97/100 of gross production
∴ 1,200 = 97/100 of gross production
∴ 1,200 × 100/97 = gross production
∴ 1,237 units = gross production

ASSESSMENT KIT ACTIVITIES

The following activities in the BPP Assessment Kit for Units 8 & 9 include topics covered in this chapter.

Activities 22 to 28
Lecturers' practice activities 12 to 15

Activity checklist

This checklist shows which performance criteria, range statement or knowledge and understanding point is covered by each activity in this chapter. Tick off each activity as you complete it.

Activity		
9.1	☐	This activity deals with Performance Criteria 9.2A regarding the presentation to management of draft budget proposals, Range Statement 9.2: types of budget (resource budgets) and data, and Unit 9 Knowledge & Understanding points (5): development of production, resource and revenue budgets from forecast sales data, (6): co-ordination of the budget system and (15): different types of budgets (resource budgets).
9.2	☐	This activity deals with Performance Criteria 9.2A regarding the presentation to management of draft budget proposals, Range Statement 9.2: types of budget (resource budgets) and data, and Unit 9 Knowledge & Understanding points (5): development of production, resource and revenue budgets from forecast sales data, (6): co-ordination of the budget system and (15): different types of budgets (resource budgets).
9.3	☐	This activity deals with Performance Criteria 9.2A regarding the presentation to management of draft budget proposals, Range Statement 9.2: types of budget (resource budgets) and data, and Unit 9 Knowledge & Understanding points (5): development of production, resource and revenue budgets from forecast sales data, (6): co-ordination of the budget system and (15): different types of budgets (resource budgets).
9.4	☐	This activity deals with Performance Criteria 9.2A regarding the presentation to management of draft budget proposals, Range Statement 9.2: types of budget (resource budgets) and data, and Unit 9 Knowledge & Understanding points (5): development of production, resource and revenue budgets from forecast sales data, (6): co-ordination of the budget system and (15): different types of budgets (resource budgets).
9.5	☐	This activity deals with Performance Criteria 9.2A regarding the presentation to management of draft budget proposals, Range Statement 9.2: types of budget (budgets for income and expenditure; resource budgets) and data, and Unit 9 Knowledge & Understanding points (5): development of production, resource and revenue budgets from forecast sales data, (6): co-ordination of the budget system and (15): different types of budgets (resource budgets).
9.6	☐	This activity deals with Performance Criteria 9.2A regarding the presentation to management of draft budget proposals, Range Statement 9.2: types of budget (resource budgets) and data, and Unit 9 Knowledge & Understanding points (5): development of production, resource and revenue budgets from forecast sales data, (6): co-ordination of the budget system and (15): different types of budgets (resource budgets).

Activity checklist (cont'd)

9.7	☐	This activity deals with Performance Criteria 9.2A regarding the presentation to management of draft budget proposals, Range Statement 9.2: types of budget (budgets for income and expenditure; resource budgets) and data, and Unit 9 Knowledge & Understanding points (5): development of production, resource and revenue budgets from forecast sales data, (6): co-ordination of the budget system and (15): different types of budgets (resource budgets).
9.8	☐	This activity deals with Unit 9 Knowledge & Understanding point (3): basic statistical methods (index numbers).
9.9	☐	This activity deals with Performance Criteria 9.2B regarding the verification that draft budget proposals include all relevant data and assumptions.
9.10	☐	This activity deals with Performance Criteria 9.2A regarding the presentation to management of draft budget proposals, Performance Criteria 9.2B regarding the verification that draft budget proposals include all relevant data and assumptions, Range Statement 9.2: types of budget (resource budgets), and Unit 9 Knowledge & Understanding points (5): development of production, resource and revenue budgets from forecast sales data, (6): co-ordination of the budget system and (15): different types of budgets (resource budgets).
9.11	☐	This activity deals with Unit 9 Knowledge & Understanding point (7): the effect of capacity constraints, other production constraints and sales constraints on budgets; limiting (key or budget) factor.
9.12	☐	This activity deals with Unit 9 Knowledge & Understanding point (7): the effect of capacity constraints, other production constraints and sales constraints on budgets; limiting (key or budget) factor.
9.13	☐	This activity deals with Unit 9 Knowledge & Understanding point (7): the effect of capacity constraints, other production constraints and sales constraints on budgets; limiting (key or budget) factor.
9.14	☐	This activity deals with Unit 9 Knowledge & Understanding point (7): the effect of capacity constraints, other production constraints and sales constraints on budgets; limiting (key or budget) factor.
9.15	☐	This activity deals with Performance Criteria 9.2A regarding the presentation to management of draft budget proposals, Performance Criteria 9.2C regarding the breaking down of budgets into periods appropriate to the organisation, Performance Criteria 9.2D regarding communication with budget holders and Unit 9 Knowledge & Understanding point (6): coordination of the budget system.

chapter 10

Budgetary control

Contents

1 Introduction
2 Responsibility centres
3 Fixed and flexible budgets
4 Preparing flexible budgets
5 Flexible budgets and budgetary control
6 Format of budget statements

Performance criteria

9.3A Check and reconcile budget figures on an ongoing basis

9.3B Correctly code and allocate actual cost and revenue data to responsibility centres

9.3C Clearly and correctly identify variances and prepare relevant reports for management

9.3D Discuss with budget holders and other managers any significant variances and help managers take remedial action

Range statement

9.3 Types of budgets: budget for income and expenditure; resource budget; fixed and flexible budgets

9.3 Responsibility centres: expense centres; profit centres

9.3 Variances: actual; potential

Knowledge and understanding

Unit 9 Accounting techniques

8 Budgets for control: flexible budgets, marginal costing

10 Analysing the significance of budget variances and possible responses required by managers

11 Presentation of budget data in a form that satisfies the differing needs of budget holders

Knowledge and understanding (cont'd)

Unit 9 Accounting principles and theory

12 Marginal and absorption costing: cost recording, cost reporting, cost behaviour

13 Uses of budgetary control: planning, co-ordinating, authorising, cost control

Unit 9 The organisation

17 The structure of the organisation and its responsibility centres and an understanding of the inter-relationships between departments and functions is required

18 Responsibility centres: expense centres; profit centres; investment centres

Signpost

The topics covered in this chapter are relevant to **Unit 9.**

You may find it useful to read through Chapters 6 and 7 on standard costing and variances before beginning this chapter.

1 Introduction

We will be looking at a number of background issues in Sections 1 and 2 before moving on to consider the most **important** topic covered in this chapter – **budgetary control** and **flexible budgeting**.

In essence, a **flexible budget shows what costs and revenues should have been for the actual level of output**. A flexible budget can then be **compared with actual results** and the **differences** between the two (**variances**) used to **highlight possible areas for management control action**. (This description should make you think of the control system we looked at in Chapter 1).

Flexible budgets and their preparation **appear regularly in exams** and so an understanding of the contents of Sections 3, 4 and 5 of this chapter is vital.

2 Responsibility centres

In order to prepare a budget for an organisation as a whole, individual budgets have to be prepared for different sections of the organisation, such as individual departments. **Each section of an organisation for which a budget is prepared is called a budget centre**. Since budgets will be made for each of these budget centres, budgetary **control reporting** (the comparison of actual results against plan) will also be **based on budget centres**.

The selection of budget centres in an organisation is therefore a **key first step in setting up a control system**.

(a) Individual **managers** should be made **responsible** for achieving the budget **targets** of a particular budget centre.

(b) **Budget centres** need to be **organised** so that **all** the **revenue** earned by an organisation, all the **costs** incurred and all the **capital employed**, are the **responsibility of someone in the organisation**.

Budgetary control and budget centres are therefore part of the overall system of responsibility accounting within an organisation.

- **Responsibility accounting** is a system of accounting that makes **revenues and costs the responsibility of particular managers** so that the performance of each part of the organisation can be **monitored** and **assessed**.
- A **responsibility centre** is a **section** of an organisation that is headed by a manager who has **direct responsibility** for its performance.

If a manager is to be responsible for the performance of his area of the business he will need to know three things.

Requirements	Examples of information
What are his resources?	Finance, stocks of raw materials, spare machine capacity, labour availability, the balance of expenditure remaining for a certain budget.
How quickly are the resources being consumed?	How fast is his labour force working, how quickly are his raw materials being used up, how quickly is available finance being consumed?
Are resources being used well?	How well are his objectives being met?

The level of detail in the information and the frequency with which it is provided needs to be considered. And the cost of providing information must be weighed against the benefit derived from it.

Traditionally, managers are given monthly reports, but this is simply because it ties in with financial reporting cycles and because it may be administratively convenient. With modern systems, however, there is a danger of **information overload**, since information technology allows the information required to be made available much more frequently.

Management accountants therefore need to find out from the managers of responsibility centres what information they need, in what form and how frequently, and then they should design a planning and control system that enables this information to be provided.

Responsibility centres are therefore usually divided into different categories. Here we shall describe cost (expense), revenue, profit and investment centres.

2.1 Responsibility centres

2.1.1 Cost centres

A **cost** (or **expense**) **centre** is **any part** of an organisation which **incurs costs.**

Cost centres can be quite small, sometimes one person or one machine or one expenditure item. They can also be quite big, for example an entire department. An organisation might establish a hierarchy of cost centres. For example, within a transport department, individual vehicles might each be made a cost centre, the repairs and maintenance section might be a cost centre, there might be cost centres for expenditure items such as rent or building depreciation on the vehicle depots, vehicle insurance and road tax. The transport department as a whole might be a cost centre at the top of this hierarchy of sub-cost centres.

To charge actual costs to a cost centre, each cost centre will have a **cost code**, and items of expenditure will be recorded with the appropriate cost code. When costs are eventually analysed, there may well be some apportionment of the costs of one cost centre to other cost centres.

Information about cost centres might be collected in terms of **total actual costs, total budgeted costs** and **total cost variances**. In addition, the information might be analysed in terms of **ratios**, such as cost per unit produced (budget and actual), hours per unit produced (budget and actual) and transport costs per tonne/ kilometre (budget and actual).

2.1.2 Revenue centres

A **revenue centre** is a **section** of an organisation which **raises revenue** but has **no responsibility for production**. A sales department is an example.

The term 'revenue centre' is **often used in non-profit-making organisations**. Revenue centres are similar to cost centres, except that whereas cost centres are for costs only, revenue centres are for recording revenues only. **Information collection and reporting** could be **based on a comparison of budgeted and actual revenues** earned by that centre.

2.1.3 Profit centres

A **profit centre** is any **section** of an organisation (for example, division of a company) which **earns revenue** and **incurs costs**. The profitability of the section can therefore be measured.

Profit centres differ from cost centres in that they **account for both costs and revenues**. The **key performance measure** of a profit centre is therefore **profit. The manager of the profit centre must be able to influence both revenues and costs** (in other words, have a say in both sales and production policies).

A profit centre manager is likely to be a fairly senior person within an organisation, and a profit centre is likely to cover quite a large area of operations. A profit centre might be an entire division within the organisation, or there might be a separate profit centre for each product, brand or service or each geographical selling area. Information requirements need to be similarly focused.

In the hierarchy of responsibility centres within an organisation, there are likely to be several cost centres within a profit centre.

2.1.4 Investment centres

An **investment centre manager** has some **say in investment policy** in his area of operations as well as being **responsible for costs and revenues**.

Several profit centres might share the same capital items, for example the same buildings, stores or transport fleet, and so investment centres are likely to include several profit centres, and provide a basis for control at a very senior management level, like that of a subsidiary company within a group.

The performance of an investment centre is measured by the return on capital employed. It shows how well the investment centre manager has used the resources under his control to generate profit.

Activity 10.1

Find out if your organisation has a system of cost, revenue, profit and/or investment centres. What is the scope of planning and control within each centre?

ATTENTION!

You should be aware that the information needs of managers of different types of responsibility centre will vary. In an exam, don't state that the manager of a cost centre will need to know how well products are selling or that the manager of a revenue centre will need to be provided with information about cost variances.

2.2 Controllable and non-controllable costs

Managers of responsibility centres should **only be held responsible for costs over which they have some control**. These are known as **controllable costs**, which are items of expenditure which can be **directly influenced** by a given manager within a given time span.

A cost which is not controllable by a junior manager might be controllable by a senior manager. For example, there may be high direct labour costs in a department caused by excessive overtime working. The junior manager may feel obliged to continue with the overtime to meet production schedules, but his senior may be able to reduce costs by hiring extra full-time staff, thereby reducing the requirements for overtime.

A cost which is not controllable by a manager in one department may be controllable by a manager in another department. For example, an increase in material costs may be caused by buying at higher prices than expected (controllable by the purchasing department) or by excessive wastage (controllable by the production department) or by a faulty machine producing rejects (controllable by the maintenance department).

Some costs are **non-controllable**, such as increases in expenditure items due to inflation. Other costs are **controllable, but in the long term rather than the short term**. For example, production costs might be reduced by the introduction of new machinery and technology, but in the short term, management must attempt to do the best they can with the resources and machinery at their disposal.

2.2.1 The controllability of fixed costs

It is often assumed that all fixed costs are non-controllable in the short run. This is not so.

Committed fixed costs are those costs arising from the possession of plant, equipment, buildings and an administration department to **support the long-term needs of the business**. These costs (depreciation, rent, administration salaries) are largely **non-controllable in the short term** because they have been committed by longer-term decisions affecting longer-term needs. When a company decides to cut production drastically, the long-term committed fixed costs will be reduced, but only after redundancy terms have been settled and assets sold.

Discretionary fixed costs, such as advertising and research and development costs, are incurred as a result of a top management decision, but could be **raised or lowered at fairly short notice** (irrespective of the actual volume of production and sales).

2.2.2 Controllability and apportioned costs

Managers should only be held accountable for costs over which they have some influence. This may seem quite straightforward in theory, but it is not always so easy in practice to distinguish controllable from uncontrollable costs. **Apportioned overhead costs provide a good example**.

Suppose that a manager of a production department in a manufacturing company is made responsible for the costs of his department. These costs include **directly attributable overhead items** such as the costs of indirect labour employed in the department and indirect materials consumed in the department. The department's overhead costs also include an apportionment of costs from other cost centres, such as rent and rates for the building it shares with other departments and a share of the costs of the maintenance department.

Should the production manager be held accountable for any of these apportioned costs?

- Managers should not be held accountable for costs over which they have no control. In this example, apportioned rent and rates costs would not be controllable by the production department manager.
- Managers should be held accountable for costs over which they have some influence. In this example, it is the responsibility of the maintenance department manager to keep maintenance costs within budget. But their costs will be partly variable and partly fixed, and the variable cost element will depend on the volume of demand for their services. If the production department's staff treat their equipment badly we might expect higher repair costs, and the production department manager should therefore be made accountable for the repair costs that his department makes the maintenance department incur on its behalf.

3 Fixed and flexible budgets

3.1 Fixed budgets

A fixed budget is a budget which **remains unchanged regardless of the volume of output** or sales achieved.

The budgets we looked at in the **previous chapter** are known as **fixed budgets**. The term 'fixed' means the following.

- The budget is **prepared on the basis of an estimated volume of production** and an **estimated volume of sales**, but no plans are made for the event that actual volumes of production and sales may differ from budgeted volumes.
- When actual volumes of production and sales during a control period (month or four weeks or quarter) are achieved, a fixed budget is **not adjusted (in retrospect) to the new levels of activity**.

Fixed budgets are generally **used for planning** and **define the broad objectives** of the organisation.

3.2 Flexible budgets

A flexible budget is a budget which is designed to **change as volumes of output change**.

Flexible budgets may be used in one of two ways.

- **At the planning stage**. For example, suppose that a company expects to sell 10,000 units of output during the next year. A master budget (the fixed budget) would be prepared on the basis of these expected volumes. However, if the company thinks that output and sales might be as low as 8,000 units or as high as 12,000 units, it may prepare **contingency flexible budgets**, at volumes of, say 8,000, 9,000, 11,000 and 12,000 units and then assess the possible outcomes.
- **Retrospectively**. At the end of each month (control period) or year, flexible budgets can be used so that the **results that should have been achieved** given the actual circumstances (the flexible budget) can be compared with the actual result. As we shall see, flexible budgets are therefore an essential factor in **(budgetary) control systems** as discussed at the beginning of the text in Chapter 1.

4 Preparing flexible budgets

Before we look at how flexible budgets are used for budgetary control purposes, we need to see how they are prepared. Underlying their preparation are the statements of **cost behaviour** included in Chapter 2. Look back to this topic if you need a reminder.

4.1 Cost behaviour and flexible budgets

Here are the main points.

- **Fixed costs** remain the same irrespective of changes in output and so will be the **same in the original and flexed budget**.
- If actual output is greater than the original budgeted output, variable costs in the flexed budget will be greater than those in the original budget.
- If actual output is less than the original budgeted output, semi-variable costs in the flexed budget will be less than those in the original budget because of the decrease in variable costs.

ATTENTION!

You must treat **fixed costs** correctly – they do not change as activity levels change and hence will be the **same in the original and flexed budgets**. The assessor has stated that flexible budgets are all about cost behaviour and so the treatment of fixed costs as though they were a variable cost will be viewed as a fundamental error.

4.2 Flexing costs and revenue

Flexing revenue is straightforward: it simply increases in line with sales volume.

For costs which are wholly fixed or wholly variable no problem arises: fixed costs remain the same and variable costs increase in line with output. But if you are presented with a cost which appears to have behaved in the past as a **semi-fixed cost**, you need to be able to **estimate the fixed and variable elements**. Depending on the data provided, you can use either the **high-low method** (see Chapter 5) or the **incremental method**.

4.2.1 Incremental method

The **incremental method** of splitting a semi-variable cost into its fixed and variable components can be used if you are given the **costs at two different activity levels**.

A semi-variable cost comprises both fixed and variable components. Given that fixed costs do not change with changes in activity level, any difference in the two costs must be due to the variable cost components.

This method is illustrated in the example which follows.

Example: preparing a flexible budget

(a) Prepare a budget for Year 6 for the direct labour costs and overhead expenses of a production department at the activity levels of 80%, 90% and 100%, using the information listed below and ignoring inflation.

(i) The direct labour hourly rate is expected to be £3.75.

(ii) 100% activity represents 60,000 direct labour hours.

(iii)

Variable indirect labour cost	£0.75 per direct labour hour
Variable consumable supplies cost	£0.375 per direct labour hour
Variable canteen cost	6% of direct and indirect labour costs

(iv) Semi-variable costs are expected to relate to the direct labour hours in the same manner as in the last two years.

In year 4, when 64,000 hours were worked, the cost was £20,800, while in year 5 the cost was £16,000 when 40,000 hours were worked.

(v) **Fixed costs**

	£
Depreciation	18,000
Maintenance	10,000
Insurance	4,000
Rates	15,000
Management salaries	25,000

(b) Calculate the **budget cost allowance (ie expected expenditure)** for Year 6 assuming that 57,000 direct labour hours are worked.

Solution

(a)

	80% level *48,000 hrs* £'000	*90% level* *54,000 hrs* £'000	*100% level* *60,000 hrs* £'000
Direct labour	180.00	202.50	225.0
Other variable costs			
Indirect labour	36.00	40.50	45.0
Consumable supplies	18.00	20.25	22.5
Canteen etc	12.96	14.58	16.2
Total variable costs (£5.145 per hour)	246.96	277.83	308.7
Semi-variable costs (W)	17.60	18.80	20.0
Fixed costs			
Depreciation	18.00	18.00	18.0
Maintenance	10.00	10.00	10.0
Insurance	4.00	4.00	4.0
Rates	15.00	15.00	15.0
Management salaries	25.00	25.00	25.0
Budgeted costs	336.56	368.63	400.7

Working

We now use the **incremental method** of splitting the mixed costs.

Step 1. **Find the variable cost of the difference in the activity level.**

	£
Total cost of 64,000 hours	20,800
Total cost of 40,000 hours	16,000
Variable cost of 24,000 hours	4,800

Step 2. **Find the variable cost per unit of activity (hour).**

Variable cost per hour (£4,800/24,000)	£0.20

Step 3. **Find the fixed costs by substitution.**

	£
Total cost of 64,000 hours	20,800
Variable cost of 64,000 hours (× £0.20)	12,800
Fixed costs	8,000

Step 4. **Calculate the semi-variable costs.**

Semi-variable costs are calculated as follows.

			£
60,000 hours	(60,000 × £0.20) + £8,000	=	20,000
54,000 hours	(54,000 × £0.20) + £8,000	=	18,800
48,000 hours	(48,000 × £0.20) + £8,000	=	17,600

(b) The budget cost allowance for 57,000 direct labour hours of work would be as follows.

		£
Variable costs	(57,000 × £5.145)	293,265
Semi-variable costs	(£8,000 + (57,000 × £0.20))	19,400
Fixed costs		72,000
		384,665

WATCH OUT FOR ...

Fixed costs and flexible budgets

In an exam do not fall into the trap of flexing fixed costs. Remember that they remain unchanged regardless of the level of activity.

You will need to use the incremental method in Activity 10.2, the high-low method in Activity 10.3.

Activity 10.2

A company manufactures a single product and has produced the following flexed budget for the year.

		Level of activity	
	70%	*80%*	*90%*
	£	£	£
Turnover	210,000	240,000	270,000
Direct materials	17,780	20,320	22,860
Direct labour	44,800	51,200	57,600
Production overhead	30,500	32,000	33,500
Administration overhead	17,000	17,000	17,000
Total cost	110,080	120,520	130,960
Profit	99,920	119,480	139,040

The budgeted fixed production overhead is £20,000.

Task

Prepare a budget flexed at the 45% level of activity.

Activity 10.3

Allied Instruments Ltd is preparing budgets for the coming year. 120,000 direct labour hours represents the expected production time (100%), but a flexible budget at 90%, 110% and 120% is required so that cost allowances can be set for these possible levels. Budget cost details are as follows.

(a) **Fixed costs per annum**

	£
Depreciation	22,000
Staff salaries	43,000
Insurances	9,000
Rent and rates	12,000

(b) **Variable costs**

Power	30p per direct labour hour
Consumables	5p direct labour hour
Direct labour	£3.50 per direct labour hour

(c) **Semi-variable costs**

An analysis of past records, adjusted to eliminate the effect of inflation, shows the following.

		Direct labour hours	*Total semi-variable costs*
			£
Last year,	Year 8	110,000	330,000
	Year 7	100,000	305,000
	Year 6	90,000	280,000
	Year 5	87,000	272,500
	Year 4	105,000	317,500
	Year 3	80,000	255,000

Task

Prepare a cost budget at 100% and flex to show cost allowances at 90%, 110% and 120% of expected level.

TOPIC LINK

Indices and flexible budgets

As you have now no doubt guessed, indices can crop up in a great variety of situations. For example, to bring them up to date, you may have to index costs within a flexible budget using an average index for the period covered by the budget.

4.3 Coding data

Whilst preparing a budget you may be required to **correct a miscoded cost or revenue**. You simply need to **deduct the amount** in question **from the category to which it has been incorrectly coded** and **add it to the correct category**.

5 Flexible budgets and budgetary control

Budgetary control involves drawing up budgets for the **areas of responsibility** of individual managers (for example production managers, purchasing managers and so on) and of regularly **comparing actual results against expected results**.

As you will know if you have worked through Part B of this text, the **differences** between actual results and expected results are called **variances** and these are used to provide a **guideline for control action** by individual managers.

Individual **managers** are held responsible for **investigating differences** between budgeted and actual results, and are then expected to take **corrective action or amend the plan** in the light of actual events.

5.1 The wrong approach to budgetary control

The wrong approach to budgetary control is to compare actual results against a fixed budget. Consider the following example.

Tree Ltd manufactures a single product, the bough. Budgeted results and actual results for June Year 2 are shown below.

	Budget	*Actual results*	*Variance*
Production and sales of the bough (units)	2,000	3,000	
	£	£	£
Sales revenue (a)	20,000	30,000	10,000 (F)
Costs:			
Direct materials	6,000	8,500	2,500 (A)
Direct labour	4,000	4,500	500 (A)
Maintenance	1,000	1,400	400 (A)
Depreciation	2,000	2,200	200 (A)
Rent and rates	1,500	1,600	100 (A)
Other costs	3,600	5,000	1,400 (A)
Total costs (b)	18,100	23,200	5,100 (A)
Profit ((a) – (b))	1,900	6,800	4,900 (F)

In this example, the **variances are meaningless for purposes of control**. They simply show variations in expenditure. Costs were higher than budget because the volume of output was also higher; variable costs would be expected to increase above the budgeted costs. There is no information to show whether control action is needed for any aspect of costs or revenue.

For control purposes, it is **necessary to know** the following.

- Has the volume of units made varied from the budget favourably or adversely?
- Were actual costs higher than they should have been to produce 3,000 boughs?
- Was actual revenue from the sale of 3,000 boughs satisfactory?

There are a number of **reasons for a physical difference between the actual volume of activity and the planned volume**.

- The original budget was not set correctly and did not represent a valid target. This raises questions about managers' forecasting ability, or other behavioural issues, which we will discuss later in the text.
- Circumstances may have changed, rendering the original budget unachievable.
- Genuine efficiencies or inefficiencies may have arisen, which require investigation.

5.2 The correct approach to budgetary control

In order to focus on identifying genuine efficiencies or inefficiencies a flexible budgeting approach to budgetary control is required. The **correct approach to budgetary control** is as follows.

- **Identify fixed and variable costs.**
- **Produce a flexible budget using marginal costing techniques.**

In the previous example of Tree Ltd, let us suppose that we have the following estimates of cost behaviour.

- Direct materials, direct labour and maintenance costs are variable.
- Rent and rates and depreciation are fixed costs.
- Other costs consist of fixed costs of £1,600 plus a variable cost per unit made and sold.

Now that the cost behaviour patterns are known, a **budget cost allowance** can be calculated for each item of expenditure. This allowance is shown in a **flexible budget** as the **expected expenditure on each item for the relevant level of activity**. The budget cost allowances are calculated as follows.

(a) Variable cost allowances = original budgets × (3,000 units/2,000 units)
eg material cost allowance = £6,000 × $^3/_2$ = £9,000

Alternatively you can calculate the **budgeted variable cost per unit** as (**budgeted cost/budgeted production level**) **to get the variable cost per unit and then multiply by 3,000**.

(b) Fixed cost allowances = as original budget (because fixed costs do **not** change as activity levels change **within the relevant range)**

(c) Semi-fixed cost allowances = original budgeted fixed costs + (3,000 units × variable cost per unit)

Calculation of budget cost allowance for other costs

Total cost = fixed cost + variable cost
∴ £3,600 = £1,600 + variable cost for 2,000 units
∴ Variable cost of 2,000 units = £2,000
∴ Variable cost per unit = £1
∴ Other cost allowance = £1,600 + (3,000 × £1) = £4,600

The **budgetary control statement** should be as follows.

	Fixed budget (a)	*Flexible budget (b)*	*Actual results (c)*	*Budget variance (b) – (c)*
Production and sales (units)	2,000	3,000	3,000	
	£	£	£	£
Sales revenue	20,000	30,000	30,000	0
Variable costs				
Direct materials	6,000	9,000	8,500	500 (F)
Direct labour	4,000	6,000	4,500	1,500 (F)
Maintenance	1,000	1,500	1,400	100 (F)
Semi-variable costs				
Other costs	3,600	4,600	5,000	400 (A)
Fixed costs				
Depreciation	2,000	2,000	2,200	200 (A)
Rent and rates	1,500	1,500	1,600	100 (A)
Total costs	18,100	24,600	23,200	1,400 (F)
Profit	1,900	5,400	6,800	1,400 (F)

Note. (F) denotes a favourable variance and **(A) an adverse or unfavourable variance**. Adverse variances are sometimes denoted as (U) for 'unfavourable'.

ATTENTION!

The analysis above is the **basic template** for practically all tasks involving flexible budgets.

- The **original budget flexed** to the actual volume
- The **actual results**
- The resulting **line by line differences** or variances (**between the flexed budget** and the **actual results**)

5.3 Budgetary control analysis

We can **analyse** the above statement as follows.

5.3.1 Impact of a difference in costs

In producing and selling 3,000 units the expected profit should have been, not the fixed budget profit of £1,900, but the flexible budget profit of £5,400. Instead, actual profit was £6,800, ie £1,400 more than we should have expected. One of the reasons for the improvement is that, **given actual output** of 3,000 units, **costs were lower than expected** (and sales revenue was exactly as expected).

	£
Direct materials cost variance	500 (F)
Direct labour cost variance	1,500 (F)
Maintenance cost variance	100 (F)
Other costs variance	400 (A)
Fixed cost variances	
Depreciation	200 (A)
Rent and rates	100 (A)
	1,400 (F)

5.3.2 Impact of a difference in sales volumes

Another reason for the improvement in profit above that in the fixed budget is the difference between budgeted and actual **sales volume.** Tree Ltd sold 3,000 boughs instead of 2,000 boughs, with the following result.

	£	£
Sales revenue increased by		10,000
Variable costs increased by:		
direct materials	3,000	
direct labour	2,000	
maintenance	500	
variable element of other costs	1,000	
Costs increased by		6,500
Profit increased by		3,500

The impact of the **increase in sales volume is an increase in profit of £3,500.** This is the **difference between the fixed budget and the flexible budget**. It is the increase in profit that should be expected simply because volume has increased.

Note that **fixed costs** are **not affected** since they should remain the same whatever the activity level.

5.3.3 Full variance analysis statement

	£	£
Fixed budget profit		1,900
Variances		
Sales volume	3,500 (F)	
Direct materials cost	500 (F)	
Direct labour cost	1,500 (F)	
Maintenance cost	100 (F)	
Other costs	400 (A)	
Depreciation	200 (A)	
Rent and rates	100 (A)	
		4,900 (F)
Actual profit		6,800

Note that the **budgeted and actual selling price were the same** (the expected sales revenue was the same as the actual sales revenue). We will see the impact of a difference between budgeted and actual selling price a little later.

TOPIC LINK

Flexible budgets and standard costing

Note the similarity between flexible budgets and standard costing. If you remember, standard costing considers the difference between what actual output should have cost and what it actually did cost.

5.4 Investigation of variances and control action

Such a statement could be prepared by the accountant and then circulated to senior management and/or operational management in a periodically-prepared budgetary control report. Operational management may then be asked to **investigate the reasons for significant variances** to see whether any corrective action is necessary.

TOPIC LINK

Action in response to variances

You need to know about the **type of action** which may be required of managers in **response to variances**. We have already looked at this issue in Chapters 1 and 7. Here are the main points you need to remember.

- Make sure that any comments you make on individual variances are relevant to the task scenario. Avoid general statements – the use of a higher quality material, for example.
- You might be asked to identify which variances are controllable and which are uncontrollable.
- You could be asked to identify when particular variances should be investigated. In your answer you would need to establish some general rules, based on materiality, controllability and variance trend.

ATTENTION!

If management are to act upon the **information contained in a budgetary control report** then it must be **presented clearly**. After the December 1999 exam the assessor commented that candidates seemed unaware of good practice in presenting data for a flexed budget. Costs should be **separated according to whether they are variable, semi-variable or fixed**. Also there should be a **clear comparison** between the flexible budget and the actual results, to **show the variances**. Pay particular attention to the presentation of your budget when you try the next activity.

5.5 Impact of a difference in selling price

In the activity which follows, you will find that when you compare your flexed budget revenue with the actual revenue there is a difference. Have a think about what this difference represents. We will let you know after the activity!

Activity 10.4

The budgeted and actual results of XYZ Ltd for September Year 1 were as follows. The company uses a marginal costing system. There were no opening or closing stocks.

	Fixed budget		*Actual*	
Sales and production	1,000 units		700 units	
	£	£	£	£
Sales revenue		20,000		14,200
Variable cost of sales:				
Direct materials	8,000		5,200	
Direct labour	4,000		3,100	
Variable overhead	2,000		1,500	
Variable costs		14,000		9,800
Contribution		6,000		4,400
Fixed costs		5,000		5,400
Profit/(loss)		1,000		(1,000)

Task

Prepare a budget that will be useful for management control purposes.

By **flexing** the budget in the statement above we **removed the effect on sales revenue** of **the difference between budgeted sales volume and actual sales volume**. But there is still a **variance of £200 (F).** This means that the **actual selling price** must have been **different** to the **budgeted selling price**, resulting in a £200 (F) **selling price variance.**

The basis used to flex the costs will depend on the type of activity carried out by the organisation or department. A manufacturing organisation might flex on the basis of units of output, distribution costs may be flexed on the basis of miles/kilometres travelled while the basis for flexing personnel costs may be number of staff.

5.6 Preparing a flexible budget – absorption costing

ATTENTION!

In 'real-world' organisations, actual results are prepared using either marginal costing or absorption costing.

Given that exams are meant to reflect the workplace, the assessor has warned that in exam tasks **actual results will be provided on an absorption costing basis on occasions.**

If the actual results (and possibly the budget data) are presented on an absorption costing basis, you may be asked to rearrange them on a marginal costing basis. In any task where this is the case, it will be **made clear** that data must be **rearranged** using marginal costing.

REMEMBER...

Cost recording versus cost behaviour

You may wish to re-read Chapter 2 before working through this example.

Example: flexible budgets and absorption costing

Consider the following data prepared on an absorption costing basis.

	Budget	*Actual results*
Volume (units)	12,000	15,000
	£	£
Turnover	240,000	315,000
Variable costs	144,000	165,000
Fixed overheads	100,000	100,000
Operating profit/(loss)	(4,000)	50,000

Here is some additional data about actual results.

	Closing stock	*Cost of sales*	*Cost of production*
	£	£	£
Variable costs	30,000	165,000	195,000
Fixed overhead	22,000	100,000	122,000

The budget assumed that there would be no closing stock. There is no opening stock.

Task

Prepare a flexible budget statement on a marginal costing basis using the above data.

Solution

Because the actual results have been prepared using **absorption costing**, **closing stock** is **valued** at **fully absorbed cost** and so **both fixed and variable costs** incurred to produce the closing stock have been **carried forward** to be set against the profit of the period when the units are sold.

When **marginal costing** is used, however, **all actual fixed overheads** incurred (those included in cost of sales (£100,000) and those included in closing stock (£22,000)) need to be **included** in the profit calculation. Marginal costing charges all fixed costs incurred during the period against profit earned during the period in question, **none** being **carried forward** in closing stock. **Closing stock** is **valued** at **variable cost** only and so only **variable costs** are **carried forward**.

Flexible budget statement

	Flexible budget	*Actual results*	*Variance*
Volume (units)	15,000	15,000	–
	£	£	£
Turnover	300,000 (W1)	315,000*	15,000 (F)
Variable costs	180,000 (W2)	165,000*	15,000 (F)
Fixed overheads	100,000*	122,000 (W3)	22,000 (A)
Operating profit	20,000	28,000	8,000 (F)

* = given

Workings

1. £240,000 × 15/12
2. £144,000 × 15/12
3. Fixed overheads in cost of sales + fixed overheads in closing stock (ie the fixed overheads in cost of production).

The actual marginal costing operating profit of £28,000 **differs** from the absorption costing operating profit of £50,000 by **£22,000**.

This difference is the **fixed overhead in closing stock** which is included in the profit calculation when marginal costing is used but not when absorption costing is used.

IMPORTANT POINT

Don't forget that management are able to manipulate results if they use absorption costing: the higher the level of production, the larger the closing stock, the larger the value of closing stock carried forward and hence the higher the profit.

5.7 Factors to consider when preparing flexible budgets

The mechanics of flexible budgeting are, in theory, fairly straightforward. In practice, however, the following points should be considered before figures are flexed.

- Separating costs into their fixed and variable elements is not always straightforward.
- Fixed costs may behave in a step-line fashion as activity levels increase/decrease.
- Account must be taken of the assumptions upon which the original fixed budget was based. Such assumptions might include the constraint posed by limiting factors, the rate of inflation and judgements about future uncertainty.

ATTENTION!

As part of your studies for Unit 8 you may well have already worked through Chapters 6 and 7, in which we looked at variances in detail and, in particular, saw how a total variance could be split into components (for example, the total materials variance into price and usage components).

The assessor has confirmed that **component variances will not** be **assessed in Unit 9**.

Activity 10.5

Explain the differences between a fixed budget and a flexible budget. Describe the way in which fixed budgets and flexible budgets are useful for planning and control.

REMEMBER...

Flexing variable costs

This can be done in two ways.

- Find the budgeted cost per unit (original budgeted cost/original budgeted volume) and then multiply by the actual volume
- Original budgeted cost × (actual volume/original budgeted volume)

Activity 10.6

Phoebe Jenson Products Ltd produces a single product and uses flexible budgets to control expenditure. The following forecasts have been prepared for the production costs to be incurred at the highest and lowest activity levels likely to be experienced in any particular period.

	Production level	
	5,000 units	*15,000 units*
	£	£
Direct material	25,000	75,000
Direct labour	10,000	30,000
Indirect material	8,000	18,000
Indirect labour	12,000	22,000
Machine rental	4,000	8,000
Rent, rates, etc	6,000	6,000

Indirect labour costs are fixed for activity levels up to and including 10,000 units. For all units produced in excess of 10,000 per period, a bonus payment of £2 per unit is paid, in addition to the fixed costs. All other variable costs and the variable part of semi-variable costs follow constant linear patterns. The variable cost per unit of indirect material is £1. Machine rental costs are stepped fixed costs. For activity levels up to and including 12,000 units one machine is needed at a rental cost of £4,000 per period. Above 12,000 units two machines are needed.

Tasks

(a) Prepare a set of flexible budgets which show the production cost allowances for the period for activity levels of 5,000 units, 10,000 units, 12,000 units and 15,000 units.

(b) During the latest period ended 30 November the company was operating at full capacity in order to build up stocks in anticipation of a sales drive. 15,000 units were produced. The actual costs incurred were recorded as follows.

	£
Direct material	69,400
Direct labour	37,700
Indirect material	15,460
Indirect labour	28,780
Machine rental	10,790
Rent, rates etc	5,800

As the management accountant at Phoebe Jensen Products Ltd, one of your tasks is to check that invoices have been properly coded. On checking the actual invoices for machine rental for the period ended 30 November, you find that one invoice for £2,790 had been incorrectly coded. The invoice should have been coded to indirect material.

After correcting of the miscoding of the invoice, present this data as a budgetary control statement for the period. Beneath your statement, write brief notes commenting on the significant variances, suggesting what further management action might be necessary.

Activity 10.7

A&B Engineering Ltd produces a single product, the LSO, on an assembly line. As budget officer you have prepared the following production budgets from the best information available, to represent the extremes of high and low volume of production likely to be encountered by the company over a three-month period.

	Production of 4,000 units	*Production of 8,000 units*
	£	£
Direct materials	80,000	160,000
Indirect materials	12,000	20,000
Direct labour	50,000	100,000
Power	18,000	24,000
Repairs	20,000	30,000
Supervision	20,000	36,000
Rent, insurance and rates	9,000	9,000

Supervision is a 'step function'. One supervisor is employed for all production levels up to and including 5,000 units. For higher levels of production an assistant supervisor (£16,000) is also required. For power, a minimum charge is payable on all production up to and including 6,000 units. For production above this level there is an additional variable charge based on the power consumed. Other variable and semi-variable costs are incurred evenly over the production range. The variable cost per unit of indirect materials is £2. The fixed cost of repairs is £10,000.

Tasks

(a) Use the table given below to prepare a set of flexible budgets for presentation to the production manager to cover levels of production over a period of three months of 4,000, 5,000, 6,000, 7,000 and 8,000 units.

	Budgets at different levels of activity				
	4,000 units	*5,000 units*	*6,000 units*	*7,000 units*	*8,000 units*
Direct materials					
Indirect materials					
Direct labour					
Power					
Repairs					
Supervision					
Rent, insurance and rates					
Total					

(b) During the three months July to September (covering most of the summer holiday period) 5,000 units were produced. Costs incurred during the three-month period were as follows.

	£
Direct materials	110,000
Indirect materials	14,000
Direct labour	70,000
Power	18,000
Repairs	30,000
Supervision	20,000
Rent, insurance and rates	8,000

Present the above figures as a budget report for presentation to the Production Manager. Write a brief note against each significant variance suggesting any investigations which might be required.

ATTENTION!

There are two main formats for a flexible budgeting task.

- The first gives you a single planning budget, as in the illustration at the beginning of Section 5 and details of cost assumptions upon which it is based. If you need to deal with **semi-variable costs**, either the **fixed element** of the cost will be **provided**, as in the example in Section 5.2 and in Activity 10.7 (repairs), **or** the **variable cost** will be **provided**, as in Activity 10.7 (indirect materials).
- The second gives you two fixed budgets, but for different levels of activity, as in Activity 10.6. You might then be told that any difference between the two budgets arises because of the change in activity level. Sometimes you are also told which costs are variable, which are fixed and which are semi-variable (although this should be clear to you from your marginal costing knowledge!). To calculate the fixed and variable elements of any semi-variable costs you need to use the incremental method, as illustrated in Section 4.2.1.

ATTENTION! ... (cont'd)
The assessor has issued the following warning:

'When answering a flexible budgeting task, you need to take special care. Are you being given the individual budgeted costs or are you being given two budgets? Each approach involves a different way of calculating unit data. One common error is to try using the incremental approach, even though the task only gives one budget. Finding the difference between the budgeted and actual costs and then dividing by the difference between the budgeted and actual volumes is a fundamental error. You are not measuring like for like: one set of data uses budgeted costs, the other actual costs.

6 Format of budget statements

You may be required to comment on the **appropriateness of a budget statement as a management report**. Here are some **features of good management reports on budgeting**.

- **Actual** and **budget** figures and **variances** should be shown for the **current control period** (say, month) so that problems are highlighted quickly.
- The same information should also be shown for the **year to date**.
- The **size of figures** (£, £'000 and so on) should be **immediately obvious**.
- It may be useful to include a **year-end forecast** (actual to date plus expected to year end).

Of course you will need to **use your common sense** in assessing a budget report. Think about **what information** it is trying to convey and to **whom**. The following activity gives you the opportunity to practice this.

REMEMBER ...

Reports

You may be required to prepare memos and reports for Unit 9 so re-read Section 3 in Chapter 4 to remind yourself of the key points on report writing covered in your earlier studies.

Activity 10.8

The following report has been prepared, relating to one product for March Year 7. This has been sent to the appropriate product manager as part of the company's monitoring procedures.

Variance report: 31 March Year 7

	Actual	*Budget*	*Variance*
Production volume (units)	9,905	10,000	95 A
Direct material (kgs)	9,800	10,000	200 F
Direct material (£)	9,600	10,000	400 F
Direct labour (hours)	2,500	2,400	100 A
Direct labour (£)	8,500	8,400	100 A
Total variable costs	18,100	18,400	300 F

The product manager has complained that the report ignores the principle of flexible budgeting and is unfair.

Task

Prepare a report addressed to the management team which comments critically on the monthly variance report. Include as an appendix to your report the layout of a revised monthly variance report which will be more useful to the product manager. Include row and column headings, but do *not* calculate the contents of the report.

Key learning points

- ☑ **Responsibility centres** can be divided into three types.
  - **Cost centres**
  - **Profit centres**
  - **Investment centres**
- ☑ **Controllable costs** are items of expenditure which can be directly influenced by a given manager within a given time span.
- ☑ It is often assumed that all fixed costs are non-controllable in the short run. This is true of **committed fixed costs** but not of **discretionary fixed costs**.
- ☑ A **fixed budget** is a budget which is designed to remain unchanged regardless of the volume of output or sales achieved. A **flexible budget** is a budget which, by recognising different cost behaviour patterns, is designed to change as volumes of output change.
- ☑ Flexible budgets can be used for **planning** or for **control** purposes.
- ☑ The fixed and variable components of semi-fixed costs can be estimated using the **high-low** and **incremental methods**. The incremental method can be used if you are given costs at two different activity levels.
- ☑ Comparison of a fixed budget with the actual results for a different level of activity is of little use for control purposes. Flexible budgets should be used to show the cost allowances for the actual level of activity.
- ☑ The differences between the components of a flexed budget and actual results are known as **variances**.
- ☑ There is a basic **template** for practically all tasks involving flexible budgets.
  - The original budget flexed to the actual volume
  - The actual results
  - The resulting line by line differences or variances (between the flexed budget and the actual results)
- ☑ You may be **given data** prepared on an **absorption costing basis** and asked to **prepare a flexible budget statement on a marginal costing basis**. The actual profits under the two costing approaches will differ because of the fixed overhead carried forward in closing stock (when absorption costing is used), rather than set against profit (when marginal costing is used).
- ☑ Be prepared to deal with the **two main formats** of flexible budgeting task.

Quick quiz

1 An extract of the costs incurred at two different activity levels is shown. Classify the costs according to their behaviour patterns and show the budget cost allowance for an activity of 1,500 units.

		1,000 units	*2,000 units*	*Type of cost*	*Budget cost allowance for 1,500 units*
		£	£		£
(a)	Fuel	3,000	6,000	....	....
(b)	Photocopying	9,500	11,000	....	....
(c)	Heating	2,400	2,400	....	....
(d)	Direct wages	6,000	8,000	....	....

2 Fill in the blank.

.... is a system of accounting that makes revenues and costs the responsibility of particular managers so that the performance of each part of the organisation can be monitored and assessed.

3 Committed fixed costs can be raised or lowered at fairly short notice. True or false?

4 Choose the correct words from those highlighted.

Three columns of figures make up the basic template for practically all tasks involving flexible budgets.

- The **original/revised** budget flexed to the **original/actual** volume
- The **original/actual** results
- The differences between the **original/flexed** budget and the **actual/revised** results

5 The fixed overheads included in the actual results in a flexible budget statement should be:

A those in closing stock only
B those in cost of sales only
C those in cost of production only
D those in closing stock plus those in cost of production

6 Choose the correct word from those highlighted.

Absorption/marginal costing is used to prepare flexible budgets.

Answers to quick quiz

1 (a) Variable £4,500
(b) Semi-variable £10,250
(c) Fixed £2,400
(d) Semi-variable £7,000

2 Responsibility accounting

3 False

4
- The original budget flexed to the actual volume
- The actual results
- The differences between the flexed budget and the actual results

5 C

6 Marginal costing

ASSESSMENT KIT ACTIVITIES

See the box at the end of Chapter 11 for details of the activities in the BPP Assessment Kit for Units 8 & 9 which include topics covered in this chapter.

Activity checklist

This checklist shows which performance criteria, range statement or knowledge and understanding point is covered by each activity in this chapter. Tick off each activity as you complete it.

Activity		
10.1	☐	This activity deals with Range Statement 9.3: responsibility centres (expense centres; profit centres) and Unit 9 Knowledge & Understanding points (17): the structure of the organisation and its responsibility centres and (18): responsibility centres.
10.2	☐	This activity deals with Range Statement 9.3: types of budgets (fixed and flexible budgets).
10.3	☐	This activity deals with Range Statement 9.3: types of budgets (fixed and flexible budgets).
10.4	☐	This activity deals with Performance Criteria 9.3C regarding the clear and correct identification of variances and Unit 9 Knowledge & Understanding points (8): budgets for control and (11): presentation of budget data in a form that satisfies the differing needs of budget holders.
10.5	☐	This activity deals with Unit 9 Knowledge & Understanding point (13): uses of budgetary control.
10.6	☐	This activity deals with Performance Criteria 9.3A regarding the checking and reconciliation of budget figures on an ongoing basis, Performance Criteria 9.3B regarding the correct coding and allocation of actual cost and revenue data to responsibility centres, Performance Criteria 9.3D regarding discussion with budget holders and other managers of any significant variances and helping managers take remedial action and Unit 9 Knowledge & Understanding point (10): analysing the significance of budget variances and possible responses required by managers.
10.7	☐	This activity deals with Performance Criteria 9.3C regarding the clear and correct identification of variances and the preparation of relevant reports for management, and Performance Criteria 9.3D regarding discussion with budget holders and other managers of any significant variances and helping managers take remedial action, and Range Statement 9.3: variances.
10.8	☐	This activity deals with Unit 9 Knowledge & Understanding point (11): presentation of budget data in a form that satisfies the differing needs of budget holders.

chapter 11

Further aspects of budgeting

Contents

1 Introduction
2 Incremental budgeting and zero based budgeting
3 Rolling budgets
4 The behavioural effects of control systems
5 Computers and budgeting

Performance criteria

9.2D Communicate with budget holders in a manner which maintains goodwill and ensure budget proposals are agreed with budget holders

Knowledge and understanding

Unit 8 Accounting principles and theory

11 Effect of accounting controls on behaviour of managers and other employees

Unit 9 Accounting techniques

4 Use of relevant computer packages

9 The effect of budgetary systems on the behaviour and motivation of managers and other employees

Unit 9 Accounting principles and theory

13 Uses of budgetary control: planning, co-ordinating, authorising, cost control

Signpost

The topics covered in this chapter are relevant to **Unit 9** but the sections on behavioural implications and spreadsheets are also relevant to standard costing systems (**Unit 8**).

1 Introduction

We begin this chapter by looking at two **alternatives to the annual process of budgeting**. Although these alternatives, **zero based budgets** and **rolling budgets**, are not specifically identified in the standards, they could well be included within the 'Uses of budgetary control' area of Knowledge and Understanding for Unit 9. Sections 2 and 3 are therefore **relevant** to your studies, **but not central**.

Section 4 is probably the **most important** in the chapter, covering as it does the effects of control systems on the behaviour of managers and other employees. We touched on this issue in Chapter 1 but consider it in more detail here.

The final topic of the chapter is the role of **computers** in budgeting. A number of past exam tasks have asked for spreadsheet formulae to be derived from task data.

2 Incremental budgeting and zero based budgeting

2.1 Incremental budgeting

The **traditional** approach to budgeting is known as **incremental** budgeting, which involves **basing next year's budget on the current year's budget plus an extra amount for estimated growth or inflation**.

Allowance would also be made for any specific **anticipated changes**, such as the opening of a new factory.

An incremental budgeting system is fairly **simple** to operate and easy to understand but it has a number of **disadvantages**.

- It assumes that activities and ways of doing things will continue in the same way, which gives management **no incentive to come up with new ideas.**
- The **budgets** may become **out of date** and no longer relate to the level of activity or the type of work being carried out. A department that is no longer important may continue to receive a large share of the organisation's resources while newer departments find it difficult to grow because they receive a relatively small share. Resources are therefore rarely allocated in the best way.
- Management has **no incentive to try and reduce costs**. In fact management are encouraged to spend up to the budget allowance so that the level of next year's budget is maintained.
- **Budgetary slack** occurs when managers overestimate their requirements in order to obtain a larger budget, within which it is easier to work and which allows them to report favourable variances. Because incremental budgets are rarely subjected to close scrutiny, the budgetary slack built into the budget is never reviewed.

Example: incremental budgeting

Suppose the budget for a canteen in a manufacturing organisation is set using incremental budgeting. The budget would continue at the same level (allowing for increases in inflation) irrespective of the changing size of the workforce or any changes in demand for its services. (For example, a larger proportion of employees perhaps prefer to bring a

packed lunch than a number of years ago). There would be no opportunity to review the service provided and no incentive to look for more cost effective ways of providing the service.

Activity 11.1

Can incremental budgeting be used to budget for rent? What about for advertising expenditure?

2.2 Zero based budgeting

Zero based budgeting (ZBB) was developed in an attempt to **overcome** some of the **problems** associated with **incremental budgeting**. The approach is the opposite to that taken in incremental budgeting and involves preparing the **budget for each cost centre from a zero base**. **Every item of expenditure** therefore has to be completely **justified** in order to be included in the budget.

2.2.1 The steps in ZBB

Step 1 Analyse the work of each department (cost centre) to identify the **activities** carried out.	
Step 2 **Describe each activity** and the associated **costs and benefits** in a **decision package**.	**Base packages** describe the minimum amount of work that must be done to carry out the activity. **Incremental packages** describe what additional work could be done, at what cost and for what benefits.
Step 3 **Evaluate and rank each package** on the basis of its benefit to the organisation.	Activities that are essential for the basic operation of the organisation should be given high priority, as will work that meets legal obligations. In an accounting department these would be minimum requirements to operate the payroll, purchase ledger and sales ledger systems, and to maintain and publish a satisfactory set of accounts.
Step 4 **Allocate the funds** available to decision packages, and hence activities, in order of priority.	This process determines which activities will be carried out and at what level. Activities that contribute nothing will receive no funds and will be discontinued.

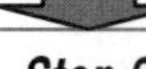

Example: decision packages

Suppose that a cost centre manager is preparing a budget for maintenance costs.

- The 'base' package would describe the minimum requirement for the maintenance work. This might be to pay for one man per shift for two shifts each day at a cost of £30,000.
- Incremental package 1 might be to pay for two men on the early shift and one man on the late shift, at a cost of £45,000. The extra cost of £15,000 would need to be justified, for example by savings in lost production time, or by more efficient machinery.
- Incremental package 2 might be for two men on each shift at a cost of £60,000. The cost-benefit analysis would compare its advantages, if any, over incremental package 1; and so on.

Activity 11.2

What might the base package and incremental packages for a personnel department cover?

2.2.2 Advantages and disadvantages of ZBB

- Inefficient and obsolete activities are identified and removed.
- Employees are forced to avoid wasteful expenditure.
- Budgetary slack should not exist.
- It takes into account changes in the business environment.
- It does not assume that existing activities will continue and so innovation is encouraged.
- Resource allocation should be improved.

2.2.3 Disadvantages of ZBB

- It is more complex and hence more costly to operate.
- The ranking process can be difficult. For example, it is difficult to rank activities which have qualitative rather than quantitative benefits – such as spending on staff welfare.
- Short-term benefits might be emphasised to the detriment of long-term benefits.
- The organisation's information systems may not be able to provide suitable information.

Activity 11.3

What might the base and incremental packages cover in your department if your organisation used ZBB?

2.2.4 Using zero based budgeting

ZBB is not particularly suitable for direct manufacturing costs, which are usually budgeted using standard costing.

ZBB is best applied to **support expenses** (expenditure incurred in departments which exist to support the essential production function). These support areas include:

- Marketing
- Finance
- Quality control
- Personnel
- Data processing
- Sales and distribution

In many organisations, these expenses make up a large proportion of the total expenditure. These activities are less easily quantifiable by conventional methods and are more **discretionary** in nature.

Example: using ZBB for discretionary costs

If ZBB were applied to advertising, decision packages might detail the expected benefits from different levels of expenditure on various forms of advertising. This might be particularly appropriate if an organisation was considering a move away from traditional forms, such as advertising in the trade press, to a web-based approach.

ZBB can also be successfully applied to **service industries** and **non-profit-making organisations** such as local and central government, educational establishments, hospitals and so on, and in any organisation where different levels of provision for each activity are possible and costs and benefits are separately identifiable.

Activity 11.4

You work for a large multinational company which manufactures paint. It has been decided to introduce zero based budgeting in place of the more traditional incremental budgeting. The manager of the research and development department has never heard of zero based budgeting.

Task

Write a report to the research and development department manager which explains the following.

(a) How zero based budgeting techniques differ from traditional budgeting
(b) How ZBB may assist in planning and controlling discretionary costs

3 Rolling budgets

Sometimes managers need the **chance to revise their plans**.

- Perhaps because it is suspected that a new competitor will enter the market at the beginning of the year, and the effect of this cannot be quantified when the budget is set.
- Perhaps because inflation is very high or is expected to rise or fall by a large amount during the course of the year.

Management may therefore decide to introduce a system of rolling budgets (also called **continuous budgets**).

A rolling budget is a budget which is **continuously updated by adding a further accounting period** (a month or quarter) **when the earlier accounting period has finished**.

Rolling budgets are an attempt to prepare targets and plans which are **more realistic and certain**, particularly with a regard to price levels, by **shortening the period between preparing budgets.**

Instead of preparing a period budget annually for the full budget period, there would be **budgets every one, two, three or four months** (three to six, or even twelve budgets each year). **Each of these budgets would plan for the next twelve months** so that the current budget is extended by an extra period as the current period ends: hence the name rolling budgets.

Suppose, for example, that a rolling budget is prepared every three months. The first three months of the budget period would be planned in great detail, and the remaining nine months in lesser detail, because of the greater uncertainty about the longer-term future. If a first continuous budget is prepared for January to March in detail and April to December in less detail, a new budget will be prepared towards the end of March, planning April to June in detail and July to March in less detail. Four rolling budgets would be prepared every 12 months on this 3 and 9 month basis, requiring, inevitably, greater administrative effort.

3.1 The advantages and disadvantages of rolling budgets

Advantages

- They **reduce the element of uncertainty** in budgeting because they concentrate detailed planning and control on short-term prospects.
- They force managers to reassess the budget regularly, and to **produce budgets** which are **up to date in the light of current events and expectations**.
- **Planning and control will be based on a recent plan** which is likely to be far more realistic than a fixed annual budget made many months ago.
- There is **always a budget which extends for several months ahead**. For example, if rolling budgets are prepared quarterly there will always be a budget extending for the next 9 to 12 months. This is not the case when fixed annual budgets are used.

Activity 11.5

What do you see as the disadvantages of rolling budgets?

3.2 Rolling budgets or updated annual budgets?

If the expected changes are not likely to be continuous there is a strong argument that routine updating of the budget is unnecessary. **Instead the annual budget could be updated whenever changes become foreseeable**, so that a budget might be updated once or twice, and perhaps more often, during the course of the year.

When a fixed budget is updated, a 'rolling' budget would probably not be prepared. If a budget is updated in month 8 of the year, the updated budget would relate to months 8 to 12. It would not be extended to month 7 of the following year.

4 The behavioural effects of control systems

Standard costing and budgetary control systems help management plan and control the organisation's resources. Control is exercised by management and staff, however, and so the **control systems** themselves can **affect** the **behaviour of employees**. Depending on the circumstances, the effect will either be to **motivate or demotivate.**

4.1 Budgets and standards as targets

Once decided, budgets and standards become targets. But **how difficult** should the targets be? And how might people react to targets which are easy to achieve, or difficult to achieve?

We looked briefly at the impact on employee behaviour of the type of standard set in Chapter 6.

Type of standard	Impact
Ideal	Some say that they provide employees with an incentive to be more efficient even though it is highly unlikely that the standard will be achieved. Others argue that they are likely to have an unfavourable effect on employee motivation because the differences between standards and actual results will always be adverse. The employees may feel that the goals are unattainable and so they will not work so hard.
Attainable	Might be an incentive to work harder as they provide a realistic but challenging target of efficiency.
Current	Will not motivate employees to do anything more than they are currently doing.
Basic	May have an unfavourable impact on the motivation of employees. Over time they will discover that they are easily able to achieve the standards. They may become bored and lose interest in what they are doing if they have nothing to aim for.

Similar comments apply to budgets.

Budgets and standards are **more likely to motivate** employees if employees accept that the budget or standard is **achievable**. If it can be achieved too easily, it will not provide sufficient motivation. If it is too difficult, employees will not accept it because they will believe it to be unachievable. In extreme circumstances, if employees believe a budget is impossible to achieve, they might be so demotivated that they attempt to prove that the budget is wrong. This is obviously the completely opposite effect to that intended.

The various **research** projects into the behavioural effects of budgeting have given **conflicting views** on certain points. There appears to be **general agreement** that a **target must fulfil certain conditions** if it is to motivate employees to work towards it.

- It must be **sufficiently difficult** to be a **challenging** target.
- It must **not be so difficult** that it is not achievable.
- It must be **accepted** by the employees as their personal goal.

Some research has considered whether the extent to which employees participate in the budget and standard-setting process affects the likelihood of the budget or standard being accepted as a personal goal.

4.2 Participation

There are basically two ways in which a budget can be set: from the **top down** (**imposed** budget) or from the **bottom up** (**participatory** budget).

4.2.1 Imposed style of budgeting

In this approach to budgeting, **top management prepare a budget with little or no input from operating personnel.** This budget is then **imposed** upon the employees who have to work to the budgeted figures.

The times when imposed budgets are **effective** are as follows.

- In newly-formed organisations, because of employees' lack of knowledge
- In very small businesses, because the owner/manager has a complete overview of the business
- When operational managers lack budgeting skills
- When the organisation's different units require precise co-ordination
- When budgets need to be set quickly

They are, of course, advantages and disadvantages to this style of setting budgets.

Advantages

- The aims of long-term plans are more likely to be incorporated into short-term plans.
- They improve the co-ordination between the plans and objectives of divisions.
- They use senior management's overall awareness of the organisation.
- There is less likelihood of input from inexperienced or uninformed lower-level employees.
- Budgets can be drawn up in a shorter period of time because a consultation process is not required.

Disadvantages

- Dissatisfaction, defensiveness and low morale amongst employees who have to work to meet the targets. It is hard for people to be motivated to achieve targets set by somebody else. Employees might put in only just enough effort to achieve targets, without trying to beat them.
- The feeling of team spirit may disappear.
- Organisational goals and objectives might not be accepted so readily and/or employees will not be aware of them.
- Employees might see the budget as part of a system of trying to find fault with their work: if they cannot achieve a target that has been imposed on them they will be punished.
- If consideration is not given to local operating and political environments, unachievable budgets for overseas divisions could be produced.
- Lower-level management initiative may be stifled if they are not invited to participate.

4.2.2 Participative style of budgeting

In this approach to budgeting, **budgets are developed by lower-level managers who then submit the budgets to their superiors**. The budgets are based on the lower-level managers' perceptions of what is achievable and the associated necessary resources.

Activity 11.6

In what circumstances might participative budgets be effective?

The **advantages** of participative budgets are as follows.

- They are based on information from employees most familiar with the department. Budgets should therefore be more realistic.
- Knowledge spread among several levels of management is pulled together, again producing more realistic budgets.
- Because employees are more aware of organisational goals, they should be more committed to achieving them.
- Co-ordination and cooperation between those involved in budget preparation should improve.
- Senior managers' overview of the business can be combined with operational-level details to produce better budgets.
- Managers should feel that they 'own' the budget and will therefore be more committed to the targets and more motivated to achieve them.
- Participation will broaden the experience of those involved and enable them to develop new skills.

Overall, participation in budget setting should give those involved a more positive attitude towards the organisation, which should lead to better performance.

There are, on the other hand, a number of **disadvantages** of participative budgets.

- They consume more time.
- Any changes made by senior management to the budgets submitted by lower-level management may cause dissatisfaction.
- Budgets may be unachievable if managers are not qualified to participate.
- Managers may not co-ordinate their own plans with those of other departments.
- Managers may include budgetary slack in their budgets. This means they have over-estimated costs or under-estimated income. Actual results are then more likely to be better than the budgeted target results.
- An earlier start to the budgeting process could be required.

The research projects do not appear to provide definite conclusions about the motivational effects of budgeting. The **attitudes of the individuals** involved have an impact.

- Some managers may complain that they are too busy to spend time on setting standards and budgeting.
- Others may feel that they do not have the necessary skills.
- Some may think that any budget they set will be used against them.

In such circumstances participation could be seen as an **added pressure rather than as an opportunity**. For such employees an imposed approach might be better.

4.2.3 Negotiated style of budgeting

At the two extremes, budgets can be dictated from above or simply emerge from below but, in practice, different levels of management often agree budgets by a process of negotiation.

- In the imposed budget approach, operational managers will try to negotiate with senior managers the budget targets which they consider to be unreasonable or unrealistic.
- Likewise senior management usually review and revise budgets presented to them under a participative approach through a process of negotiation with lower level managers.
- **Final budgets are therefore most likely to lie between what top management would really like and what junior managers believe is feasible**.

4.3 Pay as a motivator

Pay can be an **important** motivator when there is a **formal link between higher pay and achieving targets**. Individuals are likely to work harder to achieve a target if they know that they will be rewarded for their successful efforts. There are, however, **problems** with using pay as an incentive.

- Higher pay or bonuses will be tied to the achievement of short-term targets, to which there is a danger that the long-term interests of the organisation will be subordinated.

- The targets must be challenging, but fair, otherwise individuals will become dissatisfied. Pay can be a demotivator as well as a motivator!

If performance-related pay is to lead to improved performance, the following **conditions are necessary**.

- Managers need to know the organisational objectives, and budgets must tie in with these objectives.
- Managers must feel that the objectives are achievable (although they should provide a challenge) and they must want to achieve them.
- Managers must be able to influence the achievement of objectives.
- The rewards (both financial and non-financial) should motivate.
- Managers must have the skills necessary to achieve the targets.

TOPIC LINK

Conditions for motivation

You may remember that we noted in Chapter 1 that managers need to be motivated to investigate variances and take control action. The five conditions above are needed to motivate management.

There is some evidence that performance-related pay does give individuals an incentive to achieve a good performance level. On the other hand, there are **circumstances in which individual performance-related pay schemes do not work**.

- They do not work if an individual's work performance is dependent on work done by other people (and much work involves co-operation and interdependence with others).
- Performance-related pay is most effective when there is a short time-scale between effort and reward. It is less effective for long-term achievements, since effort and reward are too distant in time from each other.
- There is evidence that the effectiveness of performance-related pay wears off over time, as acceptable 'norms' of working are re-established.

A serious problem that can arise is that performance-related pay and performance evaluation systems **can encourage dysfunctional behaviour**. Many investigations have noted the tendency of managers to pad their budgets either in anticipation of cuts by superiors or to make the subsequent variances more favourable. Perhaps of even more concern are the numerous examples of managers making decisions that are contrary to the wider purposes of the organisation.

4.4 Performance evaluation

A very important **source of motivation to perform well** (to achieve budget targets, perhaps, or to eliminate variances) is, not surprisingly, being **kept informed about how actual results are progressing, and how actual results compare with target**. Individuals should not be kept in the dark about their performance.

The information fed back about actual results should obviously have the qualities of good information.

- Reports should be clear and comprehensive.
- Significant variances should be highlighted for investigation.

- Reports should be timely, which means they must be produced in good time to allow the individual to take control action before any adverse results get much worse.

Surprisingly, research evidence suggests that **all too often accounting performance measures can lead to a lack of goal congruence**. Managers try to improve their performance in terms of the performance measures used, even if this is not in the best interests of the organisation as a whole. For example, a production manager may be encouraged to achieve and maintain high production levels and to reduce costs, particularly if his or her bonus is linked to these factors. Such a manager is likely to be highly motivated. But the need to maintain high production levels could lead to high levels of slow-moving stock, resulting in an adverse effect on the company's cashflow.

Activity 11.7

Frendon Ltd has been receiving an increasing number of customer complaints about a general weakness in the quality of its products in recent months. The company believes that its future success is dependent on product quality and it is therefore determined to improve it.

Task

Explain how the budgeting system can be involved in attempts to improve product quality.

4.5 Goal congruence and dysfunctional decision making

Individuals are motivated by personal desires and interests. These desires and interests may tie in with the objectives of the organisation – after all, some people 'live for their jobs'. Other individuals see their job as a chore, and their motivations will have nothing to do with achieving the objectives of the organisation for which they work.

It is therefore important that **some of the desires, interests and goals motivating employees correspond with the goals of the organisation as a whole.** This is known as **goal congruence**. Such a state would exist, for example, if the manager of department A worked to achieve a 10% increase in sales for the department, this 10% increase being part of the organisation's overall plan to increase organisational sales by 20% over the next three years.

On the other hand, **dysfunctional behaviour** can occur if a **manager's goals are not in line with those of the organisation as a whole**. Attempts to enhance his or her own situation or performance (typically **'empire building'** – employing more staff, cutting costs to achieve favourable variances but causing quality problems in other departments) will be at the expense of the best interests of the organisation as a whole. **Participation is not necessarily the answer**. Goal congruence does not necessarily result from allowing managers to develop their own budgets.

A well designed standard costing and budgetary control system can help to ensure goal congruence: continuous feedback prompting appropriate control action should steer the organisation in the right direction.

Activity 11.8

Eskafield Industrial Museum opened ten years ago and soon became a market leader with many working exhibits. In the early years there was a rapid growth in the number of visitors but with no further investment in new exhibits, this growth has not been maintained in recent years.

Two years ago, John Derbyshire was appointed as the museum's chief executive. His initial task was to increase the number of visitors to the museum and, following his appointment, he had made several improvements to make the museum more successful.

Another of John's tasks is to provide effective financial management. This year the museum's Board of Management has asked him to take full responsibility for producing the 20X9 budget. He has asked you to prepare estimates of the number of visitors next year.

Shortly after receiving your notes, John Derbyshire contacts you. He explains that he had prepared a draft budget for the Board of Management based on the estimated numbers for 20X9. This had been prepared on the basis that:

- most of the museum's expenses such as salaries and rates are fixed costs;
- the museum has always budgeted for a deficit;
- the 20X9 deficit will be £35,000.

At the meeting with the Board of Management, John was congratulated on bringing the deficit down from £41,000 in 20X7 to £37,000 (latest estimate) in 20X8. However, the Board of Management raised two issues.

- They felt that the planned deficit of £35,000 should be reduced to £29,000 as this would represent a greater commitment.
- They also queried why the budget had been prepared without any consultation with the museum staff, ie a top down approach.

Task

Draft a memo to John Derbyshire. Your memo should:

(a) discuss the motivational implications of imposing the budget reduction from £35,000 to £29,000;
(b) consider the arguments for and against using a top-down budgeting approach for the museum.

5 Computers and budgeting

Computers can take the hard work out of budgeting: a computerised system will have a number of basic advantages over a manual system.

Activity 11.9

What advantages does a computerised system have over a manual system?

Such advantages make computers ideal for taking over the manipulation of numbers, leaving staff to get involved in the real planning process.

Budgeting is usually computerised using either a computer program written specifically for the organisation or by a commercial spreadsheet package. Both methods of computerisation of the budgeting process will **involve a mathematical model.**

A mathematical model simply represents a 'real-world' situation with mathematical relationships and formulae. An example might be the EOQ model covered in your earlier studies.

The model will consist of a number of interrelated variables. A **variable** is an item in the model which has a value. A variable in the EOQ model is ordering costs. Variables in a sales budget might include selling price and sales volumes.

Once the model has been constructed, the **same model can be used week by week, month after month, or year after year**, simply by changing the values of the variables to produce new results. For example, by changing selling price you would be able to change revenue in the sales budget.

A major advantage of budget models is their **ability to evaluate different options.** By changing the value of certain variables (for example altering the selling price of a product), management are able to assess the effect of such changes. This is sometimes known as **'what if' analysis,** as management can answer questions such as 'What if we raised selling prices by £1?', 'What if we used a cheaper material?, 'What if we increased production in May?'.

Computerised models can also incorporate actual results, period by period, and carry out the necessary calculations to **produce flexible budget control reports**.

The use of a model also allows the budget for the remainder of the year to be adjusted once it is clear that the circumstances on which the budget was originally based have changed.

Spreadsheets and budgeting

Most organisations do not have budgeting programs written for them but use standard spreadsheet packages.

Spreadsheet packages for budgeting have a number of advantages.

- Spreadsheet packages have a facility to perform **'what if' calculations** at great speed. For example, the consequences throughout the organisation of sales growth per month of nil, ½%, 1%, 1½% and so on can be calculated very quickly.
- Preparing budgets may be complex; budgets may need to go through several drafts. If one or two figures are changed, the **computer will automatically make all the computational changes to the other figures**.
- A spreadsheet model will **ensure that the preparation of the individual budgets is co-ordinated**. Data and information from the production budget, for example, will be automatically fed through to the material usage budget (as material usage will depend on production levels).

ATTENTION!

Candidates in the December 1999 exam were required to complete a spreadsheet template to show the formulae in each cell which would enable the sales budgets to be calculated.

Activity 11.10

	A	B	C	D	E	F
1	BUDGETED SALES FIGURES					
2		*Jan*	*Feb*	*Mar*	*Total*	
3		£'000	£'000	£'000	£'000	
4	North	2,431	3,001	2,189	7,621	
5	South	6,532	5,826	6,124	18,482	
6	West	895	432	596	1,923	
7	Total	9,858	9,259	8,909	28,026	
8						

Tasks

(a) In the spreadsheet shown above, which of the cells contain values (ie they have had a number typed in), and which cells contain a formula?

(b) What formula would the following cells contain?

(i) Cell B7
(ii) Cell E6
(iii) Cell E7

(c) If the February sales figure for the South changed from £5,826 to £5,731, what other figures would change as a result? Give cell references.

Key learning points

- ☑ The traditional approach to budgeting, known as **incremental budgeting**, bases the budget on the current year's results plus an extra amount for estimated growth or inflation next year. It encourages slack and wasteful spending to creep into budgets.
- ☑ The principle behind **zero based budgeting (ZBB)** is that the budget for each cost centre should be made from a zero base. Every item of expenditure has to be completely justified in order to be included in the budget.
- ☑ **Rolling budgets (continuous budgets)** are budgets which are continuously updated by adding another period (every month or quarter) and deducting the earliest period.
- ☑ Budgets and standards are most likely to **motivate** employees if employees accept that the budget/standard is achievable.
- ☑ Budgets can be set from the top down (**imposed budget**) or from the bottom up (**participatory budget).** You need to be aware of the conditions needed for either one to be the preferred approach.
- ☑ Providing certain conditions are met, **pay** can be an important motivator if there is a formal link between higher pay and achieving targets.
- ☑ An important source of motivation to perform well is being kept **informed** about how actual results compare with target.
- ☑ **Goal congruence** occurs when the goals of an individual tie in with the goals of the organisation as a whole. If this is not the case **dysfunctional behaviour** can occur.
- ☑ Make sure that you understand how to derive **spreadsheet formulae.**

Quick quiz

1 Incremental budgeting is widely used and is a particularly efficient form of budgeting. *True or false?*

2 What are the four steps of ZBB?

Step 1 ....

Step 2 ....

Step 3 ....

Step 4 ....

3 To which of the following can ZBB be usefully applied?

	Use ZBB	Do not use ZBB
Personnel		
Social services department of local government		
Direct material costs		
Sales department		
Schools		
An inefficient production department		
An efficient production department		

4 *Choose the appropriate word from those highlighted.*

A continuous budget is also known as a **periodic/rolling** budget.

5 *Match the descriptions to the budgeting style.*

Description

(a) Budget allowances are set without the involvement of the budget holder.

(b) All budget holders are involved in setting their own budgets.

(c) Budget allowances are set on the basis of discussions between budget holders and those to whom they report.

Budgeting style

Negotiated budgeting
Participative budgeting
Imposed budgeting

6 Budgetary slack is necessary to ensure that managers are able to meet their targets. *True or false?*

7 What does the spreadsheet formulae SUM(B6:B18)*C18 mean?

A Total the contents of cells B6 to B18 and C18
B Add the contents of cell B6 to those of B18 and multiply by the contents of cell C18
C Total the contents of cells B6 to B18 and multiply this total by the contents of cell C18
D Add the contents of cell B6 to the product of the contents of cells B18 and C18

Answers to quick quiz

1 False. Incremental budgeting is inefficient.

2 ***Step 1.*** Identify activities

Step 2. Draw up decision packages

Step 3. Evaluate and rank activities (decision packages)

Step 4. Allocate funds

3

	Use ZBB	Do not use ZBB
Personnel	✓	
Social services department of local government	✓	
Direct material costs		✓
Sales department	✓	
Schools	✓	
An inefficient production department	✓	
An efficient production department		✓

4 It is also known as a rolling budget.

5 (a) Imposed budgeting
(b) Participative budgeting
(c) Negotiated budgeting

6 False. Budgets should be reviewed to ensure that operational managers have not included slack.

7 C

ASSESSMENT KIT ACTIVITIES

The following activities in the BPP Assessment Kit for Units 8 & 9 include topics covered in both this chapter and Chapter 10.

Activities 27, 29 to 39
Lecturers' practice activities 16 to 21

Activity checklist

This checklist shows which performance criteria, range statement or knowledge and understanding point is covered by each activity in this chapter. Tick off each activity as you complete it.

Activity		
11.1	☐	This activity deals with Unit 9 Knowledge & Understanding point (13): uses of budgetary control.
11.2	☐	This activity deals with Unit 9 Knowledge & Understanding point (13): uses of budgetary control.
11.3	☐	This activity deals with Unit 9 Knowledge & Understanding point (13): uses of budgetary control.
11.4	☐	This activity deals with Unit 9 Knowledge & Understanding point (13): uses of budgetary control.
11.5	☐	This activity deals with Unit 9 Knowledge & Understanding point (13): uses of budgetary control.
11.6	☐	This activity deals with Performance Criteria 9.2D regarding communication with budget holders in a manner which maintains goodwill and ensuring budget proposals are agreed with budget holders.
11.7	☐	This activity deals with Unit 8 Knowledge & Understanding point (11): effect of accounting controls on behaviour of managers and other employees, and Unit 9 Knowledge & Understanding point (9): the effect of budgetary systems on the behaviour and motivation of managers and other employees.
11.8	☐	This activity deals with Performance Criteria 9.2D regarding communication with budget holders in a manner which maintains goodwill and ensuring budget proposals are agreed with budget holders, Unit 8 Knowledge & Understanding point (11): effect of accounting controls on behaviour of managers and other employees, and Unit 9 Knowledge & Understanding point (9): the effect of budgetary systems on the behaviour and motivation of managers and other employees
11.9	☐	This activity deals with Unit 9 Knowledge & Understanding point (4): use of relevant computer packages.
11.10	☐	This activity deals with Unit 9 Knowledge & Understanding point (4): use of relevant computer packages.

PART D

Core theme 3: measurement of performance

chapter 12

Performance measurement

Contents

1 Introduction
2 Performance indicators
3 Ratio analysis
4 Ratio analysis: the profit and loss account
5 Ratio analysis: linking the profit and loss account to the balance sheet
6 Ratio analysis: current assets and current liabilities
7 Limitations and strengths of ratios

Performance criteria

8.2A Analyse routine cost reports, compare them with other sources of information and identify any implications

8.2B Prepare and monitor relevant performance indicators, interpret the results, identify potential improvements and estimate the value of potential improvements

8.2D Prepare exception reports to identify matters which require further investigation

Range statement

8.2 Performance indicators to measure: efficiency, effectiveness and productivity; profitability

Knowledge and understanding

Unit 8 Accounting techniques

6 Performance indicators: efficiency, effectiveness, productivity

Signpost

This chapter is relevant to **Unit 8.**

1 Introduction

Management **measure** the **performance** of an organisation in a number of areas to **see** whether **objectives or targets are being met**.

- In the organisation as a whole
- In each of the main sub-divisions of the organisation
- In individual activities
- In relationships with customers, the market, suppliers and competitors

The process of performance measurement is carried out using a variety of **performance indicators**, which are individual measurements. We look at performance indicators **in general** in Section 2 before moving on to look at performance indicators **derived from the profit and loss account and balance sheet.** As well as being of use to management, **parties external** to the organisation can use these as a guide to how well the organisation is performing.

Exam tasks frequently require you to establish the types of indicator discussed in this chapter.

Many performance indicators are concerned with **productivity**, **efficiency** and **effectiveness**, ideas we introduced in Chapter 1. These concepts underlie the whole topic of performance measurement and so it is vital the you really understand what they mean. Go back to Chapter 1 to refresh your memory if necessary.

In the next chapter we look at additional ways of measuring performance.

2 Performance indicators

In Chapters 6 and 7 we looked at the analysis of **cost variances**. Cost variances are examples of performance indicators and can provide assistance to management in a number of ways.

- Monitoring the use of resources
- Controlling the organisation
- Planning for the future

In this chapter and the next we will look at a wide variety of performance indicators. Let's have a look at some examples and the possible uses they could have.

- The direct labour efficiency variance, which could **identify problems** with labour productivity
- Distribution costs as a percentage of turnover, which could help with the **control of costs**
- Number of hours during which labour are idle, which could indicate **how well resources are being used**
- Profit as a percentage of turnover, which could highlight **how well the organisation is being managed**
- Number of units returned by customers, which could help with **planning** production and finished stock levels

Given this **wide range of uses**, you should be able to appreciate the importance of performance indictors and their value to managers in allowing them to see where improvements in organisational performance can be made.

A performance indicator is only useful if it is given meaning in relation to something else. Here is a list of **yardsticks** against which indicators can be compared so as to become useful.

- **Standards, budgets or targets**
- **Trends over time** (comparing last year with this year, say). An upward trend in the number of rejects from a production process, say, would indicate a problem that needed investigating. The effects of inflation would perhaps need to be recognised if financial indicators were being compared over time.
- **The results of other parts of the organisation**. Large manufacturing companies may compare the results of their various production departments, supermarket chains will compare the results of their individual stores, while a college may compare pass rates in different departments.
- **The results of other organisations.** For example, trade associations or the government may provide details of key indicators based on averages for the industry.

As with all comparisons, it is vital that the performance measurement process compares **'like with like'**. There is little to be gained in comparing the results of a small supermarket in a high street with a huge one in an out-of-town shopping complex. We return to the importance of consistency in comparisons later in this chapter.

2.1 Data for performance indicators

It is possible to distinguish between quantitative data, which is capable of being expressed in numbers, and qualitative data, which can only be expressed in numerical terms with difficulty.

- An example of a **quantitative** performance measure is 'You have been late for work **twice** this week and it's only Tuesday!'.
- An example of a **qualitative** performance measure is 'My bed is **very** comfortable'.

The first measure is likely to find its way into a staff appraisal report. The second would feature in a bed manufacturer's customer satisfaction survey. Both are indicators of whether their subjects are doing as good a job as they are required to do.

Qualitative measures are by nature **subjective** and **judgmental** but this does not mean that they are not valuable. They are especially valuable when they are derived from several different sources because then they can be expressed in a mixture of quantitative and qualitative terms which is more meaningful overall.

Consider the statement 'Seven out of ten customers think our beds are very comfortable'. This is a quantitative measure of customer satisfaction as well as a qualitative measure of the perceived performance of the beds. (But it does not mean that only 70% of the total beds produced are comfortable, nor that each bed is 70% comfortable and 30% uncomfortable: 'very' is the measure of comfort.)

2.2 Productivity, efficiency and effectiveness

In general, performance indicators are established to measure productivity, efficiency and effectiveness, concepts introduced in Chapter 1.

To recap:

- Effectiveness is about meeting targets and objectives.
- Productivity is a measure of output relative to some form of input.

- Efficiency also looks at output relative to input, but it is not the same as productivity because the output is considered in terms of financial gain or value to the organisation.

Activity 12.1

Stern Ltd aims to fulfil all customer orders within six weeks from the time an order is first placed. The company had no outstanding orders for its product at the beginning of 20X2. During the year orders were placed for 16,560 units but only 13,800 units were manufactured and sold.

Task

Establish a performance measure to show how effectively Stern Ltd is meeting customers' needs.

3 Ratio analysis

Ratio analysis is one of the principal tools used to determine how well an organisation is performing. It involves the calculation of ratios or percentages using data from an organisation's management accounts or financial accounts. These figures can then be compared with budgets or targets, over time or with similar organisations.

Its main **advantage** is that ratios are often **easier to understand** than absolute measures of physical quantities or money values. For example, it is easier to understand that 'productivity in March was 94%' than 'there was an adverse labour efficiency variance in March of £3,600'.

We will be looking at three groups of ratios.

- Those which can be calculated from the profit and loss account
- Those which provide a link between figures in the profit and loss account and figures in the balance sheet
- Those which relate to the current assets and current liabilities section of the balance sheet

4 Ratio analysis: the profit and loss account

4.1 Profit margin

The profit margin **(profit to sales ratio, operating profit percentage, net margin** or **sales margin)** is calculated as **(profit ÷ sales) × 100%**, where profit is usually **operating profit.**

Operating profit is usually **used** rather than one of the several versions of profit given in company accounts (before and after interest and tax) because it is the profit derived from the main trading activities of the organisation.

The profit margin is a **key measure of efficiency for organisations with an objective to earn profit.** The ratio measures the **efficiency with which sales** (the **input**) has been **used to generate profit** (the **value of the output**).

The profit margin is a particularly useful way of analysing information.

- It provides a measure of performance for management as it is concerned with the profit over which operational management can exercise day to day control.
- Investigation of unsatisfactory profit margins enables control action to be taken, either to reduce excessive costs or, possibly, to raise selling prices (both actions hopefully improving profits).

Example: the profit to sales ratio

FOB Ltd compares its Year 1 results with Year 0 results as follows.

	Year 1	*Year 0*
	£	£
Sales	160,000	120,000
Cost of sales		
Direct materials	40,000	20,000
Direct labour	40,000	30,000
Production overhead	22,000	20,000
Marketing overhead	42,000	35,000
	144,000	105,000
Profit	16,000	15,000
Profit to sales ratio	10%	12½%

Ratio analysis on the above information shows that there is a decline in profitability in spite of the £1,000 increase in profit, because the profit margin is less in Year 1 than Year 0.

4.1.1 Manipulation of the ratio

The measure can be manipulated in a number of ways. The following actions would result in **short-term improvements in the margin**, although probably **at the expense of the organisation's long-term viability**.

- Reducing expenditure on discretionary cost items
- Depreciating assets over a longer period of time

The ratio is also **affected by the stock valuation method**. The cost of sales figure will depend on whether FIFO or LIFO, say, is used, and this will have an impact on profit.

4.2 Gross profit margin

The profit to sales ratio above was based on a profit figure which included non-production overheads. The **pure trading activities of a business can be analysed** using the gross profit margin, which is calculated as **(gross profit ÷ turnover)** × **100%**.

For FOB Ltd in the example above, the gross profit margin would be ((16,000 + 42,000)/160,000) × 100% = 36.25% in Year 1 and ((15,000 + 35,000)/120,000) × 100% = 41.67% in Year 0.

Activity 12.2

(a) How can the gross profit margin be increased?
(b) What are its limitations?

4.3 Cost/sales ratios

There are three principal ratios for analysing profit and loss account information.

- Production cost of sales ÷ sales
- Distribution and marketing costs ÷ sales
- Administrative costs ÷ sales

When **particular areas of weakness are found subsidiary ratios are used to examine them in greater depth**. For example, for production costs the following ratios might be used.

- Material costs ÷ sales value of production
- Works labour costs ÷ sales value of production
- Production overheads ÷ sales value of production

Example: cost/sales ratios

Look back to the example about FOB Ltd in Section 4.1. A more detailed analysis would show that higher direct materials are the probable cause of the decline in profitability.

	Year 1	*Year 0*
Material costs/sales	25%	16.7%

Other cost/sales ratios have remained the same or improved.

4.3.1 Percentage analysis of sales revenue

Using the information in the FOB Ltd example, it is possible to provide a complete analysis of sales revenue for years 1 and 0, to see how it is split between the various elements of cost and profit.

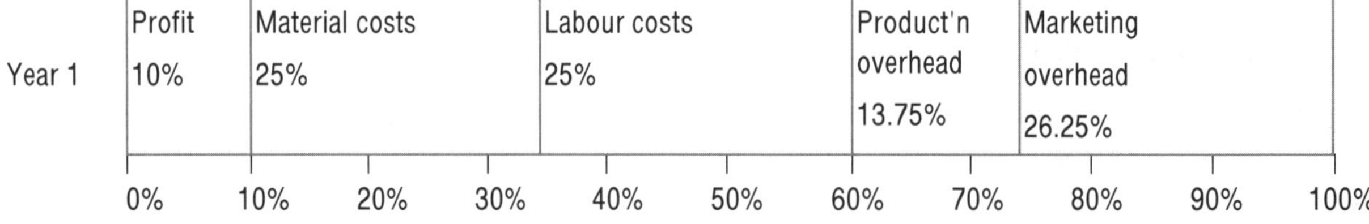

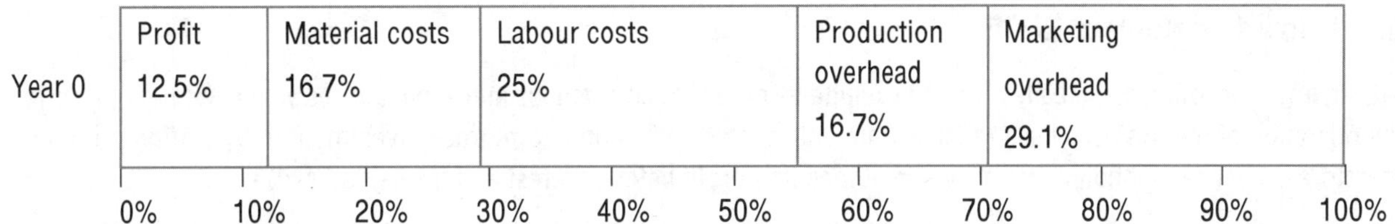

4.3.2 The impact of cost behaviour on cost/sales ratios

The ratios will be affected by whether costs are fixed or variable. An increase in turnover is often the result of an increase in sales volume. An increase in sales volume will result in an increase in variable costs but total fixed costs should remain the same (because they are not affected by changes in activity level).

How will this affect ratios?

- A variable cost should remain roughly the same percentage of turnover
- A fixed cost should decrease as a percentage of turnover as turnover increases

5 Ratio analysis: linking the profit and loss account to the balance sheet

5.1 Return on capital employed

Return on capital employed **(ROCE)** (also called **return on investment (ROI)**) is calculated as **(profit/capital employed) × 100%** and **shows how well managers have used resources under their control to generate profit**.

If an organisation's ROCE is, say, 25%, 25p of profit is generated from every £1 of resources used.

This is one of the **major measurements of efficiency** in organisations with an **objective** to earn **profit**. The ratio measures the **efficiency with which the capital employed (input)** has been **used to generate profit** (the **value of the output**).

Profits alone do not show whether the return achieved by an organisation is sufficient, because the profit measure takes no account of the volume of assets the organisation has used to generate that return. So if company A and company B have the following results, company B would have the better performance.

	A	*B*
	£	£
Profit	5,000	5,000
Sales	100,000	100,000
Capital employed	50,000	25,000
ROCE	10%	20%

The profit of each company is the same but company B only invests £25,000 to achieve these results whereas company A needs £50,000.

5.1.1 How to calculate ROCE

Management accountants usually prefer to exclude from profits all revenues and expenditures which are not related to the operation of the business itself (such as interest payable and income from trade investments). **Operating profit** is therefore often used (although you may sometimes find profit before interest and tax being used).

Similarly **all assets of a non-operational nature** (for example trade investments and intangible assets such as goodwill) **should be excluded** from capital employed.

But what is the capital employed figure? You should remember from your financial accounting studies that the idea of the balance sheet can be represented by

assets – liabilities = capital

where capital is the owner's interest in the business. The balance sheet can therefore be considered from two perspectives.

- Net assets
- Capital provided by the owners

As 'assets' includes both fixed and current assets, and 'liabilities' includes current and long-term liabilities, we can restate the equation above as:

fixed assets + current assets – current liabilities = long-term liabilities + capital

For our purposes 'capital employed' in ROCE will therefore be defined in one of two ways.

- Net assets
- Long-term liabilities + capital

ATTENTION!

Always make it clear what profit and capital employed figures you are using when calculating ROCE because of the possible variations in the way it is derived.

Profits should be related to average capital employed but, in practice, the **ratio is usually computed using the year-end assets**. Using year-end figures can, however, distort trends and comparisons. If a new investment is undertaken near to a year end and financed, for example, by an issue of shares, the capital employed will rise by the finance raised but profits will only have a month or two of the new investment's contribution.

An organisation's ROCE could be **misleading** if a large proportion of its costs are treated as revenue expenditure but could actually be viewed as investment in the future (for example, marketing, research and development and training costs) since, without these expenses, the ROCE would be much higher.

Another point to bear in mind is that ROCE tends to increase as fixed assets get older. As the accumulated depreciation charge reduces the net book value, so the value of capital employed reduces. Therefore, for a given level of profit, the calculated ROCE will increase.

5.1.2 What does the ROCE tell us?

What should we be looking for? There are **two principal comparisons** that can be made.

- The change in ROCE from one year to the next
- The ROCE being earned by other entities

These comparisons will tell us how well the organisation's management have used the resources under their control (fixed assets + current assets – current liabilities) to generate profit compared with previous years or compared with managers of other entities.

5.2 Asset turnover

This is another important ratio which **links the profit and loss account and balance sheet**. It is a measure of **how well the assets of a business are being used to generate sales** and is calculated as **(sales ÷ capital employed)**.

The **same figure for capital employed used in ROCE** is used in asset turnover.

For example, suppose two companies each have capital employed of £100,000 and Company A makes sales of £400,000 per annum whereas Company B makes sales of only £200,000 per annum. Company A is making a higher turnover from the same amount of assets, in other words twice as much asset turnover as Company B, and this will help A to make a higher return on capital employed than B. Asset turnover is **expressed as 'x times' so that assets generate x times their value in annual turnover**. Here, Company A's asset turnover is 4 times and B's is 2 times.

The **problems** associated with the **valuation of capital employed** which we looked at for ROCE apply equally to the asset turnover ratio.

The asset turnover ratio is a **key measure of productivity** for many organisations, measuring **how intensively its capital employed has been used to generate sales**.

IMPORTANT POINT

'New' fixed assets and/or a large fixed asset base can help employees achieve higher levels of productivity. Both of these factors reduce the fixed asset turnover ratio (an alternative measure of productivity) and ROCE (a measure of efficiency).

Activity 12.3

South & Brown Limited is a member of a trade association which operates an inter-company comparison scheme. The scheme is designed to help its member companies to monitor their own performance against that of other companies in the same industry.

At the end of each year, the member companies submit detailed annual accounts to the scheme organisers. The results are processed and a number of accounting ratios are published and circulated to members. The ratios indicate the average results for all member companies.

Your manager has given you the following extract, which shows the average profitability and asset turnover ratios for the latest year (Year 4). For comparison purposes, South & Brown Limited's accounts analyst has added the ratios for your company.

	Trade association average	*South & Brown Ltd*
Return on capital employed	20.5%	18.4%
Net (operating) profit margin	5.4%	6.8%
Asset turnover	3.8 times	2.7 times
Gross margin	14.2%	12.9%

Tasks

As assistant accountant for South & Brown Limited, your manager has asked you to prepare a report for the Senior Management Committee. The report should cover the following points.

(a) An explanation of what each ratio is designed to show

(b) An interpretation of South & Brown Limited's profitability and asset turnover compared with the trade association average

5.3 The link between ROCE, profit margin and asset turnover

We know that ROCE = profit/capital employed.

This could be written as ROCE = $\frac{\text{profit}}{\text{sales}} \times \frac{\text{sales}}{\text{capital employed}}$ (because the 'sales' figures can cancel each other out).

$\therefore$ **ROCE = profit margin × asset turnover**

ROCE can therefore be **increased** by **improving the profit margin** and/or **increasing asset turnover**. In other words, spending less of the sales revenue on operating costs and/or using the organisation's assets more effectively to generate sales can improve ROCE.

6 Ratio analysis: current assets and current liabilities

In this section we are going to look at a number of ratios based on the working capital component of an organisation's overall capital. **Working capital** is made up of **stock**, **debtors**, **cash** and **trade creditors,** which are within the current assets and current liabilities section of the balance sheet.

The ratios fall into two groups.

- Those that consider the **liquidity** of an organisation (its ability to pay its current liabilities when they fall due)
- Those that consider how well **stock, debtors** and **creditors** have been **controlled**

6.1 Liquidity ratios

6.1.1 Current ratio

The current ratio is the 'standard' test of liquidity and is the **ratio of current assets to current liabilities**.

The ratio is different to those we have looked at so far in that it is **presented in ratio form** (**x:1**, where **x** is the **answer given by current assets/current liabilities**).

The idea behind the current ratio is that a company should have enough current assets that give a promise of 'cash to come' to meet its future commitments to pay off its current liabilities. Obviously, a **ratio in excess of 1 should be expected**. Otherwise, there would be the prospect that the company might be unable to pay its debts on time. In practice, a ratio comfortably in excess of 1 should be expected, but what is 'comfortable' varies between different types of businesses.

Companies are not able to convert all their current assets into cash very quickly. In particular, some manufacturing companies might hold large quantities of raw material stocks, which must be used in production to create finished goods stocks. Finished goods stocks might be warehoused for a long time, or sold on lengthy credit. In such businesses, **where stock turnover is slow, most stocks are not very 'liquid' assets**, because the cash cycle is so long. For these reasons, we **calculate an additional liquidity ratio**, known as the quick ratio or acid test ratio.

6.1.2 Quick (or acid test) ratio

The quick ratio, or acid test ratio, is the **ratio of current assets less stocks to current liabilities**.

This ratio should **ideally be at least 1 for companies with a slow stock turnover**. For companies with a **fast stock turnover**, a quick ratio can be comfortably **less than 1** without suggesting that the company is in cash flow trouble.

6.1.3 Insights provided by these ratios

Both the current ratio and the quick ratio offer an indication of the company's liquidity position, but the absolute figures should not be interpreted too literally. It is often said that an acceptable current ratio is 1.5 and an acceptable quick ratio is 0.8, but these should only be used as a guide. Different businesses operate in very different ways. A supermarket, for example, might have a current ratio of 0.40 and a quick ratio of 0.16. due to low debtors (people do not buy groceries on credit), low cash (good cash management), medium stocks (high stocks but quick turnover, particularly in view of perishability) and very high creditors (many supermarkets buy their supplies of groceries on credit).

What is important is the trend of these ratios, which will show whether liquidity is improving or deteriorating. If a supermarket has traded for the last 10 years (very successfully) with current ratios of 0.40 and quick ratios of 0.16 then it ought to be able to continue in business with those levels of liquidity. If in the following year the current ratio were to fall to 0.38 and the quick ratio to 0.09, further investigation would be needed. It is the relative position that is far more important than the absolute figures.

A current ratio and a quick ratio can get bigger than they need to be, however. A company that has large volumes of stocks and debtors might be over-investing in working capital, and so tying up more funds in the business than it needs to. This would suggest poor management of debtors (credit) or stocks by the company. We consider this issue next.

Activity 12.4

The following details have been extracted from the accounts of Logic Ltd. The company's year ends on 31 March.

	Year 2	*Year 3*	*Year 4*
	£m	£m	£m
Turnover (sales)	100	103	108
Gross profit	33.0	34.0	35.6
Net profit	15	15	15
Fixed assets	64	72	68
Stock	4	4	4
Debtors	8	11	15
Creditors	5	6	6
Cash at bank	5	-	-
Bank overdraft	-	6	5

Tasks

(a) Calculate the following for each of the three years.

(i) Gross profit percentage
(ii) Net profit percentage
(iii) Quick ratio (acid test)

(b) Comment briefly on the ratios you have calculated

6.2 Ratios for the control of debtors, creditors and stock

6.2.1 Debtor days ratio

The debtor days ratio (or **average debtors' payment period** or **average age of debtors)** is a rough measure of the **average length of time it takes for a company's debtors to pay what they owe**. It is calculated as **(trade debtors/sales) × 365 days** or **(trade debtors/sales) × 12 months**.

The **estimate of debtor days is only approximate** because the balance sheet value of debtors might be abnormally high or low compared with the organisation's 'normal' level.

A supermarket should have a very low debtor days ratio since sales should not be on credit. Sales of most organisations, however, are usually made on 'normal credit terms' of payment within 30 days. Debtor days significantly in excess of this might be representative of poor management of funds of a business. However, some companies must allow generous credit terms to win customers. Exporting companies in particular may have to carry large amounts of debtors, and so their average collection period might be well in excess of 30 days.

The **trend of the collection period (debtor days) over time is probably the best guide**. If debtor days are increasing year on year, this is indicative of a poorly managed credit control function (and potentially therefore a poorly managed company).

LOOK OUT FOR ...

Unusual terminology

You might be asked to calculate what is actually a debtors days ratio although the name of the ratio might reflect the task scenario. For example, you could be asked to calculate the average age of rent arrears if you are dealing with a housing society. The type of debt will depend on the organisation.

6.2.2 Creditors' turnover

Creditors' turnover or **average age of creditors** or **creditors' payment period** provides a rough measure of the **average length of time it takes a company to pay what it owes**. It is **ideally** calculated by the formula **(creditors/purchases) × 365 days** or **(creditors/purchases) × 12 months. Cost of sales** can be used as an **approximation for purchases**.

The creditors' turnover ratio **often helps to assess a company's liquidity**; an increase is often a sign of lack of long-term finance or poor management of current assets, resulting in the use of extended credit from suppliers, increased bank overdraft and so on.

6.2.3 Stock turnover period

The stock turnover period (or **stock days** or **average age of stock**) indicates the **average number of days that items of stock are held** for and is calculated as **(stock ÷ cost of sales)** × **365 days** or **(stock ÷ cost of sales)** × **12 months**.

As with the average debt collection period, this is only an approximate estimated figure, but one which should be reliable enough for comparing changes year on year.

Presumably if we add together the stock days and the debtor days, this should give us an indication of how soon stock is convertible into cash. Both debtor days and stock days therefore give us a further indication of the company's liquidity.

6.2.4 Stock turnover

'Cost of sales ÷ stock' is termed stock turnover, and is a measure of **how vigorously** a business is **trading**.

The result of this calculation gives a measure in terms of **'number of times per year.'**

A **lengthening stock turnover period** from one year to the next indicates either a **slowdown in trading** or **a build-up in stock levels**, perhaps suggesting that the investment in stocks is becoming excessive.

When you are interpreting stock turnover data you should consider the type of organisation and the systems it operates.

- Obviously there should be a marked difference between the stock turnover of a retail organisation such as a supermarket, and a manufacturing group.
- In an organisation which operates a just in time system (one which minimises or, ideally, eliminates stock) you would expect to see very high stock turnover, but you may also notice other effects such as low storage costs and higher prices paid for supplies.

6.2.5 Working capital period

Working capital control is concerned with minimising funds tied up in net current assets while ensuring that sufficient stock, cash and credit facilities are in place to enable trading to take place. Calculation of the ratio provides some insight into working capital control.

The ratio (which is also called the **average age of working capital**) identifies **how long** it takes to **convert the purchase of stocks into cash from sales** and is calculated as **(working capital/cost of sales) × 365 days**. The ratio can also be calculated as **(working capital/ operating costs) × 365 days**.

The **lower the age** or **period**, the **better the working capital control**.

Care needs to be taken when determining the ideal ratio. Reduce it too low and there may be insufficient stock and other current assets to sustain the volume of trade. Taking too much credit from suppliers may jeopardise relationships and/or cause suppliers to increase prices.

A ratio in excess of a target indicates that working capital levels are probably too high and that management action is needed to reduce them. This may involve stringent control of debtors, a reduction in stock levels and/or a more efficient use of available credit facilities. A debtors days ratio, stock turnover period and creditors turnover period can be calculated to determine where the problem lies.

The ratio has two principal **limitations**.

- It is based on the working capital level on one particular day, which may not be representative of working capital levels throughout the entire period.
- Working capital includes a figure for stock which may be a very subjective valuation.

LOOK OUT FOR ...

Ways to check your workings

You are often provided with data about an organisation's performance over two periods, a list of performance measures for the earlier period and are then asked to calculate the same measures for the second period. You are therefore able to check how to calculate the measures by **recalculating the measures for the first period and comparing them to the values provided.** Alternatively, you are provided with industry average performance measures or performance measures for one organisation and then asked to compare them with the performance of another organisation.

You are sometimes told how to calculate more unusual ratios. The formula for the average age of working capital was provided in the December 1995 exam, for example.

Activity 12.5

Calculate liquidity and working capital ratios from the accounts of Gelton Ltd, a manufacturer of products for the construction industry. Discuss your results.

	Year 8	*Year 7*
	£m	£m
Turnover	2,065.0	1,788.7
Cost of sales	1,478.6	1,304.0
Gross profit	586.4	484.7
Current assets		
Stocks	119.0	109.0
Debtors (note 1)	400.9	347.4
Short-term investments	4.2	18.8
Cash at bank and in hand	48.2	48.0
	572.3	523.2
Creditors: amounts falling due within one year		
Loans and overdrafts	49.1	35.3
Corporation taxes	62.0	46.7
Dividend	19.2	14.3
Creditors (note 2)	370.7	324.0
	501.0	420.3
Net current assets	71.3	102.9

Notes

1 Trade debtors	329.8	285.4
2 Trade creditors	236.2	210.8

7 Limitations and strengths of ratios

7.1 Limitations of the profit and loss account and balance sheet ratios

On their own, they do not provide information to enable managers to gauge performance or make control decisions. Yardsticks are needed for comparison purposes.

The ratios used **must be carefully defined**. For example, should 'return' equal profit before interest and taxation, profit after taxation, or profit before interest, taxation and investment income?

Ratios compared over a period of time at historical cost will not be properly comparable where **inflation** in prices has occurred during the period, unless an adjustment is made to the ratios to make allowance for price level differences.

The ratios of **different companies** cannot be properly compared where each company uses a **different method to do the following**.

- Value closing stocks (for example FIFO, LIFO, or marginal/absorbed cost)
- Apportion overheads in absorption costing
- Value fixed assets (for example at net book value, replacement cost and so on)
- Estimate the life of assets in order to calculate depreciation
- Account for research and development costs
- Account for goodwill

Remember that ratios calculated using **historical costs** may not be a guide to the future.

7.2 Strengths of the profit and loss account and balance sheet ratios

We stated earlier that ratios are often **easier to understand than absolute measures** of physical quantities or money values. Ratios have other strengths too.

- It is **easier to look at changes over time** by comparing ratios in one time period with the corresponding ratios for periods in the past.
- Ratios **relate one item to another, and so help to put performance into context**. For example the profit/sales ratio sets profit in the context of how much has been earned per £1 of sales, and so shows how wide or narrow profit margins are.
- Ratios can be used as **targets,** for example for productivity. Managers will then take decisions which will enable them to achieve their targets.
- Ratios provide a way of **summarising** an organisation's results, and **comparing** them with similar organisations.

Activity 12.6

You are given summarised results of Disraeli plc as follows.

PROFIT AND LOSS ACCOUNT FOR YEAR ENDED 31 DECEMBER YEAR 1

	£'000
Turnover	60,000
Cost of sales	42,000
Gross profit	18,000
Operating expenses	15,500
Profit	2,500

BALANCE SHEET AT 31 DECEMBER YEAR 1

	£'000	£'000
Fixed assets		12,500
Current assets		
Stock	14,000	
Debtors	16,000	
Cash	500	
		30,500
Creditors due within 1 year		24,000
Net current assets		6,500
Total assets less current liabilities		19,000
Capital and reserves		19,000

Task

Calculate the following ratios, clearly showing the figures used in the calculations.

(a) Current ratio
(b) Quick/acid test ratio
(c) Stock turnover in days
(d) Debtors turnover in days
(e) Creditors turnover in days
(f) Gross profit percentage
(g) Net profit percentage
(h) ROCE
(i) Asset turnover

Activity 12.7

Comment on any limitations of the ratios used in Activity 12.6 and of comparisons made against trade association average ratios for an industry.

Key learning points

- ☑ **Performance indicators** are only useful if given meaning in relation to something else.
  - Standards, budgets, targets
  - Trends over time
  - Results of other parts of the organisation
  - Results of other organisations
- ☑ It is vital that the performance measurement process compares 'like with like'.
- ☑ **Return on capital employed (ROCE)** (also called **return on investment (ROI)**), a key measure of efficiency, is calculated as (profit/capital employed) × 100% and shows how much profit has been made in relation to the amount of resources invested.
- ☑ Another measure of efficiency is **profit margin (profit to sales ratio),** which is calculated as (profit ÷ sales) × 100% and focuses on operating activities. The pure trading activities of a business can be analysed using the **gross profit margin**, which is calculated as (gross profit ÷ turnover) × 100%.
- ☑ **Asset turnover** is a productivity measure and shows how well the assets of a business are being used to generate sales. It is calculated as (sales ÷ capital employed).
- ☑ **ROCE = profit margin × asset turnover**, and so ROCE can be increased by improving the profit margin and/or increasing turnover.
- ☑ The **current ratio** is the 'standard' test of liquidity and is the ratio of current assets to current liabilities. The **quick ratio**, or **acid test ratio**, is the ratio of current assets less stocks to current liabilities. It is the trend in these ratios that is important.
- ☑ A rough measure of the average length of time it takes for a company's debtors to pay what they owe is the **debtor days ratio** (or **average debtors' payment period** or **average age of debtors**).The **creditors' turnover** or **average age of creditors** is a rough measure of the average length of time it takes a company to pay what it owes.
- ☑ The **stock turnover period** indicates the average number of days that items of stock are held for.
- ☑ **Stock turnover** is a measure of how vigorously a business is trading.
- ☑ The **working capital period** (or **average age of working capital)** identifies how long it takes to convert the purchase of stocks into cash from sales.

Quick quiz

1 *Fill in the blanks.*

To become useful, performance indicators should be compared against yard-sticks including ……………………… , ……………………… , …………………… or …………………… .

2 What types of measure are profit margin and ROCE?

	Profit margin	*ROCE*
A	Of efficiency	Of productivity
B	Of effectiveness	Of effectiveness
C	Of productivity	Of effectiveness
D	Of efficiency	Of efficiency

3 *Choose the correct words from those highlighted.*

ROCE is usually calculated using **operating profit/gross profit** and **current assets/total assets/net assets.**

4 Asset turnover is calculated as assets ÷ sales. *True or false?*

5 *Fill in the blanks with words from the list below.*

ROCE = ……………………….. × ………………………….

Possible words

Asset turnover
Net current asset
Profit
Profit margin
Quick ratio
Total liabilities

6 *Choose the correct words from those highlighted.*

A current ratio **less than 1/in excess of 1** should normally be expected.

7 How is a stock turnover period calculated?

A (Stock ÷ cost of sales) × 12 months
B Stock ÷ purchases
C (Purchases ÷ stock) × 12 months
D Cost of sales ÷ stock

8 A decrease in the creditors' turnover ratio is a sign of poor management of current assets. *True or false?*

Answers to quick quiz

1 standards, budgets or targets
trends over time
results of other parts of the organisation
results of other organisations

2 D

3 operating profit and net assets

4 False. It is sales ÷ capital employed.

5 ROCE = profit margin × asset turnover

6 in excess of 1

7 A

8 False. An increase shows possible poor management of current assets.

ASSESSMENT KIT ACTIVITIES

See the box at the end of Chapter 13 for details of the activities in BPP's Assessment Kit for Units 8 & 9 which include topics covered in this chapter.

Activity checklist

This checklist shows which performance criteria, range statement or knowledge and understanding point is covered by each activity in this chapter. Tick off each activity as you complete it.

Activity

12.1	☐	This activity deals with Range Statement 8.2: performance indicators to measure effectiveness, and Unit 8 Knowledge & Understanding point (6): performance indicators (effectiveness).
12.2	☐	This activity deals with Range Statement 8.2: performance indicators to measure profitability.
12.3	☐	This activity deals with Performance Criteria 8.2A regarding the analysis of routine cost reports, their comparison with other sources of information and the identification of any implications.
12.4	☐	This activity deals with Performance Criteria 8.2B regarding the preparation and monitoring of relevant performance indicators and the interpretation of results, and Performance Criteria 8.2D regarding the preparation of exception reports to identify matters which require further investigation.
12.5	☐	This activity deals with Performance Criteria 8.2B regarding the preparation and monitoring of relevant performance indicators and the interpretation of results.
12.6	☐	This activity deals with Performance Criteria 8.2B regarding the preparation and monitoring of relevant performance indicators and the interpretation of results.
12.7	☐	This activity deals with Performance Criteria 8.2A regarding the analysis of routine cost reports, their comparison with other sources of information and the identification of any implications.

chapter 13

Further aspects of performance measurement

Contents

1 Introduction
2 Financial performance measures
3 Value added
4 Non-financial indicators
5 'What if' analysis
6 The balanced scorecard
7 Benchmarking
8 Measures of performance using the standard hour
9 Performance measures for non-profit-making organisations
10 Management performance measures
11 Criticisms of performance indicators

Performance criteria

8.2.B Prepare and monitor relevant performance indicators, and interpret the results

Range statement

8.2 Performance indicators to measure: financial, customer, internal business and learning and growth perspectives; productivity; unit costs; resource utilisation; quality of service

8.2 Recommendations: benchmarking

Knowledge and understanding

Unit 8 Accounting techniques

3 Basic statistical methods: index numbers

4 Use of relevant computer packages

6 Performance indicators: efficiency, effectiveness; productivity; balanced scorecard, benchmarking; unit costs; control ratios (efficiency, capacity and activity), scenario planning ('what-if' analysis)

Unit 8 Accounting principles and theory

11 Effect of accounting controls on behaviour of managers and other employees

Signpost

This chapter is relevant to **Unit 8.**

1 Introduction

We looked in Chapter 12 at the performance measures that can be derived from the profit and loss account and balance sheet. We continue our study of performance measurement in this chapter and consider a range of other performance measures.

2 Financial performance measures

The ratios we looked at in the previous chapter were all financial indicators. Financial indicators can be **absolute** figures (turnover was £1.2 million) or **relative** figures (gross profit margin was 15%).

Financial measures (or **monetary** measures) should be very familiar to you. Here are some examples, accompanied by comments from a single page of the *Financial Times.*

Measure	Example
Profit	Profit is the commonest measure of all. Profit maximisation is usually cited as the main objective of most business organisations: 'ICI increased pre-tax profits to £233m'; 'General Motors... yesterday reported better-than-expected first-quarter net income of $513 (£333m) ... Earnings improved $680m from the first quarter of last year when GM lost $167m.
Revenue	'the US businesses contributed £113.9m of total group turnover of £409m'.
Costs	'Sterling's fall benefited pre-tax profits by about £50m while savings from the cost-cutting programme ... were running at around £100m a quarter'; 'The group interest charge rose from £48m to £61m'.
Share price	'The group's shares rose 31p to 1,278p despite the market's fall'.
Cash flow	'Cash flow was also continuing to improve, with cash and marketable securities totalling $8.4bn on March 31, up from $8bn at December 31'.

As before, note that monetary amounts stated are **only given meaning in relation to something else**. Here is a list of **yard-sticks** against which financial results are usually placed so as to become measures, perhaps in the form of variances.

- Budgeted **sales**, **costs** and **profits**
- **Standards** in a standard costing system
- The **trend** over time (last year/this year, say)
- The results of **other parts of the business**
- The results of **other businesses**
- The **economy** in general
- **Future potential**

There are a number of **limitations** of using financial data to measure business performance.

- The value of money may change over time due to inflation, making comparison more difficult (see below).
- Even without inflation the price of goods may change due to technology or pricing policy.

- Accounting policies (depreciation, stock valuation) adopted by different divisions, organisations and so on can distort performance.
- Financial performance measures are only concerned with data recorded in the accounts.
- They do not take account of other key, non-financial performance indicators (see Section 4).
- As we will see in later sections, they focus on the short term, can give misleading signals and can be manipulated.

2.1 Adjusting for inflation

When comparing data over a number of periods, it may be necessary to adjust the figures for inflation, so that a 'like for like' comparison can be carried out. This is done using indices.

We saw in Chapter 4 that **to bring a figure 'more up to date'** it should be **multiplied by (recent index number/ older index number).** Such an approach can inflate past costs or prices to bring them in line with current costs and prices. Valid comparisons can then be made.

Industry indices will usually provide a more useful way of comparing results in different periods than more general indices such as the RPI. The RPI measures price changes over a varied 'basket' of retail goods and services, including housing costs. The price trends facing a wholesaler or producer in any particular industry may be very different.

Let us now look at an example which considers the way in which index numbers may be used to compare the performance over five years of a manufacturing company.

Example: using index numbers to compare performance

Charming Chairs Limited manufactures a range of chairs. The sales manager thinks performance over the past five years has been very good as sales have increased by £412,000.

Task

The finance of director disagrees, believing the increase is simply due to inflation. She has asked you to use the industry index figures below to demonstrate the validity of her view.

Year	*Turnover* £'000	*Industry index*
1	2,448	122
2	2,558	131
3	2,659	137
4	2,721	141
5	2,860	149

Solution

To put each figure into year 5 terms, multiply it by (index for year 5/index for its own year).

Year	*Actual turnover*				*Turnover at current prices*
	£'000				£'000
1	2,448	×	149/122	=	2,990
2	2,558	×	149/131	=	2,909
3	2,659	×	149/137	=	2,892
4	2,721	×	149/141	=	2,875
5	2,860	×	149/149	=	2,860

Once the effects of inflation are taken into account it can be seen that annual revenue is actually falling in 'real 'terms. Sales volumes have therefore been decreasing and the finance director is correct.

Activity 13.1

The management of ABC Ltd have noticed that the cost of one of the raw materials, M1, used in the manufacture of its product, a non-hazardous chemical mix, has been increasing dramatically over the last few years despite the fact that the number of barrels of the chemical mix produced has remained fairly static. In order to investigate whether wastage of M1 is increasing the management accountant of ABC Ltd has collected the following information on the annual expenditure on M1 from Year 1 to Year 5 and has also derived a price index for material M1 as follows.

Year	*Expenditure*	*Material M1 price index*
	£	
1	185,365	100
2	198,721	107
3	221,737	119
4	239,114	129
5	255,100	138

Task

Use the price index to convert the annual expenditure on M1 into expenditure in terms of Year 5 prices. Comment on your results.

Activity 13.2

The company directors of Melton Ltd are concerned by the increase in expenditure on fuel for sales representatives' cars over the last few years. Fuel costs have increased although there were no changes in the number of vehicles and negligible changes in the number of miles driven each year. The company accountant has gathered information on the fuel costs and has also established a price index for fuel as follows.

Year	*Expenditure on fuel*	*Fuel price index*
	£	
1	18,000	100
2	19,292	106
3	21,468	120
4	23,010	128

Task

Use the index numbers to express all fuel costs in terms of year 4 prices. All figures should be rounded to the nearest £. Comment on the results you have obtained.

Activity 13.3

(a) Describe the use of indices to allow for price and performance level changes through time.

(b) How might indices be used for inter-company performance comparisons?

2.2 Calculating averages

Performance measurement can be based on total amounts of money such as sales, costs and profits. It is often more useful to calculate indicators based on 'per unit of output', 'per machine hour', 'per employee' and so on, however, thereby producing a measure which is related to the size of the organisation in some way.

Here are some examples.

- If turnover in a tele-sales organisation totals £3.2 million and there are 40 tele-sales representatives, average turnover per representative = £3.2 million/40 = £80,000.
- If output during control period 7 is 800 units and 500 labour hours are worked, average output per labour hour = 800/500 = 1.6.

3 Value added

One way of looking at an organisation's operations is to say that the **cost of materials** – direct and indirect – purchased from outside suppliers, and the cost of services provided by other organisations, **represent the value of output** (products and services) **created by someone outside the organisation**. For example, if an organisation purchases supplies of raw materials or office stationery, the cost of the purchases represents the value of the goods produced by those suppliers. The purchasing organisation must then use the materials and services it purchases to provide goods and services of its own, which it will want to sell at a higher price to make a profit.

The **difference between the purchase costs of external materials and services and the selling prices of an organisation's own goods or services** is referred to as **value added**.

Value added = sales value – cost of purchased materials and bought-in services

3.1 Value added statements

Value added statements **show how much wealth or value has been created by an organisation's operations**, and **how the wealth has been shared by interested groups**, in particular the following.

- Shareholders and investors in debt capital of the company (the providers of capital)
- Employees (wages and salaries)
- The government (taxation)
- Amounts retained for reinvestment (retained profits and depreciation)

Value added statements can **provide additional information** to senior managers to help them in comparing the performance of different divisions.

Suppose that Witches Best Ltd makes two products B and W, each in a separate division. Revenues and costs in each division in March were as follows.

		Product B		*Product W*	
		B Division		*W Division*	
		£'000	£'000	£'000	£'000
Direct materials			60		24
Direct labour			10		10
Variable overhead:	materials	1		1	
	labour	4		4	
			5		5
Total variable costs			75		39
Fixed overhead:	materials	5		4	
	labour	5		5	
	depreciation	5		2	
			15		11
Total costs			90		50
Sales			100		60
Profit			10		10
Profit to sales ratio		(10/100)	10%	(10/60)	16.7%

Using the profit to sales ratio as a basis for company divisional performance, W appears more profitable than B. To some extent, this analysis is valid, but it is not the full story. A value added statement, and performance ratios based on value added, provide a contrast more in favour of B.

		B			*W*	
		£'000	£'000		£'000	£'000
Sales			100			60
Materials: direct		60			24	
indirect	(1 + 5)	6		(1 + 4)	5	
			66			29
Value added			34			31
Shared between						
Labour: direct		10			10	
indirect	(4 + 5)	9		(4 + 5)	9	
			19			19
Depreciation			5			2
Profit			10			10
			34			31

Ratios for comparison might be as follows.

		B		*W*
Profit to value added	(10/34)	29%	(10/31)	32%
Contribution to value added	(25/34)	74%	(21/31)	68%
Value added per £1 of labour	(34/19)	£1.79	(31/19)	£1.63

Although W has a bigger profit to value added ratio, B makes more value added per £1 of labour cost (suggesting better wealth-creation from labour effort) and has a higher ratio of contribution to value added.

This analysis does not necessarily make B more profitable than W, or a better performing product. What the analysis does is to provide information for comparison and judging performance, which adds to the more 'traditional' performance ratios of profit to sales and so on.

Activity 13.4

Is value added per employee a measure of productivity or efficiency?

There are several reasons **why a value added statement might provide a useful way of comparing the results of two or more divisions**, departments or subsidiary companies.

Firstly, managers might be in a better position to control their organisation's own inputs than the cost or usage efficiency of purchased materials and services. If this is so, value added statements **focus attention on what managers can do something about**.

Secondly, value added statements also **focus attention on how the benefits are shared out**, particularly in the following respects.

- Are employees getting paid too much for what they are doing? For example if the value added per £1 of labour cost is gradually declining over time, management will be made aware of the need to keep labour

costs under control. On the other hand, an improving value added per £1 of labour cost would suggest that there is some scope for rewarding employees more highly.

- Are enough funds being retained in the business (depreciation plus retained profits) to provide for asset replacement and internally-funded growth?

Lastly, value added in relation to labour effort and labour costs provides an excellent measure of productivity, and so **facilitates the comparison of the relative productivity** of two or more divisions.

4 Non-financial indicators

Financial measures do not convey the full picture of a company's performance, especially in a **modern business environment**. Today, organisations are competing in terms of product quality, delivery, reliability, after-sales service and customer satisfaction, but none of these variables is directly measured by a traditional accounting system.

Many companies are therefore discovering the usefulness of quantitative and qualitative **non-financial indicators (NFIs)** such as the following.

- Quality
- Number of customer complaints
- Number of warranty claims
- Lead times
- Rework
- Delivery to time
- Non-productive hours
- System (machine) down time, and so on

Unlike traditional variance reports, measures such as these can be **provided quickly** for managers, per shift or on a daily or even hourly basis as required. They are likely to be **easy to calculate**, and **easier** for non-financial managers **to understand** and therefore to use effectively.

The beauty of non-financial indicators is that **anything can be compared if it is meaningful to do so**. The measures should be **tailored to the circumstances** so that, for example, number of coffee breaks per 20 pages of text might indicate to you how hard you are studying!

However, many such measures combine elements from the chart shown below. The chart is not intended to be prescriptive or exhaustive.

Errors/failure	Time	Quantity	People
Defects	Second	Units produced	Employees
Equipment failures	Minute	Parts/components	Employee skills
Complaints	Shift	Units sold	Competitors
Returns	Cycle	Services performed	Suppliers
Stockouts	Day	kg/litres/metres	Customers
Lateness/waiting	Month	m^2/m^3	
Miscalculation	Year	Deliveries	
Absenteeism		Documents	

Traditional measures derived from these lists like 'kg (of material) per unit produced' or 'units produced per hour' are fairly obvious, but what may at first seem a fairly **unlikely combination** may also be very revealing. For example, 'miscalculations per 1,000 invoices' would show how accurately the invoicing clerk was working.

Activity 13.5

Using the above chart make up four non-financial indicators and explain how each might be useful.

TOPIC LINK

Presentation of data and NFIs

- **Pictograms** could be used to show the number of equipment failures per shift or per week, say.
- A **pie chart** could show the different reasons for returns per month, say.
- A **simple bar chart** could be used to represent in a diagrammatic form the number of complaints from each of an organisation's ten most important customers.

5 'What if' analysis

LOOK OUT FOR ...

'What if analysis'

It is one of the examiner's favourite ways of assessing performance measurement.

'What if' analysis in the context of performance measurement involves modelling the effect on an organisation of revisions to its performance indicators. For example, management may wish to know the effect on Division A's results if its efficiency ratios were improved to be the same as the average for all divisions.

A thorough understanding of performance indicators is vital in a 'what if' analysis, because **changes in one indicator or variable can have a 'knock on' effect on other variables**.

In particular you need to know how the various elements of the profit and loss account and balance sheet are linked together.

For example, assuming that there are no changes in unit variable costs and no changes in the organisation's assets, a 10% fall in sales will lead to a 10% fall in variable costs but no change in fixed costs. This should be clear from your knowledge of cost behaviour. (See Chapter 2 if you need reminding.)

The organisation's net assets will then fall by the profit from these sales, provided no dividends are paid or funds raised. This should be clear from your financial accounting studies.

The effect on individual elements of the profit and loss account and balance sheet can then be **modelled**.

For example, if the revised turnover is £3.2m and the target average age of debtors is 2.4 months, the revised forecast debtors figure will be (£3.2m/12) × 2.4 = £640,000.

This and other similar calculations will provide you with the data to develop revised performance indicators such as ROCE.

TOPIC LINK

'What if' analysis and spreadsheets

'What if' analysis (and other Unit 8 and 9 topics such as producing charts and graphs) are often performed using spreadsheets. Spreadsheets are covered in this text in Chapters 7 and 11. You should be able to apply the spreadsheet skills covered in other BPP Texts/Kits (eg Unit 4 and Unit 7) to Unit 8 and 9 topics.

If you require practice in spreadsheet construction and use, practical, hands-on examples are available in the BPP Publication *Excel Exercises for Technician*. The book is accompanied by a CD containing Excel spreadsheets.

Note that *Excel Exercises for Technician* assumes you already have basic Excel skills (to AAT Foundation Level).

Activity 13.6

Southport Ltd manufactures a particular design of barbeque. Revenue for 20X2 was £750,000. Year-end debtors were £180,000 and the year-end cash balance was £17,000.

Southport Ltd's major competitor is Freshfields Ltd, a company which sells virtually identical barbeques. Freshfields Ltd can sell its barbeques for 30% more than Southport Ltd. Freshfields Ltd's debtors have an average age of two months.

Task

Calculate Southport Ltd's cash balance at the end of 20X3 if it were able to meet the same performance criteria as Freshfields Ltd.

Activity 13.7

(a) Division Alpha's gross profit margin is 20%. Its fixed costs are £81,900 and its capital employed is £1 million. What would the division's ROCE be if the division had been able to achieve an asset turnover of 1.3 times while maintaining prices and existing capital employed?

(b) Division Beta has the following results for Year 6.

Sales	£375,000
Purchases	£95,000
Cost of sales	£185,000
NBV of fixed assets	£957,850
Operating profit	£363,000

Division Gamma reports the following performance measures.

Average age of debtors	2 months

Average age of creditors	3 months
Average age of stock	1 month

Task

Calculate Division Beta's ROCE if it has the same efficiency ratios as Division Gamma.

Activity 13.8

Tring Ltd sells product P1 for £100. Annual maximum factory capacity is 10,000 units. Results for the year ended 30 April Year 9 were as follows.

		£	£
Turnover (8,000 units)			800,000
Expenses:	Materials (variable)	240,000	
	Labour (variable)	160,000	
	Selling (variable)	40,000	
	Administration (fixed)	120,000	
			560,000
Profit			240,000

The average age of debtors is 3 months and the year-end debtors balance is £200,000. The year-end cash balance is £20,000.

Tasks

(a) Calculate the revised profit if annual output had been 90% of maximum factory capacity.

(b) Calculate the value of debtors and cash as a result of achieving an output of 90% of maximum factory capacity and an average age of debtors of 1 month.

6 The balanced scorecard

Although segments of a business may be measured by a single performance indicator such as ROCE, profit, or cost variances, it might be more suitable to use multiple measures of performance where each measure reflects a **different aspect of achievement**. Where multiple measures are used, several may be **non-financial.**

The most popular approach in current management thinking is the use of what is called a **'balanced scorecard'** consisting of a variety of indicators both financial and non-financial. The balanced scorecard focuses on four different perspectives, as follows.

Perspective	Question
Customer	What do existing and new customers value from us? This perspective gives rise to targets that matter to customers: cost, quality, delivery, inspection, handling and so on.
Internal	What processes must we excel at to achieve our financial and customer objectives? This perspective aims to improve internal processes and decision making, and may monitor aspects such as the measurement of quality and unit costs.
Innovation and learning	Can we continue to improve and create future value? This perspective considers the business's capacity to maintain its competitive position by acquiring new skills and developing new products.
Financial	How do we create value for our shareholders? This perspective covers traditional measures such as growth, profitability and shareholder value but these are set through talking to the shareholder or shareholders direct.

Performance targets are set once the key areas for improvement have been identified, and the balanced scorecard is the main monthly report.

The scorecard is **'balanced'** in the sense that managers are required to think in terms of **all four** perspectives, to prevent improvements being made in one area at the expense of another. The method had the advantages of looking at both **internal and external** matters concerning the organisation and of linking together **financial and non-financial** measures.

And because it gives a more rounded view of performance, the balanced scorecard should help to overcome the problems associated with **ensuring consistency between objectives, control systems and staff** that we considered in Chapter 1.

ATTENTION!

The balanced scorecard featured in the December 1999 exam, but the task was worded to allow candidates to answer even if they had no knowledge of the balanced scorecard concept. But don't expect the assessor always to be so helpful!

Let's look at the four perspectives and the associated performance indicators in a little more detail.

6.1 Customer perspective

In a customer-focused organisation the basic information 'Turnover is up by 14%' can be supplemented by a host of other indicators.

Indicator	What it indicates
Customer rejects/returns: total sales	Helps to monitor customer satisfaction, providing a check on the efficiency of quality control procedures.
Deliveries late: deliveries on schedule	Can be applied both to sales made to customers and to receipts from suppliers. When applied to customers it provides an indication of the efficiency of production and production scheduling.

Indicator	What it indicates
Turnover per employee	Indicates how effectively resources are being used. Customer service and quality might suffer if the ratio is too high.
Flexibility	Indicates how well a company can respond to customers' requirements, in terms of delivering the goods on time (train punctuality), responding to changing customer requirements and coping with demand (which in a service organisation can be measured by overcrowding in trains or queuing times in shops).
Number of people served and speed of service	Could be used in a shop or a bank. If it takes too long to reach the point of sale, future sales are liable to be lost.
Customer satisfaction	You have probably filled in questionnaires in fast-food restaurants or on aeroplanes without realising that you were completing a customer attitude survey for input to the organisation's management information system. A measure of customer satisfaction might be the time between order and delivery.

Example: customer satisfaction

An organisation takes orders worth £3,750,800 in Year 7. Turnover during the year is £3,190,900. What is the average delay in fulfilling orders?

Solution

	£
Orders during year	3,750,800
Turnover during year	3,190,900
Unfulfilled orders	559,900

Average delay = (£559,900/£3,190,900) $\times$ 12 = 2.1 months.

6.2 Internal perspective

6.2.1 Performance measures for materials

Traditional measures are **standard costs** for materials, and price and particularly usage **variances**. Many traditional systems also analyse **wastage**. Measures used in **modern manufacturing environments** include the number of **rejects** in materials supplied, and the **timing and reliability of deliveries** of materials.

6.2.2 Performance measures for labour

Labour costs are traditionally measured in terms of rate and efficiency **variances**. **Qualitative measures** of labour performance concentrate on matters such as **ability to communicate, interpersonal relationships** with colleagues, **customers' impressions** ('so and so was extremely helpful/rude'), and **levels of skills** attained.

Note that employee-based measures are very important when assessing the performance of the employees' *manager*. High profitability or tight cost control should not be accompanied by 100% labour turnover!

6.2.3 Performance measures for quality

We look at the topic of quality in detail in Chapter 15, but you may already be aware that it is a highly significant trend in modern business thinking.

In a manufacturing organisation, **performance measures for quality should not be confined to the production process** but must also cover the work of sales, distribution and administration departments, the efforts of external suppliers and the reaction of external customers. In many cases the measures used will be non-financial ones. They may be divided into three types.

Type of measure	Example
Measuring incoming supplies	Percentage of defective items per delivery Number of returns per supplier
Monitoring work done as it proceeds	Number of rejects per production run Ratio of waste material to used material
Measuring customer satisfaction	Complaints per 10,000 units sold Number of claims under warranty

Activity 13.9

Strides plc has been receiving an increasing number of customer complaints about a general weakness in the quality of its products in recent months. The company believes that its future success is dependent on product quality and it is therefore determined to improve it.

Task

Suggest three measures or ratios which could be used to monitor product quality at Strides plc.

Service quality is measured principally by **qualitative measures**, as you might expect, although some quantitative measures are used by some businesses. If it were able to obtain the information, for example, a retailer might use number of lost customers in a period as an indicator of service quality. Lawyers use the proportion of time spent with clients.

The following table shows the measures used to assess four quality factors and the means of obtaining the information by British Airports Authority (BAA), a mass transport service.

Service quality factors	Measures	Mechanisms
Access	Walking distances Ease of finding way around	Customer survey and internal operational data
Cleanliness/tidiness	Cleanliness of environment and equipment	Customer survey and management inspection
Comfort	Crowdedness of airport	Customer survey and management inspection
Friendliness	Staff attitude and helpfulness	Customer survey and management inspection

6.2.4 Resource utilisation

Not surprisingly performance indicators measuring resource utilisation consider **how efficiently resources are being utilised** and are usually measures of productivity.

Resource utilisation is therefore fairly **easy to measure** in **a manufacturing organisation. In service businesses** it is often more **problematic**, however, because of the complexity of the inputs to a service and the outputs from it.

Of course in some service businesses it is straightforward. The main resource of a firm of accountants, for example, is the time of various grades of staff. The main output of an accountancy firm is chargeable hours.

But in a restaurant, for example, inputs are highly **diverse**: the ingredients for the meal, the chef's time and expertise, the surroundings and the customers' own likes and dislikes. A customer attitude survey might show whether or not a customer enjoyed the food, but it could not ascribe the enjoyment or lack of it to the quality of the ingredients, say, rather than the skill of the chef.

Here are some other resource utilisation ratios for services.

Business	Input	Output
Hotel	Rooms available	Rooms occupied
Railway company	Train miles available	Passenger miles
Bank	Number of staff	Number of accounts

6.3 Innovation and learning perspective

Companies do not have to innovate to be successful, but it helps! Others will try to steal their market, and so others' innovations must at least be matched. In a modern environment in which product quality, product differentiation and continuous improvement are the order of the day, a company that can find innovative ways of satisfying customers' needs has an important **competitive advantage**.

The **innovating process can be measured** in terms of **how much it costs to develop a new product or service, how effective the process is** and **how quickly the organisation can develop new products and services**. In more concrete terms this might translate into the following indicators.

- The **amount of spending on research and development**, and whether these costs are recovered from new product/service sales (and how quickly, if so)
- The **proportion of new products/services to total products/services**
- The **time between identification of the customer need for a new product/ service and making it available**

6.4 Financial perspective

This has been covered in detail in the previous chapter and in Section 2 of this chapter.

Activity 13.10

For each of the following performance indicators, identify one balanced scorecard perspective being measured.

(a) Labour cost per unit manufactured
(b) Asset turnover
(c) Training expenditure as a percentage of sales turnover
(d) Return on capital employed
(e) Percentage of on-time deliveries
(f) Percentage of turnover generated by new products
(g) Percentage of quality control rejects

ATTENTION!

In this chapter you have seen many examples of how the same basic performance measurement techniques can be adapted to suit a variety of organisations. In the December 1999 exam candidates were required to calculate performance indicators for a police force. You must always be prepared to *apply* your understanding of the *underlying concepts* to any given situation. Of course, this comment applies to all of the methods and techniques that you have learnt in this text.

6.5 Example of a balanced scorecard

Perspective	Financial indicator	Non-financial indicator
Customer	Price Unit cost Debtor days	Lead time Defect level On-time delivery
Internal	Stock turnover Asset turnover ROCE	Time to market Trade cycle time % employee absence per month
Innovation/ learning	Spend on R&D Spend on new fixed assets	% sales from new products Training days as % of total employee days
Financial	Earnings per share Share price movement Profit margins	Market share Revenue growth %

7 Benchmarking

Benchmarking is a **comparison** exercise carried out by organisations in an attempt to improve performance. The idea is to **gather information about 'best' performance** against which an organisation can monitor and compare its own achievements.

7.1 Types of benchmarking

There are basically two types of benchmarking.

- Organisations in the **same industry** pool information about their processes, the processes are benchmarked (compared) against each other and best practice is identified.
- Organisations in **non-competing industries** but with **similar processes** participate in a benchmarking exercise. For example, a railway company and an airline company that operate on different routes could share information and compare their on-board catering operations.

7.2 Obtaining information

Financial information about competitors is **easier** to acquire than non-financial information. Information about **products** can be obtained from **reverse engineering** (buying a competitor's product and dismantling it in order to understand its content and how it is made up), **product literature**, **media comment** and **trade associations**. Information about **processes** (how an organisation deals with customers or suppliers) is more **difficult** to find.

Such information can be obtained from **group companies** or possibly **non-competing organisations in the same industry** (such as the train and airline companies mentioned above).

7.3 Why use benchmarking?

- An organisation can improve performance by learning from the experience of others.
- Benchmarking sets targets which are challenging but 'achievable'. What is *really* achievable can be discovered by examining what others have achieved: managers are able to accept that they are not being asked to perform miracles.

7.4 Disadvantages of benchmarking

- There may be problems in identifying best practice.
- It can be difficult to persuade other organisations to share information.
- Successful practices in one organisation may not transfer successfully to another. There may not be one best way of doing something.
- There is a danger of drawing incorrect conclusions from inappropriate comparisons. For example, a cross-channel ferry company might benchmark its activities (such as speed of turnaround at Dover and

Calais, cleanliness on ship) against another ferry company, whereas the real competitor is the Channel Tunnel.

- Competitors may gain too much information.

TOPIC LINK

'What if' analysis and benchmarking

An exam task might give you benchmark data and you might have to show what an organisation's results would have been had those benchmarks been achieved.

8 Measures of performance using the standard hour

Suppose Sam Ltd manufactures plates, mugs and eggcups. Production during the first two quarters of Year 5 was as follows.

	Quarter 1	*Quarter 2*
Plates	1,000	800
Mugs	1,200	1,500
Eggcups	800	900

The fact that 3,000 products were produced in quarter 1 and 3,200 in quarter 2 does not really tell us anything about Sam Ltd's performance over the two periods because plates, mugs and eggcups are so different. The fact that the production mix has changed is not revealed by considering the total number of units produced. The problem of how to **measure output when a number of dissimilar products are manufactured** can be overcome, however, by the **use of the standard hour**.

The standard time allowed to produce one plate is $^1/_2$ hour, the standard time for one mug is $^1/_3$ hour, while for an eggcup it is $^1/_4$ hour.

By measuring the standard hours of output in each quarter, a more useful output measure is obtained.

		Quarter 1		*Quarter 2*	
	Standard hours		*Standard*		*Standard*
Product	*per unit*	*Production*	*hours*	*Production*	*hours*
Plate	1/2	1,000	500	800	400
Mug	1/3	1,200	400	1,500	500
Eggcup	1/4	800	200	900	225
			1,100		1,125

The output level in the two quarters was therefore very similar.

8.1 Efficiency, activity and capacity ratios

Standard hours are useful in computing levels of efficiency, activity and capacity measured as ratios.

- The **capacity ratio** compares actual hours worked and budgeted hours, and measures the extent to which planned utilisation has been achieved.
- The **activity** or **production volume ratio compares the number of standard hours equivalent to the actual work produced and budgeted hours**.
- The **efficiency ratio** measures the efficiency of the labour force by **comparing equivalent standard hours for work produced and actual hours worked**.

Example: ratios and standard hours

Given the following information about Sam Ltd for quarter 1 of Year 5, calculate a capacity ratio, an activity ratio and an efficiency ratio and explain their meaning.

Budgeted hours	1,100 standard hours
Standard hours produced	1,125 standard hours
Actual hours worked	1,200

Solution

Capacity ratio = (Actual hours worked/budgeted hours) × 100% = (1,200/1,100) × 100% = 109%

Activity ratio = (Standard hours produced/budgeted hours) × 100% =(1,125/1,100)× 100% = 102%

The overall activity or production volume for the quarter was 2% greater than forecast. This was achieved by a 9% increase in capacity.

Efficiency ratio = (Standard hours produced/actual hours worked) × 100% = (1,125/1,200) × 100% = 94%

The labour force worked 6% below standard levels of efficiency.

9 Performance measures for non-profit-making organisations

9.1 Non-profit-making organisations (NPMOs)

NPMOs include private sector organisations such as charities and churches and much of the public sector. Commercial organisations generally have market competition and profit as the objective which guide the process of managing resources economically, efficiently and effectively. However, NPMOs **cannot** by definition **be judged by profitability** nor do they generally have to be successful against competition, so other methods of assessing performance have to be used.

Performance **indicators** should be designed to **show the extent to which an organisation has been successful in achieving its objectives**. A major problem with many NPMOs, however, particularly government bodies, is that it is extremely **difficult to define their objectives** at all, let alone find *one* which can serve a yardstick function in the way that profit does for commercial bodies.

9.2 How can performance be measured?

9.2.1 The three Es

Performance is usually judged in terms of **'value for money'**.

- **Economy** (spending money frugally)
- **Efficiency** (getting out as much as possible for what goes in)
- **Effectiveness** (getting done, by means of economy and efficiency, what was supposed to be done)

More formally, **effectiveness** is the **relationship between an organisation's outputs and its objectives**, **efficiency** is **the relationship between inputs and outputs**, and **economy** equates to **cost control** in the commercial sector.

Economy can be measured in the same way as in profit-making organisations, using budgets and variances for example.

Efficiency is difficult to measure because **outputs can seldom be measured** in a way that is generally agreed to be meaningful. (Are good exam results alone an adequate measure of the quality of teaching?)

Effectiveness is measured by comparisons with targets.

9.2.2 Alternative approaches

Performance can be judged in terms of **inputs**. This is very common in everyday life. If somebody tells you that their suit cost £1,750, for example, you would generally conclude that it was an extremely well-designed and good quality suit, even if you did not think so when you first saw it. The **drawback**, of course, is that you might also conclude that the person wearing the suit had been cheated or was a fool, or you may happen to be of the opinion that no piece of clothing is worth £1,750, designer label or not. So it is with the inputs and outputs of a NPMO.

A second possibility is to accept that performance measurement must to some extent be subjective. **Judgements** can be made **by experts** in that particular non-profit-making activity **or by the persons who fund the activity**.

Most NPMOs do not face competition but this does not mean that all NPMOs are unique. Bodies like local governments, health services and so on can **compare** their performance **against each other. Unit cost measurements** like 'cost per patient day' or 'cost of borrowing one library book' can be established to allow organisations to assess whether they are doing better or worse than their counterparts.

Example: Inputs and outputs

As a further illustration, suppose that at a cost of £40,000 and 4,000 hours (**inputs**) in an average year, two policemen travel 8,000 miles and are instrumental in 200 arrests (**outputs**). A large number of **possibly meaningful measures** can be derived from these few figures.

		£40,000	4,000 hours	8,000 miles	200 arrests
Cost	£40,000		£40,000/4,000 = £10 per hour	£40,000/8,000 = £5 per mile	£40,000/200 = £200 per arrest
Time	4,000 hrs	4,000/£40,000 = 6 minutes patrolling per £1 spent		4,000/8,000 = ½ hour to patrol 1 mile	4,000/200 = 20 hours per arrest
Miles	8,000	8,000/£40,000 = 0.2 of a mile per £1	8,000/4,000 = 2 miles patrolled per hour		8,000/200 = 40 miles per arrest
Arrests	200	200/£40,000 = 1 arrest per £200	200/4,000 = 1 arrest every 20 hours	200/8,000 = 1 arrest every 40 miles	

These measures do not necessarily identify cause and effect or personal responsibility and accountability. Actual performance needs to be **compared** to the following.

- **Standards**, if there are any
- Similar external activities
- Similar internal activities
- **Targets**
- Indices
- Over time – ie as trends

ATTENTION!

A charity provided the scenario for tasks on performance analysis in the June 1998 exam. Candidates had to calculate profit-based ratios (such as return on net assets) but then had to discuss their possible inappropriateness.

10 Management performance measures

We have not so far **distinguished between measures of performance of individual managers** and **measures of performance of what they manage**.

The distinction is very important. A very skilful manager may be put in charge of the worst division in an organisation. Although the manager may succeed in improving the division's performance, the division may continue to be a poor performer in comparison with other divisions. If the manager is assessed purely on the division's results then he will not appear to be a good performer.

The problem therefore arises as to which performance measures should be used to measure management performance and which should be used to measure the performance of the business.

It is difficult to devise performance measures that relate specifically to a manager to judge his or her performance as a manager. It is possible to calculate statistics to **assess the manager as an employee** like any other employee (days absent, professional qualifications obtained, personality and so on), but this is not the point.

As soon as the issue of ability as a manager arises it is necessary to consider him **in relation to his area of responsibility**. If we want to know how good a manager is at marketing, the only information there is to go on is the marketing performance of his division, which may or may not be traceable to his own efforts.

It is unreasonable to assess managers' performance in relation to matters that are beyond their control. Management performance measures should therefore **only include those items that are directly controllable by the manager in question.**

10.1 Possible management performance measures

Subjective measures may be used, for example ranking performance on a scale of 1 to 5. To work well it must be perceived by managers generally to be fair, which usually means that the judgement is made by somebody impartial, but close enough to the work of each manager to appreciate the efforts made and the difficulties faced.

The **judgement of outsiders** can be regarded as a measure of managerial performance. An organisation might set up a bonus scheme for directors such that they would only receive a reward if the share price outperforms the FT-SE 100 index for more than three years. This is fair in that the share price reflects many aspects of performance, but it is questionable whether all these aspects can be influenced by the directors.

Upward appraisal is used by some businesses. This involves staff giving their opinions on the performance of their managers. To be effective this requires very healthy working relationships, however.

Accounting measures can be used, but must be tailored according to what or whom is being judged.

11 Criticisms of performance indicators

11.1 Non-financial indicators versus financial measures

If performance measurement systems **focus entirely** on those items that can be **expressed in monetary terms**, managers will concentrate on only those variables and **ignore other important variables** that cannot be expressed in monetary terms.

For example, pressure from senior management to **cut costs** and **raise productivity** will produce **short-term benefits** in cost control but, in the **long term**, managerial **performance and motivation** are likely to be **affected**. Labour turnover will increase and **product quality** will **fall**.

Reductions in cost can easily be measured and recorded in performance reports. Employee morale cannot. **Performance reports** should therefore **include** not only financial measures but **other** important **variables** too, to give an indication of expected future results from current activity. The **wider implications** for the organisation of **achieving a particular indicator** should always be **considered**.

11.2 Pursuit of detailed operational goals

A danger of indicators measuring operational performance, especially non-financial indicators, is that managers might be led into pursuing detailed operational goals, becoming **blind to the overall objectives** that these goals were meant to attain.

11.3 Not measuring what is supposed to be measured

Sometimes performance indicators do not actually measure what they are supposed to be measuring.

For example, suppose that an organisation wished to measure the **efficiency of its production workforce** and used profit margin to do so.

Although **profit margin** is a key measure of efficiency (the efficiency with which sales have been used to generate profit), the **production workforce cannot directly affect the revenue earned**. Use of the indicator should therefore be **questioned**. Or maybe the organisation should **instead be measuring** the workforce's **productivity**.

11.4 Manipulating the way in which performance is measured

Suppose a poster in a doctor's surgery states that 98% of patients are seen punctually by the doctor. This sounds impressive. But you need to ask **how 'punctually' has been defined**. It could be that punctual means the patient was seen within ten minutes of the appointment time. You should also consider whether such a statement was based on the experience of all patients, or whether a **sample** was used. And if a sample was used, could it be **biased**? What if the doctor cut short the appointments of those patients he knew not to be in the sample in order to ensure those patients in the sample were seen on time.

11.5 Manipulating performance measures

We explained how the various financial performance measures could be manipulated earlier in the chapter. This is a topical area which was assessed in the December 1998 exam. As the chief assessor explains in his report, 'In the UK, there has been extensive press coverage about how some railway operating companies have used performance indicators to their own advantage. Examples include the timetabling of journeys to take longer than before so that there would be less chance of trains not arriving on time, and defining arriving not more than 15 minutes late as 'arriving on time'.

ATTENTION!

What you need to be able to do for tasks on performance measurement

- **Calculation of a range of performance indicators**. Some might be applicable to many organisations, such indicators including ROCE and profit margin. Others might only be relevant to a particular type of organisation, such as the average time to arrive at an accident for an ambulance service.
- **Development of new performance indicators** to measure particular aspects of the organisation (such as efficiency, effectiveness or productivity), or the four perspectives of the balanced scorecard, or perhaps for benchmarking purposes. The task will tell you what needs to be measured and you will be provided with a range of data to choose from.

  For example, if the task related to a restaurant you might be asked to develop a possible measure of waiter/waitress productivity and a possible measure of customer satisfaction using the task data provided.
- **Criticise existing indicators**. Is the indicator measuring what it is supposed to be measuring? Is the measurement process being manipulated? (See Section 11.)
- **Discuss the role of, and effect on, managers in setting performance measures and being measured**. (See Section 10.)
- **Forecast future performance indicators** using **'what if' analysis** (see Section 5).

Key learning points

- ☑ **Financial performance measures** may need to be adjusted for the effects of **inflation** so that a 'like for like' comparison can be carried out. This is done using index numbers.
- ☑ **Averaging** can produce a measure which is related to the size of the organisation in some way.
- ☑ **Value added** = sales value – cost of purchased materials and bought-in services.
- ☑ **Non-financial indicators (NFIs)** are particularly useful in a modern business environment.
- ☑ Be aware of the fact that performance measures can be **manipulated.**
- ☑ '**What if' analysis** is one of the examiner's favourite ways of assessing performance measurement.
- ☑ The **balanced scorecard** focuses on four different perspectives (customer, internal, innovation and learning, financial).
- ☑ **Benchmarking** involves comparing processes with organisations in the same industry or in non-competing industries to identify best practice.
- ☑ **Capacity ratio** = $\frac{\text{actual hours worked}}{\text{budgeted hours}} \times 100\%$

  This measures the extent to which planned utilisation has been achieved.
- ☑ **Activity (production volume) ratio** = $\frac{\text{standard hours produced}}{\text{budgeted hours}} \times 100\%$
- ☑ **Efficiency ratio** = $\frac{\text{standard hours produced}}{\text{actual hours worked}} \times 100\%$

  This measures the efficiency of the workforce.
- ☑ Performance of **non-profit-making organisations (NPMOs)** is usually judged in terms of **'value for money'**.
- ☑ **Management performance** might be assessed using subjective measures, the judgement of outsiders, upward appraisal and/or accounting measures.
- ☑ Be aware that performance indicators may not be measuring what they are supposed to measure, and that the way in which performance is measured can very easily be **manipulated**.

Quick quiz

1 Which of the following is not a disadvantage of using financial data to measure business performance?

   A The value of money may change over time due to inflation, making comparisons more difficult.
   B Accounting policies adopted by different organisations can distort performance.
   C They tend to focus on the long term.
   D They are easily manipulated.

2 *Choose the appropriate words from those highlighted.*

   To bring a figure more 'up to date' it should be multiplied by (**recent/older** index number ÷ **recent/older** index number).

3 Value added per £ of labour is a measure of efficiency. *True or false?*

4 An organisation has an ROCE of 10%. Another organisation has the same capital employed but makes more profit. Its ROCE is therefore higher. *True or false?*

5 Which of the following is not a perspective of the balanced scorecard?

   A Financial
   B Competitive
   C Customer
   D Internal

6 *Match the term to the definition.*

Terms	*Definitions*
Economy	Getting done, by means of the other two terms, what was supposed to be done
Efficiency	Spending money frugally
Effectiveness	Getting out as much as possible for what goes in

Answers to quick quiz

1 C They focus on the short term.

2 It should be multiplied by (recent index number ÷ older index number).

3 True

4 True

5 B

6

Economy	Spending money frugally
Efficiency	Getting out as much as possible for what goes in
Effectiveness	Getting done, by means of the other two terms, what was supposed to be done

ASSESSMENT KIT ACTIVITIES

The following activities in the BPP Assessment Kit for Units 8 & 9 include topics covered in both this chapter and Chapter 12.

Activities 40 to 51
Lecturers' practice activities 22 to 27

Activity checklist

This checklist shows which performance criteria, range statement or knowledge and understanding point is covered by each activity in this chapter. Tick off each activity as you complete it.

Activity		
13.1	☐	This activity deals with Unit 8 Knowledge & Understanding point (3): basic statistical methods (index numbers).
13.2	☐	This activity deals with Unit 8 Knowledge & Understanding point (3): basic statistical methods (index numbers).
13.3	☐	This activity deals with Unit 8 Knowledge & Understanding point (3): basic statistical methods (index numbers).
13.4	☐	This activity deals with Range Statement 8.2: performance indicators to measure productivity, and Unit 8 Knowledge & Understanding point (6): performance indicators (productivity).
13.5	☐	This activity deals with Performance Criteria 8.2B regarding the preparation of relevant performance indicators.
13.6	☐	This activity deals with Unit 8 Knowledge & Understanding point (6): performance indicators (scenario planning/'what-if' analysis).
13.7	☐	This activity deals with Unit 8 Knowledge & Understanding point (6): performance indicators (scenario planning/'what-if' analysis).
13.8	☐	This activity deals with Unit 8 Knowledge & Understanding point (6): performance indicators (scenario planning/'what-if' analysis).
13.9	☐	This activity deals with Performance Criteria 8.2B regarding the preparation of relevant performance indicators, Range Statement 8.2: performance indicators to measure internal business perspective, and Unit 8 Knowledge & Understanding point (6): performance indicators (balanced scorecard).
13.10	☐	This activity deals with Performance Criteria 8.2B regarding the preparation of relevant performance indicators, Range Statement 8.2: performance indicators to measure financial, customer, internal business, and learning and growth perspectives, and Unit 8 Knowledge & Understanding point (6): performance indicators (balanced scorecard).

PART E

Core issues

chapter 14

Cost management I

Contents

1 Introduction
2 Cost reduction
3 Life cycle costing
4 Target costing

Performance criteria

8.2C Consult relevant specialists and assist in identifying ways to reduce costs and enhance value

Range statement

8.2 Recommendations: efficiencies; modifications to work processes

Knowledge and understanding

Unit 8 Accounting principles and theory

9 Cost management: life cycle costing; target costing (including value engineering)

Unit 8 The organisation

14 The contribution of functional specialists in an organisation (eg marketing, design, engineering, quality control etc) to cost reduction and value enhancement

Signpost

The topics covered in this chapter are relevant to **Unit 8.**

1 Introduction

It has been argued that **traditional management accounting approaches** are **not effective** in **managing costs** in **today's environment**.

One reason for this lies in the fact that, nowadays, the **costs of a product** are **determined** when it is being **designed**, **not** when it is in **production**. The materials that will be used and the machines and labour required are largely determined at the design stage. In the car industry it is estimated that 85% of all product costs are determined by the end of the testing stage. Management accountants, however, continue to direct their efforts to the **production stage**, when only a **small proportion of costs are manageable**.

This has created the **need** for **additional controls at the design stage**, the **point** at which **most costs** are **committed**. In this chapter we will be looking at two approaches which attempt to provide such control, life cycle costing and target costing.

We begin this chapter, however, with a general section on cost reduction.

In the next chapter we consider two other approaches to managing costs in the modern business environment, activity based costing and total quality management.

ATTENTION!

The topics covered in Sections 3 and 4 of this chapter are new areas of knowledge and understanding under the revised standards for Unit 8. The AAT has confirmed that these topics will **not** be assessed during the changeover between the old and new standards. If cost management (as covered in this chapter) is assessed in exams up to and including that in December 2004, it will be restricted to cost reduction (Section 2 of this chapter). Afterwards all aspects of cost management will be assessable. (The contents of Chapter 15 are assessable immediately.)

We recommend that you work through Sections 3 and 4, however, for a full understanding of the topic of cost management.

2 Cost reduction

Budgetary control and **standard costing** are examples of **cost control techniques**. Cost control is all about **keeping costs within predetermined limits** (usually standard cost). If actual costs differ from planned costs by an excessive amount, cost control action is necessary.

Cost reduction is different. It aims to **reduce costs below a previously accepted level, without adversely affecting the quality of the product** or service being provided.

Significant **cost reduction** can be **achieved** simply by using a **little common sense**. Here are some examples.

- **Improve the efficiency of materials usage** by reducing levels of wastage.
- **Improve labour productivity** by giving pay incentives or changing work methods to eliminate unnecessary procedures.
- **Improve the efficiency of equipment usage** by achieving a better balance between preventive maintenance and machine 'down time' for repairs.

- **Reduce material costs** by taking advantage of bulk purchase discounts or by improving stores control.
- **Reduce labour costs** by replacing people with machinery or by improving work methods following a work study (see below).
- **Save on finance costs** by taking advantage of early payment discounts or reassessing sources of finance.
- **Improve control over spending decisions** so that junior managers are not able to commit an organisation without consideration of long-term cost. For example, the hire of two office assistants at wages of £200 per week each would cost £200,000 over a ten-year period. Such a decision might be taken by an office manager whereas the purchase of a piece of machinery for the same cost would probably need board authorisation.

Activity 14.1

How can wastage be reduced?

A successful **cost reduction programme** will **cover all aspects** of an organisation's activities, systems and products and will be **supported by senior management**.

As well as the common sense ways of reducing costs, there are a number of formal techniques that can improve products or services, reduce waste, simplify systems and hence reduce costs.

2.1 Value analysis

Value analysis involves **assessing the value of every aspect of a product** (or service) in order to **devise ways of achieving** the product's (or service's) **purpose** as **economically** as possible while **maintaining** the required standard of **quality** and **reliability**.

Conventional cost reduction techniques aim to **produce a particular design of a product as cheaply as possible. Value analysis,** on the other hand, tries to **find the least-cost method of making a product that achieves its intended purpose.**

A value analysis assessment is likely to be carried out by a **team of experts** from the engineering, technical production and finance departments. It will involve the systematic investigation of every source of cost and every technique of production with the aim of getting rid of all unnecessary costs. An **unnecessary cost** is a cost that **does not add value**.

2.1.1 Value-adding activity

Value is **only added** to a product **while it is actually being processed**. Whilst it is being inspected for quality, moving from one part of the factory to another, waiting for further processing and held in store, value is not being added. Non value-adding activities should therefore be eliminated.

A **value-adding activity cannot be eliminated without the customer perceiving a deterioration in the performance, function or other quality of a product**.

Activity 14.2

Which of the following are value-adding activities?

(a) Setting up a machine so that it drills holes of a certain size
(b) Repairing faulty production work
(c) Painting a car, if the organisation manufactures cars
(d) Storing materials

2.1.2 Areas of special importance in a value analysis

Area	Method
Product design	At the design stage value analysis is called value engineering. The designer should be cost conscious and avoid unnecessary complications. Simple product design can avoid production and quality control problems, thereby resulting in lower costs.
Components and material costs	The purchasing department should beware of lapsing into habit with routine buying decisions. It has a crucial role to play in reducing costs and improving value by procuring the desired quality materials at the lowest possible price.
Production methods	These ought to be reviewed continually, on a product-by product basis, especially with changing technology.

2.1.3 Typical considerations in value analysis

- **Can the function of the product be achieved in another way**, using less expensive methods?
- **Are all the functions of the product essential**, or can some be removed without affecting quality?
- **Can a cheaper substitute material be found** which is as good, if not better, than the material currently used?
- **Can unnecessary weight or embellishments be removed** without reducing the product's attractions or desirability?
- **Can a new product/service be standardised** so it can be produced in conjunction with existing products/services?
- **Is it possible to use standardised components** (or to make components to a particular standard) thereby reducing the variety of units used and produced? **Variety reduction (standardisation)** is cost effective because it allows a range of finished products to be produced from a common, relatively small pool of

components. In general, if there are fewer product varieties, production is more straight-forward, which makes it easier to automate and so costs are likely to reduce. Fitted kitchens, for example, come in a wide variety of colours and finishes but it is only the cupboard doors that differ; the bodies of the cupboards are standardised.

Activity 14.3

Standardisation of parts and components might offer enormous cost reduction potential for some manufacturing industries. Can you think why this might be the case? What are the disadvantages of standardisation?

- **Is it possible to reduce the number of components,** for example could a product be assembled safely with a smaller number of screws?

The origins of value analysis were in the engineering industry, but it **can be applied to services or to aspects of office work**.

If applied thoroughly and on a **continuous** basis, value analysis should result in a planned, ongoing search for cost reductions.

2.2 Work study

Work study is used to **determine the most efficient methods of using labour, materials and machinery**. There are two main parts to work study.

- **Method study** involves **systematically recording** and **critically examining** existing and proposed **ways of doing work**. The aim of this is to **develop** and **apply easier** and **more effective methods**, and so **reduce costs**.
- **Work measurement** involves **establishing the time for a qualified worker** to carry out a **specified job** at a **specified level of performance**.

Areas where work study can be applied

- Plant facilities, layout and space utilisation
- Analysis, design and improvement of work systems (say forms used or the telephone system), work places and work methods
- Setting standards
- Determining the most profitable, alternative combinations of personnel, materials and equipment

2.3 Organisation and methods (O&M)

Organisation and methods (O&M) is a term for **techniques**, including method study and work measurement, that are used to **examine clerical, administrative and management procedures in order to make improvements**.

O&M is **primarily concerned with office work** and looks in particular at areas such as the following.

- Organisation
- Office layout
- Office mechanisation
- Duties
- Staffing
- Methods of procedure
- Documentation and the design of forms

Work study and O&M are perhaps associated in your mind with establishing standard times for work, but the real aim is to decide the most efficient methods of getting work done. More efficient methods and tighter standards will improve efficiency and productivity, and so reduce costs.

2.4 Difficulties with introducing cost reduction programmes

- There may be **resistance from employees** to the pressure to reduce costs, usually because the nature and purpose of the campaign has not been properly explained to them, and because they feel threatened by the change.
- The programme may be limited to a small area of the business with the result that **costs are reduced in one cost centre, only to reappear as an extra cost in another**.
- Cost reduction campaigns are **often introduced as a rushed, desperate measure** instead of a carefully organised, well thought-out exercise.
- **Long-term factors** must be considered. Reduction in expenditure on maintenance, advertising or research and development in the short term could have serious long-term consequences.
- It is becoming increasingly apparent that the **key area** for cost reduction is **product design**. Once manufacturing begins there is less scope for reducing costs, especially if production is heavily automated.

3 Life cycle costing

3.1 The product life cycle

Every product goes through a life cycle (a concept we covered in Chapter 8). The costs incurred over a product's life cycle can be illustrated by the generic curves in the following diagram.

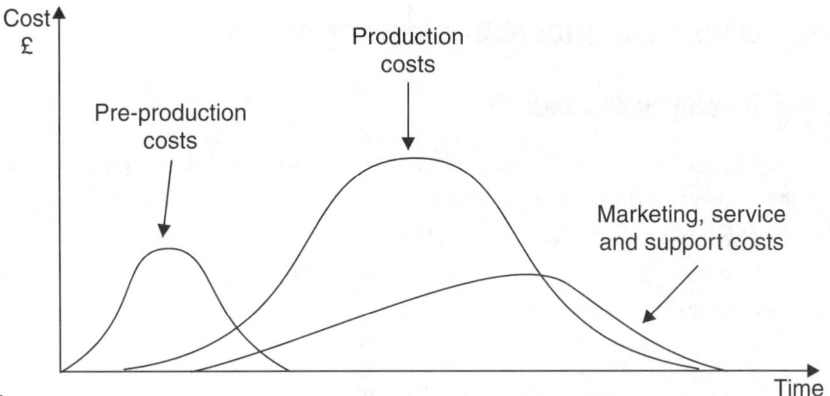

The horizontal axis measures the **duration of the life cycle**, which can last from, say, **18 months to several hundred years**. Children's crazes and fad products have very short lives while some products, such as binoculars (invented in the eighteenth century), can last a very long time.

3.2 What are life cycle costs?

A product's life cycle costs are incurred throughout its life, **from the design stage** through **development** to market **launch**, **production and sales**, to its eventual **withdrawal** from the market. Life cycle costs include the following components.

- Research and development costs, such as the costs of design and testing
- Technical data costs, which are the cost of purchasing any technical data required
- Training costs, including initial operator training and skills updating
- Production costs
- Distribution costs
- Marketing costs, including the costs of customer service, field maintenance and brand promotion
- Inventory costs, which are the costs of holding spare parts, warehousing and so on
- Retirement and disposal costs, which are the costs occurring at the end of a product's life

3.3 Traditional management accounting systems versus life cycle costing

Traditional management accounting systems are **based on the financial accounting year** and so tend to **dissect** a product's **life cycle** into a series of **annual sections**, **focusing** in particular on reporting costs at the stage of the life cycle during which the product is **physically produced**. Rather than assessing a product's profitability over its entire life, **profitability** is **assessed** on a **periodic basis.**

But because of the **commitment of a large proportion** of a product's **costs** during the **early stages** of its life cycle, as mentioned in the Introduction to this chapter, the **total revenue** earned by a product should be **compared** with **all the costs** incurred over its **entire life cycle**.

Life cycle costing tracks and **accumulates actual costs and revenues** attributable to each product **over the entire product life cycle, including the pre-production stage**. A product's **profitability** can therefore be determined at the **end** of its **economic life**.

3.4 Other problems with traditional accounting systems

3.4.1 Research and development costs

Traditional management accounting systems do not tend to relate **research and development costs** to the products that caused them. Instead the costs are **written off on an annual basis against the revenue generated by existing products**. This makes the **existing products seem less profitable** than they really are, so potentially they could be **scrapped too early**. If research and development costs are **not related** to the product that caused them, the **true profitability** of that product **cannot be assessed**.

3.4.2 Non-production costs

Traditional management accounting systems usually total all **non-production costs** and record them as a **period expense**. With **life cycle costing** these **costs** are **traced to individual products** over complete life cycles.

- The total of these costs for each individual product is reported and compared with revenues generated in the future.
- The **visibility** of such costs increases.
- **Individual product profitability** is easier to understand if all costs are attributed to products.
- As a consequence, **more accurate information** is available on an organisation's success or failure in **developing new products**. In today's competitive environment, where the ability to produce new and updated versions of products is paramount to the survival of an organisation, this information is vital.
- When an entire product life is analysed, **cost reduction**, **cost minimisation** and **revenue expansion opportunities** are more apparent than if management attempt to maximise profit on a year by year basis.

3.5 Maximising the return over the product life cycle

3.5.1 Design costs out of products

Between 70% to 90% of a product's life cycle costs are determined by decisions made early in the life cycle, at the design or development stage. Careful design of the product and manufacturing and other processes will keep cost to a minimum over the life cycle.

3.5.2 Minimise the time to market

This is the time from the conception of the product to its launch.

Competitors watch each other very carefully to determine what types of product their rivals are developing. If an organisation is launching a new product it is vital to get it to the market place as soon as possible. This will give the product as long a period as possible without a rival in the market place and should mean increased market share in the long run.

A product's life span may not proportionally lengthen if its launch is delayed and so sales may be permanently lost. It is not unusual for a product's overall profitability to fall by 25% if its launch is delayed by six months. This means that it is usually worthwhile incurring extra costs to keep the launch on schedule or to speed it up.

3.5.5 Minimise breakeven time

A short breakeven time (the time for revenue earned to equal costs incurred) is very important in keeping an organisation liquid. The sooner the product is launched the quicker the research and development costs will be repaid, providing the organisation with funds to develop further products.

3.5.4 Maximise the length of the life span

Product life cycles are not predetermined; they are set by the actions of management and competitors. Once developed, some products lend themselves to a number of different uses; this is especially true of materials, such as plastic, PVC, nylon and other synthetic materials. The life cycle of the material is then a series of individual product curves nesting on top of each other as shown below.

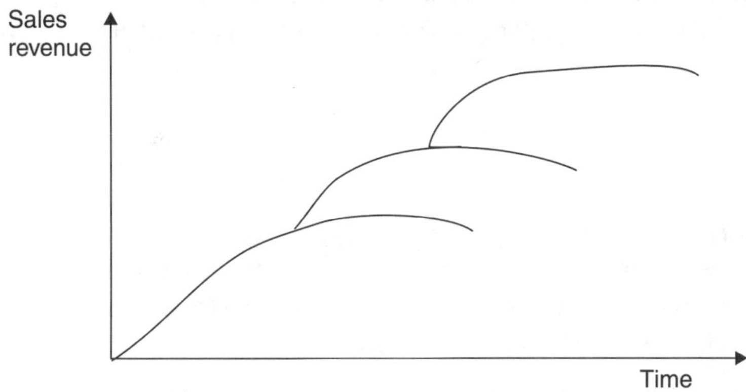

By entering different national or regional markets one after another an organisation may be able to maximise revenue. Resources can then be applied efficiently, and sales in each market maximised. In today's fast moving world, however, an organisation could lose out to a competitor if it failed to establish an early presence in a particular market.

3.5.5 Minimise product proliferation

If products are updated or superseded too quickly, the life cycle is cut short and the product may just cover its research and development costs before its successor is launched.

3.6 Service life cycles

A service organisation will have services that have life cycles. The only difference is that the research and development stages will not exist in the same way and will not have the same impact on subsequent costs. The different processes

that go to form the complete service are important, however, and consideration should be given in advance as to how to carry them out and arrange them so as to minimise cost.

4 Target costing

Japanese companies developed target costing as a **response to the problem of controlling and reducing costs over the entire product life cycle**, but **especially** during the **design and development stages**. It has been used successfully **by car manufacturers** in particular, including Toyota and Mercedes Benz.

4.1 The relationship between cost, price and profit

Target costing requires managers to change the way they think about the relationship between cost, price and profit.

4.1.1 The traditional approach

The traditional approach is to **develop a product**, **determine the expected standard production cost** of that product and then **set a selling price** (probably **based on cost**), with a **resulting profit or loss**. Costs are **controlled** through **variance analysis** at monthly intervals.

4.1.2 The target costing approach

The target costing approach is to **develop a product concept** and the primary specifications for performance and design and then to **determine the price customers would be willing to pay** for that concept. The **desired profit margin** is **deducted from the price**, **leaving** a figure that represents **total cost**. This is the **target cost**. The product must be capable of being produced for this amount otherwise it will not be manufactured.

During the product's life the **target cost** will be **continuously reviewed and reduced** so that the **price can fall**. Continuous **cost reduction techniques** must therefore be used.

4.2 Achieving the target cost

If the **anticipated product cost** (based on the design specifications) is **above the target cost**, the product must be **modified** so that it is cheaper to produce.

The total target cost can be split into broad cost categories such as development, marketing, manufacturing and so on. A team of designers, engineers, marketing and production staff, as well as the management accountant, should then endeavour to produce a product with planned development, marketing, manufacturing (and so on) costs below the target costs. Any of the cost reduction techniques we covered in Section 2 could be used.

If any of the target costs cannot be achieved given the product design, other individual targets must be reduced, the product redesigned yet again or scrapped.

4.2.1 Value engineering

One way of achieving target cost levels is to apply value engineering.

Value engineering is similar to value analysis, which we looked at in Section 2, but whereas **value analysis** is **cost reduction (whilst assuring standards of quality and reliability) during production, value engineering** is **cost avoidance or cost reduction before production**.

Key learning points

- ☑ Nowadays the costs of a product are determined when it is designed, not when it is in production. Additional controls are therefore needed at the design stage, the point at which most costs are committed. Life cycle costing and target costing can provide such control.
- ☑ **Cost reduction** aims to reduce costs below a previously accepted level, without adversely affecting the quality of the product being produced or service being provided.
- ☑ **Value analysis** involves assessing the value of every aspect of a product (or service) in order to devise ways of achieving the product's (or service's) purpose as economically as possible whilst maintaining the required standard of quality and reliability.
- ☑ Other techniques of cost reduction include **variety reduction (standardisation), work study** and **O&M**.
- ☑ A product's **life cycle costs** are incurred throughout its life, from the design stage to its eventual withdrawal from the market.
- ☑ Traditional management accounting systems are based on the financial accounting year and so tend to dissect a product's life cycle into a series of annual sections, focusing in particular on reporting costs at the production stage of the life cycle. Rather than assessing a product's profitability over its entire life, profitability is assessed on a periodic basis.
- ☑ **Life cycle costing** tracks and accumulates actual costs and revenues attributable to each product over the entire product life cycle, including the pre-production stage. A product's profitability can therefore be determined at the end of its economic life.
- ☑ Traditionally, a product is developed, its expected standard production cost determined and a selling price (probably based on cost) set, with a resulting profit or loss. Costs are controlled through monthly variance analysis.
- ☑ The **target costing** approach is to develop a product concept and the primary specifications for performance and design and then to determine the price customers would be willing to pay for that concept. The desired profit margin is deducted from the price, leaving a figure that represents total cost. This is the target cost. The product must be capable of being produced for this amount otherwise it will not be manufactured.
- ☑ During the product's life the target cost will be continuously reviewed and reduced so that the price can fall. Continuous cost reduction techniques must therefore be used.
- ☑ **Value engineering** is cost reduction before production.

Quick quiz

1 *Choose the correct words from those highlighted.*

Cost reduction/control is about regulating the costs of operating a business and keeping costs within acceptable limits whereas **cost reduction/control** is a planned and positive approach to reducing expenditure.

2 *Fill in the blanks.*

(a) .... is a way of raising productivity by reorganising work.

(b) .... involves systematically recording and critically examining existing and proposed ways of doing work in order to develop and apply easier and more effective methods and reduce costs.

(c) .... involves establishing the time for a qualified worker to carry out a specified job at a specified level of performance.

3 Life cycle costing is the profiling of cost over a product's production life. *True or false?*

4 *Choose the correct words from those highlighted.*

Between 70% to 90% of a product's life cycle costs are determined by decisions made **early/late** in its life cycle.

Minimising/maximising the time to market and/or **minimising/maximising** the length of the lifespan are ways of maximising the return over a product's life cycle.

5 When target costing is in use, a product concept is developed. What is determined next?

A Profit margin
B Price
C Full cost
D Production cost

Answers to quick quiz

1 The first term should be cost control, the second term cost reduction.

2 Work study
Method study
Work measurement

3 False. It is profiling over its entire life.

4 early
minimising
maximising

5 B

ASSESSMENT KIT ACTIVITIES

See the box at the end of Chapter 15 for details of the activities in the BPP Assessment Kit for Units 8 & 9 on cost management.

Activity checklist

This checklist shows which performance criteria, range statement or knowledge and understanding point is covered by each activity in this chapter. Tick off each activity as you complete it.

Activity		
14.1	☐	This activity deals with Performance Criteria 8.2C regarding providing assistance in identifying ways to reduce costs and enhance value and Range Statement 8.2: recommendations.
14.2	☐	This activity deals with Performance Criteria 8.2C regarding providing assistance in identifying ways to reduce costs and enhance value and Range Statement 8.2: recommendations.
14.3	☐	This activity deals with Performance Criteria 8.2C regarding providing assistance in identifying ways to reduce costs and enhance value and Range Statement 8.2. recommendations.

chapter 15

Cost management II

Contents

1 Introduction
2 The reasons for the development of ABC
3 ABC and using it to calculate product costs
4 Types of activity and their associated overhead cost
5 Merits and limitations of ABC
6 Activity based budgeting
7 The importance of quality
8 Quality and value
9 Total Quality Management (TQM)
10 Quality assurance procedures
11 Costs of quality
12 Standard costing in a total quality environment

Performance criteria

8.1E Analyse the effect of organisational accounting policies on reported costs

8.2C Consult relevant specialists and assist in identifying ways to reduce costs and enhance value

8.2E Make specific recommendations to management in a clear and appropriate form

Range statement

8.1 The build up of costs: activity-based costing

8.2 Performance indicators to measure: cost of quality

8.2 Recommendations: efficiencies; modifications to work processes

Knowledge and understanding

Unit 8 Accounting principles and theory

9 Cost management: activity based costing; principles of Total Quality Management (including cost of quality)

Unit 8 The organisation

14 The contribution of functional specialists in an organisation (eg marketing, design, engineering, quality control etc) to cost reduction and value enhancement

1 Introduction

As we saw in the previous chapter, both life cycle costing and target costing are most effective during a product's planning and design stage.

Although **activity based costing (ABC)** and **Total Quality Management (TQM)** are also **relevant** at these **early stages of the product life cycle**, they can **also be applied successfully at subsequent stages**.

Activity based costing is part of the necessary **knowledge and understanding** for Unit 8. As you will discover as you work through the chapter, it is an **alternative method of dealing with overheads** to traditional absorption costing (which we revisited in Chapter 2).

Supporters of activity based costing claim it can **help with cost reduction and cost management** – hence its inclusion in Unit 8.

Quality is an **area of knowledge and understanding** which, if appropriately **controlled** and **managed**, can **allow management to enhance value**.

We will begin our study of this topic by looking at the techniques and methods used to ensure that quality products are produced or quality services provided.

Given the way in which quality is likely to be assessed, **Sections 11 and 12** are the **central** sections on quality, however.

- Section 11 covers the costs associated with preventing poor quality, with appraising the level of quality achieved and with failing to achieve the level of quality required.
- Section 12 looks at how easy or difficult it is to operate a standard costing system within an organisation attempting to control and manage quality.

2 The reasons for the development of ABC

2.1 In the past

Most organisations used to produce **only a few products**. **Direct labour costs** and **direct material costs** accounted for the **largest proportion** of total costs and so it was these variable costs that needed to be **controlled**.

Overhead costs were only a **very small fraction** of total costs and so it did not particularly matter what absorption costing bases were used to apportion overheads to products.

2.2 Nowadays

Costs tend to be **fixed** and **overheads huge**.

Manufacturing is **capital and machine intensive** rather than labour intensive and so direct labour might account for as little as 5% of a product's cost. For example, furniture is no longer made by skilled workers. Instead complicated expensive machines are programmed with the necessary skills and workers become machine minders.

Advanced manufacturing technology (such as robotics) has had a significant impact on the level of overheads. For example, the marginal cost of producing a piece of computer software might be just a few pounds but the fixed (initial) cost of the software development might run into millions of pounds.

Many resources are used in **support activities** such as setting-up, production scheduling, first item inspection and data processing. These support activities help with the manufacture of a wide range of products and are **not**, in general, **affected by changes in production volume**. They tend to **vary** instead in the **long term** according to the **range** and **complexity** of the products manufactured.

The wider the range and the more complex the products, the more support services will be required. Suppose factory X produces 10,000 units of one product, the Alpha. Factory Y also produces 10,000 units, made up of 1,000 units each of ten slightly different versions of the Alpha. Consider the setting-up activity.

- Factory X will only need to set-up once.
- Factory Y will have to set-up the production run at least ten times for the ten different products and so will incur more set-up costs.

2.2.1 Problems of using absorption costing in today's environment

Overhead absorption rates might be 200% or 300% of unit labour costs. Unit **costs** are **distorted** and so cost information is **misleading**.

Overheads are **not controlled** because they are hidden within unit production costs rather than being shown as individual totals.

Products bear an arbitrary share of overheads which **do not reflect the benefits** they receive.

Absorption costing **assumes** all products **consume all resources** in **proportion** to their **production volumes**.

- It tends to **allocate too great a proportion** of overheads to **high volume products** (which cause relatively little diversity and hence use fewer support services).
- It tends to **allocate too small a proportion** of overheads to **low volume products** (which cause greater diversity and therefore use more support services).

Activity based costing (ABC) attempts to overcome these problems.

3 ABC and using it to calculate product costs

3.1 Major ideas behind ABC

Activities cause costs.	Activities include ordering and despatching.
↓	
The costs of an activity are caused or driven by factors known as **cost drivers**.	The cost of the ordering activity might be driven by the number of orders placed, the cost of the despatching activity by the number of despatches made.
↓	
The costs of an activity are assigned to products on the basis of the number of the activity's cost driver products generate.	If product A requires 5 orders to be placed, and product B 15 orders, ¼ (ie 5/(5 + 15)) of the ordering cost will be assigned to product A and ¾ (ie 15/(5 + 15)) to product B.

3.2 Cost drivers

For those costs that **vary with production levels in the short term**, ABC uses **volume-related cost drivers** such as labour hours or machine hours. The cost of oil used as a lubricant on machines would therefore be added to products on the basis of the number of machine hours, since oil would have to be used for each hour the machine ran.

For costs that **vary with some other activity and not volume of production**, ABC uses **transaction-related cost drivers** such as the number of production runs for the production scheduling activity.

3.3 Calculating product costs using ABC

Step 1

Identify an organisation's major activities.

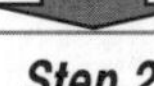

Step 2

Identify the factors (cost drivers) which cause the costs of the activities.

Step 3

Collect the costs associated with each activity into **cost pools**.

Cost pools are equivalent to cost centres used with traditional absorption costing.

Step 4

Charge the costs of activities to products on the basis of their usage of the activities. A product's usage of an activity is measured by the number of the activity's cost driver it generates.

Suppose the cost pool for the ordering activity totalled £100,000 and that there were 10,000 orders (orders being the cost driver). Each product would therefore be charged with £10 for each order it required. A batch requiring five orders would therefore be charged with £50.

Example: ABC

Suppose that Cooplan Ltd manufactures four products, W, X, Y and Z. Output and cost data for the period just ended are as follows.

	Output	*No of production runs in the period*	*Material cost per unit*	*Direct labour hours per unit*	*Machine hours per unit*
	Units		£		
W	10	2	20	1	1
X	10	2	80	3	3
Y	100	5	20	1	1
Z	100	5	80	3	3
		14			

Direct labour cost per hour is £5. Overhead costs are as follows.

	£
Short-run variable costs	3,080
Set-up costs	10,920
Production and scheduling costs	9,100
Materials handling costs	7,700
	30,800

Task

Calculate product costs using absorption costing and ABC.

Solution

Using absorption costing and an absorption rate based on either direct labour hours or machine hours, the product costs would be as follows.

	W	*X*	*Y*	*Z*	*Total*
	£	£	£	£	£
Direct material	200	800	2,000	8,000	11,000
Direct labour	50	150	500	1,500	2,200
Overheads *	700	2,100	7,000	21,000	30,800
	950	3,050	9,500	30,500	44,000
Units produced	10	10	100	100	
Cost per unit	£95	£305	£95	£305	

* £30,800 ÷ 440 hours = £70 per direct labour or machine hour

Using activity based costing and assuming that the number of production runs is the cost driver for set-up costs, production and scheduling costs and materials handling costs and that machine hours are the cost driver for short-run variable costs, unit costs would be as follows.

	W	*X*	*Y*	*Z*	*Total*
	£	£	£	£	£
Direct material	200	800	2,000	8,000	11,000
Direct labour	50	150	500	1,500	2,200
Short-run variable overheads (W1)	70	210	700	2,100	3,080
Set-up costs (W2)	1,560	1,560	3,900	3,900	10,920
Production and scheduling costs (W3)	1,300	1,300	3,250	3,250	9,100
Materials handling costs (W4)	1,100	1,100	2,750	2,750	7,700
	4,280	5,120	13,100	21,500	44,000
Units produced	10	10	100	100	
Cost per unit	£428	£512	£131	£215	

Workings

1	£3,080 ÷ 440 machine hours	=	£7 per machine hour
2	£10,920 ÷ 14 production runs	=	£780 per run
3	£9,100 ÷ 14 production runs	=	£650 per run
4	£7,700 ÷ 14 production runs	=	£550 per run

Summary

Product	Absorption costing Unit cost	ABC Unit cost	Difference
	£	£	£
W	95	428	+ 333
X	305	512	+ 207
Y	95	131	+ 36
Z	305	215	– 90

The figures suggest that the traditional volume-based absorption costing system is flawed.

- It under allocates overhead costs to low-volume products (here, W and X) and over allocates overheads to higher-volume products (here Z in particular).
- It under allocates overhead costs to less complex products (here W and Y with just one hour of work needed per unit) and over allocates overheads to more complex products (here X and particularly Z).

IMPORTANT POINT

You must be able to calculate unit and total costs using ABC. Do the activity below to make sure that you can!

Activity 15.1

Having attended a AAT course on activity based costing (ABC) you decide to experiment by applying the principles of ABC to the four products currently made and sold by your company. Details of the four products and relevant information are given below for one period.

Product	*P1*	*P2*	*P3*	*P4*
Output in units	120	100	80	120
Costs per unit:	£	£	£	£
Direct material	40	50	30	60
Direct labour	28	21	14	21

The four products are similar and are usually produced in production runs of 20 units.

The total of the production overhead for the period has been analysed as follows.

	£
Set up costs	5,250
Stores receiving	3,600
Inspection/quality control	2,100
Materials handling and despatch	4,620

You have ascertained that the following 'cost drivers' are to be used for the costs shown.

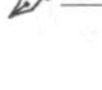

Cost	Cost driver
Set up costs	Number of production runs
Stores receiving	Requisitions raised
Inspection/quality control	Number of production runs
Materials handling and despatch	Orders executed

The number of requisitions raised on the stores was 20 for each product and the number of orders executed was 42, each order being for a batch of 10 of a product.

Task

Calculate the total costs and unit costs for each product using activity based costing.

4 Types of activity and their associated overhead cost

Overheads can be associated with different sorts of activity.

Overhead associated with ...	Detail	Examples of overheads
Unit related activities	Incurred in line with units produced or hours worked	Cost of lubricating oil is related to machine hours
Batch related activities	Incurred if a number of products are made using the same facilities	Two models of car on the same production line (so that line is rearranged when other car is produced)
Product sustaining activities	Level of overhead driven by the number of different products	Type approval of vehicles (eg deliberate crashing of vehicles in order to meet safety standards)
Facility sustaining activities	Required to support the upkeep of the factory and the managerial infrastructure that makes production possible	Factory security Factory insurance

Activity 15.2

A company manufactures two products, Superior and Deluxe, using the same equipment and similar processes. An extract of the production data for these products in one period is shown below.

	Superior	*Deluxe*
Quantity produced (units)	5,000	7,000
Direct labour hours per unit	1	2
Machine hours per unit	3	1
Set-ups in the period	10	40
Orders handled in the period	15	60

Overhead costs	£
Activity	220,000
Relating to production run set-ups	20,000
Relating to handling of orders	45,000
	285,000

Task

Calculate the production overheads to be absorbed by one unit of each of the products using the following costing methods and comment on your results.

(a) A traditional costing approach using a direct labour hour rate to absorb overheads
(b) An activity based costing approach, using suitable cost drivers to trace overheads to products

5 Merits and limitations of ABC

5.1 Merits

ABC produces **more accurate cost information** as it reflects the resources actually consumed by a product.

Management should have a **greater understanding of why costs are incurred**. They should therefore be able to **control the level of costs by controlling the level of cost drivers**. For example, if setting-up costs are driven by the number of set-ups, careful production planning should limit the number of different products made on a particular production line. The amount of costs saved will depend on the accuracy of the cost drivers chosen, however.

TOPIC LINK

ABC and cost reduction

ABC might help with an organisation's attempts at reducing costs.

'Long term, its major benefit might be its influence on management behaviour. By separating overheads into activities and then identifying drivers, ABC begins to highlight the forces behind overheads. As such, no longer need overheads be treated as a black hole which sucks in costs but about which little is known. Instead by identifying the causes of overheads, ABC allows their contribution to profitability to be questioned and recognises their controllability by management.'

('Activity based costing: taking control of fixed overheads', John Watts, Chief Assessor, *Summing Up*, February 2000, pp18-21)

5.2 Limitations

- Some measure of (arbitrary) **cost apportionment may still be required** at the cost pooling stage for items like rent, rates and building depreciation.
- Can a **single cost driver** explain the cost behaviour of all items in its associated pool?
- Unless costs are caused by an **activity** that is **measurable** in **quantitative terms** and which can be related to production output, cost drivers will not be usable. What drives the cost of the annual external audit, for example?
- ABC is sometimes introduced because it is **fashionable**, not because it will be used by management to provide meaningful product costs or extra information. If management is not going to use ABC information, an absorption costing system may be simpler to operate.

5.2.1 Factors which impact on the effectiveness of introducing ABC

ABC is basically a way of apportioning overheads between products so as to produce more accurate/product costs for planning, control and decision-making purposes. In this respect there is no point in applying it unless an organisation's product mix contains at least two products (otherwise all overheads are attributable to the single product produced).

In modern organisations with significant levels of support department overheads, ABC provides an effective method of attributing them to products.

One of the principal disadvantages of ABC is that it may be **difficult to collect the information required** to enable ABC to be introduced.

- The various activities within the organisation need to be established (possibly using observation and employee interviews) and cost drivers identified.
- A database of activities, their occurrence, their cost and cost drivers needs to be set up. This is a **huge wealth of information which may not have been recorded before**.
- Information collection and retrieval systems may therefore need to be expanded and improved.
- Although developments in information technology allow for more sophisticated information systems, the **cost** of required changes and improvements **may outweigh the anticipated benefits** of ABC and make its introduction unsuitable.

ABC is likely to be more effective in an organisation in which **managers embrace change**. If there is resistance to change it may be difficult to sell the benefits of ABC to management and they may be unwilling to participate in its implementation.

6 Activity based budgeting

At its **simplest**, activity based budgeting (ABB) is merely the **use of costs determined using ABC as a basis for preparing budgets**.

More formally, activity based budgeting involves **defining the activities that underlie the financial figures in each function** and **using the level of activity to decide how much resource should be allocated, how well it is being managed** and to **explain divergences from budget**.

ABB therefore incorporates the following **ideas**.

- Activities drive costs and the aim is to **control the causes (drivers) of costs** rather than the costs themselves, so that in the long term, costs will be better managed and better understood.
- Most departmental **activities** are **driven by demands and decisions beyond the immediate control of the manager responsible for the department's budget**.

  The cost of setting up new personnel records and of induction training would traditionally be the responsibility of the personnel manager.

  In reality such costs are driven by the number of new employees required by managers other than the personnel manager.

Example: ABB

A stores department has two main activities, receiving deliveries of raw materials from suppliers into stores and issuing raw materials to production departments. Two major cost drivers, the number of deliveries of raw materials and the number of production runs, have been identified. Although the majority of the costs of the department can be attributed to the activities, there is a small balance, termed 'department running costs', which includes general administration costs, part of the department manager's salary and so on. Based on activity levels expected in the next control period, cost driver volumes of 250 deliveries of raw materials and 120 production runs have been budgeted.

On the basis of budgeted departmental costs and the cost analysis, the following budget has been drawn up for the next control period.

Cost	*Total* £'000	*Costs attributable to receiving deliveries* £'000	*Costs attributable to issuing materials* £'000	*Dept running costs* £'000
Salaries – management	25	8	12	5
Salaries – stores workers	27	13	12	2
Salaries – administration	15	4	5	6
Consumables	11	3	5	3
Information technology costs	14	5	8	1
Other costs	19	10	6	3
	111	43	48	20
Activity volumes		250	120	
Cost per unit of cost driver		£172	£400	£20,000

Note the following.

- The apportionment of cost will be subjective to a certain extent. The objective of the exercise is that the resource has to be justified as supporting one or more of the activities. Costs cannot be hidden.
- The cost driver rates of £172 and £400 can be used to calculate product costs using ABC.
- Identifying activities and their costs helps to focus attention on those activities which add value and those that do not.
- The budget has highlighted the cost of the two activities.

7 The importance of quality

In the past, many organisations focused on **quantity** – producing as many 'units' as possible as cheaply as possible. **Customers** used to accept late delivery of the same old unreliable products from organisations which appeared to care little for their customers. But **now** they **want more.**

- New products
- High levels of quality
- On-time delivery
- Immediate response to their requests

Businesses **today** are therefore **concentrating** on **quality** in the hope of becoming the success stories of the 21st century.

8 Quality and value

8.1 Quality

Quality means 'the **degree of excellence of a thing'** – how well made it is, or how well it is performed if it is a service, how well it serves its purpose, and how it measures up against its rivals.

The quality of a product or service has also been defined as 'its **fitness for the customer's purpose'.**

So if we are looking for an **'excellent' product** or service, we expect it to be **completely satisfactory for its purpose** from the **point of view of the customer.**

The **degree** to which a product or service is **fit for its purpose** will depend on the product or service in question.

- **Cost**. Customers expect some products to be cheap because of their short life. Pencils and daily newspapers are examples.
- **Life**. Other products are expected to last for longer and to be reliable and hence are more expensive. Televisions are an example.
- **Manner of production**. With some products, customers expect the use of highly skilled labour and/or expensive raw materials. A meal in a highly–commended restaurant is an example.
- **Esteem**. If a customer is looking for esteem or status from a product, the product is likely to have a high price, a designer label and/or expensive package. An example is designer-label clothing.

A **quality service** is likely to be **efficient**, be provided by **courteous staff** who have **knowledge of the service** and take place within a **pleasant environment**. For example, if a train arrives on time, is clean and the guard gives out accurate announcements over the tannoy, many customers would feel they had enjoyed a quality service.

8.2 Value

The **value** of a product or service **to a customer** can therefore be considered in terms of its **fitness for purpose** and the **prestige or esteem attached**. From the **point of view of the producer of the product or the provider of the service,** however, other aspects are important.

- All organisations need to control costs and so the **cost of making the product or providing the service** is one aspect.
- The other aspect, the product's or service's **selling price** (its **market value),** is of importance to profit-making organisations.

The value of a product therefore has four distinct aspects.

- **Cost value** is the cost of producing and selling an item/providing a service.
- **Exchange value** is the market value of the product or service.
- **Use value** is what the product or service does, the purpose it fulfils.
- **Esteem value** is the prestige the customer attaches to a product.

Activity 15.3

Classify the following features of a product, using the types of value set out above.

(a) The product can be sold for £27.50.
(b) The product is available in six colours to suit customers' tastes.
(c) The product will last for ten years.

8.2.1 Enhancing value

The **producer** of a product or **provider** of a service will want to **increase exchange value** (the selling price) **without increasing cost value. To do this, the value the customer attaches** to the product or service **must be enhanced** (its **use value** or its **esteem value**) so that they will pay the higher price.

- Extended opening hours may add to the use value of a local shop.
- The esteem value of certain products such as expensive jewellery can be increased by increasing the price!

We will now turn out attention to specific techniques for reducing costs and enhancing value.

9 Total Quality Management (TQM))

If the level of quality is to be controlled, a **control system** is needed.

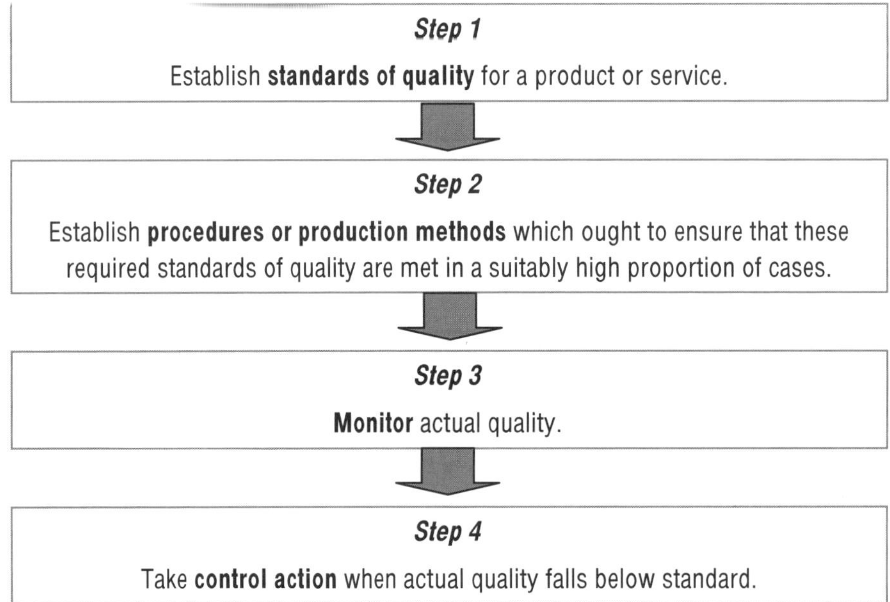

Step 1
Establish standards of quality for a product or service.
Step 2
Establish procedures or production methods which ought to ensure that these required standards of quality are met in a suitably high proportion of cases.
Step 3
Monitor actual quality.
Step 4
Take control action when actual quality falls below standard.

TOPIC LINK

Control systems and TQM

The relationship between quality control systems and the general control systems examined in Chapter 1 should be evident.

Activity 15.4

How is this system of control similar to budgetary control and standard costing control systems?

How might the postal service control quality? It might establish a standard that 90% of first class letters will be delivered on the day after they are posted, and 99% will be delivered within two days of posting.

- Procedures would have to be established for ensuring that these standards could be met (attending to such matters as frequency of collections, automated letter sorting, frequency of deliveries and number of staff employed).
- Actual performance could be monitored, perhaps by taking samples from time to time of letters that are posted and delivered.
- If the quality standard is not being achieved, management should take control action (employ more postmen or advertise the use of postcodes again).

Quality management becomes **total (Total Quality Management (TQM)) when it is applied to everything a business does**.

9.1 Get it right, first time

One of the basic principles of TQM is that the **cost of preventing mistakes is less than the cost of correcting them** once they occur. The aim should therefore be **to get things right first time**. Every mistake, delay and misunderstanding, directly costs an organisation money through **wasted time and effort**, including time taken in pacifying customers. The **lost potential for future sales because of poor customer service must also be taken into account.**

9.2 Continuous improvement

A second basic principle of TQM is dissatisfaction with the *status quo*: the belief that it is **always possible to improve** and so the aim should be to **'get it more right next time'**.

10 Quality assurance procedures

Because TQM embraces every activity of a business, quality assurance procedures **cannot be confined to the production process** but must also cover the work of sales, distribution and administration departments, the efforts of external suppliers, and the reaction of external customers.

10.1 Quality assurance of goods inwards

The quality of output depends on the quality of input materials. Quality control should therefore include **procedures over acceptance and inspection of goods inwards** and **measurement of rejects**. Each supplier can be given a 'rating' for the quality of the goods they tend to supply, and preference with purchase orders can be given to well-rated suppliers. This method is referred to as 'vendor rating'.

Where a **quality assurance scheme** is in place the supplier guarantees the quality of goods supplied and allows the customers' inspectors access while the items are being manufactured. The **onus is on the supplier to carry out the necessary quality checks**, or face cancellation of the contract.

Suppliers' quality assurance schemes are being used increasingly, particularly where extensive sub-contracting work is carried out, for example in the motor industries. One such scheme is **BS EN ISO 9000** certification. A company that gains registration has a certificate testifying that it is operating to a structure of written policies and procedures which are designed to ensure that it can consistently deliver a product or service to meet customer requirements.

10.2 Inspection of output

This will take place at various key stages in the production process and will provide a continual check that the production process is under control. The aim of inspection is *not* really to sort out the bad products from the good ones after the work has been done. The **aim is to satisfy management that quality control in production is being maintained.**

The **inspection of samples** rather than 100% testing of all items will keep inspection costs down, and smaller samples will be less costly to inspect than larger samples. The greater the confidence in the reliability of production methods and process control, the smaller the samples will be.

TOPIC LINK

We looked at sampling in Chapter 3.

10.3 Monitoring customer reaction

Some sub-standard items will inevitably be produced. Checks during production will identify some bad output, but other items will reach the customer who is the ultimate judge of quality. **Complaints ought to be monitored** in the form of letters of complaint, returned goods, penalty discounts, claims under guarantee, or requests for visits by service engineers. Some companies actually survey customers on a regular basis.

10.4 Employees and quality

10.4.1 Empowerment

Workers themselves are frequently the best source of information about how (or how not) to improve quality. **Empowerment** therefore has two key aspects.

- Allowing workers to have the **freedom to decide how to do** the necessary work, using the skills they possess and acquiring new skills as necessary to be an effective team member.
- Making workers **responsible** for achieving production targets and for quality control.

10.4.2 Quality circles

A quality circle is a group of employees who meet regularly to discuss **problems of quality** and **quality control** in their area of work, and perhaps to suggest ways of improving quality.

10.5 Quality control and inspection

A distinction should be made between **quality control** and **inspection**.

Quality control involves setting controls for the process of manufacture or service delivery. It is aimed at **preventing the manufacture of defective items** or the provision of defective services.

Inspection is a technique of **identifying when defective items are being produced at an unacceptable level.** Inspection is usually carried out at three main points.

- Receiving inspection – for raw materials and purchased components
- Floor or process inspection for WIP
- Final inspection or testing for finished goods

11 Costs of quality

When we talk about quality-related costs you should remember that a concern for **good quality saves money**; it is **poor quality that costs money.**

IMPORTANT POINT!

You need to be able to define the following terms in the exam.

Prevention costs are the costs of any action taken to investigate, prevent or reduce defects and failures.

Appraisal costs are the costs of assessing the quality achieved.

Internal failure costs are the costs arising within the organisation of failing to achieve the required level of quality.

External failure costs are the costs arising outside the organisation of failing to achieve the required level of quality (after transfer of ownership to the customer).

Quality-related cost	Example
Prevention costs	Quality engineering Design/development of quality control/inspection equipment Maintenance of quality control/inspection equipment Administration of quality control Training in quality control
Appraisal costs	Acceptance testing Inspection of goods inwards Inspection costs of in-house processing Performance testing
Internal failure costs	Failure analysis Re-inspection costs Losses from failure of purchased items Losses due to lower selling prices for sub-quality goods Costs of reviewing product specifications after failures

Quality-related cost	Example
External failure costs	Administration of customer complaints section Costs of customer service section Product liability costs Cost of repairing products returned from customers Cost of replacing items due to sub-standard products/marketing errors

The **introduction of TQM** will cause a **drop** in **internal and external failure costs** but **prevention and appraisal costs** will **increase**. Management need to **ensure** that the **cost savings** are **never outweighed by** the **additional costs**.

ATTENTION!

In an exam you might be asked to suggest quality-related costs in a particular environment, such as external failure costs that could occur in a management accounting department. Alternatively you might have to identify the four general headings (or classifications) which make up the cost of quality, and provide examples (**not** necessarily related to the scenario) of each type.

Example: cost of poor quality

A manufacturer's inspection procedures indicate that one faulty item out of every 1,000 good items produced is sent to a customer. The management regards this as acceptable, as a replacement will be supplied free of charge. Unit sales are 10,000,000 per year, and each unit costs £20 to manufacture and makes a profit of £5. It is probable that every customer who buys a faulty product will return it, and will thenceforth buy a similar product from another company. The average customer buys two units a year. Marketing costs per new customer are £10 per year.

(a) What is your best estimate of the net cost of this policy for a year?
(b) What name(s) would you give to quality-related costs of this type?
(c) Could the situation be improved by incurring other types of quality-related cost?

Solution

(a) Presumed number of bad units delivered a year = 10,000,000/1,000= 10,000

	£
Cost of defects 10,000 × £20	200,000
Cost of free replacement 10,000 × £20	200,000
Manufacturing cost	400,000
Marketing costs for replacement customers £10 × 10,000	100,000
Gross cost of poor quality	500,000
Less income from original sale	250,000
Net cost of poor quality	250,000

Although the cost of the original defective item is recovered, the company **does not get it right first time**. The company has still suffered the cost of the replacement and the cost of replacing the customer by marketing to new customers.

(b) The cost of replacements is an external failure cost; the cost of defects and the new marketing costs are internal failure costs.

(c) It appears that the manufacturer already incurs *appraisal* costs, since there are inspection procedures for goods about to be despatched. The reason(s) for the fault should be established (a further *internal failure* cost) and the extent of the problem should be more precisely ascertained (further *appraisal* costs), since it is not certain that all dissatisfied customers return their goods, though it is highly likely that their business is lost. Once this has been done it will be possible to decide whether, by spending more on *prevention*, the overall cost of poor quality can be reduced.

11.1 Traditional accounting systems and the cost of quality

Traditionally, the **costs** of **scrapped units, wasted materials and reworking** have been **lost within the costs of production** by incorporating the costs of an expected level of loss (a normal loss) to the costs of good production. **Other costs of poor quality have been included within production or marketing overheads.** So such costs are not only **considered as inevitable** but are not highlighted for management attention.

Traditional accounting reports **tend also to ignore the hidden but real costs of excessive stock levels** (held to enable faulty material to be replaced without hindering production) **and the facilities necessary for storing that stock**.

The introduction of a system of **just-in-time (JIT)** purchasing and manufacturing should eradicate such costs, however. A just-in-time production system is driven by demand from customers for finished products. Components on a production line are only produced when needed for the next stage of production. Stocks of work in progress and finished goods are therefore not needed. In a just-in-time purchasing system, materials are not delivered until they are needed in production, thereby eradicating stock of raw materials.

To **implement a TQM programme, costs of quality** must be **highlighted separately** within accounting reports so that *all* employees are aware of the cost of poor quality.

11.2 Explicit and implicit costs of quality

Explicit costs of quality are those that are recorded in accounting records, to be separately highlighted with the implementation of a TQM programme.

Implicit costs of quality are not recorded in accounting records. They tend to be of two forms.

- **Opportunity costs** such as the loss of future sales to a customer dissatisfied with faulty goods
- **Costs which tend to be subsumed** within other account headings such as costs which result from the disruptions caused by stockouts due to faulty purchases

Activity 15.5

Elyard Ltd defines the cost of quality as the total of all costs incurred in preventing faults in production of its single product, plus the costs involved in correcting faults once they have occurred. It only includes explicit costs of quality.

Task

Determine which of the following costs Elyard Ltd would include in the cost of quality.

(a) Remedial work required as a result of faulty raw material
(b) Cost of customer support department which deals with faulty products
(c) Loss of customer goodwill following delivery of faulty products
(d) Cost of detailed inspection of raw materials due to poor quality of supplies
(e) Cost of products returned by customers due to faults
(f) Sales revenue lost as a result of returns in (e)

12 Standard costing in a total quality environment

TOPIC LINK

Standard costing and quality

We looked at standard costing in Chapters 6 and 7.

It has been argued that traditional variance analysis is unhelpful and potentially misleading in the modern organisation, and causes managers to focus their attention on the wrong issues.

Standard costing concentrates on **quantity** and ignores other factors contributing to an organisation's effectiveness. In a **total quality** environment, however, quantity is not an issue, **quality** is. Effectiveness in such an environment therefore centres on high quality output (produced as a result of high quality input); the cost of failing to achieve the required level of effectiveness is not measured in variances, but in terms of the **internal and external failure costs** which would not be identified by traditional standard costing analysis.

Standard costing might measure, say, **labour efficiency** in terms of individual tasks and the level of **output**. In a **total quality environment**, the effectiveness of labour is more appropriately measured in terms of **re-working** required, **returns** from customers, **defects** identified in subsequent stages of production and so on.

In a **TQM** environment there are likely to be **minimal rate variances** if the workforce are paid a guaranteed weekly wage. Fixed price contracts, with suppliers guaranteeing levels of quality, are often a feature, and so there are likely to be **few, if any, material price and usage variances.**

So **can standard costing and TQM exist together?**

- Predetermined standards conflict with the TQM philosophy of continual improvement.
- Continual improvements should alter quantities of inputs, prices and so on, whereas standard costing is best used in a stable, standardised, repetitive environment.

- Standard costs often incorporate a planned level of scrap in material standards. This is at odds with the TQM aim of 'zero defects'.

On the other hand, variance analysis can contribute towards the aim of improved product quality. Can you think how? The following activity tests this point.

Activity 15.6

Acton plc has been receiving an increasing number of customer complaints about a general weakness in the quality of its products in recent months. The company believes that its future success is dependent on product quality and it is therefore determined to improve it.

Task

Describe the contribution that variance analysis can make towards the aim of improved product quality.

Activity 15.7

(a) What are the potential benefits of training for quality?
(b) What are the potential benefits of quality control?

Activity 15.8

Read the following extract from an article in the *Financial Times* and then explain how the bank could monitor the impact of the initiative.

'If you telephone a branch of Lloyds Bank and it rings five times before there is a reply; if the person who answers does not introduce him or herself by name during the conversation; if you are standing in a queue with more people in it than the number of tills, then something is wrong.'

'If any of these things happen then the branch is breaching standards of customer service set by the bank since last July ... the "service challenge" was launched in the bank's 1,888 branches last summer after being tested in 55 branches ...'

'Lloyds already has evidence of the impact. Customers were more satisfied with pilot branches ... than with others.'

Key learning points

- ☑ An alternative to the traditional method of accounting for overhead costs – absorption costing – is **activity based costing (ABC)**. ABC involves the identification of the factors (**cost drivers**) which cause the costs of an organisation's major activities. Costs of an activity are charged to products on the basis of the products' usage of the activity (the number of the activity's cost driver they generate).
- ☑ When using ABC, for costs that vary with production levels in the short term, the cost driver will be volume related (labour or machine hours). Overheads that vary with some other activity (and not volume of production) should be traced to products using transaction-based cost drivers such as production runs or number of orders received.
- ☑ Although ABC has obvious merits, it does have a number of limitations.
- ☑ At its simplest, **activity based budgeting (ABB)** is merely the use of costs determined using ABC as a basis for preparing budgets. More formally, activity based budgeting involves defining the activities that underlie the financial figures in each function and using the level of activity to decide how much resource should be allocated, how well it is being managed and to explain divergencies from budget.
- ☑ In the **past,** organisations focused on **quantity**. Customers now want more and so businesses today are concentrating on **quality.**
- ☑ **Total quality management (TQM)** has two basic principles.
  - Get it right first time (**zero defects**)
  - Get it more right next time (**continuous improvement**)
- ☑ **Quality assurance procedures** should not be confined to the production process but must also cover the work of sales, distribution and administration departments, the efforts of external suppliers and the reaction of external customers.
- ☑ **Quality control** happens at various stages in the process of designing a product or service.
- ☑ **Quality control** is aimed at preventing the manufacture of defective items or the provision of defective services. **Inspection** is a technique for identifying when defective items are being produced at an unacceptable level.
- ☑ The costs associated with a concern for quality are **prevention costs**, **appraisal costs**, **internal failure costs** and **external failure costs**.
- ☑ **Explicit costs** of quality are those that are recorded in accounting records, to be separately highlighted. **Implicit costs** of quality are not recorded in accounting records.
- ☑ It may be difficult for standard costing and TQM to exist together.

Quick quiz

1 *Choose the correct words from those highlighted.*

Traditional costing systems tend to allocate **too great/too small** a proportion of overheads to high volume products and **too great/too small** a proportion of overheads to low volume products.

2 *Fill in the blanks.*

The major ideas behind ABC are as follows.

(a) Activities cause ....

(b) Producing products creates demand for the ....

(c) Costs are assigned to a product on the basis of the product's consumption of the ....

3 Match the most appropriate cost driver to each cost.

Costs	*Cost driver*
(a) Set-up costs	Number of machine hours
(b) Short-run variable costs	Number of production runs
(c) Materials handling and despatch	Number of orders executed

4 When ABC is used, some measure of (arbitrary) cost apportionment may still be required at the cost pooling stage for items like rent, rates and building depreciation. True or false?

5 *Choose the correct words from those highlighted.*

Overheads that support the upkeep of the factory and the managerial infrastructure that makes production possible are associated with **unit related/batch related/product sustaining/facility sustaining** activities.

6 The cost of inspecting a product for quality is a value-added cost. *True or false?*

7 *Which of the following is/are correct?*

(a) Cost of conformance = cost of prevention + cost of internal failure
(b) Cost of conformance = cost of internal failure + cost of external failure
(c) Cost of non-conformance = cost of internal failure + cost of external failure
(d) Cost of conformance = cost of appraisal + cost of prevention
(e) Cost of non-conformance = cost of prevention + cost of appraisal
(f) Cost of non-conformance = cost of appraisal + cost of external failure

8 *Match the cost to the correct cost category.*

Costs

(a) Administration of quality control
(b) Product liability costs
(c) Acceptance testing
(d) Losses due to lower selling prices for sub-quality goods

Cost categories

- Prevention costs
- Appraisal costs
- Internal failure costs
- External failure costs

9 *Match the terms to the correct definitions.*

Terms
Cost value
Exchange value
Use value
Esteem value

Definitions

(a) The prestige the customer attaches to the product
(b) The market value of the product
(c) What the product does
(d) The cost of producing and selling the product

10 *Choose the correct word from those highlighted.*

Explicit/implicit costs of quality are not recorded in accounting records.

11 *Fill in the blanks.*

There are two basic principles of TQM.

....

....

12 The aim of TQM is for a process to go out of control less than 10% of the time. *True or false?*

Answers to quick quiz

1 Too great to high volume
Too small to low volume

2 (a) Costs
(b) Activities
(c) Activities

3 (a) Number of production runs
(b) Number of machine hours
(c) Number of orders executed

4 True

5 facility sustaining

6 False

7 (c) and (d) are correct.

8 (a) Prevention costs
(b) External failure costs
(c) Appraisal costs
(d) Internal failure costs

9

Cost value	(d)
Exchange value	(b)
Use value	(c)
Esteem value	(a)

10 Implicit

11 Get it right, first time
Continuous improvement

12 False

ASSESSMENT KIT ACTIVITIES

The following activities in the BPP Assessment Kit for Units 8 & 9 include topics covered in this chapter.

Activities 52 to 56
Lecturers' practice activities 28 and 29

Activity checklist

This checklist shows which performance criteria, range statement or knowledge and understanding point is covered by each activity in this chapter. Tick off each activity as you complete it.

Activity		
15.1	☐	This activity deals with Performance Criteria 8.1E regarding analysis of the effect of organisational accounting policies on reported costs, and Unit 8 Knowledge & Understanding point (9): cost management (activity based costing).
15.2	☐	This activity deals with Performance Criteria 8.1E regarding analysis of the effect of organisational accounting policies on reported costs, and Unit 8 Knowledge & Understanding point (9): cost management (activity based costing).
15.3	☐	This activity deals with Performance Criteria 8.2C regarding the identification of ways to enhance value.
15.4	☐	This activity deals with Unit 8 Knowledge & Understanding point (9): cost management (principles of Total Quality Management).
15.5	☐	This activity deals with Unit 8 Knowledge & Understanding point (9): cost management (principles of Total Quality Management (including cost of quality)).
15.6	☐	This activity deals with Performance Criteria 8.2C regarding the identification of ways to reduce costs and enhance value, and Range Statement 8.2: recommendations (efficiencies; modifications to work processes).
15.7	☐	This activity deals with Performance Criteria 8.2C regarding the identification of ways to reduce costs and enhance value.
15.8	☐	This activity deals with Performance Criteria 8.2C regarding the identification of ways to reduce costs and enhance value and Performance Criteria 8.2E regarding the making of specific recommendations to management in a clear and appropriate form.

Answers to activities

Chapter 1

Answer 1.1

Productivity can be measured by looking at average services performed per employee.

	Budget	*Actual*	*Rise*
Service M	175 (W)	195	+11.4%
Service N	157.5	185	+17.5%
Service P	210	358.75	+70.8%

Working

For example, 875/5 = 175

What comments would you make about the results of these calculations? How well is the business doing?

Answer 1.2

(a) The workplace has been effective because it met (and exceeded) the target of 12,400 units.

(b) Old productivity = 12,000/24 = 500 units per employee

Productivity in period 6 = 12,460/25 = 498.4 units per employee

There has been a fall in productivity, so the bonuses should not be paid. Note, however, that production has increased by over 3% $(((12{,}460 - 12{,}000)/12{,}000) \times 100\%)$

(c) We can measure efficiency as (profit/costs) × 100%

Old profit	= £(600,000 – 360,000) = £240,000
New revenue	= 12,460 × £49 = £610,540
New profit	= £(610, 540 – 373,800) = £236,740
Old efficiency	= (240,000/360,000) × 100% = 67%
New efficiency	= (236,740/373,800) × 100% = 63%

Efficiency has fallen.

Answer 1.3

Here are some examples.

Productivity Number of orders per man day
Telephone calls per telemarketing man day
Sales (£) per man day
Sales (£) or number of orders per £ of labour

Efficiency Profit per £ of labour; Profit per man day
Profit per £ of sales; Profit per telephone call

Effectiveness Actual orders as a % of target orders

Chapter 2

Answer 2.1

Items (a) and (b) are direct labour costs of the items produced in the 42 hours worked in week 5.

Overtime premium, item (c), is usually regarded as an overhead expense, because it is 'unfair' to charge the items produced in overtime hours with the premium. Why should an item made in overtime be more costly just because, by chance, it was made after the employee normally clocks off for the day?

Group bonus scheme payments (d) are usually overhead costs, because they cannot normally be traced directly to individual products or jobs.

In this example, there were £168 in direct costs and £36 in indirect costs.

Answer 2.2

- A percentage of direct materials cost
- A percentage of direct labour cost
- A percentage of prime cost
- A rate per machine hour
- A rate per direct labour hour
- A rate per unit
- A percentage of factory cost (for administration overhead)
- A percentage of sales or factory cost (for selling and distribution overhead)

Answer 2.3

(a) Hourly overhead absorption rate for department A = £24,000 ÷ 10,000 = £2.40
Hourly overhead absorption rate for department B = £21,000 ÷ 30,000 = £0.70

(b)

					£
Materials					100.00
Direct labour	(A)		2	× £10	20.00
	(B)		12	× £5	60.00
Overhead (machine hours)		(A)	20	× £2.40 (from (a))	48.00
Overhead (labour hours)		(B)	12	× £0.70 (from (a))	8.40
					236.40

(c)

	Direct cost £	*Indirect cost* £	*Total wages* £
Active hours			
20 at basic rate (× £5)	100		100
Overtime premium (2 × £2.50)		5	5
Idle time (22 hours × £5)		110	110
	100	115	215

Answer 2.4

Fixed overhead absorption rate = £100,000/5,000 = £20 per unit
Fixed overhead absorbed into production = £20 × 5,300 = £106,000

Answer 2.5

The overhead recovery rate is £180,000/45,000 = £4 per machine hour.

		£
(a)	Actual overhead	170,000
	Absorbed overhead (45,000 × £4)	180,000
	Over-absorbed overhead	10,000

The reason for the over-absorption is that although the actual and budgeted machine hours are the same, actual overheads cost less than expected.

		£
(b)	Actual overhead	180,000
	Absorbed overhead (40,000 × £4)	160,000
	Under-absorbed overhead	20,000

The reason for the under-absorption is that although budgeted and actual overhead costs were the same, fewer machine hours were worked than expected.

		£
(c)	Actual overhead	170,000
	Absorbed overhead (40,000 × £4)	160,000
	Under-absorbed overhead	10,000

The reason for the under-absorption is a combination of the reasons in (a) and (b).

Answer 2.6

Overhead absorbed = £23,840

Overhead absorption rate (OAR) = £10

∴ Actual activity level = £23,840 ÷ £10 = 2,384 labour hours.

Under-absorbed overhead = OAR × (budgeted activity level – actual activity level)

∴ £1,790 = £10 × (budgeted activity level – 2,384)

∴ 179 + 2,384 = budgeted activity level

∴ 2,563 labour hours = budgeted activity level

Answer 2.7

Overhead absorption rate = £25,000/5,000 = £5 per unit

	£
Charged to cost of sales = number of units sold (5,500) × £5	27,500
Carried forward in closing stock = (6,000 – 5,500) × £5	2,500
Over-absorbed overhead = £(25,000 – 2,500 – 27,500)	
or = (5,000 – 6,000) × £5	(5,000)
	25,000

Answer 2.8

	£	£
Selling price per unit		1009.99
Marginal cost per unit		
Direct material	320	
Direct labour	192	
Variable production overhead	132	
		644.00
Contribution per unit		365.99

We do *not* include absorbed fixed overheads in the calculation of marginal cost per unit and contribution per unit.

Answer 2.9

	(a) *15,000 Deltas*		*(b)* *20,000 Deltas*	
	£	£	£	£
Sales (at £10)		150,000		200,000
Opening stock	–		–	
Variable production cost	120,000		120,000	
	120,000		120,000	
Less value of closing stock (at marginal cost)	30,000		–	
Variable cost of sales		90,000		120,000
Contribution		60,000		80,000
Less fixed costs		45,000		45,000
Profit/(loss)		15,000		35,000
Profit (loss) per unit		£1		£1.75
Contribution per unit		£4		£4

Answer 2.10

Absorption costing profit statement

	£	£
Revenue		64,000
Cost of production		
Material and labour (£7.50 × 4,000)	30,000	
Absorbed fixed overhead (4,000 × £5*)	20,000	
Cost of sales	50,000	
Under-absorbed overhead (£(28,000 – 20,000))	8,000	
Total		58,000
Profit		6,000

*£25,000/5,000

Answer 2.11

Absorption costing profit statement

	£	£
Revenue		64,000
Cost of production		
Material and labour (£7.50 × 5,000)	37,500	
Absorbed fixed overhead (5,000 × £5)	25,000	
	62,500	
Less closing stock (1,000 × £(7.50 + 5))	(12,500)	
Cost of sales	50,000	
Under-absorbed overhead (£(28,000 – 25,000))	3,000	
Total costs		53,000
Profit		11,000

Answer 2.12

Marginal costing profit statement

	£	£
Revenue		64,000
Variable cost of production		
Material and labour	37,500	
Less closing stock (1,000 × £7.50)	7,500	
Cost of sales		30,000
Contribution		34,000
Fixed costs		28,000
Profit		6,000

Chapter 3

Answer 3.1

- The staff in the sales department might deliberately distort the results of their investigation, perhaps understating the forecast so that they are more likely to achieve any sales target based on the forecast.
- The sales staff might only contact those customers with which they have a good relationship.
- The customers might give incorrect information.
- The customers might refuse to provide information unless given a discount, say.

Answer 3.2

The possibility of sampling error is particularly great with small samples because they are unlikely to accurately reflect the characteristics of the population being studied

For example, suppose the sales personnel of the organisation in Activity 3.1 were to contact only ten of the organisation's 500 customers, and those ten happened to be the customers to whom the highest volume of sales were made. If their expected demand levels were used as the basis for calculating an expected average demand per customer, the forecast average would be far greater than the actual average.

Answer 3.3

(a) The manufacturer could try to supply the coffee to a **random sample** of coffee drinkers, and then ask for their views. Such samples are taken in such a way that every member of the population (in this case, all coffee drinkers and perhaps all potential coffee drinkers) has an equal chance of being selected for the sample. The main advantage of random sampling is that it allows mathematical analysis of the data to be carried out. The main disadvantage is that a random sample can be difficult and expensive to collect. The manufacturer may well find that it is impossible to compile a list of all coffee drinkers from which to select a sample.

(b) **Stratified sampling** may well be appropriate. The population would first be divided into groups, perhaps by age or by weekly coffee consumption, and then samples would be selected from each group (reflecting the proportion of the population in the group). The main advantage of stratified sampling is that it ensures that each group is represented in the sample. The main disadvantage is that preliminary work is needed to determine which groupings are likely to be useful and the proportion of the population in each group.

(c) **Cluster sampling** may well be a practical alternative, giving some of the benefits of both random sampling and stratified sampling. The population could be divided geographically into those who drink coffee at home in different regions of the country and those who purchase cups of coffee from coffee houses and/or cafes within these regions. A sample of regions could be selected, and a sample of roads (for home coffee drinkers) and coffee houses/cafes in each selected region could be chosen. All consumers in the chosen roads and coffee houses/ cafes would then form the sample. The main advantage of cluster sampling is its relative cheapness. The main disadvantage is that the sample obtained will not be truly random, so some forms of statistical analysis will not be possible.

(d) **Quota sampling** has the advantage of being even cheaper than cluster sampling, but the disadvantage of producing a sample which is even further from being random. Researchers would simply visit a selection of homes and coffee houses/cafes and interview the first coffee drinkers they met until they had fulfilled some quota (say ten men and ten women).

Answer 3.4

Reducing non-response for interviews

- The success of interviews relies on the quality of interaction between respondent and interviewer. Interviewers who appear/sound pleasant, interesting and interested in the respondent and who convincingly persuade the respondent that his/her views are important will produce lower rates of refusal.
- If someone is 'not at home' the interviewer should call back.
- Respondents can be promised gifts/monetary reward.

Reducing non-response for postal questionnaires

- Contact respondents prior to despatching the questionnaire to ask whether they would be prepared to aid the study by completing a questionnaire.
- Include a covering letter to explain why the data are being collected and to put the respondent in the appropriate frame of mind.
- Include a freepost/stamped addressed envelope for ease of reply.
- Provide a gift or monetary incentive upon questionnaire completion.
- Address the respondent by name.
- Use postal or telephone follow up reminders.
- Carefully select a target audience who have particular interest in the topic.

Answer 3.6

(a), (b) and (d)

Economic Trends and the **Singapore Business Times** are both sources of secondary external data. Historic expenditure data of canteen costs were not collected specifically for the preparation of forecasts, and are therefore also secondary data. Data collected through personal interview for a particular project are a primary source of data.

Answer 3.7

Some aspects of an organisation's external environment will be more important for the organisation than others. Just what the most important aspects are will vary from organisation to organisation.

- **Competitors**. (What competitors are doing, how successful they are and how much of a threat they are)

- **Suppliers**. (Suppliers and potential suppliers, their prices, product or service quality and delivery dates and so on)
- **Customers**. An organisation should always try to be aware of the needs of its customers, to identify changes in these needs, to recognise potential market segments, and to assess the size of a potential market. Customer awareness is vital for new product development and successful selling.
- **Legal changes**. Changes in the law might affect how an organisation operates, and any such changes should be monitored.
- **Political changes**. Some organisations are affected by national or local politics. The defence equipment industry is just one such example. If politics can be important, the organisation should try to monitor political decisions at both national and local level.
- **Financial and economic conditions**. Most organisations have to monitor developments in financial and economic conditions. For example, a large company's treasury department must be aware of current money market interest rates and foreign exchange rates.
- **Social changes**. Changes in the age structure of the population, or in social attitudes can affect demand for consumer goods, for example, over the long term.

An organisation should then establish the following.

- The most appropriate sources for obtaining this information
- The individuals or departments whose task it should be to gather and disseminate the information
- The form in which the information should be disseminated through the organisation

Sources of information include the following.

- Suppliers' price lists and brochures
- Published reports and accounts (of competitors, suppliers and business customers)
- Government reports (often, reports on specific topics)
- Government statistics
- External databases, provided by specialist organisations through a network such as Prestel

Answer 3.8

Primary data

Primary data is data collected first hand. The data is collected for a specific purpose and the collector is fully aware of both how it has been gathered and the subsequent processing it has undergone. As a result the accuracy, relevance, limitations or inadequacies of the data are fully understood by the investigator and there can be control over the method of collection. Primary data is also more likely to be more up to date than secondary data. The disadvantage of primary data is that it can be very expensive to acquire because a substantial labour force is usually required to collect it. Only organisations with large amounts of money, such as the government or big companies, are usually capable of collecting primary data.

Retailers will be interested in the items they have sold over a period (day, week, month, year) to enable them to reorder items of stock as stock levels become low. Data on daily/weekly sales collected by the retailer is primary data. A public transport organisation may collect data on how its customers would react to a fare increase following an increase in the frequency of a service. The data collected directly from the customers would be primary data.

Secondary data

Secondary data is data which has already been collected elsewhere, for some other purpose, but which can be used or adapted for a current enquiry. There are two obvious advantages to using secondary data. Time and effort does not have to be expended in collecting the data and hence it is cheaper than primary data. Secondary data is also often far more complex than an ordinary organisation could hope to collect as primary data (having more than likely been collected by the government or another large organisation who have the appropriate resources).

There are, however, disadvantages to using secondary data.

- The data may not always be up to date for the required purpose. Either the data was collected quite some time ago or the data takes considerable time to collect, process, print and distribute.
- The data may not be entirely suitable for the purpose it is being used for.
- The investigator will not be aware of the data collection methods used. Although it can be assumed valid techniques are used to collect data for published official statistics, other data may have been collected from too small a sample or from using a poorly designed questionnaire. The data may have been analysed in a particular way so as to make a particular point.
- Some terms used in the data and its subsequent analysis may be ambiguous. Employees, for example, may refer to full-time employees or full-time and part-time employees, or full-time equivalent employees.
- Data may have been collected from a number of different sources and hence conclusions drawn from badly 'mixed' data could be invalid.
- Published data may contain errors due to typing or printing.

A prime example of secondary data used by business is the large amount of official statistics published by the Government. The Index of Average Earnings, for example, is used in wage negotiations. A mail order firm may use the results of a survey undertaken by a credit card company (which analyses the salary and occupation of its customers) for advertising purposes. New pay structures could be devised by an organisation by using information on job times and skills breakdowns which they had originally compiled for job costing purposes.

Chapter 4

Answer 4.1

(a) $\frac{72j+16}{16} = 10$

$16 \times \frac{72j+16}{16} = 10 \times 16$ — $\times$ both sides by 16

$72j + 16 = 160$

$72j + 16 - 16 = 160 - 16$ — deduct 16 from both sides

$72j = 144$

$j = 2$

(b) Kgs purchased × cost per kg = total cost
Kgs purchased × £16.50 = £29,700
(Kgs purchased × £16.50)/£16.50 = £29,700/£16.50 — divide both sides by £16.50
Kgs purchased = 1,800

Answers 4.2 and 4.3

Secondary statistics are supporting figures that are supplementary, and which clarify or amplify the main pieces of information. A major example of secondary statistics is percentages.

We can show either of the following.

(a) The percentage of the total sales in each region of each product
(b) The percentage of the total sales of each product made in each region

Approach (a)

Analysis of sales

	Region							
Products	*A*		*B*		*C*		*Total*	
	£m	%	£m	%	£m	%	£m	%
Alpha	0.5	8.3	0.5	16.7	0.1**	10	1.1	11
Beta	0.5*	8.3	0.4*	13.3	0.2**	20	1.1	11
Gamma	1.5	25.0	1.1	36.7	0.3**	30	2.9	29
Delta	3.5	58.4	1.0	33.3	0.4**	40	4.9*	49
Total	6.0	100.0	3.0	100.0	1.0	100	10.0	100

* Balancing figure to make up the column total
** Balancing figure then needed to make up the row total

Approach (b)

Analysis of sales

	Products									
Regions	*Alpha*		*Beta*		*Gamma*		*Delta*		*Total*	
	£m	%	£m	%	£m	%	£m	%	£m	%
A	0.5	0.455	0.5	0.454	1.5	0.517	3.5	0.714	6.0	60
B	0.5	0.455	0.4	0.364	1.1	0.379	1.0	0.204	3.0	30
C	0.1	0.090	0.2	0.182	0.3	0.104	0.4	0.082	1.0	10
	1.1	1.000	1.1	1.000	2.9	1.000	4.9	1.000	10.0	100

Answer 4.4

(a)

	Sales (thousands)			
Company	*1960*	*1970*	*1980*	*1990*
Accurate Vision Ltd	1,810	3,248	5,742	4,932
Best View Ltd	2,114	1,288	3,038	3,138
Clear Cut Ltd	448	1,618	2,228	1,506
Others	874	676	1,646	618
Total	5,246	6,830	12,654	10,194

(b)

	Sales (percentages)			
Company	*1960*	*1970*	*1980*	*1990*
Accurate Vision Ltd	34.5	47.6	45.4	48.4
Best View Ltd	40.3	18.8	24.0	30.8
Clear Cut Ltd	8.5	23.7	17.6	14.8
Others	16.7	9.9	13.0	6.0
Total	100.0	100.0	100.0	100.0

(c) Accurate Vision Ltd was the second largest producer in 1960, but was the market leader in 1970, 1980 and 1990, with an apparently secure grip on nearly half the market.

Best View Ltd's share of the market dropped sharply between 1960 and 1970, but the company has since been steadily recovering market share.

Clear Cut Ltd did very well between 1960 and 1970, but has not been able to sustain its growth rate, and has lost market share since 1970.

Other companies have maintained a small and variable market share. There is no sign of a serious challenge to the three main companies.

Answer 4.5

We have chosen to use a pie chart as this format enables the relative sizes of the components to be displayed. You might have used some form of bar chart.

To convert the components into degrees of a circle, we can use either the percentage figures or the actual cost figures.

(a) Using the percentage figures, the total percentage is 100%, and the total number of degrees in a circle is 360°. To convert from one to the other, we multiply each percentage value by 360°/100% = 3.6.

	Standard product		*Deluxe product*	
	%	Degrees	%	Degrees
Wood	35	126	20	72
Metal	15	54	50	180
Plastic	45	162	20	72
Glass	5	18	10	36
	100	360	100	360

(b) Using the actual cost figures, we would multiply each cost by (number of degrees/total cost), which is 360/2,000= 0.18 for product 1, and 360/2,500= 0.144 for product 2.

	Standard product		*Deluxe product*	
	£'000	Degrees	£'000	Degrees
Wood	700	126	500	72
Metal	300	54	1,250	180
Plastic	900	162	500	72
Glass	100	18	250	36
	2,000	360	2,500	360

A pie chart could be drawn for each product, as follows. A protractor is used to measure the degrees accurately to obtain the correct sector sizes.

Standard product

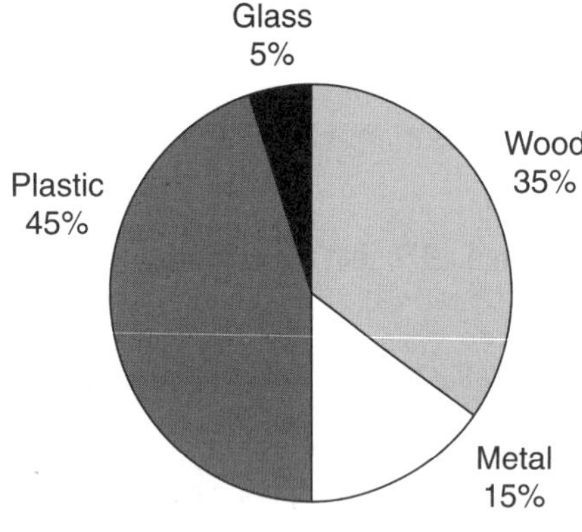

Deluxe product

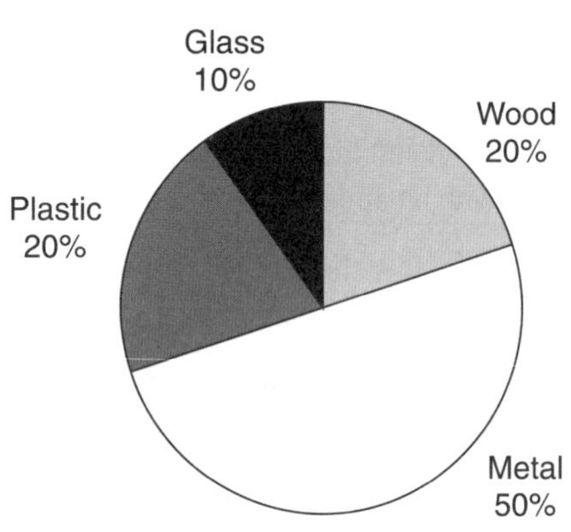

Answer 4.6

(a)

Product	*Year 1*	*Year 2*	*Year 3*
	£'000	£'000	£'000
A	3,579	2,961	2,192
K	857	893	917
E	62	59	70
	4,498	3,913	3,179

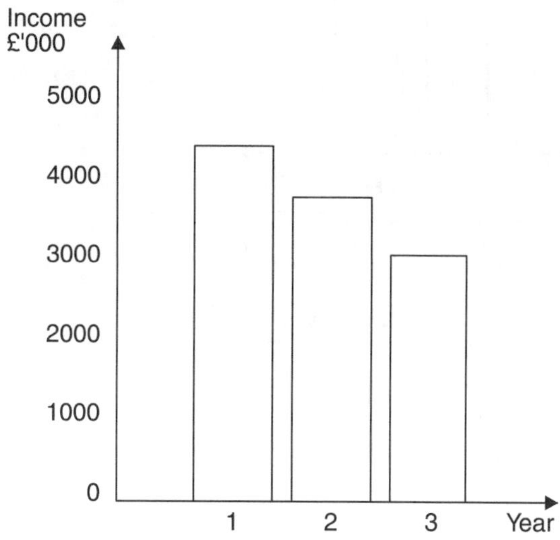

(b)

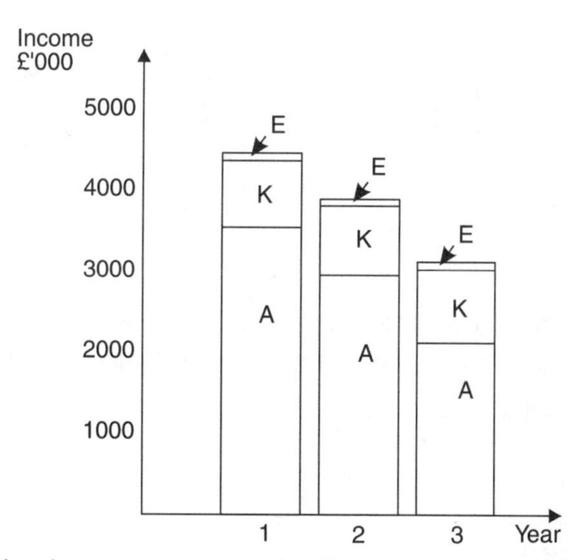

(c)

Product	*Year 1*		*Year 2*		*Year 3*	
	£'000	%	£'000	%	£'000	%
A	3,579	80	2,961	76	2,192	69
K	857	19	893	23	917	29
E	62	1	59	1	70	2
	4,498	100	3,913	100	3,179	100

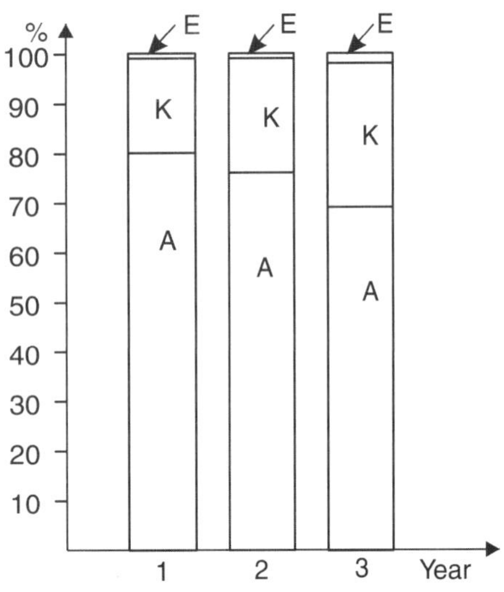

(d)

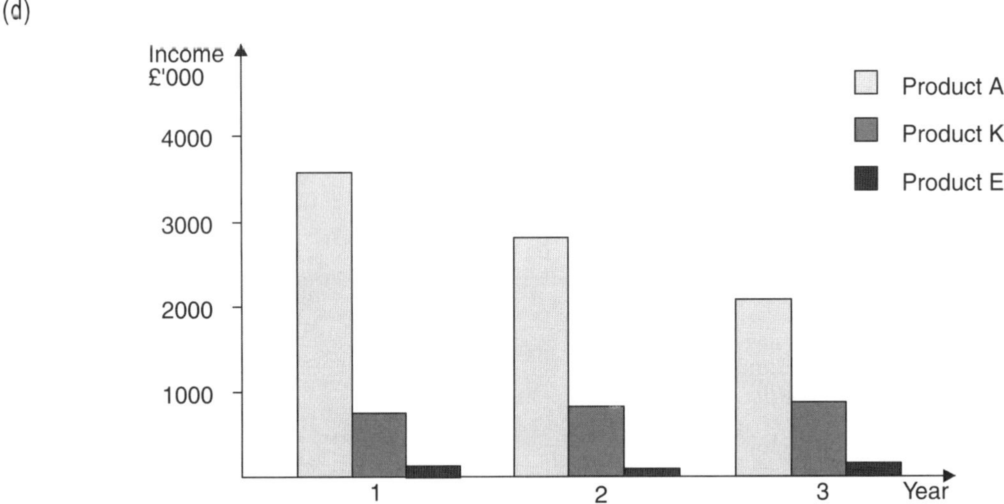

Answer 4.7

Let us first look at the overall opinions of the 200 people surveyed regarding both British and non-British motorbikes. For British motorbikes, the percentages who agreed with each of the four statements made were as follows.

British motorbikes are:	% Agree
easy to get serviced	55.5
economical	68.0
reliable	62.0
comfortable	65.0

It can be seen that the overall percentages who were happy about the economy, reliability and comfort of British motorbikes were more or less the same, but rather fewer people agreed that servicing was easy.

Turning to non-British motorbikes, the overall opinions expressed were as follows.

Non-British motorbikes are:	% Agree
easy to get serviced	46.0
economical	72.0
reliable	79.5
comfortable	46.5

The picture here is somewhat different in that about the same proportion (46%) agreed that the motorbikes were easy to get serviced and that they were comfortable whereas a markedly higher proportion (about 75%) were happy with economy and reliability.

Comparing British and non-British motorbikes overall, the picture can be represented by the following bar chart.

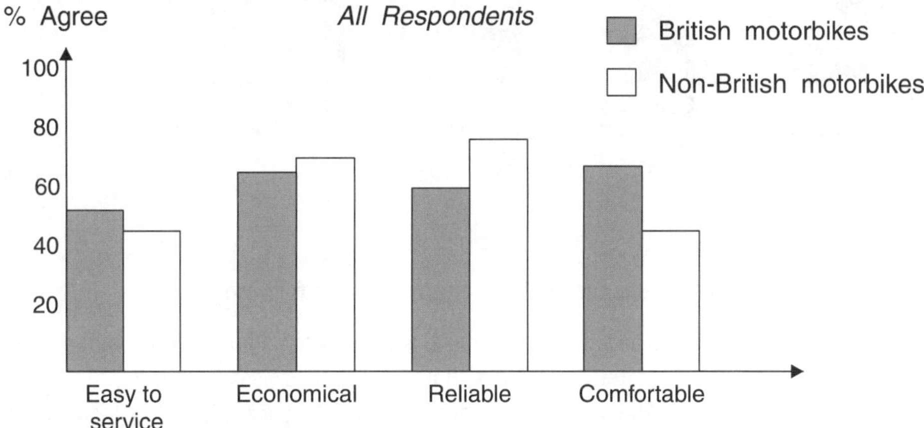

There is not much difference in terms of both ease of servicing and economy, but non-British motorbikes seem to score more highly for reliability whereas British motorbikes seem to be more acceptable as regards comfort.

Looking more closely at the data, it is possible to contrast the opinions of those respondents who bought British motorbikes with those who bought non-British motorbikes. For the purchasers of British motorbikes, their attitudes as regards British and non-British motorbikes are represented in the following bar chart.

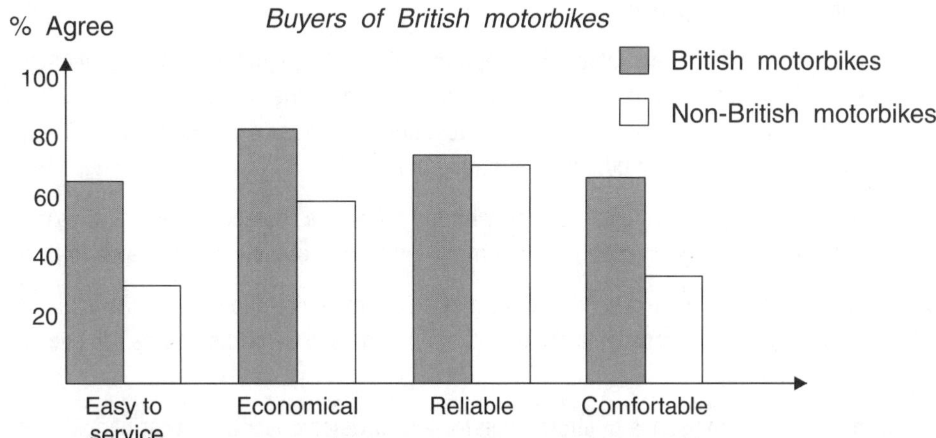

As would be expected, the attitudes of this group are biased towards British motorbikes, and the only factor where British and non-British motorbikes are at all close is reliability. When one looks at the purchasers of non-British motorbikes, the same sort of picture emerges. As can be seen from the following bar chart, buyers of non-British

motorbikes favour non-British motorbikes for all features except comfort where, as with reliability in the previous case, there is very little to choose between British and non-British motorbikes.

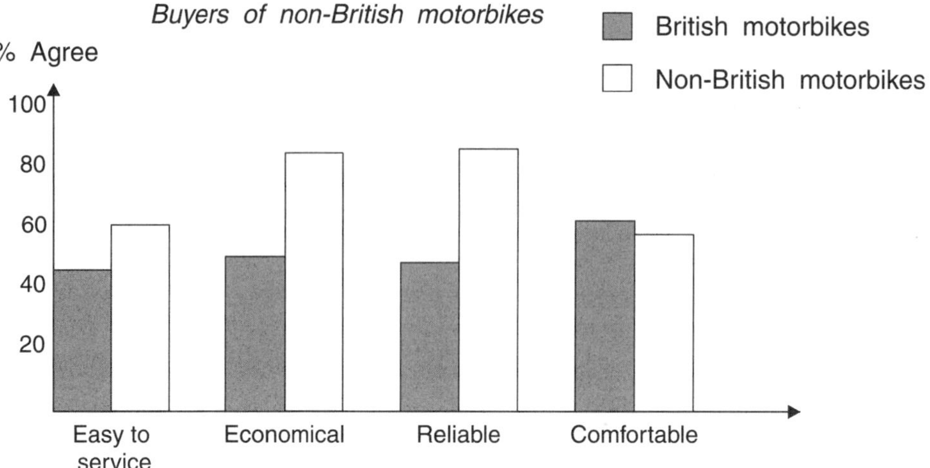

Answer 4.8

(a) The graph is extremely unclear and could be improved in the following ways.

- The axes are not labelled. The horizontal axis (the x axis) should represent the independent variable, being time in this case. So it should be labelled Year 1, Year 2, ... Year 6. Similarly the vertical axis (the y axis) should represent the dependent variable, being profits in this case.
- An indication should be given of whether the profits have been adjusted in any way. In particular, it would be useful to have profit figures adjusted for inflation, so that the changes in profits shown by the graph are all changes in real terms.
- The graph has no heading. Every graph should have a title explaining what variables are being displayed against each other. In the given case the heading could be 'Profits of divisions 1, 2, 3 and 4 during the period Year 1 to Year 6'.
- Crosses should be marked on the graph to indicate the points plotted. The given graph merely has smooth curves which presumably pass through where the crosses should be. Marking the actual points will help the reader of the graph to judge how much estimation has been carried out in trying to draw the best curves through the points.
- A graph should not be overcrowded with too many lines. Graphs should always give a clear, neat impression. The given graph has too many lines on it for a clear impression to be given.
- If the data to be plotted is derived from calculations, there should be a neat table showing the actual figures accompanying the graph, stating the source of the figures. No such information is given here.

(b) We wish to show a time series of information for four divisions over a six-year period. Possible methods of presenting the data are pie charts and component bar charts. You could also use a simple historigram, a method of data presentation that we will encounter in the next chapter.

On balance, a vertical component bar chart would seem to be the most suitable in this instance. This would show both how total profits (of all divisions together) have changed from year to year and the components of each year's total.

Answer 4.9

- Avoid 'jargon', overly technical terms and specialist knowledge the user may not share.
- Keep vocabulary, sentence and paragraph structures as simple as possible, for clarity (without patronising an intelligent user).
- Bear in mind the type and level of detail that will interest the user and be relevant to his/her purpose.
- In a business context, the user may range from senior manager to junior supervisor, to non-managerial employee (such as in the case of minutes of a meeting) to complete layman (customer, press and so on). Vocabulary, syntax and presentation, the amount of detail gone into, the technical matter included and the formality of the report structure should all be influenced by such concerns.

Answer 4.10

- Who is the user?
- What type of report will be most useful to him/her?
- What exactly does he/she need to know, and for what purpose?
- How much information is required, how quickly and at what cost?
- Do you need to give judgements, recommendations etc (or just information)?

Answer 4.11

This is one suggestion as to how the sentence could be rewritten.

'Despite thorough investigations it has been impossible to find an explanation for the differences that have been occurring between petty cash records and the petty cash float. It is clear the investigations should now be carried out at a higher level.'

Answer 4.12

(a) Increase = 395 – 370 = 25 index points
(b) % increase = ((395 – 370)/370) × 100% = 6.8%
(c) Price inflation = increase in RPI = 6.8%

Answer 4.13

Planned cost = 100/2 = £50, actual cost = 100/2.2 = £45.45 and so the difference is £4.55

Chapter 5

Answer 5.1

Here are some suggestions.

- Sales of ice cream will be higher in summer than in winter, and sales of overcoats will be higher in autumn than in spring.
- Shops might expect higher sales shortly before Christmas, or in their winter and summer sales.
- Sales might be higher on Friday and Saturday than on Monday.
- The telephone network may be heavily used at certain times of the day (such as mid-morning and mid-afternoon) and much less used at other times (such as in the middle of the night).

Answer 5.2

(a) Cyclical variations
(b) Seasonal variations (August and February sales higher than sales in other months)
(c) Random variations (huge decrease after glass found)
(d) Seasonal variations (sales very high towards Christmas)
(e) Increasing trend
(f) Decreasing trend

Answer 5.4

The trend in sales is upward.

Answer 5.5

Quarter	*1*	*2*	*3*	*4*
	%	%	%	%
Variation, Year 1	*95.6	102.7	105.3	91.4
Variation, Year 2	101.0	103.9	107.7	87.5
Average variation	98.3	103.3	106.5	89.5
Adjustment	0.6	0.6	0.6	0.6
Adjusted average variation	98.9	103.9	107.1	90.1

* (350/366) × 100%

Answer 5.6

Week	*Day*	*Data* £'000	*7-day total* £'000	*Trend* £'000	*Daily variation* £'000
1	S	13			
	M	5			
	T	7			
	W	9	82	11.71	− 2.71
	T	11	83	11.86	− 0.86
	F	14	83	11.86	+ 2.14
	S	23	85	12.14	+ 10.86
2	S	14	86	12.29	+ 1.71
	M	5	86	12.29	− 7.29
	T	9	88	12.57	− 3.57
	W	10	90	12.86	− 2.86
	T	11	91	13.00	− 2.00
	F	16	92	13.14	+ 2.86
	S	25	91	13.00	+ 12.00
3	S	15	93	13.29	+ 1.71
	M	6	95	13.57	− 7.57
	T	8	96	13.71	− 5.71
	W	12	98	14.00	− 2.00
	T	13			
	F	17			
	S	27			

Calculation of variation factors

Week	*Sun*	*Mon*	*Tues*	*Wed*	*Thurs*	*Fri*	*Sat*	*Total*
1				−2.71	−0.86	+2.14	+10.86	
2	+1.71	−7.29	−3.57	−2.86	−2.00	+2.86	+12.00	
3	+1.71	−7.57	−5.71	−2.00				
	+3.42	−14.86	−9.28	−7.57	−2.86	+5.00	+22.86	
Average	+1.71	−7.43	−4.64	−2.52	−1.43	+2.50	+11.43	−0.38
	+0.05	+0.05	+0.05	+0.05	+0.06	+0.06	+0.06	+0.38
	+1.76	−7.38	−4.59	−2.47	−1.37	+2.56	+11.49	0

Answer 5.7

T = £47,500

S = −13.3%

Forecast Y = £47,500 × (100 − 13.3)%
= £41,182.50

Answer 5.8

Month 8: Trend = 1,344 × 120% = 1,613
Month 9: Trend = 1,613 × 120% = 1,936
Month 10: Trend = 1,936 × 120% = 2,323
Month 11: Trend = 2,323 × 120% = 2,788

∴ Forecast month 9 = 1,936 units (no seasonal variation)
Forecast month 11 = 2,788 units × 110% = 3,067 units

Answer 5.9

(a) (i) Seasonal variations are regular patterns of fluctuations which occur over the year. For example, the seasonal variation for quarter 1 is minus 50 units. This indicates that the sales volume for quarter 1 is on average 50 units below the general trend in sales. Similarly the sales volume for quarter 2 is generally 22 units above the general trend

(ii) A trend line is the underlying direction in which a time series is moving. The trend is determined by removing the effect of seasonal variations from data, usually by using the technique of moving averages. In the data provided, the monthly sales volume appears to be increasing by an average of 45 units in each quarter, after eliminating the seasonal variations. This is the underlying trend in the data, which the analyst suggests should be used to project the sales data into the future. This is known as extrapolating the trend, that is, continuing its general direction as a basis for the sales forecast.

(b) **Working**

Calculating the average quarterly increase in the trend.

Year	*Quarter*	*Trend* Units	*Increase in trend* Units
3	4	3,407	
4	1	3,452	45
	2	3,496	44
	3	3,541	45
	4	3,587	46
			180

Average = 180/4 = 45 units

Sales volume forecast for year 5

Quarter	*1*	*2*	*3*	*4*
	Units	Units	Units	Units
Trend	3,632	3,677	3,722	3,767
Seasonal adjustment	−50	+22	+60	−32
Forecast	3,582	3,699	3,782	3,735

Answer 5.10

(a)

	Quarter 1	*Quarter 2*	*Quarter 3*	*Quarter 4*
	Units	Units	Units	Units
Actual sales volumes	420,000	450,000	475,000	475,000
Seasonal variation	+25,000	+15,000	0	–40,000
Deseasonalised sales volumes	395,000	435,000	475,000	515,000

(b) The deseasonalised sales volumes (trend) show an increase of 40,000 units per quarter.

	Quarter 1	*Quarter 2*	*Quarter 3*	*Quarter 4*
	Units	Units	Units	Units
Trend	555,000 (W1)	595,000 (W2)	635,000 (W3)	675,000 (W4)
Seasonal variations	+25,000	+15,000	0	–40,000
Forecast sales volumes	580,000	610,000	635,000	635,000

Workings

1 515,000 + 40,000
2 555,000 + 40,000
3 595,000 + 40,000
4 635,000 + 40,000

(c) MEMORANDUM

To: Marketing Assistant
From: Assistant to the Management Accountant
Date: XX June 20X8
Subject: **Time series analysis and forecasting**

Following our meeting yesterday, at which you expressed concern over your level of understanding of time series analysis and forecasting, I set out below explanations of some of the principal terms used in preparing sales forecasts and analysing sales trends and the role of these concepts in analysing a time series and preparing forecasts.

(i) **Explanation of terminology**

Seasonal variations are short-term fluctuations in sales around the trend in sales, due to different circumstances which affect sales at different times of the year. For example, a quarter 2 seasonal variation of 15,000 units for product P means that in quarter 2 sales volumes are 15,000 units higher than the underlying trend in sales whereas in quarter 4 sales volumes are 40,000 units below the underlying trend in sales. Of course, for other organisations, seasonal variations occur with the days of the week, weeks of the month and so on. A supermarket, for example, is likely to experience higher sales on a Saturday than a Monday.

Data from which the seasonal variations have been removed is termed **deseasonalised (seasonally-adjusted) data** and represents the trend, the underlying long-term movement in the values of the data recorded. The deseasonalised sales volumes for product P show an upward trend, the rate of increase being 40,000 units per quarter. When just one year's actual data is viewed in isolation, the seasonal variations hide this upward trend. Before seasonally adjusting the data there appears to be a decreasing rate of growth in sales volumes.

(ii) **The role of seasonal variations and deseasonalised data in time series analysis and forecasting**

Forecasts using seasonal variations and deseasonalised data rely on one major assumption: that the trend will continue in the future, outside the time period for which actual data is available. There are various methods of extrapolating (projecting) the trend into the future. For the purposes of project P we can assume that the trend in sales volume will be an increase of 40,000 units per quarter and therefore for every quarter after that for which we have data (quarter 4 of last year) we add 40,000 to the deseasonalised data value for quarter 4 to determine the trend value for the future quarter. We then adjust this trend value by the appropriate seasonal variation (upward for a positive variation, downward for a negative variation) to give us the actual forecast.

I hope this information is useful. If I can be of any further assistance please do not hesitate to contact me.

Answer 5.11

x = 0 corresponds to Year 0 quarter 1 and so x = 23 corresponds to Year 5 quarter 4.
Trend sales level = 300 – (4.7 × 23) = 191.9 ie 191,900 units
Seasonally-adjusted sales level = 191.9 + 15 = 206.9 ie 206,900 units

Answer 5.12

(a)

Quarter		*x value of quarter*	*Trend value* (100 + 5x)	*Seasonal variation* %	*Forecast* Units
Year 1	1st	20	200	0	200
	2nd	21	205	–20	164 (W1)
	3rd	22	210	+40	294 (W2)
	4th	23	215	–20	172

Workings

1 Forecast = 205 × ((100 – 20)/100)% = 164
2 Forecast = 210 × ((100+40)/100)% = 294

(b)

Quarter		*Forecast volume* Units	× *Price*	× *Inflation* %	=	*Forecast revenue* £
Year 1	1st	200	× 1,000	× 1.00		= 200,000
	2nd	164	× 1,000	× 1.02		= 167,280
	3rd	294	× 1,000	× 1.02^2		= 305,878
	4th	172	× 1,000	× 1.02^3		= 182,528

(c) Forecast = £305,878
Exchange rate = 9.77 Kr to £1
∴ Forecast in Kr = 305,878 × 9.77 = 2,988,428.1 Kr

(d) The forecasts in (b) assume that both the trend and pattern of seasonal variations will continue as in the past and that there will be no unforeseen events which might affect sales. They also assume that inflation will continue to run at 2% per quarter and that prices will continue to be revised in line with inflation. The underlying assumption is that the linear regression equation provided does describe the actual trend in sales.

(e) Assuming that the regression equation describes the actual trend, the trend in sales has risen by five units per quarter from a starting point of sales of 100 units at time 0. Sales show marked seasonal variation, peaking at 40% above the trend in each third quarter and having troughs of 20% below trend in the second and fourth quarters. First quarter sales are very close to the level of the trend.

Answer 5.13

Hours of study would be the independent variable and examination results the dependent variable.

Answer 5.14

Variable cost per unit = £(5,100 – 3,750)/4,500
= £0.30

Answer 5.15

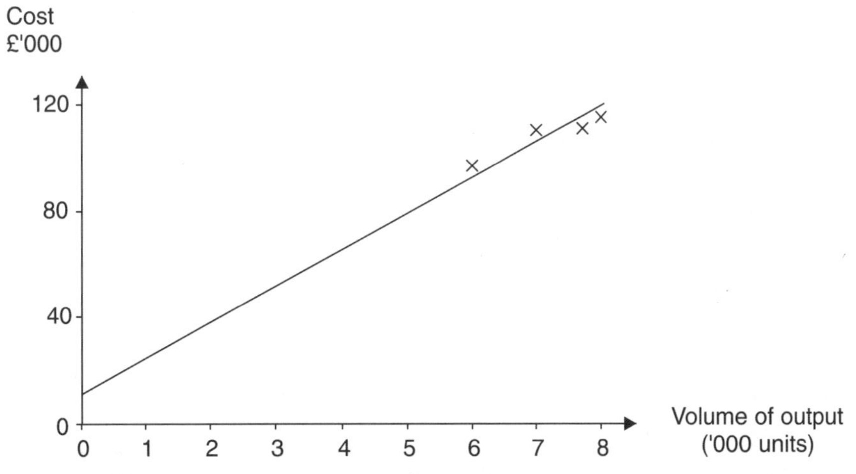

The point where the line cuts the vertical axis (approximately £12,000) is the fixed cost (the cost if there is no output). If we take the value of one of the plotted points which lies close to the line and deduct the fixed cost from the total cost, we can calculate the variable cost per unit.

Total cost for 8,000 units = £115,000
Variable cost for 8,000 units = £(115,000 – 12,000) = £103,000
Variable cost per unit = £103,000/8,000 = £12.875

∴ Forecast production cost of 6,900 units = £12,000 + (£12.875 × 6,900) = £100,837.50

Answer 5.16

	Units		£
High units	3,000	total cost =	220
Low units	2,100	total cost =	184
	900		36

Variable cost per unit = £36/900 = £0.04

Substituting:

	£
Total cost of 3,000 units	220
Variable costs (3,000 × £0.04)	120
Fixed cost	100

Total cost in July = £(100 + (2,750 × 0.04)) = £210

Answer 5.17

The disadvantage of the scattergraph method for estimating costs is that the line of best fit is drawn by visual judgement and so is only a subjective approximation of total cost.

The major drawback to the high-low method is that only two historical cost records from previous periods are used in the cost estimation. Unless these two records are a reliable indicator of costs throughout the relevant range of output, which is unlikely, only a 'loose approximation' of fixed and variable costs will be obtained.

Answer 5.18

y = 28 + 2.6x and if 17,000 units are produced, x = 17
∴ y = 28 + (2.6 × 17) = 72.2
∴ Budgeted costs = £72,200

Answer 5.19

Year	*Cost*		*Adjusted cost*
	£		£
0	145,000	× 100/100	145,000
1	179,200	× 100/112	160,000
2	209,100	× 100/123	170,000
3	201,600	× 100/144	140,000
4	248,000	× 100/160	155,000

Answer 5.20

Forecast at Year 0 price levels

	£
Fixed cost	80,000
Variable cost (85,000 × £1)	85,000
	165,000

Forecast at Year 5 price levels = £165,000 × $\frac{180}{100}$ = £297,000

Chapter 6

Answer 6.1

STANDARD COST CARD - PRODUCT JK66

Direct materials	*Cost*	*Requirement*	£	£
D1	£1 per kg	7 kgs	7	
D2	£2 per litre	4 litres	8	
D3	£3 per m	3 m	9	
				24
Direct labour				
Skilled	£10 per hour	8 hours	80	
Semi-skilled	£5 per hour	4 hours	20	
				100
Standard direct cost				124
Variable production overhead	£2.50 per hour	8 hours		20
Standard variable cost of production				144
Fixed production overhead	£6.25 (W) per hour	8 hours		50
Standard full production cost				194

Working

Overhead absorption rate = $\frac{£250,000}{5,000 \times 8}$ = £6.25 per skilled labour hour

Answer 6.2

- Deciding how to incorporate inflation into planned unit costs
- Agreeing on a performance standard (attainable or ideal)
- Deciding on the quality of materials to be used (a better quality of material will cost more, but perhaps reduce material wastage)
- Estimating materials prices where seasonal price variations or bulk purchase discounts may be significant
- Finding time to construct accurate standards as standard setting can be a time-consuming process
- Incurring the cost of setting up and maintaining a system for establishing standards
- Dealing with behavioural problems, managers responsible for achieving standards possibly resisting the use of a standard costing control system for fear of being blamed for any adverse variances

Answer 6.3

(a)

	£
Material (4m × £5)	20
Labour (3 hrs × £15)	45
	65

(b)

	£
Material	20
Labour	45
Fixed overhead (3 hrs × £10)	30
	95

Answer 6.4

(a) (i) **Marginal costing**

	Total cost of production		Unit cost
	£		£
Material (20,000 × £10)	200,000	(£200,000 ÷ 5,000)	40
Labour (15,000 × £8)	120,000	(£120,000 ÷ 5,000)	24
	320,000		64

(ii) **Absorption costing**

	Total cost of production		Unit cost
	£		£
Material (as above)	200,000		40
Labour (as above)	120,000		24
Fixed overheads	240,000	(£240,000 ÷ 5,000)	48
	560,000		112

Alternatively you could have added the fixed overhead components to the marginal costs calculated in (i).

(b) (i) **Marginal costing**

	Total cost of production		Unit cost
	£		£
Material	214,137	(£214,137 ÷ 5,150)	41.58
Labour	148,320	(£148,320 ÷ 5,150)	28.80
	362,457		70.38

(ii) **Absorption costing**

	Total cost of production	Unit cost
	£	£
Material (as above)	214,137	41.58
Labour (as above)	148,320	28.80
Fixed overheads (£48 × 5,150)	247,200	48.00
	609,657	118.38

Alternatively, you could have added the fixed overhead component over to the marginal costs.

Answer 6.5

Standard full cost of actual production = (4,200 × £12) = £50,400

Answer 6.6

(a)

Product	Standard hrs per unit	Budgeted production	Budgeted labour hrs
	Hrs	Units	Hrs
Harlequin	2	500	1,000
Joker	3	1,000	3,000
Jester	4	1,500	6,000
			10,000

(b) Absorption rate = budgeted expenditure/budgeted labour hours
= £600,000/10,000 = £60 per hr

(c) Budgeted labour hours for Harlequin = 1,000 hrs
∴ Budgeted overhead attributable to Harlequin = 1,000 × £60 = £60,000

(d) Actual absorption rate = actual expenditure/budgeted labour hours
= £780,000/10,000 = £78 per unit

Actual overhead attributable to Harlequin = 1,000 × £78 = £78,000

(e) Actual labour rate = £5,390/550 = £9.80 per hr

(f) Actual material cost = £22,050/1,260 = £17.50 per kg

(g) Standard absorption cost of actual production = standard absorption cost per unit × actual production

Standard absorption cost per unit

	£
Material (£20 × 5 kgs)	100
Labour (£10 × 2 hrs)	20
Fixed factory overhead (£60 × 2 hrs)	120
	240

∴ Standard absorption cost of actual production = £240 × 200 = £48,000

(h) Actual absorption cost of actual production = actual absorption cost per unit × actual production

Actual absorption cost per unit

	£
Material (£17.50 × 6.3 kgs*)	110.25
Labour (£9.80 × 2.75 hrs**)	26.95
Fixed factory overheads (£78 per hr × 2 hrs)	156.00
	293.20

Note how in this example the actual fixed factory overhead absorbed is based on actual absorption rate and standard hours.

* 1,260 kgs/200 units

** 550 hrs/200 units

Answer 6.7

Purchased material	Extract price variance	Material valued at standard cost	Extract usage variance	Standard cost of production
	£15		£40	
£1,025	£1,025	£1,040	£1,000	£1,000
(a)	(b)	(c)	(d)	(e)

(Not to scale)

Rectangles (a) and (b)

The standard cost of the materials purchased (520 kgs × £2) = £1,040 is greater than the actual cost and so the variance of £(1,040 – 1,025) = £15 is added to the 'actual rectangle' to give the 'standard rectangle'.

Rectangles (d) and (e)

Standard cost of the material that should have been used = 100 × £10 = £1,000, which is less than the standard cost of the material that was used.

(a) **The material price variance.** This is the difference between what 520 kgs should have cost (rectangle (c)) and what 520 kgs did cost (rectangle (a)).

	£
520 kgs of material should have cost (× £2)	1,040
but did cost	1,025
Material price variance	15 (F)

The variance is favourable because the material cost less than it should have.

(b) **The direct material usage variance.** This is the difference between how many kilograms of material should have been used to produce 100 units (rectangle (e)) and how many kilograms were used (rectangle (c)), valued at the standard cost per kilogram.

100 units should have used (×(£10 ÷ £2 per kg) ie 5kgs)	500 kgs
but did use	520 kgs
Usage variance in kgs	20 kgs (A)
× standard cost per kilogram	× £2
Usage variance in £	£40 (A)

The variance is adverse because more material than should have been used was used.

Answer 6.8

(a) % increase (1.7/(5.8 – 1.7)) × 100% = 41.5%

(b) Revised standard cost = £12.92 × 1.15 = £14.86

Answer 6.9

Hours paid for	Extract rate variance	Actual hours valued at standard rate	Extract efficiency variance	Standard cost of production
	£2,100		£400	
£17,500	£15,400	£15,400	£15,000	£15,000
(a)	(b)	(c)	(d)	(e)

(Not to scale)

(a) **The labour rate variance**. The rate variance is a comparison of what the hours paid should have cost and what they did cost.

	£
3,080 hours of grade Z labour should have cost (× £5)	15,400
but did cost	17,500
Labour rate variance	2,100 (A)

Actual cost is greater than standard cost. The variance is therefore adverse.

(b) **The labour efficiency variance**. The variance is calculated by taking the amount of output produced (1,500 units of product X) and comparing the time it should have taken to make them, with the actual time spent making them. Once again, the variance in hours is valued at the standard rate per labour hour.

1,500 units of product X should take (× 2 hrs)	3,000 hrs
but did take	3,080 hrs
Labour efficiency variance in hours	80 hrs (A)
× standard rate per hour	× £5
Labour efficiency variance in £	£400 (A)

Answer 6.10

Shaping department

	£
16,875 hours should have cost (× £4)	67,500
but did cost	70,875
Labour rate variance	3,375 (A)
7,500 units should have taken (× 2 hrs)	15,000 hrs
but did take	16,875 hrs
Variance in hours	1,875 hrs (A)
× standard rate per hour	× £4
Labour efficiency variance in £	£7,500 (A)

Moulding department

	£
15,750 hours should have cost (× £3.50)	55,125
but did cost	56,700
Labour rate variance	1,575 (A)
9,000 units should have taken (× 1.5 hrs)	13,500 hrs
but did take	15,750 hrs
Variance in hours	2,250 hrs
× standard rate per hour	× £3.50
Labour efficiency variance in £	£7,875 (A)

Answer 6.11

(a) **Price variance – M1**

	£
7,800 kgs should have cost (× £20)	156,000
but did cost	159,900
Price variance	3,900 (A)
Usage variance – M1	
800 units should have used (× 10 kgs)	8,000 kgs
but did use	7,800 kgs
Usage variance in kgs	200 kgs (F)
× standard cost per kilogram	× £20
Usage variance in £	£4,000 (F)

Price variance – M2

	£	
4,300 units should have cost (× £6)	25,800	
but did cost	23,650	
Price variance	2,150	(F)

Usage variance – M2

800 units should have used (× 5 l)	4,000	
but did use	4,300	
Usage variance in litres	300	(A)
× standard cost per litre	× £6	
Usage variance in £	£1,800	(A)

(b) **Labour rate variance**

	£	
4,200 hours should have cost (× £6)	25,200	
but did cost	24,150	
Rate variance	1,050	(F)

Labour efficiency variance

800 units should have taken (× 5 hrs)	4,000 hrs	
but did take	4,200 hrs	
Efficiency variance in hours	200 hrs	(A)
× standard rate per hour	× £6	
Efficiency variance in £	£1,200	(A)

(c) Overhead absorption rate per labour hour = £50/5 = £10

Budgeted expenditure = £50 × 900 = £45,000

Actual output in hours = 800 × 5 = 4,000

To plot a line which has a gradient the same as the overhead absorption rate per hour we need to know two points through which it passes. If 5,000 labour hours are worked, overhead absorbed = £10 × 5,000 = £50,000. If 4,000 labour hours are worked, overhead absorbed = £10 × 4,000 = £40,000. The line therefore passes through (4,000, 40,000) and (5,000, 50,000).

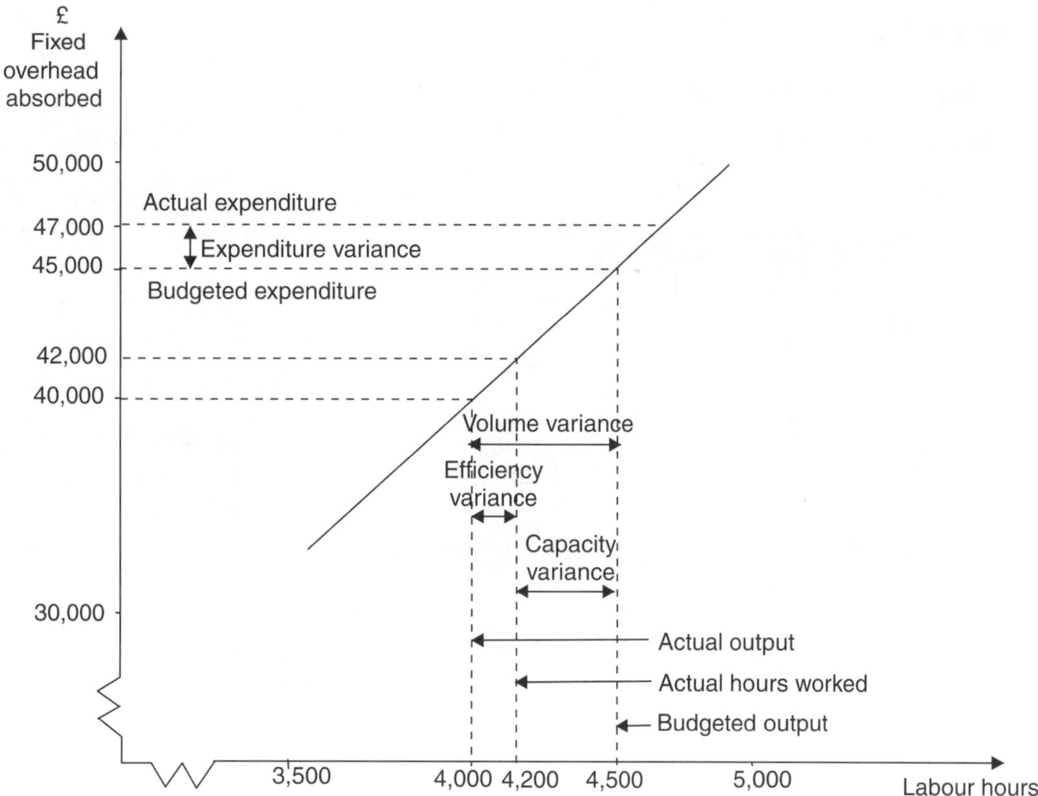

Expenditure variance = £45,000 – £47,000 = £2,000 (A). The variance is adverse because the actual expenditure is greater than the budgeted expenditure.

Volume variance is the difference between actual output and budgeted output. In monetary terms this is (800 – 900) units × £50 per unit = £5,000. The variance is adverse because the actual output is less than the budgeted output and so less overhead will be absorbed than expected.

Efficiency variance is the difference between actual output in standard hours and actual hours. In monetary terms this is (4,000 – 4,200) hrs × £10 per hour = £2,000. The variance is adverse because 4,200 hours of work should have been produced but only 4,000 were produced and so less overheads were absorbed than should have been.

Capacity variance is the difference between budgeted output and actual hours worked = (4,500 – 4,200) hrs × £10 per hour = £3,000. The variance is adverse because we would expect production levels to be less than budgeted if fewer hours are worked.

Answer 6.12

Overhead absorption rate per cup	= £75,000/50,000
	= £1.50
Overhead absorption rate per hour	= £75,000/(50,000 × 0.25)
	= £6
or	= £1.50/0.25
	= £6

Answer 6.13

Actual rate per hour = £900/200 = £4.50

Both variances are favourable.

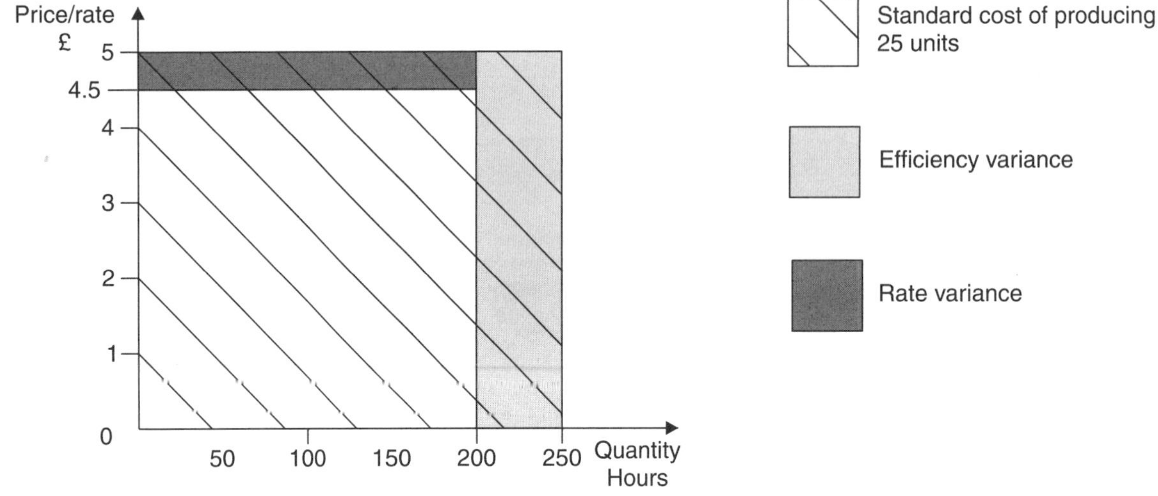

Answer 6.14

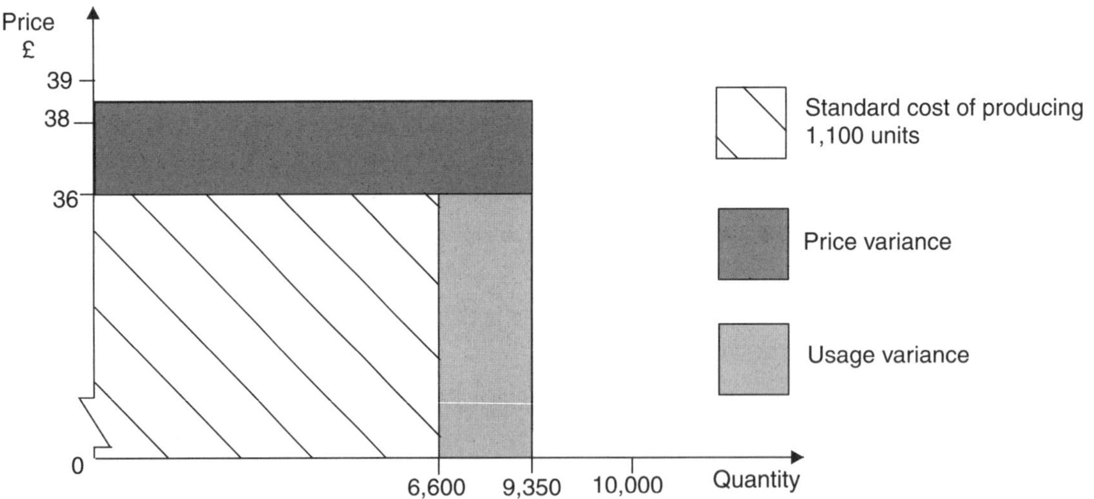

Standard cost per litre = £237,600/6,600 = £36
Actual cost per litre = £359,975/9,350 = £38.50
Both variances are adverse.

Note that we have not drawn this graph to scale.

Answer 6.15

Standard cost of production. This is clearly 3,000 units × standard cost of £33 per unit = £99,000.

(a) (i)

	£
9,750 units of leather were purchased and cost	45,400
but should cost (× £ 5)	48,750
Leather price variance	3,350 (F)

(ii)

3,200 shoes were made and used	9,750 units
but 3,200 units should use (× 3 units)	9,600 units
Usage variance in units	150 units (A)
× standard cost per unit of leather	× £5
Leather usage variance in £	£750 (A)

(iii) **Other materials**. We are not given a breakdown into units of material and price per unit of material, and so the only materials variance we can calculate is the total cost variance.

	£
3,200 shoes did cost	9,500 in other materials
but should cost (× £3)	9,600
Other materials cost variance	100 (F)

(b) (i)

	£
5,850 hours were paid for and cost	24,100
but should cost (× £4)	23,400
Direct labour rate variance	700 (A)

(ii)

3,200 shoes took	5,850 hours
but should take (× 1.5 hrs)	4,800 hours
Efficiency variance, in hours	1,050 hours (A)
× standard cost per labour hour	× £4
Direct labour efficiency variance in £	£4,200 (A)

(c)

	£
Actual fixed overheads absorbed (3,200 × £9)	28,800
Actual fixed overheads incurred	31,500
Total fixed overhead variance	2,700 (A)

(i) **Fixed overhead expenditure variance**. This is under absorption or over absorption of overhead because actual fixed overhead expenditure differed from budgeted expenditure.

	£
Budgeted fixed overhead (£9 × 3,000)	27,000
Actual fixed overhead	31,500
Expenditure variance	4,500 (A)

The expenditure variance also indicates over-spending above budget by £4,500, and a control report should attempt to pinpoint the source of this excessive overhead spending.

(ii) **Fixed overhead volume variance.** This is under-absorbed or over-absorbed overhead caused by a difference between actual and budgeted production volume.

Budgeted production volume of M25	3,000 units
Actual production volume	3,200 units
Total volume variance, in units or std hours	200 units (F)
× standard fixed overhead cost per unit	× £9
Total volume variance in £	£1,800 (F)

Producing a bigger quantity than budgeted will create over absorption of fixed overhead, and so is a favourable variance. The fixed overhead total volume variance of 200 units (F) means that the company produced 200 units of output more than budgeted in period 7. The reason for this must have been either working more efficiently than expected (an efficiency variance) or working more production hours than expected (a capacity variance).

(iii) **Fixed overhead efficiency variance.** This is the same variance in hours as the direct labour efficiency variance and is valued in £ at the standard fixed overhead rate per hour.

1,050 hrs (A) × £6 per hour	£6,300 (A)

(iv) **Fixed overhead capacity variance.** This is the difference between actual and budgeted production hours.

Budgeted production hours (3,000 units × 1.5 hrs)	4,500 hours
Actual production hours	5,850 hours
Volume capacity variance in hours	1,350 hours (F)
× standard fixed overhead rate per hour	× £6
Volume capacity variance in £	£8,100 (F)

The capacity and efficiency variances add up to the total volume variance of £1,800(F).

The variances can now be summarised in a reconciliation statement.

SURE FIRE SHOES LTD
RECONCILIATION STATEMENT FOR PERIOD 7

	£	£	£
Standard cost of production (3,200 × £33)			105,600
Variances	(F)	(A)	
Leather: price	3,350		
usage		750	
Other materials	100		
Direct labour: rate		700	
efficiency		4,200	
Fixed overhead expenditure		4,500	
Fixed overhead efficiency		6,300	
Fixed overhead capacity	8,100		
Total variances	11,550	16,450	4,900 (A)
Actual cost of production			110,500

Answer 6.16

(a)

(i)	6,600 kg of materials should cost (× £4)	£ 26,400
	but did cost	25,080
	Material price variance	1,320 (F)

(ii)	1,300 units should use (× 5 kg)	6,500 kgs
	but did use	6,600 kgs
	Material usage variance (kg)	100 kgs (A)
	× standard price per kg	× £4
	Material usage variance (£)	£400 (A)

(iii)		£
	5,330 hours should cost (× £6)	31,980
	but did cost	32,513
	Labour rate variance	533 (A)

(iv)	1,300 units should take (× 4 hours)	5,200 hrs
	but did take	5,330 hrs
	Labour efficiency variance (hours)	130 hrs (A)
	× standard rate per hour	× £6
	Labour efficiency variance (£)	£780 (A)

		£
(v)	Budgeted overheads (1,200 × £16)	19,200
	Actual overheads	22,000
	Fixed overhead expenditure variance	2,800 (A)

(vi)	Labour efficiency variance	130 hrs (A)
	× standard absorption rate per hour	× £4
	Fixed overhead efficiency variance	£520 (A)
(vii)	Budgeted hours of work (4 hrs × 1,200)	4,800 hrs
	Actual hours of work	5,330 hrs
	Variance in hours	530 hrs (F)
	× standard absorption rate per hour	× £4
	Fixed overhead capacity variance	£2,120 (F)

(b) **Variance report: May Year 1**

			£
Expected costs (W)			78,000
Materials variance	920	(F)	
Labour variance	(1,313)	(A)	
Fixed overhead variance	(1,200)	(A)	
			1,593 (A)
Actual costs			79,593

Working: expected costs

	£
Material (20 × 1,300)	26,000
Labour (24 × 1,300)	31,200
Fixed overheads (16 × 1,300)	20,800
	78,000

Alternatively, 1,300 units at £60 = £78,000.

Answer 6.17

(a)

	£
19,500 kg should have cost (× £8)	156,000
but did cost (× £8.50)	165,750
Direct material price variance	9,750 (A)

4,500 units should have used (× 4.3 kg)	19,350 kg
but did use	19,500 kg
Variance in kg	150 kg (A)
× standard cost per kg	× £8
Direct material usage variance in £	£1,200 (A)

	£
6,740 hours should have cost (× £4)	26,960
but did cost	26,286
Direct labour rate variance	674 (F)

4,500 units should have taken (× 1.5 hrs)	6,750 hrs
but did take	6,740 hrs
Variance in hours	10 hrs (F)
× standard rate per hour	× £4
Direct labour efficiency variance in £	£40 (F)

(b) **Reconciliation of standard direct cost of production with actual direct cost for June**

Actual production = 4,500 units

	£	£
Standard cost of production = 4,500 × £40.40		181,800
Direct cost variances		
Direct material price	9,750 (A)	
Direct material usage	1,200 (A)	
		10,950 (A)
Direct labour rate	(674) (F)	
Direct labour efficiency	(40) (F)	
		(714) (F)
Actual direct cost of production		192,036

Note. We *add* an adverse variance because we are totalling costs and an adverse variance implies greater costs.

Answer 6.18

CAVANAGH LTD : RECONCILIATION STATEMENT FOR PERIOD ENDED 26 MAY

			£
Standard costs for actual production (£23.40 (W2) × 9,500)			222,300
Cost variances	(F)	(A)	
	£	£	
Materials price		2,470	
Materials usage		2,850	
Labour rate		9,045	
Labour efficiency	17,500		
Fixed overhead expenditure	1,238		
Fixed overhead efficiency	4,760		
Fixed overhead capacity		6,460	
	23,498	20,825	2,673 (F)
Actual costs			219,627

The variances are calculated as follows.

	£
9,500 units × 26 kg each should cost (× £0.30)	74,100
but did cost	76,570
Materials price variance	2,470 (A)

9,500 units should use (× 25kg)	237,500 kgs
but did use (× 26kg)	247,000 kgs
Usage variance in kg	9,500 kgs (A)
× standard cost per kg	× £0.30
Materials usage variance in £	£2,850 (A)

	£
20,250 hours should cost (× £5)	101,250
but did cost	110,295
Labour rate variance	9,045 (A)

9,500 units should take (× 2.5 hours)	23,750 hrs
but did take	20,250 hrs
Efficiency variance in hours	3,500 hrs (F)
× standard cost per hour	× £5
Labour efficiency variance in £	£17,500 (F)

	£
Budgeted fixed overhead expenditure	34,000
Actual fixed overhead expenditure	32,762
Fixed overhead expenditure variance	1,238 (F)

Labour efficiency variance in hours	3,500 hrs (F)
× standard absorption rate per hour (W1)	× £1.36
Fixed overhead efficiency variance	£4,760 (F)

Budgeted hours of work (10,000 × 2.5 hrs)	25,000 hrs
Actual hours of work	20,250 hrs
Variance in hours	4,750 hrs (A)
Standard fixed overhead rate per hour (W1)	× £1.36
Fixed overhead capacity variance in £	£6,460 (A)

Workings

1 Standard fixed overhead rate per hour = budgeted fixed overhead/standard hours = $\frac{£34,000}{25,000}$ = £1.36

2

	£
Materials	7.50
Direct wages	12.50
Fixed overhead (34,000 ÷ 10,000 units)	3.40
Standard cost per unit	23.40

Chapter 7

Answer 7.1

An adverse material price variance

Answer 7.2

The higher price might reflect higher quality materials. These materials might be easier to work and hence there may be a favourable labour efficiency variance (and corresponding favourable fixed overhead efficiency variance) and a favourable materials usage variance.

Answer 7.3

(a) Control action might be required to improve the accuracy of the recording system so that measurement errors do not occur.

(b) Control action might be required to set up a system to frequently review and update standards.

(c) Investigation of variances in this category should highlight the cause of the inefficiency or efficiency. It should also lead to control action to ensure the inefficiency is not repeated or action to compound the benefits of the efficiency. For example, stricter supervision may be required to reduce wastage levels and the need for overtime working. The purchasing department could be encouraged to continue using suppliers of good quality materials.

(d) Control action will not be necessary provided the variance falls within a predictable range.

Answer 7.4

			£
(a)	(i)	Variable production cost should be (1,000 × £195)	195,000
		but was (W1)	207,360
		Variable production cost variance	12,360 (A)
		Check	£
		Wages (from (ii))	3,360 (A)
		Materials (from (iii))	9,000 (A)
			12,360 (A)
			£
	(ii)	5,200 hours should cost (× £9)	46,800
		but did cost	48,360
		Direct wages rate variance	1,560 (A)

1,000 units should take (× 5 hours)	5,000 hrs
but did take	5,200 hrs
Direct wages efficiency variance in hrs	200 hrs (A)
× standard rate per hour	× £9
Direct wages efficiency variance in £	£1,800 (A)

(iii)

	£
10,000 kg should cost (× £15)	150,000
but did cost	144,000
Direct materials price variance	6,000 (F)

1,000 units should use (× 10kg)	10,000 kgs
but did use (W2)	11,000 kgs
Direct materials usage variance in kgs	1,000 kgs (A)
× standard cost per kg	× £15
Direct materials usage variance in £	£15,000 (A)

Workings

1

	£
Total wages	48,360
Direct materials (W2)	159,000
Variable production cost	207,360

2

	kg	Standard cost £	£
Opening stock	4,000	15	60,000
Purchases	10,000	–	144,000
	14,000		204,000
Closing stock	(3,000)	15	(45,000)
Production	11,000		159,000

(b) To: Production manager
From: A Technician
Subject: **Commentary on variances arising in the week ending 9th November Year 1**

Variable production cost variance. The total variance is an adverse one of £12,360. This represents over 6% of total standard production cost. Investigation is clearly warranted to identify what control action is required to bring costs back into line with budget. The total variance may be analysed into its different components to give a clearer idea of where problems are arising, as follows.

Direct wages rate variance. An adverse variance arises because the labour force were paid an average of (£48,360/5,200) = £9.30 per hour instead of the standard cost of £9 per hour. This is probably due to the short-term need to recruit temporary labour at rates more expensive than standard. Those permanent workers not absent may also have been asked to do high levels of overtime working. The production manager and/or the personnel department should be contacted for further information.

Direct wages efficiency variance. An adverse variance of £1,800 has arisen because the labour force took 200 hours more to produce 1,000 units than the standard allowance. The production manager

should be asked to explain the variance. One possible cause is lack of training of the temporary workers, but the material variances may also offer a clue as to the explanation.

Materials price variance. Materials were purchased for £14.40 per kg in the week (a price £0.60 less than standard) giving rise to a favourable price variance of £6,000. The new purchasing manger has therefore managed to buy cheaper materials. However this appears to have been at the expense of quality, to judge from the usage variance.

Materials usage variance. 1,000 kg more than standard were used to make 1,000 units. This seems most likely to be because cheaper, poor quality materials were purchased, probably resulting in excessive waste. It is possible that the need for rectification work due to poor materials is another reason why the labour force was less efficient than standard.

Answer 7.5

(a) (i)

	£
2,100 kg should have cost (× £4.90)	10,290
but did cost	9,660
Direct material price variance	630 (F)

(ii)

400 units should have used (× 4.5 kg)	1,800 kgs
but did use	2,100 kgs
Variance in kgs	300 kgs (A)
× standard cost per kg	× £4.90
Direct material usage variance	£1,470 (A)

(iii)

	£
4,000 hrs should have cost (× £3.50)	14,000
but did cost	16,000
Direct labour rate variance	2,000 (A)

(iv)

400 units should have taken (× 10.3 hrs)	4,120 hrs
but did take	4,000 hrs
Variance in hours	120 hrs (F)
× standard rate per hour	× £3.50
Direct labour efficiency variance	£420 (F)

(b) **Reconciliation of standard direct cost of production with actual direct cost for November**

		£	£
Standard direct cost of production (400 × £58.10)			23,240
Direct cost variances			
Direct material	– price	630 (F)	
	– usage	1,470 (A)	
			840 (A)
Direct labour	– rate	2,000 (A)	
	– efficiency	420 (F)	
			1,580 (A)
Actual direct cost of production			25,660

(c) **LINNEY LTD**
MEMORANDUM

To: Production manager
From: Assistant accountant
Date: 12 December Year 4
Subject: **Direct cost variances for November**

As you requested, I detail below explanations of the direct cost variances and possible suggestions as to their cause in November.

(i) **The meaning of the variances**

Direct material price variance. This variance shows the saving or overspending which resulted from paying a lower or higher price than standard for the direct material used in the period. The favourable variance indicates that a lower than standard price was paid.

Direct material usage variance. This shows the saving or overspending, at standard prices, which resulted from using less or more material than standard to produce the period's output. The adverse variance indicates that more material was used than standard.

Direct labour rate variance. This variance shows the saving or overspending which resulted from paying a lower or higher hourly rate than standard for the hours worked in the period. The adverse variance indicates that a higher than standard hourly rate was paid.

Direct labour efficiency variance. This variance shows the saving or overspending, at standard rates, which resulted from working less or more hours than standard to produce the period's output. The favourable variance indicates that less hours were worked than standard.

(ii) Possible causes of the variances include the following.

Favourable direct material price variance

- Bulk discounts were received which were not allowed for in the standard.
- The standard price of material was set too high.
- A lower quality material was purchased, at a lower price than standard.
- Effective negotiations by the buyer secured a price lower than the standard.

Adverse direct material usage variance

- Material wastage was higher than allowed in the standard.
- The standard usage was set too low.
- There was a higher than standard level of rejects.
- Material was stolen.

Adverse direct labour rate variance

- High levels of overtime were paid (with the premium included in direct labour cost).
- The standard wage rate was set too low.
- A higher grade of labour was used.
- Bonus payments were higher than standard.

Favourable direct labour efficiency variance

- Employees were working faster than standard.
- More skilled employees were used.
- There were savings through the learning effect not accounted for in the standard.
- The standard labour time was set too high.
- The material was easy to process, leading to savings against the standard time.

(iii) Examples of interdependence, where one variance can be related to another, include the following. (*Note.* You were only required to provide two examples.)

The favourable material price variance may indicate that poor quality material was purchased, leading to high wastage, rejects and an adverse usage variance. The favourable material price variance may have been due to bulk discounts. The consequent excess stocks may, however, have led to deterioration and write-offs, hence the adverse usage variance.

Direct workers may have been of a higher grade than allowed for in the standard, resulting in higher hourly rates, hence the adverse rate variance. The higher skill level may, however, have led to time savings and, therefore, the favourable efficiency variance. Higher than standard bonus payments may have caused the adverse labour rate variance, but the bonuses may have been due to faster working, hence the favourable efficiency variance. Faster working resulted in the favourable efficiency variance, but less care may have been taken over weighing and handling the material, hence the adverse material usage variance.

If you require any further information, please do not hesitate to contact me.

(d) **LINNEY LTD**
MEMORANDUM

To: Production manager
From: Assistant accountant
Date: 12 December Year 4
Subject: **Determining the standard price per kg of material**

As requested I detail below the information which would be needed to determine the standard price of material, and possible sources of the information.

(i)	The information which is needed	(ii)	Possible sources
(1)	Type and quality of material		Technical specification
(2)	Quantity and timing of purchases, for determining any bulk discounts		Production and purchasing schedules
(3)	Past trend in prices		Historical records of the company
			Supplier records
			Government statistics
			Trade association statistics
			Movements in price indices
(4)	Future trend in prices		Discussions/negotiations with suppliers
			Trade association forecasts
			Financial press forecasts
			Government forecasts of key indices
(5)	Carriage costs to be added		Historical records of company
			Supplier records
(6)	Type of standard to be set, such as an average price for the year, or a price which increases with inflation		Company policy on standard setting

Answer 7.6

REPORT ON RESULTS FOR SEPTEMBER YEAR 5

1 **TERMS OF REFERENCE**

This report provides a management accounting interpretation of the company's results for September Year 5. The report was prepared by A N Employee, Management Accountant and submitted to A Boss, General Manager, on XX October Year 5.

2 **METHOD**

Using the management accounting department's variance report for September Year 5 and actual cost data for the month, the company's results were analysed.

3 **FINDINGS**

Total variance. The total variance may only be 1.57% of total costs but this total disguises a number of significant adverse and favourable variances which need investigating.

Materials variances. The fact that there is a favourable price variance and an adverse usage variance could indicate interdependence. The purchasing department may have bought cheap materials but these cheaper materials may have been more difficult to work with so that more material was required per unit produced. The possibility of such an interdependence should be investigated. Whether or not there is an interdependence, both variances do require investigation since they represent 5.5% (usage) and 3.5% (price) of the actual material cost for the month.

Labour variances. Again there could be an interdependence between the adverse efficiency variance and the favourable rate variance, less skilled (and lower paid) employees perhaps having worked less efficiently than standard. Discussions with management should reveal whether this is so. Both variances need investigation since they represent a high percentage (compared with 1.57%) of the actual labour cost for the month (3.75% for the utilisation variance, 1.875% for the rate variance).

Fixed overhead variances. The cause of the favourable price variance, which represents 6% of the total overhead costs for the month, should be encouraged. The adverse overhead variances in total represent 6.67% of actual overhead cost during the month and must therefore be investigated. The capacity variance signifies that actual hours of work were less than budgeted hours of work. The company is obviously working below its planned capacity level. Efforts should therefore be made to increase production so as to eradicate this variance.

4 **CONCLUSION**

It is not the total of the monthly variances which should be considered but the individual variances, as a number of them represent significant deviations from planned results. Investigations into their causes should be performed and control action taken to ensure that either performance is back under control in future if the cause of the variance can be controlled, or the forecasts of expected results are revised if the variance is uncontrollable.

Answer 7.7

(a) Revised standard = £20 × (105/75) = £28

	£	
300 labour hours should have cost (using original standard of £20)	6,000	
300 labour hours should have cost (using revised standard of £28)	8,400	
Variance due to updating the standard	2,400	(A)

The variance is adverse because the revised standard rate per hour is higher.

(b)

	£	
300 labour hours should have cost (× £28)	8,400	
but did cost	7,500	
Variance due to other reasons	900	(F)

(c) Total variance = variance due to updating the standard + variance due to other reasons
= £2,400 (A) + £900 (F) = £1,500 (A)

If the variance had been set at the more realistic rate of £28, the variance would have been £900 (F), not £1,500 (A).

Answer 7.8

Revised standard = £10 × 315.81/350.9 = £9
Actual cost per kg = £16,000/2,000 = £8

Variance due to price change (index)

	£
2,000 kgs at original standard price (× £10)	20,000
2,000 kgs at indexed price (× £9)	18,000
	2,000 (F)

Variance due to other reasons

	£
2,000 kgs should have cost (× £9)	18,000
but did cost (× £8)	16,000
	2,000 (F)

Answer 7.9

\$ cost of purchases = 1,600 × \$10 = \$16,000

	£
Contract cost of purchases should have been (\$16,000 ÷ \$1.60)	10,000
but cost of purchases was (\$16,000 ÷ \$1.68)	9,524
Price variance due to exchange rate movements	476 (F)

Answer 7.10

Variance due to contract and purchasing manager's efficiency

If it were not for the contract and the purchasing manager's efficiency, a price of £16.20 per litre would have been paid instead of a price of £13 per litre.

	£	
1,725 litres would have cost (× £16.20)	27,945	
but did cost (× £13)	22,425	
	5,520	(F)

Variance due to out-of-date standard

We need to know what the variance would have been if there had been no contract so we compare the cost at the out-of-date standard and the cost at market price.

	£	
1,725 litres should have cost (× £12, the out-of-date standard)	20,700	
but would have cost (× £16.20)	27,945	
	7,245	(A)

Total variance

This compares the out-of-date standard cost (£12) and the price actually paid (£13).

	£	
1,725 litres should have cost (× £12)	20,700	
but did cost (× £13)	22,425	
	1,725	(A)

Check. £7,245 (A) + £5,520 (F) = £1,725 (A)

The apparent inefficiency of the purchasing department as represented by the total adverse variance was due to using an out-of-date standard. The purchasing department has actually been efficient (as represented by the favourable variance of £5,520).

Answer 7.11

(a) =C4–B4.

(b) =(D6/B6)*100

(c) =(D9/B9)*100. Note that in (c) you cannot simply add up the individual percentage differences. This is because the percentages are based on very different quantities.

Chapter 8

Answer 8.1

(a) **REPORT**

To: The Managing Director
From: A Technician
Date: 26 June Year 4
Subject: **Information relating to future trends of the company**

Introduction

The company's business has suffered badly from the housing market recession which has accompanied the general economic recession of recent years. This report explains how different sources of information might be of value in assessing future trends for the company. The relevance, reliability and timeliness of each source is commented on.

(i) **Official employment statistics**

Relevance. Labour rates are important in costing and estimating for the construction industry. Labour rates in the industry can be compared with the company's rates. Employment statistics give an indication of the strength of the economy, but the direction of the trend lags behind the general trend in economic activity.

Reliability. Labour rates statistics rely on companies' returns, which may not be reliable. Unemployment statistics depend upon the definition of unemployment adopted by the government, and the basis of the statistics has been changed from time to time.

Timeliness. Employment statistics only become available after a delay of up to two months.

(ii) **New housing starts**

Relevance. The number of new dwellings started indicates the construction industry firms' perception of the demand for new houses. When the number of new dwellings started begins to increase again after the recession, it could indicate the beginning of recovery in the housing market.

Reliability. As an indicator of planned construction over future months, the figures provide a useful measure of business confidence, at least in respect of the construction industry.

Timeliness. This information becomes available fairly quickly.

(iii) **Retail and wholesale price indices**

Relevance. The UK government makes available price indices for retail and wholesale prices divided into different sectors. Wholesale price indices covering building materials show the trend in prices for the raw materials of the business. The trend in the retail prices index is monitored closely by the government and so can signal possible changes in economic policy. In an economic recession, interest rates are generally cut to encourage economic recovery, but if retail price inflation rises later, the government may raise interest rates again to dampen inflationary

pressures in the economy. If interest rates rise, mortgages for first-time buyers become more expensive and demand for low-cost housing is then likely to fall.

Reliability. The main price indices are calculated using sophisticated statistical methods, based on a large sample of items for which prices are recorded monthly. The resulting indices are therefore highly reliable indicators, provided that it is understood which particular range of items is covered by each particular index.

Timeliness. The monthly price indices become available with little delay: soon after the middle of the following month.

(iv) **Building societies' information**

Relevance. Some of the major building societies in the UK publish monthly data on trends in house prices based on the houses on which they grant mortgages. The Halifax Building Society publishes such information with details of the regional breakdown and the split between different types of house and buyer. Information on price trends for new first-time buyer homes in different regions is a very specific indicator of likely trends in selling prices which the company will face in the immediate future. Trends in the value of mortgages granted is an indicator of buyer confidence in the housing market.

Reliability. Different building societies' figures often show slightly different trends in the short term because they are based on different samples. In the UK the figures for the Halifax are reliable because the Halifax is one of the largest societies, and its figures are adjusted to compensate for changes in the mix of property in its sample from month to month. The trend in the volume of mortgages granted is rather unreliable as a general indicator unless the figures for all financial institutions are added together: a rise in mortgages granted by building societies could indicate an increase in building societies' market share rather than a general trend in the housing market.

Timeliness. Monthly data is made available within a few working days of the end of the month to which they relate.

(v) **Population statistics**

Relevance. Population statistics are relevant to the medium to long-term state of the market for low-cost houses. Of particular interest is the future trend of population in the age bands of potential customers for such housing. First-time buyers tend to be people aged in their 20's. Future growth or decline of this group means that the company's potential customer base is going to expand or contract. Increases in the birth rate could signal a future trend of the creation of more households which will need housing.

Reliability. In Britain, data is compiled from comprehensive 10-yearly censuses plus other sources. Although the age profile or make-up of the population in future years can be extrapolated fairly accurately from current population data, such data needs to be treated with some caution because market trends over the shorter term can have a more significant impact, as was seen in the recent recession.

Timeliness. As these statistics are relevant mainly to medium-term and long-term forecasting, the data available on an annual basis is sufficient for the needs of the company.

(vi) **Trade association cost figures**

Relevance. Figures of average costs of construction firms published by the trade association are specific to the industry and may indicate trends affecting our own company. If regional data is available, then this might indicate where the company should be concentrating its construction efforts. However, good information on average costs is also available from the company's own accounting records.

Reliability. The trade association figures are likely only to cover its own members, and these members may not all make full returns if they are not required to do so or if they do not wish to publicise commercially sensitive information.

Timeliness. Figures of this sort may take some time to collect and so may not be available in time to be useful in indicating current short-term trends.

(vii) **Financial press surveys**

Relevance. The main advantage of surveys of the construction industry appearing in the financial press is that they can provide narrative information on the industry rather than purely quantitative statistics. Surveys might cover topics such as regional trends, the number of firms entering or leaving the industry, marketing, land prices, the size of 'land banks' held by companies in the industry or other topics relevant to the company.

Reliability. Qualitative information is unfortunately subject to selective bias, but reputable publications are likely to produce well balanced surveys. The Financial Times regularly produces industry surveys in supplements to the main paper.

Timeliness. Surveys may be produced only infrequently, possibly on an irregular basis.

Conclusion

Quantitative and qualitative information of various kinds and from various sources relevant to the business and to future trends in the industry is available.

(b) Time series information, such as of price or cost changes through time, will be subject to short-term changes but over a longer period it is possible to draw a trend line to indicate the general direction in which the variable is moving. This might be done by visual judgement or alternatively a trend line can be determined by regression analysis. **Extrapolating the trend line** involves extending this trend line outside the range of known data to future periods so as to forecast the future trend.

Cyclical fluctuations are variations in time series data which occur over a longer period than seasonal variations and which follow a regular cycle. One of the most often cited 'cycles' is the business cycle (or 'trade cycle') which is the cyclical variation in the general level of economic activity between 'boom' (rapidly expanding output) and recession (falling output).

Seasonal variations may occur over different periods according to the nature of the data under examination. In the case of the construction industry, such variations are those which occur over an annual period: for example, the level of building activity is much affected by the seasonal changes in weather at different times of the year.

A **moving average** is an average of data recorded over a number of fixed periods. By recording such averages over an extended period, short-term fluctuations in data are 'ironed out' of the series. For

example, a moving average of housing starts could be based on a period of 12 months. One moving average would be calculated by adding the monthly data for each month from May Year 3 to April Year 4 inclusive and dividing by 12. The next figure in the moving average series will be calculated similarly from the data in the period June Year 3 to May Year 4.

A **leading indicator** is an indicator which anticipates a trend in the main series of data. In other words, if the main series follows a particular pattern or trend, then the leading indicator follows approximately the same pattern or trend but earlier. In this case, it is stated that changes in capital equipment expenditure suggest (but weakly) that similar changes in industry trends will follow later.

Chapter 9

Answer 9.1

(a) **Production budget**

Use production = sales + closing stock – opening stock

	Units	Units
Budgeted sales		280
Closing stock	5	
Opening stock	30	
Decrease in stock		(25)
Budgeted production		255

(b) **Materials usage budget**

Production	255 units
× usage per unit	× 7 kgs
Total budgeted usage in kgs	1,785 kgs
× budgeted cost per kg	× £50
Total budgeted usage in £	£89,250

(c) **Labour utilisation budget – grade O**

Budgeted production	255 units
× hrs per unit	× 2 hrs
Total budgeted labour hrs	510 hrs
× budgeted cost per hr	× £15
Budgeted labour cost	£7,650

Labour utilisation budget – grade R

Budgeted production	255 units
× hrs per unit	× 3 hrs
Total budgeted labour hrs	765 hrs

Note that the budgeted labour cost is not dependent on the hours worked.

Budgeted labour cost = 16 × £280 × 4 weeks = £17,920
Total labour budget in £ = £(17,920 + 7,650) = £25,570

Answer 9.2

To determine materials purchases we first need to draw up a production budget.

Remember sales + closing stock – opening stock = production

Production budget

	Superior model Units	*Standard model* Units
Sales volume	1,500	2,200
Add closing stock	200	250
Minus opening stock	(150)	(200)
Production	1,550	2,250

Remember material used in production + closing stock – opening stock = purchases

Materials purchases budget

	Kgs
Material required for superior model (1,550 × 5 kgs)	7,750
Material required for standard model (2,250 × 4 kgs)	9,000
Total material required for production	16,750
Add closing stock	1,500
Minus opening stock	(800)
Material purchases	17,450

Answer 9.3

		kgs
Wood issued to production	(chest: 450 × 25 kgs)	11,250
	(wardrobe: 710 × 40 kgs)	28,400
		39,650
Add closing stock (39,650 × 115% × 15 days/25 days)*		27,359
Less opening stock		(40,000)
Purchases		27,009

*Production in period 2 will be 15% higher than that in period 1 and so closing stock must take this into account.

Answer 9.4

To calculate material purchase requirements, it is first of all necessary to calculate the budgeted production volumes and material usage requirements.

	Frothy Fruit		*Fruit Smoothie*	
	Units	Units	Units	Units
Sales		8,000		6,000
Provision for losses		50		100
Closing stock	600		600	
Opening stock	1,500		300	
(Decrease)/increase in stock		(900)		300
Production budget		7,150		6,400

	Milk		Fresh fruit	
	Litres	Litres	Kg	Kg
Usage requirements				
To produce 7,150 units of Frothy Fruit		21,450		28,600
To produce 6,400 units of Fruit Smoothie		32,000		12,800
Usage budget		53,450		41,400
Provision for losses		500		200
		53,950		41,600
Closing stock	5,000		3,500	
Opening stock	6,000		2,800	
(Decrease)/increase in stock		(1,000)		700
Material purchases budget		52,950		42,300

	Milk		Fresh fruit
Cost per unit	£0.30 per litre		£0.70 per kg
Cost of material purchases	£15,885		£29,610
Total purchases cost		£45,495	

Answer 9.5

(a) **Sales budget (revenue)**

	X	Y	Z	Total
	£'000	£'000	£'000	£'000
Sales team 1	180	550	360	1,090
Sales team 2	300	770	540	1,610
Total	480	1,320	900	2,700

(b) **Production budget (units)**

	X	Y	Z
Opening stock	(1,000)	(1,200)	(1,500)
Closing stock	1,200	1,000	1,800
Sales	8,000	12,000	10,000
Production	8,200	11,800	10,300

(c) **Material purchases budget (kgs)**

	Plastic	Metal
	kgs	kgs
Opening stock	(5,000)	(7,500)
Closing stock	8,000	10,000
Used in production (W)	77,550	87,250
Required purchases	80,550	89,750

Material purchases budget (£)

	Plastic	Metal	Total
Required purchases (kgs)	80,550	89,750	
Cost per kg	£3	£2	
Cost of purchases	£241,650	£179,500	£421,150

(d) **Labour cost budget**

	X	Y	Z	Total
Production (units)	8,200	11,800	10,300	30,300

	Department 1	Department 2	Total
X (8,200 × 0.75/1.50)	6,150	12,300	18,450
Y (11,800 × 1.25/2.00)	14,750	23,600	38,350
Z (10,300 × 2.00/2.50)	20,600	25,750	46,350
Budgeted labour hours	41,500	61,650	103,150
× labour rate per hour	£4	£3	
Budgeted labour cost	£166,000	£184,950	£350,950

(e) **Cost of production budget**

	X		Y		Z		Total	
	£	£	£	£	£	£	£	£
Cost of plastic used (W)	49,200		106,200		77,250		232,650	
Cost of metal used (W)	49,200		94,400		30,900		174,500	
Total cost of materials used		98,400		200,600		108,150		407,150
Cost of labour – dept 1								
(6,150/14,750/20,600 × £4)	24,600		59,000		82,400		166,000	
Cost of labour – dept 2								
(12,300/23,600/25,750 × £3)	36,900		70,800		77,250		184,950	
Total cost of labour		61,500		129,800		159,650		350,950
Cost of production		159,900		330,400		267,800		758,100

Working

Material used in production

	X	Y	Z	Total
Production (units)	8,200	11,800	10,300	
Plastic used per unit (kgs)	2	3	2.5	
Total plastic required (kgs)	16,400	35,400	25,750	77,550
Cost of plastic used (× £3)	£49,200	£106,200	£77,250	£232,650
Metal used per unit (kgs)	3	4	1.5	
Total metal required (kgs)	24,600	47,200	15,450	87,250
Cost of metal used (× £2)	£49,200	£94,400	£30,900	£174,500

Answer 9.6

Production budget

Remember production = sales + closing stock – opening stock

	Dec	*Jan*	*Feb*	*Mar*	*Apr*
	Units	Units	Units	Units	Units
Opening stock (W1)	(3,500)	(4,000)	(5,500)	(4,250)	(5,000)
Sales	14,000	16,000	22,000	17,000	20,000
Closing stock (W2)	4,000	5,500	4,250	5,000	6,000
Production	14,500	17,500	20,750	17,750	21,000

Note how closing stock in one month is opening stock in the next and so you only need to calculate one closing stock figure.

Workings

1 Opening stock = 25% × sales of month in question

December = 25% × 14,000
January = 25% × 16,000
February = 25% × 22,000
March = 25% × 17,000
April = 25% × 20,000

2 Closing stock = 25% × sales of following month

April = 25% × 24,000

Material purchases budget

As usual, for material purchases you need to use material purchases = material used in production + closing stock – opening stock.

	Dec	*Jan*	*Feb*	*Mar*
	Units	Units	Units	Units
Opening stock (W1)	(1,450)	(1,750)	(2,075)	(1,775)
Production (from (a))	14,500	17,500	20,750	17,750
Closing stock (W2)	1,750	2,075	1,775	2,100
Purchases	14,800	17,825	20,450	18,075

Again, closing stock in one month is opening stock in the next.

Workings

1 Opening stock = 10% × production of month in question (eg December = 10% × 14,500)
2 Closing stock = 10% × production of following month (March = 10% × 21,000 (from (a))

Answer 9.7

(a) **Revenue budget**

Service			£
1	£20 × 10,584	=	211,680
2	£25 × 6,804	=	170,100
3	£30 × 5,292	=	158,760
4	£40 × 7,560	=	302,400

(b) No of employees/department = $\frac{\text{budgeted chargeable hours}}{35 \times 48}$ × 100/90 (non-chargeable time)

Service			
1	(10,584 × 100/90)/(35 × 48)	=	7.0
2	(6,804 × 100/90)/(35 × 48)	=	4.5
3	(5,292 × 100/90)/(35 × 48)	=	3.5
4	(7,560 × 100/90)/(35 × 48)	=	5.0

The business should employ the following staff, assuming part-time staff work $17\frac{1}{2}$ hours a week for 48 weeks of the year.

Service	*Number of full time*	*Number of part time*
1	7	–
2	4	1
3	3	1
4	5	–
Total	19	2

(c) **Direct wages budget**

		£
Service 1	£8 an hour × 7.0 employees × 35 hours a week × 48 weeks =	94,080
Service 2	£10 an hour × 4.5 employees × 35 hours a week × 48 weeks =	75,600
Service 3	£11 an hour × 3.5 employees × 35 hours a week × 48 weeks =	64,680
Service 4	£14 an hour × 5.0 employees × 35 hours a week × 48 weeks =	117,600
Total		351,960

Answer 9.8

Revised standard price = (recent index number/older index number) × original standard price = 190/150 × £10 = £12.67.

Answer 9.9

(a) (i) Good production = (100 – 10)% = 90%
Gross production = 100/90 × 810 units = 900 units

(ii) Faulty units = 10/90 × 810 units = 90 units (or 900 units – 810 units)

(b) Gross production = 100/95 × 475 units = 500 units

Answer 9.10

(a) **Production budget**

	P1	*P2*
	Units	Units
Opening stock	(600)	(800)
Closing stock (85%)	510	680
Sales	10,000	6,000
	9,910	5,880

(b) **Raw materials purchases budget**

You need to take account of the 3% of material M2 that is spilt.

Required inputs of this material are as follows:

Per P1 100/97 × 4 litres = 4.124 litres
Per P2 100/97 × 8 litres = 8.247 litres

	M1	*M2*
	kg	kg
Opening stock	(400)	(200)
Production (per (a))		
P1 (9,910 × 10kg/4.124 litres)	99,100	40,869
P2 (5,880 × 6 kg/8.247 litres)	35,280	48,492
	133,980	89,161
Closing stock (85%)	340	170
	134,320	89,331
Cost per kg	£1.50	£4.00
Purchase cost	£201,480	£357,324

(c) **Production cost budget**

	£
Materials	
Opening stock (400 kg × £1.20 + 200 kg × £3)	1,080
Purchases £(201,480 + 357,324)	558,804
	559,884
Closing stock (340 kg × £1.50 + 170 kg × £4)	(1,190)
	558,694
Skilled labour (W1)	497,880
Variable overhead (W2)	165,960
Fixed overhead	315,900
	1,538,434

Workings

1 **Labour hours budget**

	P1	*P2*
Units produced per (a)	9,910	5,880
Hours per unit	6	4
Total hours	59,460	23,520

(59,460 + 23,520) = 82,980 hours × £6 = £497,880

2 **Variable overheads budget**

82,980 hrs × £2 = £165,960

Answer 9.11

	Hrs
Available labour	1,400
Hours required to meet contracted sales of S (1,800 × 0.5)	(900)
Hours available for production of R	500

Production budget

S	1,800 units
R (500 ÷ $^1/_6$ hr)	3,000 units

Answer 9.12

	Control period 1	*Control period 2*	*Control period 3*	*Control period 4*
Material required (production × 8 kgs)	3,200	4,480	2,800	7,120
Maximum material available from Little Ltd	4,000	4,000	4,000	4,000
Initial (shortage)/excess of material	800	(480)	1,200	(3,120)
Rescheduled purchases	(480)	480	(1,200)	1,200
Final (shortage)/excess of material	320	-	-	(1,920)

Coombe Ltd will be unable to meet the production budget in control period 4 because of a shortage of material.

Answer 9.13

Labour budget

	Period 1	*Period 2*	*Period 3*
Production (units)	7,000	5,600	9,100
Labour hrs required per unit	× 2	× 2	× 2
Labour hrs required	14,000	11,200	18,200
Basic labour hrs available	14,000	14,000	14,000
Surplus hrs/(overtime hrs)	–	2,800	(4,200)

In period 3, 4,200 hours of overtime are needed to produce the required number of units. There are 2,800 surplus labour hours available in period 2, however. If an extra 1,400 (2,800 ÷ 2) units were produced in period 2, using the surplus hours available, the need for overtime would be reduced to 1,400 hours (4,200 – 2,800), saving 1,400 × £10 = £14,000.

Answer 9.14

Reducing deterioration and obsolescence in stores by reducing stock levels (although the risk of stockouts is associated with such a policy).

Reducing the rate of rejects, either by lowering quality requirements or improving quality (perhaps by implementing a Total Quality Management programme – which we will be looking at in Chapter 15).

Finding alternative suppliers (although they would need to be carefully vetted for quality and reliability).

Sourcing finished units from outside suppliers (provided the price charged by the outside supplier is less than the marginal cost per unit).

Answer 9.15

Tutorial note. In task (a)(iii), given that there is a shortage of raw materials the original production and sales budget cannot be achieved and so revised profit-maximising budgets need to be prepared. These budgets need to be based on the contribution per limiting factor (raw materials) from the two products.

(a) (i) **Material purchases budget - weeks 1 to 13 20X8**

20,000 kgs × £5 per kg = £100,000.

(ii) **Materials issued to production budget - weeks 1 to 13 20X8**

	Kgs	£
Opening stock	6,000	30,000
Purchases	20,000	100,000
Closing stock	(6,600)	(33,000)
Issues to production	19,400	97,000

(iii) **Sales volume and turnover budget - weeks 1 to 13 20X8**

		Alpha		*Beta*
		£		£
Selling price		36.00		39.00
Variable costs				
material	(2 kgs × £5)	10.00	(1.5kg × £5)	7.50
labour	(2.5 hrs × £4*)	10.00	(2.785 hrs × £4*)	11.14
		20.00		18.64
Contribution per unit		16.00		20.36
Kgs of material required per unit		2 kgs		1.5 kgs
Contribution per kg of material		£8		£13.57
Priority for production		2nd		1st

* £169,260 ÷ 42,315 hrs = £4 per hour

The calculations above indicate that the Beta should be produced up to its maximum demand and then the Alpha produced using the remaining raw material.

We therefore need to produce the 9,000 units of Betas, which will use 9,000 × 1.5 kgs = 13,500 kgs of raw material. This leaves (19,400 (see (b)) – 13,500) 5,900 kgs with which to make 5,900 ÷ 2 kgs = 2,950 units of Alpha, a reduction of (6,900 – 2,950) 3,950 units compared with the original budget. If the closing stocks have to remain the same the sales budget for Alphas will have to be reduced by 3,950 units (ie to 6,500 – 3,950 = 2,550 units).

Revised sales budget

	Sales volume	*Selling price per unit*	*Sales revenue*
	Units	£	£
Alpha	2,550	36.00	91,800
Beta	7,800	39.00	304,200
			396,000

(iv) **Labour hours and cost budget - weeks 1 to 13 20X8**

Product	*Production*	*Labour hours per unit*	*Total labour hours*	*Labour cost per hour*	*Total labour cost*
	Units	Hrs	Hrs	£	£
Alpha	2,950	2.500	7,375	4	29,500
Beta	9,000	2.785	25,065	4	100,260
			32,440		129,760

(v) **Number of employees required budget - weeks 1 to 13 20X8**

Labour hours required	32,440
Number of weeks work this represents (÷ 35)	926.86
Within a 13-week period, this requires (÷ 13)	71.3 employees

(b) REPORT

To: George Phillips
From: Trainee Accountant
Date: 20 November 20X7
Subject: **Issues raised at budget meeting**

This report contains information on a number of issues raised at the recent management meeting to discuss the 20X8 budget.

(i) **Reducing staff numbers**

The use of labour standards implies that our organisation's labour costs are variable. This would be the case if the workforce were paid on a piecework basis but, in common with most organisations, we pay our employees either weekly or monthly a certain amount regardless of the volume of output achieved. Labour costs are fixed but only in the short term. The size of the workforce can always be reduced or increased within, say, two or three months (subject to notice periods and the pool of available workers). Theoretically an organisation would not continue to employ workers that were surplus to requirements in the longer term but in practice a number of factors would have to be considered.

(1) The **financial costs of making employees redundant** and possible **recruitment and retraining** in the future **versus the financial cost of continuing to employ unproductive employees** needs to be borne in mind.

(2) As pointed out by the production manager, those **staff made redundant may be loathe to work for us again** if there is a chance that they will be made redundant again.

(3) It could be **difficult** and/or it would **take time** to **replace** such highly-trained staff.

(4) If **new employees** had to be taken on, the **quality of output** may not be up to our normal standard during their training period. This would have a detrimental effect on our efforts to re-enter the market.

(5) It may be possible to purchase the raw material from **another source** and meet sales demand for both products, in which case all current employees would be required.

(6) It may be possible to use an **alternative raw material**.

Given the above it would probably be **inadvisable to lay off workers**, especially as it is quite likely that the shortage is not long term or an alternative supplier can be found.

(ii) **Key factors**

It is true that in most instances sales is an organisation's key factor. Most businesses only produce as many products as they can sell. But sales demand is by no means the only key factor. **Any of an organisation's resources can be a key factor** and so machine capacity, distribution and selling resources, the availability of trained personnel or the availability of cash could limit the number of units an organisation can produce. What's more, **key factors can change over time**. An organisation might usually be limited by the number of units it can sell but if specialised machinery suddenly breaks down and cannot be repaired or replaced immediately, machine capacity will become the key factor.

It is therefore vital that an organisation's **key factor is identified before the budget is prepared** so that the managers can work towards a budget that is actually achievable. There is little point in the sales department having targets that can never be attained because the budgeted production levels cannot be met due to shortage in machine capacity.

An organisation should **attempt to overcome the constraints of the key factor**, however. If machine capacity is the key factor, an organisation should look into the possibility of subcontracting work, of looking for alternative suppliers or of looking for alternative machinery that will perform the same task. Such solutions will of course impact on other resources which then become key factors. For example, an alternative machine may exist but may be far too expensive and so cash will become the key factor.

Key factors must therefore be identified before the budget is set and the situation must be **continuously reviewed** in case another resource has become the key factor, in which case the key factor must be overcome or the budget amended to reflect what is actually achievable.

If I can provide any further assistance on the matters covered in this report, please do not hesitate to contact me.

Chapter 10

Answer 10.2

Flexible budget for a 45% level of activity

	£ per 1%		£
Turnover (W1)	3,000		135,000
Variable costs:			
Direct materials (W1)	254		11,430
Direct labour (W1)	640		28,800
Production overhead (W2)	150		6,750
			46,980
Fixed costs:		£	
Production overhead (W2)		20,000	
Administration overhead		17,000	
			37,000
Total budget cost allowance			83,980
Budgeted profit			51,020

Workings

1 Alternatively, instead of finding £ per 1%, the variable costs and revenue can be found by multiplying one of the original budgeted figures by (actual volume/original budget volume).

Using 70%:

Turnover	= £210,000 × 45%/70% =	£135,000
Direct materials	= £17,780 × 45%/70% =	£11,430
Direct labour	= £44,800 × 45%/70% =	£28,800

2 Production overhead is a semi-variable cost.

Using the **incremental approach:**

Variable cost of (90% – 70%) = £(33,500 – 30,500)
∴ Variable cost of 20% = £3,000

∴ Variable cost per 1% change in activity = £3,000/20 = £150
Fixed cost = £33,500 – (90 × £150) = £20,000

Answer 10.3

Use the high-low method to determine the fixed and variable elements of the semi-variable cost.

	Hours	£
High – Year 8	110,000	330,000
Low – Year 3	80,000	255,000
Change	30,000	75,000

∴ Variable cost per hour = £75,000/30,000 = £2.50 per hour

Substitute this into the Year 8 figures.

	£
Variable cost for 110,000 hours	275,000
Total cost	330,000
∴ Fixed cost	55,000

The required budgets can now be prepared.

Company Z – cost budget

Level of productive time	90%	100%	110%	120%
Direct labour hours	108,000	120,000	132,000	144,000
Fixed costs	£	£	£	£
Depreciation	22,000	22,000	22,000	22,000
Staff salaries	43,000	43,000	43,000	43,000
Insurances	9,000	9,000	9,000	9,000
Rent and rates	12,000	12,000	12,000	12,000
Semi-variable costs – fixed element	55,000	55,000	55,000	55,000
Total fixed cost	141,000	141,000	141,000	141,000
Variable costs				
Power	32,400	36,000	39,600	43,200
Consumables	5,400	6,000	6,600	7,200
Direct labour	378,000	420,000	462,000	504,000
Semi-variable costs – variable element	270,000	300,000	330,000	360,000
Total variable cost	685,800	762,000	838,200	914,400
Total cost budget	826,800	903,000	979,200	1,055,400

Answer 10.4

We need to prepare a flexible budget for 700 units.

	Budget		*Flexed budget*	*Actual*	*Variances*
	1,000 units	Per unit	700 units	700 units	
	£	£	£	£	£
Sales revenue	20,000	20	14,000	14,200	200 (F)
Variable costs					
Direct material	8,000	8	5,600	5,200	400 (F)
Direct labour	4,000	4	2,800	3,100	300 (A)
Variable overhead	2,000	2	1,400	1,500	100 (A)
	14,000	14	9,800	9,800	
Contribution	6,000	6	4,200	4,400	
Fixed costs	5,000	N/A	5,000	5,400	400 (A)
Profit/(loss)	1,000		(800)	(1,000)	200 (A)

You could have calculated the flexed budget variable costs as original budget figure × 700/1,000.

Answer 10.5

Fixed and flexible budgets: the differences

A fixed budget will not change to take into account variations in production, sales or expenses actually experienced. A flexible budget can do this by adjusting expected total costs for the level of production achieved. The original budget based on a given volume is 'flexed' to the actual volume by analysing budgeted costs over budgeted volume and multiplying by actual units produced.

Fixed and flexible budgets: their uses

Both sorts of budget are used essentially for cost control, although they also provide management with a yardstick to measure achievement and may thus encourage the attainment of objectives.

Fixed budgets are useful at the planning stage as they provide a common ground for the preparation of all the many types of budget. At the end of the period, actual results may be compared with the fixed budget and analysed for control. However, this analysis may be distorted by uncorrected errors underlying the estimates on which the fixed budget was constructed.

A flexible budget may be needed at the planning stage to complement the master budget; output may be budgeted at a number of different possible levels for instance. During the period the flexible budget may then be updated to the actual level of activity and the results compared. As a result flexible budgets assist management control by providing more dynamic and comparable information. Relying only on a fixed budget would give rise to massive variances; since forecast volume is very unlikely to be matched, the variances will contain large volume differences. Flexible budgets are more likely to pinpoint actual problem areas on which control may be exercised.

Answer 10.6

(a) **Initial workings**

Direct material: linear variable cost at £5 per unit

Direct labour: linear variable cost at £2 per unit

Indirect material: variable cost = £1 per unit
fixed cost = £8,000 – (5,000 × £1) = £3,000

Flexible budget cost allowances

	5,000 units	*10,000 units*	*12,000 units*	*15,000 units*
	£	£	£	£
Direct material	25,000	50,000	60,000	75,000
Direct labour	10,000	20,000	24,000	30,000
Indirect material	8,000	13,000	15,000	18,000
Indirect labour	12,000	12,000	16,000	22,000
Machine rental	4,000	4,000	4,000	8,000
Rent, rates etc	6,000	6,000	6,000	6,000

(b) **Budgetary control statement for the period ending 30 November**

	Actual 15,000 units	*Budget 15,000 units*	*Variance*
	£	£	£
Direct material	69,400	75,000	5,600 (F)
Direct labour	37,700	30,000	7,700 (A)
Indirect material	*18,250	18,000	250 (A)
Indirect labour	28,780	22,000	6,780 (A)
Machine rental	**8,000	8,000	–
Rent, rates etc	5,800	6,000	200 (F)
	167,930	159,000	8,930 (A)

* £(15,460 + 2,790)
** £(10,790 – 2,790)

Comments

Direct material. A large favourable variance. May indicate that bulk discounts are available for higher volumes. Management should investigate so that further budget projections are more accurate.

Direct and indirect labour. Both large adverse variances. Perhaps bonus or overtime payments were higher than expected. Investigation into the cause is necessary in case bonus or overtime payments are not being properly controlled.

Indirect material and rent, rates etc. Small variances, probably not significant.

Activity 10.7

(a)

	Budgets at different levels of activity				
	4,000 units	*5,000 units*	*6,000 units*	*7,000 units*	*8,000 units*
	£	£	£	£	£
Direct materials (W1)	80,000	100,000	120,000	140,000	160,000
Indirect materials (W2)	12,000	14,000	16,000	18,000	20,000
Direct labour (W3)	50,000	62,500	75,000	87,500	100,000
Power (W4)	18,000	18,000	18,000	21,000	24,000
Repairs (W5)	20,000	22,500	25,000	27,500	30,000
Supervision (W6)	20,000	20,000	36,000	36,000	36,000
Rent, insurance and rates (W7)	9,000	9,000	9,000	9,000	9,000
Total	209,000	246,000	299,000	339,000	379,000

Workings

1 **Direct materials**

4,000 units cost £80,000 and 8,000 units cost £160,000. A doubling of units leads to a doubling of cost. Direct materials is therefore a variable cost.

Cost per unit = £80,000/4,000 = £20. Example: budget for 6,000 units = 6,000 × £20 = £120,000.

2 **Indirect materials**

A doubling of production does not result in a doubling of cost. Indirect materials is therefore a mixed cost.

Consider the total cost of 4,000 units.

	£
Variable cost (4,000 × £2)	8,000
Total cost	12,000
Fixed cost	4,000

The total cost of indirect materials is therefore based on a fixed cost of £4,000 plus a variable cost of £2 per unit. Example: budget for 6,000 units = £4,000 + £(6,000 × 2) = £16,000.

3 **Direct labour**

This is obviously a variable cost since double the production leads to double the cost.

Cost per unit = £50,000/4,000 = £12.50. Example: budget for 6,000 units = 6,000 × £12.50 = £75,000.

4 **Power**

If the minimum charge is payable on all production up to and including 6,000 units then it is paid on production of 4,000 units and is £18,000. This represents a fixed cost at all levels of production. On production over 6,000 units there is a variable charge based on power consumed.

Production of 8,000 units will have incurred the variable charge on 2,000 units. This variable charge for 2,000 units = £(24,000 – 18,000) = £6,000. The charge per unit = £6,000/2,000 = £3.

For production up to 6,000 units, the budget is £18,000. For production over 6,000 units, the budget is £18,000 plus £3 per unit over 6,000 units.

Example: budget for 7,000 units = £18,000 + ((7,000 – 6,000) × £3) = £21,000

5 **Repairs**

This is obviously a mixed cost.

Consider the total cost of 4,000 units.

	£
Fixed cost	10,000
Total cost	20,000
Variable cost of 4,000 units	10,000

∴ Variable cost per unit = £10,000/4,000 = £2.50

Example: budget for 6,000 units = £10,000 + £(6,000 × £2.50) = £25,000

6 **Supervision**

We are told supervision is a step cost. For 4,000 and 5,000 units the budget will be £20,000. Over 5,000 units, the budget will be £20,000 + £16,000 = £36,000. Example: budget for 6,000 units = £36,000.

7 **Rent, insurance and rates**

The cost does not change despite a doubling of production and hence it is a fixed cost. Example: budget for 6,000 units = £9,000.

(b) **REPORT**

To: Production Manager
From: A Technician
Date: XX October Year 7
Subject: **Operating costs – July to September**

1 **INTRODUCTION**

This report provides a review of operating costs incurred during the three-month period from July to September. Actual costs incurred during the period have been compared with budgeted results and differences highlighted. The budgeted results are those costs which should have been expected at the actual level of activity during the three-month period (that is, at output of 5,000 units).

Suggestions for those variances (differences between actual and budgeted results) which may require investigation have been made as necessary. (A) denotes an adverse variance and (F) a favourable variance.

2 **FINDINGS**

Cost	*Budgeted cost at output of 5,000 units*	*Actual cost*	*Variance*
	£	£	£
Direct materials	100,000	110,000	10,000 (A)
Indirect materials	14,000	14,000	–
Direct labour	62,500	70,000	7,500 (A)
Power	18,000	18,000	–
Repairs	22,500	30,000	7,500 (A)
Supervision	20,000	20,000	–
Rent, insurance and rates	9,000	8,000	1,000 (F)
	246,000	270,000	24,000 (A)

Direct materials variance. The cause of this variance needs investigating. It may have arisen because of price increases, careless purchasing or a change in the material standard or because of defective material, excessive waste, theft or stricter quality control.

Direct labour variance. Again an investigation is needed. An investigation may discover that the variance is due to a wage rate increase or because excessive overtime has been worked, although this is unlikely since production levels were fairly low. Alternatively, an investigation may reveal it being due to a cause such as machine breakdown, non-availability of material or excessive lost time.

Repairs variance. This variance should be investigated since it may indicate that capital equipment needs replacing. If so, the equipment should be replaced as soon as possible so as to avoid a total stoppage of production. On the other hand, it could indicate that the original budget was incorrect.

Rent, insurance and rates variance. This should be a fixed cost and so the variance is more than likely an expenditure variance. An investigation should reveal that either the original budget was incorrect or that a one-off exceptional payment has not been necessary.

3 **CONCLUSION**

The findings laid out in the previous section indicate that actual results for the three-month period from July to September were not as good as expected, costs being £24,000 higher than anticipated. The variances highlighted by the budget statement should therefore be investigated and their cause determined so as to ascertain whether original budgets and standards were incorrect or whether cost control needs tightening.

If you require any further information then please do not hesitate to contact me.

Answer 10.8

REPORT

To: Management Team
From: Management Accountant
Date: 17 April Year 7
Subject: **Format of variance report**

Following my meeting with Mr Product Manager last week, I have undertaken a review of the format of the variance report used throughout the organisation. I have concluded that, because of the way in which the information is presented, the report could be potentially misleading for users. I therefore recommend that the format be adapted as follows.

- Information about volumes (hrs, kgs and so on) should be reported separately in order to make the report less confusing and easier to read and understand. All information on the monthly variance report except that concerning production volumes should be monetary.
- The volume variances (those in hrs, kgs and so on) should be converted into monetary amounts in order that the financial implications of the variances are obvious.
- Instead of calculating variances by comparing actual results and the original fixed budget results, actual results should be compared with budget results flexed to the actual production volumes. The flexed results provide a far more realistic and fair target against which to measure actual results. For example, the direct labour (£) variance is currently calculated by comparing the budgeted labour cost of producing 10,000 units with the actual labour cost of producing 9,905 units. A revised format should show a direct labour (£) variance calculated by comparing the actual direct labour cost with the budgeted direct labour cost of producing 9,905 units.
- The report shows no flexed budget figures (the results which should have been expected at the actual production level achieved). A flexed budget column should therefore be included on the report.
- The report does not provide a narrative description of any known reasons for the variances. Explanations would increase the report's user friendliness.
- The report should use the principles of exception reporting, highlighting the most important variances in order to direct management attention to areas where action is most urgently required.

- Controllable fixed costs (if they exist) should be included on the report and separately identified.
- Information about cumulative results to date is needed. This will be particularly important when costs are subject to unpredictable monthly fluctuations. Management control is then more likely to concentrate on the cumulative trend in costs and variances.

A recommended layout for the monthly variance report is shown in the Appendix to this report. An identical format could be used for the presentation of cumulative results to date.

APPENDIX
MONTHLY VARIANCE REPORT

	Original fixed budget	*Flexed budget*	*Actual results*	*Variances*		*Total variance*		*Notes*
				Quantity	*Price*			
	Units	Units	Units	£	£	£	%	
Production volume	X	X	X					
Variable costs								
Direct material	X	X	X	X	X	X	X	
Direct labour	X	X	X	X	X	X	X	
Total variable costs	X	X	X			X	X	
Controllable fixed costs	X	X	X		X	X	X	
Total costs	X	X	X			X	X	

The notes column could be used to provide an explanation of the reasons for various variances occurring and/or to highlight important variances.

Chapter 11

Answer 11.1

Incremental budgeting is appropriate for budgeting for rent, which may be estimated on the basis of current rent plus an increment for the annual rent increase. Advertising expenditure, on the other hand, is not so easily quantifiable and is more discretionary in nature. Using incremental budgeting for advertising expenditure could allow slack and wasteful spending to creep into the budget.

Answer 11.2

The base package might cover the recruitment and dismissal of staff. Incremental packages might cover training, pension administration, trade union liaison, staff welfare and so on.

Answer 11.4

REPORT

To: R&D manager
From: Management accountant
Date: 1 January Year 3
Subject: Zero based budgeting

(a) The traditional approach to budgeting works from the premise that last year's activities will continue at the same level or volume, and that next year's budget can be based on last year's costs plus an extra amount to allow for expansion and inflation. The term 'incremental' budgeting is often used to describe this approach.

Zero based budgeting (ZBB) quite literally works from a zero base. The approach recognises that every activity has a cost and insists that there must be quantifiable benefits to justify the spending. ZBB expects managers to choose the best method of achieving each task by comparing costs and benefits. Activities must be ranked in order of priority.

(b) A discretionary cost is not vital to the continued existence of an organisation in the way that, say, raw materials are to a manufacturing business. ZBB was developed originally to help management with the difficult task of allocating resources in precisely such areas. Research and development is a frequently cited example; others are advertising and training. Within a research and development department ZBB will establish priorities by ranking the projects that are planned and in progress. Project managers will be forced to consider the benefit obtainable from their work in relation to the costs involved. The result may be an overall increase in R&D expenditure, but only if it is justified.

Answer 11.5

- They involve more time, effort and money in budget preparation.
- Frequent budgeting might have an off-putting effect on managers.

Answer 11.6

- In well-established organisations, because systems are in place and past experience can be used as a basis for forward planning
- In very large businesses, where senior management do not have enough knowledge of all of the organisation's activities to enable them to draw up budgets
- When operational managers have strong budgeting skills
- When the organisation's different units act autonomously

Answer 11.7

The budget planning stage should include quality targets in addition to cost information. In AB plc's case, where product quality is essential for the firm's survival, quality targets should be considered at the same time as costs. For example, more expensive materials might have to be purchased to maintain a certain level of quality. Quality is therefore one of the factors shaping the budget

In addition, there should be a budgeted level of defects. This does not mean that defects are acceptable. It is likely, however, that the introduction of quality procedures will be a cumulative process. The budgeted level of defects should therefore reduce from year to year.

At production and post production stage, the various cost and quality measures outlined in the budget should be identified and compared with budget levels.

Answer 11.8

Tutorial note. In task (b) you may have felt that the top-down approach to budgeting was more appropriate at the museum. Justify your answer and you will receive marks.

MEMORANDUM

To: John Derbyshire
From: Accounting Technician
Date: 5 October 20X8
Subject: **Behavioural aspects of budgeting**

(a) **Motivational implications of imposing the budget reduction**

When setting budgets, certain managers establish a budgeted figure and then add on a bit extra (when budgeting costs) or take off a bit (when estimating revenue) 'just in case'. This extra, which is known as **budgetary slack**, is included or deducted 'just in case' they haven't estimated accurately, costs turn out to be higher than expected or revenue lower than expected or there is some other unforeseeable event which stops them meeting their budget target.

This slack **needs to be removed** from the budget. Senior management therefore have to make an estimate of the slack and ask for the budget submitted by the lower-level manager to be adjusted accordingly. If the manager has not incorporated slack, this can be very demotivating; the entire

budgeting process has to begin again and costs reduced/revenues increased to the level required. Moreover, the manager is likely to feel no sense of ownership of the budget, it having been imposed on him/her, and hence he or she will be less inclined to make efforts to meet the targets.

The size of the reduction/increase will determine the effect on morale; a small change is likely to have less effect than a large change.

Given that the Board of Management appear to have requested the reduction from £35,000 to £29,000 with no reason to believe that you have incorporated budgetary slack (£35,000 being £2,000 less than the estimated deficit for 20X8), it is likely have a negative impact on both your motivation and that of other museum staff.

(b) **Top-down budgeting**

In the top-down or **imposed** approach to budgeting, **top management prepare a budget with little or no input from operating personnel** and it is then imposed upon the employees who have to work to the budgeted figures.

In the **bottom-up** or **participatory** approach to budgeting, **budgets are developed by lower-level managers** who then submit the budgets to their superiors. The budgets are based on lower-level managers' perceptions of what is achievable and the associated necessary resources.

Imposed budgets tend to be effective in newly-formed organisations and/or in very small businesses whereas participatory budgets are most often seen in more mature organisations, of medium to large size.

The imposed style of budgeting uses senior management's awareness of total resource availability, decreases the possibility of input from inexperienced or uninformed lower-level employees and ensures that an organisation's strategic plans are incorporated into planned activities.

On the other hand, the bottom-up approach ensures that information from employees most familiar with each department's needs and constraints is included, knowledge spread among several levels of management is pulled together, morale and motivation is improved and acceptance of and commitment to organisational goals and objectives by operational managers is increased. What's more, they tend to be more realistic.

Given that the museum is well established and in view of the advantages set out above, the **bottom-up approach** would seem to be the **more suitable** of the two approaches for the museum.

Answer 11.9

Here are some suggestions.

- A computer has the ability to process a larger volume of data.
- A computerised system can process data more rapidly than a manual system.
- Computerised systems tend to be more accurate than manual systems.
- Computers have the ability to store large volumes of data in a readily accessible form.

Answer 11.10

(a) Cells containing values are: B4, B5, B6, C4, C5, C6, D4, D5 and D6. Cells containing formulae are B7, C7, D7, E4, E5, E6 and E7.

(b) (i) =B4+B5+B6 *or better* =SUM(B4:B6)

(ii) =B6+C6+D6 *or better* =SUM(B6:D6)

(iii) =E4+E5+E6 *or better* =SUM(E4:E6) Alternatively, the three monthly totals could be added across the spreadsheet: = SUM (B7: D7)

(c) The figures which would change, besides the amount in cell C5, would be those in cells C7, E5 and E7.

Chapter 12

Answer 12.1

Stern Ltd appears to make, on average, 13,800/12 = 1,150 units per month. There is a waiting list of (16,560 – 13,800) = 2,760 units, and so the average delay in supplying customers is 2,760/1,150 = 2.4 months. Stern Ltd is therefore not attaining its objective to fulfil orders within six weeks.

Answer 12.2

(a) It can be increased by raising prices and/or by negotiating lower prices with suppliers.

(b) It is affected by the stock valuation method used and takes no account of differences in organisation's cost structures.

Answer 12.3

SOUTH & BROWN LIMITED
REPORT

To: Senior Management Committee
From: Assistant accountant
Date: 12 December Year 4
Subject: **Profitability and asset turnover ratios**

We have received the Trade Association results for year 4 and this report looks in detail at the profitability and asset turnover ratios.

(a) What each ratio is designed to show

(i) **Return on capital employed (ROCE)/Return on investment (ROI)**. This ratio shows the percentage rate of profit which has been earned on the capital invested in the business, that is the return on the resources controlled by management. The expected return varies depending on the type of business and it is usually calculated as follows.

Return on capital employed = (Profit before interest and tax/capital employed) × 100%.

Other profit figures can be used, as well as various definitions of capital employed.

(ii) **Net operating profit margin**. This ratio shows the operating profit as a percentage of sales. The operating profit is calculated before interest and tax and it is the profit over which operational mangers can exercise day to day control. It is the amount left after all direct costs and overheads have been deducted from sales revenue.

Net operating profit margin = (Operating profit/sales revenue) × 100%

(iii) **Asset turnover**. This ratio shows how effectively the assets of a business are being used to generate sales.

Asset turnover = (Sales revenue/capital employed)

If the same figure for capital employed is used as in ROCE, than ratios (i) to (iii) can be related together: (i) ROCE = (ii) net operating profit margin × (iii) asset turnover.

(iv) **Gross margin**. This ratio measures the profitability of sales.

Gross margin = (Gross profit/sales revenue) × 100%

The gross profit is calculated as sales revenue less the cost of goods sold, and this ratio therefore focuses on the company's manufacturing and trading activities.

(b) **South & Brown Limited's profitability and asset turnover**

South & Brown Limited's ROCE is lower than the trade association average, possibly indicating that the company's assets are not being used as profitably as in the industry as a whole.

South & Brown Limited's operating profit margin is higher than the trade association average, despite a lower than average gross profit margin. This suggests that non-production costs are lower in relation to sales value in South & Brown Limited than in the industry as a whole.

South & Brown Limited's asset turnover ratio is lower than the trade association average. This may mean that assets are not being used as effectively in our company as in the industry as a whole, which could be the cause of the lower than average ROCE.

South & Brown Limited's gross profit margin is lower than the trade association average. This suggests either that South & Brown Limited's production costs are higher than average, or that selling prices are lower than average.

If you would like further information please do not hesitate to contact me.

Answer 12.4

(a)

		Year 2	*Year 3*	*Year 4*
(i)	Gross profit %	(33/100) × 100% = 33%	(34/103) × 100% = 33%	(35.6/108) × 100% = 33%
(ii)	Net profit %	(15/100) × 100% = 15%	(15/103) × 100% = 14.56%	(15/108) × 100% = 13.9%
(iii)	Quick ratio	(8 + 5)/5 = 2.6	11/(6 + 6) = 0.9	15/(6 + 5) = 1.4

(b) Turnover has risen only slightly over the three years with the gross profit margin remaining high at 33%. This suggests that selling prices and costs have been increased only in line with inflation.

Net profit margin has fallen. While the fall is not great it indicates that expenditure on overheads has increased. The fall should be investigated and an attempt made to ensure that the trend does not continue.

The quick ratio fell sharply in Year 3, although it has since recovered. The more worrying aspect of the changes to working capital is that there is less cash (a bank overdraft) and more debtors. It is worth enquiring whether this is due to poor credit control or extending credit in an effort to boost or maintain sales.

It appears from the above that the company is showing a healthy profit, but needs to pay attention to working capital. It should be emphasised, however, that it is difficult to draw conclusions without knowing the sector in which Logic operates or any details about the performance of its competitors.

Answer 12.5

	Year 8		Year 7	
Current ratio	(572.3/501.0)	= 1.14	(523.2/420.3)	= 1.24
Quick ratio	(453.3/501.0)	= 0.90	(414.2/420.3)	= 0.99
Debtors' payment period	(329.8/2,065.0)	× 365 = 58 days	(285.4/1,788.7)	× 365 = 58 days
Stock turnover period	(119.0/1,478.6)	× 365 = 29 days	(109.0/1,304.0)	× 365 = 31 days
Creditors' turnover period	(236.2/1,478.6)	× 365 = 58 days	(210.8/1,304.0)	× 365 = 59 days

Gelton Ltd is a manufacturing group serving the construction industry, and so would be expected to have a comparatively lengthy debtors' turnover period, because of the relatively poor cash flow in the construction industry. It is clear that management compensates for this by ensuring that they do not pay for raw materials and so on before they have sold their stocks of finished goods (hence the similarity of debtors' and creditors' turnover periods).

Gelton Ltd's current ratio is a little lower than average but its quick ratio is better than average and very little less than the current ratio. This suggests that stock levels are strictly controlled, which is reinforced by the low stock turnover period. It would seem that working capital is tightly managed, to avoid the poor liquidity which could be caused by a high debtors' turnover period and comparatively high creditors.

Answer 12.6

(a)	Current ratio	= (Current assets/current liabilities)	= (30,500/24,000) = 1.27
(b)	Acid test ratio	= (Current assets – stock/current liabilities)	= (16,500/24,000) = 0.6875
(c)	Stock turnover	= (Stock/cost of sales) × 365 days	= (14,000/42,000) × 365 = 122 days
(d)	Debtors turnover	= (Debtors/sales) × 365 days	= (16,000/60,000) × 365 = 97 days
(e)	Creditors turnover	= (Creditors/cost of sales) × 365 days	= (24,000/42,000) × 365 = 209 days
(f)	Gross profit %	= (Gross profit/sales) × 100%	= (18,000/60,000) × 100% = 30%
(g)	Net profit %	= (Net profit/sales) × 100%	= (2,500/60,000)× 100% = 4.2%
(h)	ROCE	= (Profit/capital employed) × 100%	= (2,500/19,000) × 100% = 13.16%
(i)	Asset turnover	= (Sales/capital employed)	= (60,000/19,000) = 3.2 times

Answer 12.7

There are a number of limitations of which management should be aware before drawing any firm conclusions from a comparison of these ratios.

- The ratios are merely averages, based on year-end balance sheet data, which may not be representative.
- These ratios could be affected by any new investment towards the end of the financial year. Such investment would increase the value of the assets or capital employed, but the profits from the investment would not yet have accumulated in the profit and loss account. Generally, newer assets tend to depress the asset turnover and hence the ROCE in the short term. It is possible that this is the cause of our company's lower asset turnover and ROCE.

- Although the trade association probably makes some attempt to standardise the data, different member companies may be using different accounting policies, for example in calculating depreciation and valuing stock.
- There are different formulae for calculating one or more of the ratios. For example, as noted above, there are a variety of ways of calculating capital employed. It is likely, however, that the trade association would provide information on the basis of calculation of the ratios.
- The member companies will have some activities in common, hence their membership of the trade association. Some may, however, have a diversified range of activities, which will distort the ratios and make direct comparison difficult.

Chapter 13

Answer 13.1

Year	*Expenditure*	*Adjustment for price movement*	*Expenditure in Year 5 terms*
	£		£
1	185,365	× 138/100	255,804
2	198,721	× 138/107	256,294
3	221,737	× 138/119	257,140
4	239,114	× 138/129	255,796
5	255,100	× 138/138	255,100

The increases in expenditure are obviously principally due to increases in the price of material M1. When expenditure is adjusted to Year 5 terms it is evident that expenditure has not varied significantly in real terms.

Answer 13.2

Year	*Expenditure*	*Adjustment for movement in fuel price index*	*Expenditure at year 4 prices*
	£	£	£
1	18,000	× 128/100	23,040
2	19,292	× 128/106	23,296
3	21,468	× 128/120	22,899
4	23,010	× 128/128	23,010

The increases in expenditure on fuel are mainly the result of increases in fuel prices. When expenditure is adjusted to year 4 prices it is possible to see that expenditure has not varied significantly in real terms.

Answer 13.3

(a) One of the major advantages of indices is that they can give a very fast overview of the changes that have taken place within a business, since a single figure – 100 – is understood to represent a certain level of performance at a certain point in time and different figures represent changes in that performance. For example if sales income has grown from an index figure of 100 to 150 during a year, and in the same period costs have fallen from 100 to 85 it is likely that the organisation has performed well. Where a mass of data is presented for several periods, such measures will be far more easily appreciated than the absolute figures.

Further light is shed by indices of price levels. If prices generally have increased by a large amount an increase in sales income from 100 to 150 is less impressive, and a reduction in costs from 100 to 85 more so.

(b) For many types of business, published information in the form of key indicators of the state of the industry is available. Thus whereas an organisation may not be able to obtain much detailed information about its competitors, it will be able to compare its performance against the industry average by the use of such 'indices'. To continue the example in (a), if a company finds that in the industry as a whole there

has been an average increase in sales income from 100 to 200 and its increase is only to 150 it can see that it is performing relatively less well than its rivals.

If forecast information for the industry as a whole is published, the indices will enable the organisation to set targets.

Within a group of companies such information may be prepared internally and used for comparisons in a similar way.

Answer 13.4

Value added per employee is a measure of efficiency.

Answer 13.5

Here are four suggested indicators, showing you how to use the chart.

(a) Services performed late v total services performed
(b) Total units sold v total units sold by competitors (indicating market share)
(c) Documents processed per employee
(d) Equipment failures per 1,000 units produced

There are many other possibilities. Don't forget to explain how the ones that you chose might be useful.

Answer 13.6

	£	£
Original cash balance		17,000
Original sales revenue	750,000	
Additional sales revenue (£750,000 × 30%)	225,000	
	975,000	
Increase in cash balance due to additional revenue		225,000
Year-end debtors (£975,000 × 2/12)	162,500	
Original debtors	180,000	
Reduction in debtors	17,500	
∴ Increase in cash balance due to debtors paying more quickly		17,500
Revised cash balance		259,500

Answer 13.7

(a) Asset turnover = turnover ÷ capital employed

∴ Turnover would be 1.3 × £1 million = £1.3 million

Gross profit = 20% of sales = £260,000

Operating profit = £260,000 – fixed costs of £81,900 = £178,100

Capital employed = £1 million

ROCE = (£178,100/£1m) × 100% = 17.81%

(b)

	£
NBV of fixed assets	957,850
Debtors = 2/12 × £375,000	62,500
Creditors = 3/12 × £95,000	(23,750)
Stock = 1/12 × £185,000	15,417
	1,012,017

Operating profit = £363,000.

ROCE = (£363,000/£1,012,017) × 100% = 35.9%.

Answer 13.8

(a) 8,000 units = 80% of maximum factory capacity.

If output had been 90% of maximum factory capacity, turnover would have been (£800,000 × 90%)/80% = (£800,000 × 0.9)/0.8 = £900,000. (Alternatively you could find the number of units produced at 90% of factory capacity and multiply by the selling price per unit = 9,000 × £100 = £900,000.)

Variable expenses only would increase.

Current variable expenses = £(560,000 – 120,000) = £440,000

Variable expenses would be (£440,000 × 90%)/80% = (£440,000 × 0.9)/0.8 = £495,000. (Alternatively you could find the variable cost per unit (£440,000/8,000 = £55) and multiply by 9,000 = £495,000.)

Revised profit = revised turnover – revised variable costs – original fixed costs = £(900,000 – 495,000 – 120,000) = £285,000.

(b) If the average age of debtors is one month, the measure = £900,000/12 (ie one month's worth of revised turnover) = £75,000.

		£
Revised cash balance	= original cash balance	20,000
	+ reduction in debtors (£(200,000 – 75,000))	125,000
	+ additional turnover (£(900,000 – 800,000))	100,000
		245,000

Answer 13.9

Measures or ratios which could be used to monitor product quality include the following. (You only had to provide three.)

- Defects per 100 units produced
- Customer returns per 100 units sold
- Number of customer complaints per month
- Number of warranty claims per month
- Number of replacement units provided each month
- Preventative costs as % of total maintenance costs

Answer 13.10

(a) Internal perspective (the improvement of internal processes)
(b) Internal perspective (the intensity of asset usage)
(c) Innovation and learning perspective, or possibly the internal perspective
(d) Financial perspective
(e) Customer perspective, or possibly the internal perspective
(f) Innovation and learning perspective
(g) Internal perspective, or possibly the customer perspective

Chapter 14

Answer 14.1

Here are some suggestions

- Changing the specifications for cutting solid materials
- Introducing new equipment that reduces wastage in processing or handling materials
- Identifying poor quality output at an earlier stage in the operational processes
- Using better quality materials

Answer 14.2

All but (c) are non value-adding activities.

Answer 14.3

If a manufacturer has fewer types of components to manufacture, he will be able to increase the length of production runs, and so reduce production costs. Non-standard parts tend to be produced in small runs, and unit costs will be higher as a consequence.

Standardisation also helps to cut purchasing cost because there are fewer items to buy and stock. The company can purchase in bulk, and so perhaps obtain bulk purchase discounts. It may also be possible to buy standard parts from more than one supplier, and so purchasing will be more competitive.

The disadvantage of standardisation is that it may result in a loss of sales revenue or customer loyalty.

Chapter 15

Answer 15.1

	P1	P2	P3	P4
	£	£	£	£
Direct material	4,800	5,000	2,400	7,200
Direct labour	3,360	2,100	1,120	2,520
Production overhead (W):				
Set up costs	1,500	1,250	1,000	1,500
Stores receiving	900	900	900	900
Inspection/quality control	600	500	400	600
Material handling and despatch	1,320	1,100	880	1,320
Total cost	12,480	10,850	6,700	14,040
Unit costs	(÷120) £104	(÷ 100) £108.50	(÷ 80) £83.75	(÷ 120) £117

Working

Overhead costs will be divided in the following ratios, depending upon the number of production runs, requisitions or orders per product.

	P1	P2	P3	P4
Production runs	6	5	4	6
Requisitions raised	20	20	20	20
Orders executed	12	10	8	12

Answer 15.2

(a) **Traditional costing approach**

	Direct labour hours
Superior product = 5,000 units × 1 hour	5,000
Deluxe product = 7,000 units × 2 hours	14,000
	19,000

∴ Overhead absorption rate = £285,000/19,000 = £15 per hour

Overhead absorbed would be as follows.

Superior product	1 hour × £15	= £15 per unit
Deluxe product	2 hours × £15	= £30 per unit

(b) **ABC approach**

		Machine hours
Superior product	= 5,000 units × 3 hours	15,000
Deluxe product	= 7,000 units × 1 hour	7,000
		22,000

Using ABC the overhead costs are absorbed according to the **cost drivers**.

	£			
Machine-hour driven costs	220,000	÷	22,000 m/c hours	= £10 per m/c hour
Set-up driven costs	20,000	÷	50 set-ups	= £400 per set-up
Order driven costs	45,000	÷	75 orders	= £600 per order

Overhead costs are therefore as follows.

		Superior product		*Deluxe product*
		£		£
Machine-driven costs	(15,000 hrs × £10)	150,000	(7,000 hrs × £10)	70,000
Set-up costs	(10 × £400)	4,000	(40 × £400)	16,000
Order handling costs	(15 × £600)	9,000	(60 × £600)	36,000
		163,000		122,000
Units produced		5,000		7,000
Overhead cost per unit		£32.60		£17.43

These figures suggest that the Deluxe product absorbs an unrealistic amount of overhead using a direct labour hour basis. Overhead absorption should be based on the activities which drive the costs, in this case machine hours, the number of production run set-ups and the number of orders handled for each product.

Answer 15.3

(a) Exchange value
(b) Esteem value
(c) Use value

Answer 15.4

Standard costing and budgetary control systems also require standards to be set, actual results to be monitored and control action to be taken if actual results differ from those expected.

Answer 15.5

(c) and (f) would not be included because they would not be recorded within the accounting records and hence are implicit costs.

Answer 15.6

Variance analysis can be used to enhance product quality and to keep track of quality control information. This is because variance analysis measures both the planned use of resources and the actual use of resources in order to compare the two.

As variance analysis is generally expressed in terms of purely quantitative measures, such as quantity of raw materials used and price per unit of quantity, issues of quality would appear to be excluded from the reporting process. Quality would appear to be an excuse for spending more time, say, or buying more expensive raw materials.

Variance analysis, as it currently stands, therefore needs to be adapted to take account of quality issues.

(a) Variance analysis reports should routinely include measures such as defect rates. Although zero defects will be most desirable, such a standard of performance may not be reached at first. However there should be an expected rate of defects: if this is exceeded then management attention is directed to the excess.

(b) The absolute number of defects should be measured *and* their type. If caused by certain materials and components this can shed light on, say, a favourable materials price variance which might have been caused by substandard materials being purchased more cheaply. Alternatively, if the defects are caused by shoddy assembly work this can shed light on a favourable labour efficiency variance if quality is being sacrificed for speed.

(c) It should also be possible to provide financial measures for the cost of poor quality. These can include direct costs such as the wages of inspection and quality control staff, the cost of time in rectifying the defects, and the cost of the materials used in rectification.

(d) Measures could be built into materials price and variance analysis, so that the materials price variance as currently reported includes a factor reflecting the quality of materials purchased.

Answer 15.7

(a) The potential benefits of training for quality include improved quality of output, improved productivity and greater job satisfaction and commitment on the part of employees.

(b) The benefits of quality control come from savings in quality-related costs, from improvements in customer relations and hopefully (because of the quality of the final product) increased sales revenue due to increased sales demand.

Answer 15.8

A wide variety of answers is possible. The article goes on to explain how the bank has monitored the initiative.

(a) It has devised a 100 point scale showing average satisfaction with branch service.

(b) It conducts a 'first impressions' survey of all new customers.

(c) There is also a general survey carried out every six months which seeks the views of a weighted sample of 350 customers per branch.

(d) A survey company telephones each branch anonymously twice a month to test how staff respond to enquiries about products.

(e) A quarter of each branch's staff answer a monthly questionnaire about the bank's products to test their knowledge.

(f) Groups of employees working in teams in branches are allowed to set their own additional standards. This is to encourage participation.

(g) Branches that underperform are more closely watched by 24 managers who monitor the initiative.

Index

ABB, 397
ABC, 396
Absorption costing, 27, 289, 389
Accounting measures, 366
Acid test ratio, 333
Activator, 9
Activity based budgeting, 397
Activity based costing, 388
Activity ratio, 363
Actual cost of actual production, 153
Advanced manufacturing technology (AMT) 389
Advice bureaux, 61
Appraisal costs, 403
Asset turnover, 331
Attainable standard, 144, 307
Average age of creditors, 335
Average age of debtors, 334
Average age of stock, 335
Average age of working capital, 336
Average debtors' payment period, 334
Average earnings index, 86
Averages, 349

Balanced scorecard, 355
Banks, 60
Bar charts, 75
Base packages, 303
Base period, 81
Basic standard, 144, 307
Batch related activities, 394
Behaviour, 307
Behavioural effects of control systems, 307
Behavioural implications of standards, 143
Benchmarking, 361
Bias, 47
Biased sample, 47
Boom, 230
Bottom up budgeting, 308
Breakeven time, 381
Browsers, 61
BS EN ISO 9000, 402
Budget, 223
Budget centre, 274
Budget cost allowance, 280, 285
Budget guidelines, 225
Budget policy, 225
Budget preparation timetable, 225
Budget review, 227
Budget statements, 295
Budget system, 244
Budget variance, 286
Budgetary control, 284
Budgetary slack, 302, 310
Budgeted profit and loss account, 249
Budgets covering more than one period, 246
Budgets for more than one product, 246

Capital employed, 330
Capital expenditure budgets, 253
Cash flow, 346
CATI, 57
Cell, 213
Census, 47
Closed system, 11
Cluster sampling, 54
Coding data, 284
Coincident indicator, 231
Committed fixed costs, 277
Comparator, 9
Competitive advantage, 359
Composite index numbers, 82
Computer-assisted telephone interviewing, 57
Computers, 313
Consultancies, 61
Continuous budgets, 306
Continuous improvement, 401
Contribution, 32
Contribution per unit of limiting factor, 262
Control, 6
Control action, 288
Control systems 8, 141, 145, 400
Controllability, 199
Controllable costs, 277
Co-ordination of budgets, 226, 244
Corporate planning, 222
Cost behaviour, 26, 279
Cost centres, 275
Cost control, 374
Cost drivers, 390
Cost forecasting, 121
Cost management, 373
Cost of living index, 80
Cost of production budgets, 244
Cost of sales budgets, 245

Cost pools, 391
Cost reduction, 374, 395
Cost value, 400
Cost/sales ratios, 328
Costs, 346
Costs of quality, 403
Creditors' payment period, 335
Creditors' turnover, 335
Current standard, 144, 307
Customer perspective, 356
Customer satisfaction, 357
Cyclical variations, 98, 230

Data, 44
Debtor days ratio, 334, 340
Decision packages, 303
Decision-making framework, 224
Decline, 229
Dependent variable, 77, 121
Depression, 230
Deriving standard and actual information, 147
Deseasonalisation, 110
De-trended series, 106
Diagrams, 74
Direct cost, 27
Directly attributable overhead, 278
Discretionary costs, 305
Discretionary fixed costs, 278
Dysfunctional decision making, 312

E-commerce, 61
Economic indicators, 230
Economy, 364
Effectiveness, 16, 324, 364
Effector, 9
Efficiency, 17, 324, 364
Efficiency ratio, 363
Efficient calculations, 72, 149
Electronic data interchange (EDI), 61
Empire building, 312
Empowerment, 402
Equation, 70
Esteem value, 400
Exchange rates, 83, 209
Exchange value, 400
Expense centre, 275
Explicit costs of quality, 405
External failure costs, 403
External sources of data, 56
Extrapolation, 114, 127

Face to face interview, 56
Facility sustaining activities, 394
Feedback, 6, 8, 146
Feedback information, 12
Financial accounting, 5
Financial measures, 366
Financial newspapers, 60
Financial performance measures, 346
Financial perspective, 359
Fixed budget, 278
Fixed costs, 26
Fixed overhead (volume) capacity variance, 171
Fixed overhead (volume) efficiency variance, 171
Fixed overhead capacity variance, 167, 170
Fixed overhead efficiency variance, 167, 170
Fixed overhead expenditure variance, 163, .165, 170, 171
Fixed overhead total variance, 171
Fixed overhead variances, 162
Fixed overhead variances
and absorption costing, 163
Fixed overhead variances
and marginal costing, 163
Fixed overhead volume variance, 164, 166, 170, 171
Flexible budgets, 279
Flexing costs and revenue, 279
Focus groups, 57
Forecasting, 14, 96, 128, 227
Forecasting problems, 130
Forecasts, 96, 227
Formulae, 213
Full costs, 28

Get it right, first time, 401
Goal congruence, 312
Good information, 87
Google, 62
Governments, 60
Graphical calculation of variances, 173
Graphs, 77, 103
Gross domestic product (GDP), 231
Gross profit margin, 327
Group discussions, 57

Growth, 229
Guaranteed weekly wage, 241

High-low method, 123
Historigram, 96
Home page, 62
Human system, 11

Ideal standard, 144, 307
Implicit costs of quality, 405
Imposed budget, 308
Incremental budgeting, 302
Incremental method, 280
Incremental packages, 303
Independent variable, 77, 121
Index numbers, 80, 128, 207
Index numbers of producer prices (PPI), 86
Index of labour rates, 86
Index of retail sales, 86
Index points, 80
Indices, 255, 347
Indices and variances, 208
Indirect cost, 27
Inefficiency, 256
Inflation, 128, 212, 347
Information, 46
Information bureaux, 61
In-house sources of data, 55
Innovation and learning perspective, 359
Inputs, 7
Inspection, 403
Internal failure costs, 403
Internal perspective, 357
Internal source of data, 55
Internet, 61
Interpolation, 127
Interviews, 56
Introduction, 229
Investigation of variances, 288
Investment centres, 276

Jargon, 431
Judgement of outsiders, 366
Just-in-time (JIT), 405

Key budget factor, 225

Labour standards, 143
Labour utilisation budgets, 241
Labour variances, 159
Lagging indicator, 231
Leading indicator, 231
Libraries, 61
Life cycle costing, 378
Limiting budget factor, 225
Limiting factor analysis, 262
Limiting factors, 260, 269
Line charts, 75
Line of best fit, 122
Linear regression analysis, 119, 126
Liquidity ratios, 332
Long-term plan, 223
Long-term planning, 222

Management accounting 4
Management control, 225
Management control action, 199
Management performance measures, 365
Manipulating performance, 37
Manipulating performance measures, 367
Manipulation, 14
Marginal costing, 32, 289
Marginal costs, 26
Market research, 228
Material variances, 154
Materiality, 199
Materials purchases budget, 241
Materials usage budget, 241
Mathematical model, 99, 314
Maturity, 229
Measurement errors, 12
Mechanical systems, 11
Method study, 377
Microsoft Internet Explorer, 61
Mixed costs, 26
Model, 99, 314
Monetary measures, 346
MORI, 61
Motivation, 12, 307
Moving averages, 100
Multi-period/single product budget, 246
Multiplicative model, 108
Multistage sampling, 52

Negative feedback, 10
Negotiated style of budgeting, 310
Net margin, 326
NFIs, 352
Non-controllable costs, 277
Non-financial indicators, 352, 366
Non-profit-making organisations, 363
Non-random sampling, 53
NPMOs, 363

Objective, 12, 15, 223
Open system, 11
Operating profit percentage, 326
Operational control, 224
Operational planning, 224
Organisation and methods (O & M), 378
Outputs, 7
Over-absorbed overhead, 30
Overhead, 27

Participation, 308
Participatory budget, 308
Patterns in numbers, 70
Pay, 310
Penalty clauses in contracts, 264
Percentages, 158
Performance evaluation, 311
Performance indicators, 324
Performance measures for labour, 357
Performance measures for materials, 357
Performance measures for non-profit-making organisations, 363
Performance standards, 144
Performance-related pay schemes, 311
Periodic budget, 306
Personal interview, 57
Pictograms, 75
Pie charts, 75
Planning, 6, 222
Population, 46
Positive feedback, 11
Postal questionnaires, 58
Power (^), 214
Presentation of data, 72, 353
Prevention costs, 403
Primary data, 45
Primary external sources of data, 56
Principal budget factor, 225, 228, 238
Process, 7
Product life cycle, 229, 378
Product proliferation, 381
Product sustaining activities, 394
Production budgets, 239
Production volume ratio, 363
Productivity, 16, 324
Profit, 346
Profit centres, 276
Profit margin, 326
Profit to sales ratio, 327
Proportional model, 108

Qualitative data, 45
Qualitative performance measures, 325
Quality, 358, 398
Quality assurance procedures, 401
Quality assurance schemes, 402
Quality circles, 402
Quality control, 403
Quantitative data, 45
Quantitative performance measures, 325
Quasi-random sampling, 51
Quota sampling, 53

Random number tables, 50
Random sampling, 49
Ratio analysis, 326
Rearranging equations, 70, 149
Recession, 230
Reconciliation statements, 176
Recording costs, 27
Recovery, 230
Reference works, 61
Rejects, 256
Reporting costs, 27
Reports, 79, 201, 295
Rescheduling, 261
Research organisations, 61
Residual, 118
Resource budgets, 241
Resource utilisation, 359
Responsibility accounting, 274
Responsibility centres, 274

Retail Prices Index (RPI), 83
Return on capital employed (ROCE), 329
Return on investment (ROI), 329
Revenue, 346
Revenue centres, 276
Robotics, 389
Rolling budgets, 306

Sales budget, 226, 238
Sales forecasting, 228
Sales margin, 326
Sample, 47
Sampling, 49, 59
Sampling error, 48
Sampling frame, 49
Saturation, 229
Scattergraph method, 121
Search engine, 62
Seasonal component, 106
Seasonal variations, 98, 106
Seasonally adjusted data, 110
Secondary data, 45
Secondary external sources of data, 59
Secondary sources of data, 228
Selling price variance, 289
Semi-fixed costs, 26
Semi-variable costs, 26
Sensor, 8
Service quality, 358
Share price, 346
Shopping mall intercept surveys, 57
Short-term planning, 223
Single product/multi-period budget, 246
Spreadsheets, 213, 314
Standard, 8, 140
Standard cost cards, 141
Standard cost of actual production, 153
Standard costing, 145, 406
Standard costing and TQM, 406
Standard costs, 140
Standard hour, 362
Standardisation, 376
Stepped costs, 27
Stock days, 335
Stock turnover, 335
Stock turnover period, 335
Store intercept surveys, 57
Strategic planning, 224
Strategies, 223, 234
Stratified sampling, 51
Subdivision of variances, 206
Subjective judgement, 364
Subjective measures, 366
Sum function, 213
Surveys, 56
Systematic sampling, 51
Systems, 7
Systems approach to management accounting, 7

Tabulation, 73
Tactical planning, 225
Tactics, 225
Telephone interviews, 57
Time series, 96
Time series analysis, 96
Timing differences, 30
Top down budgeting, 308
Topic, 61
Total cost, 150, 382
Total Quality Management (TQM), 14, 400
TQM, 14, 400
Trade cycle, 98, 230
Trade journals, 60
Trend, 97

Under-absorbed overhead, 30
Unit cost, 19, 150
Unit cost measurements, 364
Unit related activities, 394
Upward appraisal, 366
Use value, 400

Value, 399
Value added, 349
Value added statements, 350
Value analysis, 375
Value engineering, 383
Value for money, 364
Value-adding activity, 376
Variable, 70
Variable costs, 26

Variance trend, 199
Variances, 9, 145, 286, 324
Variety reduction, 376
Vendor rating, 401

Waste, 256
Website, 61
'What if' analysis, 314, 353
Work measurement, 377++
Work study, 377
Working capital control, 336
Working capital period, 336
World Wide Web (www), 61

Yard-sticks, 324, 346

Zero based budgeting (ZBB), 303

See overleaf for information on other
BPP products and how to order

AAT Order

To BPP Professional Education, Aldine Place, London W12 8AW
Tel: 020 8740 2211. Fax: 020 8740 1184
E-mail: Publishing@bpp.com Web:www.bpp.com

Mr/Mrs/Ms (Full name)

Daytime delivery address

Postcode

Daytime Tel E-mail

FOUNDATION (£14.95 except as indicated)	5/03 Texts	5/03 Kits	Special offer	8/03 Passcards	Tapes
Units 1 & 2 Receipts and Payments	☐	☐		Foundation	
Unit 3 Ledger Balances and Initial Trial Balance	☐		Foundation Sage Bookeeping and Excel Spreadsheets CD-ROM free if ordering all Foundation Text and Kits, including Units 21 and 22/23 ☐	£6.95 ☐	£10.00 ☐
Unit 4 Supplying Information for Mgmt Control	☐				
Unit 21 Working with Computers (£9.95) (6/03)	☐				
Unit 22/23 Healthy Workplace/Personal Effectiveness (£9.95)	☐				
Sage and Excel for Foundation (CD-ROM £9.95)	☐				
INTERMEDIATE (£9.95 except as indicated)					
Unit 5 Financial Records and Accounts	☐	☐		£5.95 ☐	£10.00 ☐
Unit 6/7 Costs and Reports (Combined Text £14.95)	☐				
Unit 6 Costs and Revenues		☐		£5.95 ☐	£10.00 ☐
Unit 7 Reports and Returns		☐		£5.95 ☐	
TECHNICIAN (£9.95 except as indicated)					
Unit 8/9 Managing Performance and Controlling Resources	☐	☐		£5.95 ☐	£10.00 ☐
Spreadsheets for Technician (CD-ROM)	☐				
Unit 10 Core Managing Systems and People (£14.95)	☐		Spreadsheets for Technicians CD-ROM free if take Unit 8/9 Text and Kit ☐		
Unit 11 Option Financial Statements (A/c Practice)	☐	☐		£5.95 ☐	£10.00 ☐
Unit 12 Option Financial Statements (Central Govnmt)	☐	☐			
Unit 15 Option Cash Management and Credit Control	☐	☐		£5.95 ☐	
Unit 17 Option Implementing Audit Procedures	☐	☐		£5.95 ☐	
Unit 18 Option Business Tax (FA03)(8/03 Text & Kit)	☐	☐		£5.95 ☐	
Unit 19 Option Personal Tax (FA 03)(8/03 Text & Kit)	☐	☐		£5.95 ☐	
TECHNICIAN 2002 (£9.95)					
Unit 18 Option Business Tax FA02 (8/02 Text & Kit)	☐	☐			
Unit 19 Option Personal Tax FA02 (8/02 Text & Kit)	☐	☐			
SUBTOTAL	£	£	£	£	£

TOTAL FOR PRODUCTS £

POSTAGE & PACKING

Texts/Kits	**First**	**Each extra**	
UK	£3.00	£3.00	£
Europe*	£6.00	£4.00	£
Rest of world	£20.00	£10.00	£
Passcards			
UK	£2.00	£1.00	£
Europe*	£3.00	£2.00	£
Rest of world	£8.00	£8.00	£
Tapes			
UK	£2.00	£1.00	£
Europe*	£3.00	£2.00	£
Rest of world	£8.00	£8.00	£

TOTAL FOR POSTAGE & PACKING £

(Max £12 Texts/Kits/Passcards - deliveries in UK)

Grand Total (Cheques to *BPP Professional Education*)

I enclose a cheque for (incl. Postage) £

Or charge to Access/Visa/Switch

Card Number

Expiry date Start Date

Issue Number (Switch Only)

Signature

We aim to deliver to all UK addresses inside 5 working days; a signature will be required. Orders to all EU addresses should be delivered within 6 working days. All other orders to overseas addresses should be delivered within 8 working days. * Europe includes the Republic of Ireland and the Channel Islands.

See overleaf for information on other
BPP products and how to order

Mr/Mrs/Ms (Full name)

Daytime delivery address

Postcode

Daytime Tel E-mail

OTHER MATERIAL FOR AAT STUDENTS	8/03 Texts	3/03 Text
FOUNDATION (£5.95)		
Basic Mathematics	☐	
INTERMEDIATE (£5.95)		
Basic Bookkeeping (for students exempt from Foundation)	☐	
FOR ALL STUDENTS (£5.95)		
Building Your Portfolio (old standards)		☐
Building Your Portfolio (new standards)	☐	
	£	£

AAT Order

To BPP Professional Education, Aldine Place, London W12 8AW

Tel: 020 8740 2211. Fax: 020 8740 1184

E-mail: Publishing@bpp.com Web:www.bpp.com

TOTAL FOR PRODUCTS £

POSTAGE & PACKING

	First	Each extra	
Texts/Kits			
UK	£3.00	£3.00	£
Europe*	£6.00	£4.00	£
Rest of world	£20.00	£10.00	£
Passcards			
UK	£2.00	£1.00	£
Europe*	£3.00	£2.00	£
Rest of world	£8.00	£8.00	£
Tapes			
UK	£2.00	£1.00	£
Europe*	£3.00	£2.00	£
Rest of world	£8.00	£8.00	£

TOTAL FOR POSTAGE & PACKING £

(Max £12 Texts/Kits/Passcards - deliveries in UK)

Grand Total (Cheques to *BPP Professional Education*)

I enclose a cheque for (incl. Postage) £

Or charge to Access/Visa/Switch

Card Number

Expiry date Start Date

Issue Number (Switch Only)

Signature

We aim to deliver to all UK addresses inside 5 working days; a signature will be required. Orders to all EU addresses should be delivered within 6 working days. All other orders to overseas addresses should be delivered within 8 working days. * Europe includes the Republic of Ireland and the Channel Islands.

Review Form & Free Prize Draw – Units 8 and 9 Managing Performance and Controlling Resources (5/03)

All original review forms from the entire BPP range, completed with genuine comments, will be entered into one of two draws on 31 January 2004 and 31 July 2004. The names on the first four forms picked out on each occasion will be sent a cheque for £50.

Name: ______________________ **Address:** ______________________

____

____

How have you used this Interactive Text?
(Tick one box only)

- ☐ Home study (book only)
- ☐ On a course: college ______________________
- ☐ With 'correspondence' package
- ☐ Other ______________________

Why did you decide to purchase this Interactive Text? *(Tick one box only)*

- ☐ Have used BPP Texts in the past
- ☐ Recommendation by friend/colleague
- ☐ Recommendation by a lecturer at college
- ☐ Saw advertising
- ☐ Other ______________________

During the past six months do you recall seeing/receiving any of the following?
(Tick as many boxes as are relevant)

- ☐ Our advertisement in *Accounting Technician* magazine
- ☐ Our advertisement in *Pass*
- ☐ Our brochure with a letter through the post

Which (if any) aspects of our advertising do you find useful?
(Tick as many boxes as are relevant)

- ☐ Prices and publication dates of new editions
- ☐ Information on Interactive Text content
- ☐ Facility to order books off-the-page
- ☐ None of the above

Have you used the companion Assessment Kit for this subject? ☐ **Yes** ☐ **No**

Your ratings, comments and suggestions would be appreciated on the following areas

	Very useful	*Useful*	*Not useful*
Introduction	☐	☐	☐
Chapter contents lists	☐	☐	☐
Examples	☐	☐	☐
Activities and answers	☐	☐	☐
Key learning points	☐	☐	☐
Quick quizzes and answers	☐	☐	☐

	Excellent	*Good*	*Adequate*	*Poor*
Overall opinion of this Text	☐	☐	☐	☐

Do you intend to continue using BPP Interactive Texts/Assessment Kits? ☐ Yes ☐ No

Please note any further comments and suggestions/errors on the reverse of this page.

The BPP author of this edition can be e-mailed at: alisonmchugh@bpp.com

Please return this form to: Janice Ross, BPP Professional Education, FREEPOST, London, W12 8BR

Review Form & Free Prize Draw (continued)

Please note any further comments and suggestions/errors below

Free Prize Draw Rules

1. Closing date for 31 January 2004 draw is 31 December 2003. Closing date for 31 July 2004 draw is 30 June 2004.
2. Restricted to entries with UK and Eire addresses only. BPP employees, their families and business associates are excluded.
3. No purchase necessary. Entry forms are available upon request from BPP Professional Education. No more than one entry per title, per person. Draw restricted to persons aged 16 and over.
4. Winners will be notified by post and receive their cheques not later than 6 weeks after the relevant draw date.
5. The decision of the promoter in all matters is final and binding. No correspondence will be entered into.